ANNUAL EDITIONS

Education 11/12

Thirty-Eighth Edition

EDITOR

Dr. Rebecca B. Evers
Winthrop University

Dr. Rebecca Evers, an associate professor in Counseling, Leadership, and Educational Studies at the Richard W. Riley College of Education, attended Illinois College to earn a BA in English education in 1966, an MA in the Rehabilitation Teaching of the Adult Blind from Western Michigan University in 1969, and an EdD in Special Education from Northern Illinois University in 1994. She is actively involved in researching methods to determine and assess the quality of teacher candidate's dispositions. Her primary focus is dispositions for providing equitable access to learning for students with disabilities and other exceptional needs.

ANNUAL EDITIONS: EDUCATION, THIRTY-EIGHTH EDITION

Published by McGraw-Hill, a business unit of The McGraw-Hill Companies, Inc., 1221 Avenue of the Americas, New York, NY 10020. Copyright © 2011 by The McGraw-Hill Companies, Inc. All rights reserved. Previous editions © 2010, 2009, and 2008. No part of this publication may be reproduced or distributed in any form or by any means, or stored in a database or retrieval system, without the prior written consent of The McGraw-Hill Companies, Inc., including, but not limited to, in any network or other electronic storage or transmission, or broadcast for distance learning.

Some ancillaries, including electronic and print components, may not be available to customers outside the United States.

Annual Editions® is a registered trademark of The McGraw-Hill Companies, Inc.

Annual Editions is published by the **Contemporary Learning Series** group within the McGraw-Hill Higher Education division.

1 2 3 4 5 6 7 8 9 0 QDB/QDB 1 0 9 8 7 6 5 4 3 2 1 0

ISBN 978–0–07–805076–3
MHID 0–07–805076–6
ISSN 0272–5010

Managing Editor: *Larry Loeppke*
Developmental Editor: *Dave Welsh*
Permissions Coordinator: *DeAnna Dausener*
Marketing Specialist: *Alice Link*
Senior Project Manager: *Joyce Watters*
Design Coordinator: *Margarite Reynolds*
Buyer: *Susan K. Culbertson*
Media Project Manager: *Sridevi Palani*

Compositor: Laserwords Private Limited
Cover Image: Inset: Photodisc Collection/Getty Images; Background: Getty Images/Blend Images

Library in Congress Cataloging-in-Publication Data
Main entry under title: Annual Editions: Education. 2011/2012.
 1. Education—Periodicals. I. Evers, Rebecca B., *comp.* II. Title: Education.
658'.05

www.mhhe.com

Editors/Academic Advisory Board

Members of the Academic Advisory Board are instrumental in the final selection of articles for each edition of ANNUAL EDITIONS. Their review of articles for content, level, and appropriateness provides critical direction to the editors and staff. We think that you will find their careful consideration well reflected in this volume.

ANNUAL EDITIONS: Education 11/12
38th Edition

EDITOR

Dr. Rebecca B. Evers
Winthrop University

ACADEMIC ADVISORY BOARD MEMBERS

Amy Aidman
Emory University

Maribeth Andereck
William Carey University

Frank Aycock
Appalachian State University

Felicia Blacher-Wilson
Southeastern Louisiana University

Christopher Boe
Pfeiffer University

Lynn M. Burlbaw
Texas A & M University

Xiaomei Cai
University of Delaware

Robert C. Cienkus
Loyola University, Water Tower Campus

John Connor
Daytona State College

Evia L. Davis
Langston University

Anthony DeFalco
Long Island University

Charles Dittrich
Gettysburg College

Saran Donahoo
Southern Illinois University

Celina Echols
Southeastern Louisiana University

Paula Egelson
College of Charleston

Jennifer J. Endicott
University of Central Oklahoma

Stephanie Evans
California State University

La Vonne Fedynich
Texas A & M University Kingsville

Hussein Fereshteh
Bloomsburg University of Pennsylvania

Joan Fingon
California State University—Los Angeles

Kathleen E. Fite
Texas State University—San Marcos

Tami Foy
Azusa Pacific University

Josephine Fritts
Ozarks Technical Community College

Katherine Fry
Brooklyn College

Allan Futrell
University of Louisville

Robert E. Gates
Bloomsburg University of Pennsylvania

Christine M. Von Der Haar
Indiana University

Laura Haniford
University of New Mexico

J. Merrell Hansen
Brigham Young University

Judy Hassen
Pacific Lutheran University

Jason Helfer
Knox College

Harvey R. Jahn
Radford University

Brenda Campbell Jones
Azusa Pacific University

Richard Kennedy
Mount Olive College

Kathleen P. King
Fordham University—New York

Brian Kitteridge
Southern Utah University

Lawrence D. Klein
Central Connecticut State University

Douglas R. Knox
New Mexico Highlands University

Anne Meis Knupfer
Purdue University

Connie Krosney
Union Institute and University

Margaret A. Laughlin
University of Wisconsin—Green Bay

Robert Leahy
Stetson University

Pamela Lenz
Gannon University—Erie

Rebecca Letellier-Spearman
Strayer University

Kim Livengood
Angelo State University

Mark Malisa
Northeastern University

Leanna Manna
Villa Maria College

John W. McNeeley
Daytona State College

Charlotte Metoyer
National Louis University

Todd Miklas
Canisius College

Greg Morris
Grand Rapids Community College

Editors/Academic Advisory Board continued

Maria Anotonieta Pacino
Azusa Pacific University

James Van Patten
Florida Atlantic University

Karen Petitto
West Virginia Wesleyan College

Dorothy A. Pilla
Tufts University

Patricia Pollifrone
Gannon University—Erie

Patricia Reynolds
University of Mary Washington

Doug Rice
Sacramento State University

George Rodman
Brooklyn College of CUNY

Mike Romanowski
Ohio Northern University

William C. Root
Augusta State University

Daniel Rozmiarek
Towson University

Max L. Ruhl
Northwest Missouri State University

Terry M. Salem
Eastern Illinois University

Michael Schmierbach
College of Charleston

Stephen T. Schroth
Knox College

Charles Matt Seimears
Emporia State University

Patricia A. Shaw
University of Wisconsin Whitewater

Nancy Strow Sheley
California State University

Ralph Shibley
University of Rio Grande

Dick Shoemaker
Ball State University

John R. Shoup
California Baptist University

Mark Sidelnick
University of North Carolina

Juanita M. Simmons
University of Missouri

Robert J. Taggart
University of Delaware

Monte M. Tatom
Freed-Hardeman University

Thomas Walsh
Kean University

Robert Welker
Wittenberg University

Ali R. Zohoori
Bradley University

Preface

In publishing ANNUAL EDITIONS we recognize the enormous role played by the magazines, newspapers, and journals of the public press in providing current, first-rate educational information in a broad spectrum of interest areas. Many of these articles are appropriate for students, researchers, and professionals seeking accurate, current material to help bridge the gap between principles and theories and the real world. These articles, however, become more useful for study when those of lasting value are carefully collected, organized, indexed, and reproduced in a low-cost format, which provides easy and permanent access when the material is needed. That is the role played by ANNUAL EDITIONS.

The public conversation on the purposes and future direction of education is lively as ever. Alternative visions and voices regarding the broad social aims of schools, and the preparation of teachers continue to be presented. *Annual Editions: Education 11/12* attempts to reflect current mainstream as well as alternative visions as to what education ought to be. This year's edition contains articles on important issues facing educators, such as educational reforms, teacher preparation, teaching of reading and mathematics, managing student behavior, and creating communities of caring learners and diversity.

We face a myriad of quandaries in our schools today, not unfamiliar in our history as a nation, which are not easily resolved. Issues regarding the purposes of education, as well as the appropriate methods of educating, have been debated throughout the generations of literate human culture. Today, we are asking ourselves and others to provide our children a *quality education* for the 21st century. But first we must answer the questions: What is a quality education? and How do we provide such an education for all children? There will always be debates over the purposes and the ends of "education," as it depends on what the term means at a given place or time. This is because each generation must continuously reconstruct the definition of "education" based upon its understanding of "justice," "fairness," and "equity" in human relations, and each generation must locate and position its understanding of social justice and personal responsibility for our children and youth.

All of this is occurring as the United States continues to experience important demographic shifts in its cultural makeup. Furthermore, our ability to absorb children from many cultures into our schools has become a challenge in troubled economic times. Teachers in large cities have worked with immigrant populations since this nation began, but now schools in mid-size cities and rural towns are experiencing increasing numbers of children who speak a language other than English. Several articles in this edition address teaching methods for English Language Learners throughout the units on diversity, caring communities, and managing student behavior. Further, we address the larger issues of teaching reading and mathematics and the use of technology.

To provide opportunities for reading and discussion, we have included a new unit on technology. The technological breakthroughs in the information sciences are having an impact on how people learn. The rate of change in how we learn and obtain information is increasing at a rapid pace that will certainly continue. The articles in this section address how technology can change the fundamental delivery of content and expand options for personalizing learning, as well as articles on research on the effects of technology use on our children.

In assembling this volume, we make every effort to stay in touch with movements in educational studies and with the social forces at work in schools. Members of the advisory board contribute valuable insights, and the production and editorial staffs at the publisher, McGraw-Hill Contemporary Learning Series, coordinate our efforts.

The readings in *Annual Editions: Education 11/10* explore the social and academic goals of education, the current conditions of the nation's educational system, the teaching profession, and the future of American education. In addition, these selections address the issues of change, and the moral and ethical foundations of schooling. As always, we would like you to help us improve this volume. Please rate the material in this edition on the postage-paid *article rating form* provided at the back of this book and send it to us. We care about what you think. Give us the public feedback that we need.

Rebecca B. Evers
Editor

Contents

Preface v
Correlation Guide xi
Topic Guide xii
Internet References xiv

UNIT 1
Reformatting Our Schools

Unit Overview xviii

1. **'Quality Education Is Our Moon Shot'**, Joan Richardson, *Phi Delta Kappan,* September 2009
Richardson interviews Arne Duncan, U.S. Secretary of Education, regarding the plans for revision of No Child Left Behind and the implementation of President Obama's four areas of educational policies and school reform. 3

2. **Duncan's Strategy Is Flawed,** ASBJ Reader's Panel, *American School Board Journal,* February 2010
These letters to the Reader's Panel reflect a variety of thought regarding the educational policies and strategies of the Secretary of Education, Arne Duncan. 8

3. **Response to Intervention (RTI): What Teachers of Reading Need to Know,** Eric M. Mesmer and Heidi Anne E. Mesmer, *The Reading Teacher,* December 2008/January 2009
Educational law, Individuals with Disabilities Education Act, introduced Response to Intervention (RTI) as a method for establishing eligibility for special education services. These authors explain the five step process. A vignette of a real student provides an example of teacher duties and responsibilities when implementing RTI. 9

4. **Responding to RTI,** Anthony Rebora, *Teacher Magazine,* April 2010
In this interview, Richard Allington explains his views that RTI may be the last best hope for achieving full literacy in the United States. Throughout his career, Allington has advocated for intensifying instructional support for struggling readers, but he is critical of the actual implication of RTI in many schools. 18

UNIT 2
Preparing Teachers to Teach All Students in All Schools

Unit Overview 22

5. **Reluctant Teachers, Reluctant Learners,** Julie Landsman, Tiffany Moore, and Robert Simmons, *Educational Leadership,* March 2008
These authors suggested a primary reason for reluctant students is teachers who are reluctant to authentically engage with students who do not look, act, or talk like the teacher. They discuss how and why this happens. Finally, they offer suggestions that teachers can use immediately to prevent or change the possiblity that their actions are affecting student learning and behavior. 25

The concepts in bold italics are developed in the article. For further expansion, please refer to the Topic Guide.

6. **Musing: A Way to Inform and Inspire Pedagogy through Self-Reflection,** Jane Moore and Vickie Fields Whitfield, *Reading Teacher,* April 2008

   In order to deal with the social and educational issues facing teachers, these authors suggest that teacher engage in self-reflection. Musing allows teachers to grow and defend their teaching practices. After explaining the reasons to reflect and three levels of reflection, they offer questions to guide personal musings.   **29**

7. **All Our Students Thinking,** Nel Noddings, *Educational Leadership,* February 2008

   This is a thoughtful piece about teaching our students to think at all levels rather than merely making them memorize facts. As our world is changing, all citizens, whether employed in blue, pink, or white collar jobs, must be life-long learners who can think independently and solve problems effectively.   **32**

8. **Start Where Your Students Are,** Robyn R. Jackson, *Educational Leadership,* February 2010

   Jackson asserts that every classroom has its own currency which is a medium of exchange. This currency is the behavior students engage in to learn knowledge and skills in the class. She describes the conflict that results when the currency desired by students is not acknowledged and used by the teacher.   **36**

9. **Should Learning Be Its Own Reward?,** Daniel T. Willingham, *American Educator,* Winter 2007–2008

   The debate surrounding the use of rewards in school settings and for academic achievement has long been a stalemate between the "should" and "should not" advocates. Perhaps this article will offer answers to your questions or give you more support as you struggle to make decisions in your classroom.   **40**

10. **Learning to Love Assessment,** Carol Ann Tomlinson, *Educational Leadership,* December 2008

    As a novice teacher, the author was apprehensive about how to assess her students. She describes her journey from fearing assessment to using informative assessment to improve her teaching and student learning.   **46**

UNIT 3
Cornerstones to Learning: Reading and Math

Unit Overview   **50**

11. **Print Referencing during Read-Alouds: A Technique for Increasing Emergent Readers' Print Knowledge,** Tricia A. Zucker, Allison E. Ward, and Laura M. Justice, *The Reading Teacher,* September 2009

    Read-alouds are a popular daily activity in early childhood classrooms. While this activity helps young children learn comprehension and word skills, teachers rarely teach print referencing skills that students will need in higher grades as books become more print based and have fewer pictures for reference.   **52**

12. **You Gotta See It to Believe It: Teaching Visual Literacy in the English Classroom,** Robyn Seglem and Shelbie Witte, *Journal of Adolescent and Adult Literacy,* November 2009

    In the 1990s, the concept of literacy changed and became less narrowly defined. Seglem and Witte state that students need instruction in order to understand and use images so that they are able to think, learn, and express themselves in terms of images.   **60**

13. **You Should Read This Book!,** Jennifer Hartley, *Educational Leadership,* March 2008

    The author of this article, a teacher, shares her multi-trial process to developing a sustained silent reading program in her classroom. Teachers and parents will be able to use her information to support students.   **67**

14. **Do Girls Learn Math Fear from Teachers?,** *Teacher Magazine,* January 26, 2010

    Perhaps because your students model themselves after adults of the same gender and female teachers may be anxious about their personal math ability, young girls in this study indicated that "boys are good at math and girls are good at reading."   **70**

The concepts in bold italics are developed in the article. For further expansion, please refer to the Topic Guide.

15. **How Mathematics Counts,** Lynn Arthur Steen, *Educational Leadership,* November 2007

    The author reports the pressure some school professionals feel to sacrifice other content areas in order to ensure that students make "adequate yearly progress" in Mathematics. In the end, she suggests three important ingredients that would help students understand the need for math literacy as adults. — 71

16. **Textbook Scripts, Students Lives,** Jana Dean, *Rethinking Schools,* Spring 2008

    This teacher found that the pacing found in textbook publishers manuals and pacing guides were problematic in her school because they did not connect to the reality of her students' daily lives and the examples simply did not reach her students or link to their experiences. So in this article, she describes what she did about that dilemma. — 76

UNIT 4
Creating Caring Communities of Learners

Unit Overview — 80

17. **Creating Intentional Communities to Support English Language Learners in the Classroom,** Judith Rance-Roney, *English Journal,* May 2008

    In our increasingly diverse classrooms, teachers must find ways to teach and support students who do not speak English as a native language. Rance-Roney suggests that we form intentional learning communities. The suggestions in this article will help teachers support English Language Learners as well as invest all students in creating an inclusive classroom culture. — 82

18. **Cultivating Optimism in the Classroom,** Richard Sagor, *Educational Leadership,* March 2008

    One reason students drop-out of school is that they do not see any reason to invest time and energy in something that does not have a meaning in their lives. Sagor recommends strategies and actions for educators to use to build student optimism and thereby creating a culture in which they will put forth their best efforts. — 87

19. **Teachers Connecting with Families—In the Best Interest of Children,** Katharine C. Kersey and Marie L. Masterson, *Young Children and Families,* September 2009

    Long standing research supports the theory that when parents are involved in school, their child's achievement improves. But how can teachers connect with all parents? Kersey and Masterson offers practical suggestions for building bridges and strong ties to families; including suggestions to overcoming parent reluctance, sharing information, and maintaining parents' involvement throughout the year. — 91

20. **How Not to Talk to Your Kids: The Inverse Power of Praise,** Po Bronson, *New York Magazine,* February 2007

    Bronson quotes research data that 85% of American parents think it is important to tell their children that they are smart. However, a growing body of research finds that this behavior from parents may not be having the desired affect, in fact, quite the opposite affect. — 95

21. **Democracy and Education: Empowering Students to Make Sense of Their World,** William H. Garrison, *Phi Delta Kappan,* January 2008

    The author makes a case for empowering students with freedom and personal responsibility for their learning. He asserts that democratic social institutions are produced when persons have the freedom to learn from experiences, build on the experiences, and use this knowledge to direct future experiences. — 100

The concepts in bold italics are developed in the article. For further expansion, please refer to the Topic Guide.

UNIT 5
Addressing Diversity in Your School

Unit Overview — 102

22. **Meeting Students Where They Are: The Latino Education Crisis,** Patricia Gándara, *Educational Leadership,* February 2010

    Gándara asserts that Latino students are the most poorly educated of our children. They begin school lacking the skills most of their peers have and the gap is never removed or decreased. After presenting the data to support her assertions, the author offers suggestions to change the outcomes from Latino students. — 104

23. **What Does Research Say about Effective Practices for English Learners?,** Rhoda Coleman and Claude Goldenberg, *Kappa Delta Pi Record,* Winter 2010

    While students who are ELL may be able to communicate with their English-speaking peers and teachers, they may not be able to use academic English as well as their native speaking peers. Coleman and Goldenberg provide information about methods to support learning academic English for successful learning. — 110

24. **Becoming Adept at Code-Switching,** Rebecca S. Wheeler, *Educational Leadership,* April 2008

    Students who do not hear or speak Standard English in their community need a teacher who understands the need to teach code-switching. The author offers suggestions with examples to teachers who teach students from diverse cultural and linguistic backgrounds. — 114

25. **The Myth of the "Culture of Poverty,"** Paul Gorski, *Educational Leadership,* April 1, 2008

    Gorski explains how we came to believe that a culture of poverty exists. He examines a set of false stereotypes which recent research has proven to be false. Another point is that teachers who believe in the stereotypes are in danger of engaging in classism. The author finishes with a list of actions teachers need to follow to promote equality and equity in their schools. — 117

26. **Books That Portray Characters with Disabilities: A Top 25 List for Children and Young Adults,** Mary Anne Prater and Tina Taylor Dyches, *Teaching Exceptional Children,* March/April 2008

    Teachers and parents will find this list of books very helpful in teaching children about their siblings or classmates with disabilities. Further, the books also offer role models for all children. Be sure to review the authors' guidelines for book selection to help you find additional books. — 121

UNIT 6
Rethinking Discipline: Getting the Behavior You Want and Need to Teach Effectively

Unit Overview — 128

27. **The Under-Appreciated Role of Humiliation in the Middle School,** Nancy Frey and Douglas Fisher, *Middle School Journal,* January 2008

    Many of us can think back to bad days in middle school and remember the humiliation as peers laughed at us or called us names. The authors discuss the long term effects of humiliation on young adolescents and strategies for reducing that humiliation. — 131

28. **Tackling a Problematic Behavior Management Issue: Teachers' Intervention in Childhood Bullying Problems,** Laura M. Crothers and Jered B. Kolbert, *Intervention in School and Clinic,* January 2008

    The issue of bullying has been highlighted by the recent violent events caused by persons who were bullied by their peers. These authors suggest that bullying is a classroom management issue and offer eight strategies to address bullying behaviors. Teachers at all grades levels will find these strategies helpful. — 139

The concepts in bold italics are developed in the article. For further expansion, please refer to the Topic Guide.

29. **The Power of Our Words,** Paula Denton, *Educational Leadership,* September 2008

While bullying by peers can have a negative impact on a person's life so can the words spoken by teachers. Denton uses examples of teacher language that can negatively shape students' thoughts, feelings, and experiences. Finally, Denton suggests five guiding principles for using positive language. **147**

30. **Marketing Civility,** Michael Stiles and Ben Tyson, *American School Board,* March 2008

These authors cite data from a study of bullying in a suburban high school that indicate bullying is not just an urban school issue. They suggest six school-wide efforts that can change a school's climate. **150**

31. **Classwide Interventions: Effective Instruction Makes a Difference,** Maureen A. Conroy et al., *Teaching Exceptional Children,* July/June 2008

Two case studies, one of a classroom that works and one that has challenges, anchor this article. The authors posit that there are six universal classroom tools for effective instruction that when used will positively and preventively reduce behavior problems. **152**

32. **Developing Effective Behavior Intervention Plans: Suggestions for School Personnel,** Kim Killu, *Intervention in School and Clinic,* January 2008

Inclusive classrooms may have students with persistent behavior problems. Also, federal law requires that students in IEPs also be included in Behavior Intervention Plans (BIPs). Teachers will find this article on assessing and planning interventions helpful, as they strive to manage persistent behavior problems that are resistant to typical management strategies. **159**

UNIT 7
Technology: Are We Effectively Using Its Potential in Our Schools?

Unit Overview **170**

33. **"For Openers: How Technology Is Changing School,"** Curtis J. Bonk, *Educational Leadership,* April 2010

One lesson learned in the aftermath of Hurricanes Katrina and Rita was that technology could help learning continue even if the schools no longer existed. Mr. Bonk shares stories of how the internet has helped students and offers predictions for future uses for educational purposes. **172**

34. **Tech Tool Targets Elementary Readers,** Katie Ash, *Education Week,* March 18, 2010

Ms. Ash describes how a Game Boy-like device is being used by 15 states to improve the reading skills of very young students in grades K through 2. This device was developed by a non-profit organization that based the concept on the *One Laptop per Child* initiative. **176**

35. **Digital Tools Expand Options for Personalized Learning,** Kathleen Kennedy Manzo, *Digital Directions,* February 3, 2010

In this article, Manzo describes technology tools and methods used by teachers to find technology that would help them differentiate between instructions. Experts recommend a variety of tools and activities to address individual needs. Schools that have used technology for this purpose share their experiences. **178**

36. **Effects of Video-Game Ownership on Young Boys' Academic and Behavioral Functioning: A Randomized, Controlled Study,** Robert Weis and Brittany C. Cerankosky, *Psychological Science,* February 18, 2010

Using 64 boys, ages 6—9, researchers conducted an experimental study of the effects of playing video games, on development of reading and writing skills. This was a naturalistic study with no researcher interference on the frequency or duration of children's play. Results will be of interest to parents and teachers of young males. **181**

Test-Your-Knowledge Form **188**
Article Rating Form **189**

The concepts in bold italics are developed in the article. For further expansion, please refer to the Topic Guide.

Correlation Guide

The *Annual Editions* series provides students with convenient, inexpensive access to current, carefully selected articles from the public press. **Annual Editions: Education 11/12** is an easy-to-use reader that presents articles on important topics such as *learning, diversity, behavior management,* and many more. For more information on *Annual Editions* and other *McGraw-Hill Contemporary Learning Series* titles, visit www.mhhe.com/cls.

This convenient guide matches the units in **Annual Editions: Education 11/12** with the corresponding chapters in three of our best-selling McGraw-Hill Education textbooks by Fraser, Sadker et al., and Spring.

Annual Editions: Education 11/12	Teach, 1/e, by Fraser	Teachers, Schools, and Society, 9/e, by Sadker et al.	American Education, 14/e, by Spring
Unit 1: Reformatting Our Schools	**Chapter 4:** Including Everyone: Who Sometimes Gets Overlooked in School? **Chapter 6:** Curriculum and Standards: What Will I Teach? **Chapter 10:** Legal, Ethical, and Economic Responsibilities: How Can We Make Our Classrooms Fair? **Chapter 11:** Politics: What Is Its Place in Education? **Chapter 12:** Public Education: What Is Its Purpose in a Democratic Society?	**Chapter 5:** Reforming America's Schools **Chapter 6:** Curriculum, Standards, and Testing **Chapter 9:** Financing and Governing America's Schools	**Chapter 1:** The History and Goals of Public Schooling **Chapter 7:** Power and Control at State and National Levels: Political Party Platforms, High-Stakes Testing, and School Violence
Unit 2: Preparing Teachers to Teach All Students in All Schools	**Chapter 1:** Teaching: Is It for Me? **Chapter 2:** Good Teaching: What Is Its Impact? **Chapter 5:** Philosophical and Psychological Theories: How Do Children Learn? **Chapter 6:** Curriculum and Standards: What Will I Teach? **Chapter 7:** Motivating, Managing, and Assessing: How Will I Teach? **Chapter 13:** Developing a Plan and Personal Philosophy: Where Do I Go from Here?	**Chapter 1:** Becoming a Teacher **Chapter 2:** Different Ways of Learning **Chapter 3:** Teaching Your Diverse Students **Chapter 6:** Curriculum, Standards, and Testing **Chapter 8:** Philosophy of Education **Chapter 11:** Teacher Effectiveness **Chapter 12:** Your First Classroom	**Chapter 6:** Local Control, Choice, Charter Schools, and Home Schooling **Chapter 8:** The Profession of Teaching
Unit 3: Cornerstones to Learning: Reading and Math	**Chapter 6:** Curriculum and Standards: What Will I Teach?	**Chapter 6:** Curriculum, Standards, and Testing	
Unit 4: Creating Caring Communities of Learners	**Chapter 1:** Teaching: Is It for Me? **Chapter 2:** Good Teaching: What Is Its Impact? **Chapter 4:** Including Everyone: Who Sometimes Gets Overlooked in School?	**Chapter 4:** Student Life in School and at Home	**Chapter 8:** The Profession of Teaching **Chapter 6:** Local Control, Choice, Charter Schools, and Home Schooling
Unit 5: Addressing Diversity in Your School	**Chapter 3:** Student Diversity: Who Will I Teach? **Chapter 4:** Including Everyone: Who Sometimes Gets Overlooked in School? **Chapter 6:** Curriculum and Standards: What Will I Teach?	**Chapter 3:** Teaching Your Diverse Students **Chapter 7:** The History of American Education	**Chapter 2:** Education and Equality of Opportunity **Chapter 3:** Equality of Educational Opportunity: Race, Gender, and Special Needs **Chapter 4:** Student Diversity **Chapter 5:** Multicultural and Multilingual Education
Unit 6: Rethinking Discipline: Getting the Behavior You Want and Need to Teach Effectively	**Chapter 2:** Good Teaching: What Is Its Impact? **Chapter 7:** Motivating, Managing, and Assessing: How Will I Teach?	**Chapter 4:** Student Life in School and at Home **Chapter 11:** Teacher Effectiveness **Chapter 12:** Your First Classroom	**Chapter 9:** Textbooks, Curriculum, E-Learning, Cyber Bullying, and Global Models of Curriculum and Instruction
Unit 7: Technology: Are We Effectively Using Its Potential in Our Schools?	**Chapter 5:** Philosophical and Psychological Theories: How Do Children Learn?		**Chapter 9:** Textbooks, Curriculum, E-Learning, Cyber Bullying, and Global Models of Curriculum and Instruction

Topic Guide

This topic guide suggests how the selections in this book relate to the subjects covered in your course. You may want to use the topics listed on these pages to search the Web more easily.

On the following pages a number of websites have been gathered specifically for this book. They are arranged to reflect the units of this Annual Editions reader. You can link to these sites by going to www.mhhe.com/cls

All the articles that relate to each topic are listed below the bold-faced term.

Authentic learning
- 15. How Mathematics Counts
- 16. Textbook Scripts, Students Lives
- 18. Cultivating Optimism in the Classroom
- 21. Democracy and Education: Empowering Students to Make Sense of Their World
- 35. Digital Tools Expand Options for Personalized Learning

Assessment and research
- 10. Learning to Love Assessment

Behavior management
- 8. Start Where Your Students Are
- 9. Should Learning Be Its Own Reward?
- 27. The Under-Appreciated Role of Humiliation in the Middle School
- 28. Tackling a Problematic Behavior Management Issue: Teachers' Intervention in Childhood Bullying Problems
- 29. The Power of Our Words
- 30. Marketing Civility
- 31. Classwide Interventions: Effective Instruction Makes a Difference
- 32. Developing Effective Behavior Intervention Plans: Suggestions for School Personnel

Bullying
- 27. The Under-Appreciated Role of Humiliation in the Middle School
- 28. Tackling a Problematic Behavior Management Issue: Teachers' Intervention in Childhood Bullying Problems
- 29. The Power of Our Words
- 30. Marketing Civility

Caring communities of learners
- 17. Creating Intentional Communities to Support English Language Learners in the Classroom
- 18. Cultivating Optimism in the Classroom
- 19. Teachers Connecting with Families—In the Best Interest of Children
- 20. How Not to Talk to Your Kids: The Inverse Power of Praise
- 21. Democracy and Education: Empowering Students to Make Sense of Their World
- 28. Tackling a Problematic Behavior Management Issue: Teachers' Intervention in Childhood Bullying Problems
- 29. The Power of Our Words
- 30. Marketing Civility
- 31. Classwide Interventions: Effective Instruction Makes a Difference

Critical thinking skills
- 7. All Our Students Thinking
- 15. How Mathematics Counts

Disability
- 26. Books That Portray Characters with Disabilities: A Top 25 List for Children and Young Adults
- 31. Classrwide Interventions: Effective Instruction Makes a Difference
- 32. Developing Effective Behavior Intervention Plans: Suggestions for School Personnel

Discipline
- 28. Tackling a Problematic Behavior Management Issue: Teachers' Intervention in Childhood Bullying Problems
- 32. Developing Effective Behavior Management Plans: Suggestions for School Personnel

Diversity
- 5. Reluctant Teachers, Reluctant Learners
- 22. Meeting Students Where They Are: The Latino Education Crisis
- 23. What Does Research Say about Effective Practices for English Learners?
- 24. Becoming Adept at Code-Switching
- 25. The Myth of the "Culture of Poverty"
- 26. Books that Portray Characters with Disabilities: A Top 25 List for Children and Young Adults

Education policies
- 1. 'Quality Education is Our Moon Shot'
- 2. Duncan's Strategy Is Flawed
- 3. Response to Intervention (RTI): What Teachers of Reading Need to Know
- 4. Responding to RTI
- 33. "For Openers: How Technology Is Changing School"

Engaging students
- 5. Reluctant Teachers, Reluctant Learners
- 7. All Our Students Thinking
- 8. Start Where Your Students Are
- 9. Should Learning Be Its Own Reward?
- 21. Democracy and Education: Empowering Students to Make Sense of Their World
- 22. Meeting Students Where They Are: The Latino Education Crisis

English language learners
- 17. Creating Intentional Communities to Support English Language Learners in the Classroom
- 22. Meeting Students Where They Are: The Latino Education Crisis
- 23. What Does Research Say about Effective Practices for English Learners?
- 24. Becoming Adept at Code-Switching

Families
- 19. Teachers Connecting with Families—In the Best Interest of Children
- 20. How Not to Talk to Your Kids: The Inverse Power of Praise
- 25. The Myth of the "Culture of Poverty"

Future of education
- 1. 'Quality Education Is Our Moon Shot'
- 2. Duncan's Strategy Is Flawed

Gaming
- 34. Tech Tool Targets Elementary Readers
- 36. Effects of Video-Game Ownership on Young Boys' Academic and Behavioral Functioning: A Randomized, Controlled Study

Gender issues
14. Do Girls Learn Math Fear from Teachers?

Inclusion
17. Creating Intentional Communities to Support English Language Learners in the Classroom
25. The Myth of the "Culture of Poverty"
26. Books That Portray Characters with Disabilities: A Top 25 List for Children and Young Adults
28. Tackling a Problematic Behavior Management Issue: Teachers' Intervention in Childhood Bullying Problems
29. The Power of Our Words
31. Classwide Interventions: Effective Instruction Makes a Difference
32. Developing Effective Behavior Intervention Plans: Suggestions for School Personnel
35. Digital Tools Expand Options for Personalized Learning

Internet
33. "For Openers: How Technology Is Changing School"
36. Effects of Video-Game Ownership on Young Boys' Academic and Behavioral Functioning: A Randomized, Controlled Study

Literacy
4. Responding to RTI
11. Print Referencing during Read-Alouds: A Technique for Increasing Emergent Readers' Print Knowledge
12. You Gotta See It to Believe It: Teaching Visual Literacy in the English Classroom
13. You Should Read This Book!
34. Tech Tool Targets Elementary Readers

Mathematics
14. Do Girls Learn Math Fear from Teachers?
15. How Mathematics Counts

Middle school students
27. The Under-Appreciated Role of Humiliation in the Middle School

Multicultural education
17. Creating Intentional Communities to Support English Language Learners in the Classroom
22. Meeting Students Where They Are: The Latino Education Crisis
23. What Does Research Say about Effective Practices for English Learners?
24. Becoming Adept at Code-Switching

No child left behind
1. 'Quality Education is Our Moon Shot'
2. Duncan's Strategy Is Flawed

Parents
19. Teachers Connecting with Families—In the Best Interest of Children
20. How Not to Talk to Your Kids: The Inverse Power of Praise

Problem solving
6. Musing: A Way To Inform and Inspire Pedagogy through Self-Reflection
7. All Our Students Thinking

Reading
3. Response to Intervention (RTI): What Teachers of Reading Need to Know
11. Print Referencing during Read-Alouds: A Technique for Increasing Emergent Readers' Print Knowledge
13. You Should Read This Book!
34. Tech Tool Targets Elementary Readers

Real world relevance in schools
7. All Our Students Thinking
15. How Mathematics Counts
16. Textbook Scripts, Students Lives
21. Democracy and Education: Empowering Students to Make Sense of Their World

Reformatting our schools
1. 'Quality Education is Our Moon Shot'
2. Duncan's Strategy Is Flawed
7. All Our Students Thinking
21. Democracy and Education: Empowering Students to Make Sense of Their World
33. "For Openers: How Technology Is Changing School"

Reinforcement
8. Start Where Your Students Are
9. Should Learning Be Its Own Reward?

Reflection
6. Musing: A Way to Inform and Inspire Pedagogy through Self-Reflection

Response to intervention
3. Response to Intervention (RTI): What Teachers of Reading Need to Know
4. Responding to RTI

Skill gaps
22. Meeting Students Where They Are: The Latino Education Crisis
34. Tech Tool Targets Elementary Readers
35. Digital Tools Expand Options for Personalized Learning

Special education
26. Books That Portray Characters with Disabilities: A Top 25 List for Children and Young Adults
28. Tackling a Problematic Behavior Management Issue: Teachers' Intervention in Childhood Bullying Problems
32. Developing Effective Behavior Intervention Plans: Suggestions for School Personnel

Stereotypes
14. Do Girls Learn Math Fear from Teachers?
25. The Myth of the "Culture of Poverty"
26. Books That Portray Characters with Disabilities: A Top 25 List for Children and Young Adults

Teacher preparation
3. Response to Intervention (RTI): What Teachers of Reading Need to Know
5. Reluctant Teachers, Reluctant Learners
14. Do Girls Learn Math Fear from Teachers?
33. "For Openers: How Technology Is Changing School"

Technology
33. "For Openers: How Technology Is Changing School"
34. Tech Tool Targets Elementary Readers
35. Digital Tools Expand Options For Personalized Learning
36. Effects of Video-Game Ownership on Young Boys' Academic and Behavioral Functioning: A Randomized, Controlled Study

Internet References

The following Internet sites have been selected to support the articles found in this reader. These sites were available at the time of publication. However, because websites often change their structure and content, the information listed may no longer be available. We invite you to visit www.mhhe.com/cls for easy access to these sites.

Annual Editions: Education 11/12

General Sources

Education Week on the Web
www.edweek.org

At this Education Week home page you will be able to open its archives, read special reports on education, keep up on current events in education, look for job opportunities, and access articles relevant to educators today.

Educational Resources Information Center
www.eric.ed.gov

This invaluable site provides links to all ERIC sites: clearinghouses, support components, and publishers of ERIC materials. You can search the ERIC database, find out what is new, and ask questions about ERIC.

National Education Association
www.nea.org

Something about virtually every education-related topic can be accessed via this site of the 2.3-million-strong National Education Association.

National Parent Information Network/ERIC
www.npin.org

This is a clearinghouse of information on elementary and early childhood education as well as urban education. Browse through its links for information for parents and for people who work with parents.

U.S. Department of Education
www.ed.gov

Explore this government site for examination of institutional aspects of multicultural education. National goals, projects, grants, and other educational programs are listed here as well as many links to teacher services and resources.

UNIT 1: Reformatting Our Schools

U.S. Department of Education: Overview of the Educational Recovery Act
www.ed.gov/policy/gen/leg/recovery/programs.html

This page offers links to the various recovery acts passed during 2009. Here, you can learn what the acts are and how they are being implemented to improve public schools.

American School Board Journal
www.asbj.com

The National School Boards Association publishes a monthly magazine where educational issues of national interest are discussed. They offer the journal free of cost online and solicit reader comments at http://www.asbj.com/readerpanel. Further, at the Resources tab, they offer links to special reports and a topic archive that are rich sources of information on current topics.

The Response to Intervention Action Network
www.rtinetwork.org

The goal of the RTI Action Network, sponsored by the National Center for Learning Disabilities, is to inform educators and families about the large-scale implementation of RTI so that each child has equitable access to instruction and that struggling students are identified early, in order to receive the necessary supports to meet their individual needs. Materials and links offered at this website cover all grade levels and content areas. They bring leaders to the website to answer questions and offer webinars.

Teacher Magazine
www.edweek.org/tsb/articles/2010/04/12/02allington.h03.html

This link to Teacher Magazine will allow you to read or make comments in response to Dr. Richard Allington's article about Response to Intervention. In addition, in this online copy of the article you will find a link to allow you to sign up for the Education Week Teacher Book Club.

Wrightslaw
www.wrightslaw.com/info/rti.index.htm

Wrightslaw is the website of a lawyer who specializes in special education law and has argued special education cases before the U.S. Supreme Court. The link above leads you to his page on Response to Intervention where you will find additional links to national experts who helped frame the law and who offer their perspective on RTI.

The Bill & Melinda Gates Foundation
www.gatesfoundation.org/topics/Pages/high-schools.aspx

The Gates Foundation provides grants and donations to schools. Visit this website to learn how they are working to improve educational opportunities across the country.

What Works Clearinghouse
www.ies.ed.gov/ncee/wwc

The Clearinghouse is a source for programs with scientific evidence that they work. You are able to create a summary of the research findings on a topic, such as beginning reading, and then read summaries of the research on all of the reviewed programs.

The Center for Comprehensive School Reform and Improvement
www.centerforcsri.org

Information about research-based strategies and assistance for schools wishing to make positive changes is available on this U.S. Department of Education sponsored website. You can search their database by topic, listen to podcasts, and view videos to learn how schools are working to reform the educational experience for students.

Internet References

Unit 2: Preparing Teachers to Teach All Students in All Schools

Mindsteps
www.mindstepsinc.com/resources.asp

Author Robyn Jackson has a consulting company called Mindsteps. You will need to register to view much of the site, but there is no charge to become a member of the website. She provides a variety of free resources on her website.

Edutopia
www.edutopia.org

Project-based learning can be used to teach problem solving and critical thinking skills. This website has many video examples and articles about how teachers are integrating the real world into their teaching.

Teacher Magazine
www.edweek.org/ew/section/blogs/index.html

Blogs offer one way to reflect on teaching and living the teaching life. Three such blogs are offered below, however, you can find many more at the link above. Nancy Flanagan is a K-12 music teacher from Michigan. Read her blog at: http://teacherleaders.typepad.com/teacher_in_a_strange_land Donalyn Miller is a 6th grade teacher in Texas who loves to inspire children to read. See what she has to say at: http://blogs.edweek.org/teachers/book_whisperer

Jim Randels and Kalamu ya Salaam reflect on the teaching of writing in two New Orleans High Schools at: http://blogs.edweek.org/edweek/nola_voices.

North Central Regional Educational Laboratory
www.ncrel.org/sdrs/areas/issues/methods/assment/as700.htm

This Web page provides information about the changing role of assessment and the reasons why we must change how we assess student learning. The hyperlinks take you to additional information on a variety of assessment topics as well as illustrative cases.

Wrightslaw
www.wrightslaw.com/advoc/articles/tests_measurements.html

Peter and Pamela Wright founded this website for parents and teachers who work with students who have disabilities. However, all teachers will find their explanation of tests and measurements, statistics, and how to understand test scores very informative.

Unit 3: Cornerstones to Learning: Reading and Math

The National Council of Teachers of English (NCTE)
www.ncte.org/search?q=teaching+ELL

NCTE provides teaching strategies for supporting language learning for students who are not native English speakers. In addition, they provide information about other resources and professional readings.

National Council of Teachers of Mathematics
www.nctm.org

The National Council of Teachers of Mathematics (NCTM) has a resource rich website for any teacher who wants professional development, suggestions for teaching, or is interested in attending conferences and workshops. Membership in this professional organization offers opportunities to network with teachers who share an interest in mathematics.

International Association of Reading
www.reading.org/General/Default.aspx

This international association for reading offers resources on many reading topics such as adolescent literacy, reading comprehension, the history of reading, Response to Intervention, and technology. In addition, they provide information on conferences, workshops, and books about teaching reading.

Visible Thinking
www.pzweb.harvard.edu/vt/index.html

Visible Thinking is one of several programs that are part of Project Zero at Harvard University. The goal is to help students develop thinking dispositions that support thoughtful learning—In the arts, and across school subjects. Also visit the Artful Thinking website at www.pzweb.harvard.edu/tc/index.cfm.

Jim Trelease's Read-aloud Home Page
www.trelease-on-reading.com

Did you know you can use rain gutters for book shelves? Or do you know where to find an online interview with a favorite author? Or do you know how to read a book you don't want to read? Answers can be found on the website noted above.

Literature Circles Resource Center
www.litcircles.org

The comprehensive website will help you start a literature circle in your classroom. Begin with the link to *How to use this site.*

Read, Write, Think
www.readwritethink.org

This resource rich website is sponsored by the International Reading Association and National Council of Teachers of English. You can find lesson plans, student materials, and Web resources for teaching language and reading.

National Library of Virtual Manipulatives
www.nlvm.usu.edu/en/nav/vlibrary.html

This site sponsored by Utah State University offers a wide variety of online manipulatives that teachers and students can use to enhance learning of mathematical principals.

Unit 4: Creating Caring Communities of Learners

Read Write Think Connection
www.readwritethink.org/lessons/lesson_view.asp?id=987

In Rance-Roney's article, she mentions a lesson plan for peer interviews so that classmates could learn about their peers and understand their similarities and differences. The link above takes you to that lesson plan with all of its handouts and teaching materials.

Education World
www.educationworld.com/a_curr/curr302.shtml

Here is another view point on praising children to raise their self-esteem.

Teacher Vision
www.teachervision.fen.com/education-and-parents/resource/3730.html

This website has links to many topics of interest to all teachers. The link above will take you to a page of tips, strategies, and free *printables* to use as you collaborate and consult with parents of your students. Under the tab *Classroom Management* you will find more information about conduction effective and collaborative conferences with parents.

Internet References

Coalition of Essential Schools
www.essentialschools.org

The Coalition is about creating and sustaining personalized, equitable, and intellectually challenging schools. While you will have access to many resources on this website, if you register you can participate in blogs and discussions online.

The National Coalition for Parent Involvement in Education (NCPIE)
www.ncpie.org

On this website you will find information and ideas about research, programs, and policies to increase family involvement in education. You will find access to resources, tools, and legislative updates to assist you in promoting parent and family involvement in their child's education.

Unit 5: Addressing Diversity in Your School

The Literacy Web
www.literacy.uconn.edu/index.htm

The University of Connecticut sponsors this website devoted to literacy. You will find many useful resources for teaching reading to all students. If you are interested in teaching English Language Learners, go to the Literacy Topics page and scroll down to find the link to ESL/EFL.

New Horizons for Learning
www.newhorizons.org

This site has many resources for teachers who work with diverse students. The topics addressed by the group are news from the neurosciences, teaching strategies, student voices, lifelong learning, and special needs. Resources include articles to read online, lists of additional recommended reading, and related links.

National Association for Multicultural Education (NAME)
www.nameorg.org

NAME is a professional organization for persons interested in multicultural education. However, there are many resources available for nonmember teachers in their Resource Center.

Everything ESL
www.everythingesl.net

You WILL find everything at this website! This veteran teacher offers lesson plans ready to use, teaching tips, discussion topics where you can ask questions and read teaching tips from other teachers, and links to additional resources.

The National Research Center on the Gifted and Talented
www.gifted.uconn.edu/nrcgt

From this website, learn about research-based models, read articles, and link to organizations for students who are gifted/talented.

Circle of Inclusion
www.circleofinclusion.org

Educators who work with young children will find the resources on this website useful. You will find information about inclusion and accommodation strategies, augmentative communication, and downloadable forms.

Special Education Law Blog
www.specialedlaw.blogs.com

Charlie Fox, an attorney specializing in Special Education, blogs on a wide variety of topics relating to teaching, living with, and working with persons who have disabilities.

LD Online
www.ldonline.org

LD OnLine is a national educational service of WETA-TV, the PBS station in Washington, D.C., in partnership with seven leading special education professional organizations. Topics of interest to both teachers and parents include resources for teaching and living with persons who have LD, including opportunities to ask questions of leading experts in the field.

Council for Exceptional Children (CEC)
www.cec.sped.org

CEC is the largest professional organization devoted to teaching students with exceptional needs, including gifted and talented students. You will find information about membership, research-based practices, conferences at state and national levels, and news of policy and advocacy.

Unit 6: Rethinking Behavior Management: Getting the Behavior You Want and Need to Teach Effectively

The OSEP Technical Assistance Center of Positive Behavior Interventions & Supports (PBIS)
www.pbis.org/school/what_is_swpbs.aspx

Positive Behavior Interventions & Supports is being used across the country as a behavior management system. This website provides a comprehensive overview of this method used to change inappropriate behaviors and teach positive social behaviors. You can find this information by clicking on the link, *School-Wide PBS*.

Bully OnLine
www.bullyonline.org

Need to know more about bullying? This is the place to go. One reason you may want to visit this website is that they discuss all of the places where children and teens can be bullied and offer suggestions for helping victims outside school.

Teaching Tolerance
www.tolerance.org

Teaching Tolerance offers a two-part series on *The ABCs of Classroom Management*. The first part offers articles and videos on Democratic Classroom, Positive Behavior, and Authentic Relationships. Part two covers Engaging Curriculum, Being Culturally Responsive, and Motivation.

National Education Association: Classroom Management
www.nea.org/tools/ClassroomManagement.html

Need a quick tip to solve a management problem? This website has many of them.

Teacher Vision
http://teachervision.fen.com

Once at the homepage, look for the link to Class Management for information about topics for positive behavior management, lesson planning advice, and other topics of interest to all teachers.

Center for Safe and Responsible Internet Use
www.cskcst.com

As more and more children have unsupervised access to the Internet, CyberBullying has risen. Teachers can raise awareness in their students. You will find the link to CyberBullying at the top of the home page; scroll down for articles, a poster, and informational guides for students and parents.

Internet References

Unit 7: Technology: Are We Effectively Using Its Potential in Our Schools?

Educational Technology
www.edtech.sandi.net

Are you concerned that you do not know enough to help your students learn with technology. Visit the San Diego School District website link found above. Under the category of Resources you will find helpful tutorials, lesson plans, and other resources to get you started teaching with technology.

Curriculum Connections
www.edtech.sandi.net/old305/handouts/digitalclassroom/curriculumconnections.html

This is a comprehensive resource for lesson plans, teaching materials, and online resources for your students. Content is offered by grade level and content area. You will find resources to U.S. national parks, libraries, zoos, and many other websites that will enhance your teaching and student learning.

Open Thinking Wiki
http://couros.wikispaces.com/TechAndMediaLiteracyVids

This wiki is meant as a resource for courses I teach related to ICT in education and media studies. The creator, Alec Couros, is the ICT Coordinator of the Faculty of Education, University of Regina. The link about will take you to a page of resources all teachers will find helpful.

No limits 2 learning: Celebrating human potential through assistive technology
www.nolimitstolearning.blogspot.com

Lon Thornburg is an educator and assistive technology specialist and trainer. His blog is updated regularly with the latest information on technology tools that all students can use. However, he does offer clear descriptions and reviews that all of us can understand.

Quest Garden
www.questgarden.com

Looking for a way to include Project-based Learning into your lesson plans? This is the website for you. Regardless of the content area, topic, or size of your class you will find a Web Quest you can use at this site. All Web Quests found here have been peer previewed.

Go2web20
www.go2web20.net

Some schools and teachers do not have the funds to purchase software every year. At Go2Web20 you will find 68 pages of Web 2.0 tools and applications. Some of these are just for fun, but many can be used for educational purposes. Enjoy searching here.

UNIT 1
Reformatting Our Schools

Unit Selections
1. **'Quality Education Is Our Moon Shot',** Joan Richardson
2. **Duncan's Strategy Is Flawed,** ASBJ Reader's Panel
3. **Response to Intervention (RTI): What Teachers of Reading Need to Know,** Eric M. Mesmer and Heidi Anne E. Mesmer
4. **Responding to RTI,** Anthony Rebora

Learning Outcomes
After reading this unit, you will be able to:

- Explain the issues that make revisions of the No Child Left Behind (NCLB) Act necessary.
- Discuss the merits of the five strategies that Secretary Duncan thinks will support school improvement under a new NCLB Act.
- Synthesize the public responses to the policies and strategies suggested for the revision of NCLB.
- Construct your own response to the policies and strategies suggested for the revision of NCLB.
- Paraphrase each of the levels of Response to Intervention (RtI) process.
- Explain how to complete each of the five steps to implementation of RtI.
- Prepare a plan for using the RtI process in your classroom.
- Present an argument for or against the implementation of RtI in general education classrooms.
- Assess the criticism of RtI's value as a method for finding and remediating students who are struggling to learn.

Student Website
www.mhhe.com/cls

Internet References
U.S. Department of Education: Overview of the Educational Recovery Act
www.ed.gov/policy/gen/leg/recovery/programs.html
American School Board Journal
www.asbj.com
The Response to Intervention Action Network
www.rtinetwork.org
Teacher Magazine
www.edweek.org/tsb/articles/2010/04/12/02allington.h03.html
Wrightslaw
www.wrightslaw.com/info/rti.index.htm
The Bill & Melinda Gates Foundation
www.gatesfoundation.org/topics/Pages/high-schools.aspx
What Works Clearinghouse
www.ies.ed.gov/ncee/wwc
The Center for Comprehensive School Reform and Improvement
www.centerforcsri.org

As school districts have implemented "No Child Left Behind" (NCLB) legislation, they have restructured the schools to emphasize core content proficiency. In other words, the emphasis has been on preparing students to meet college entrance requirements. We are left to decide the equity issues involved. We are also left to answer the most fundamental question of all: What constitutes a "well-educated high school graduate?" What educational background should the person have? We are a democratic society, committed to the free education of all our citizens, but are we accomplishing that goal? Under the Clinton administration, Goals 2000 was established under the *Educate America Act.* Two of these goals are important to the discussion of what constitutes a well-educated graduate. First, are we keeping students in school? Second, are they prepared with the necessary skills that will enable them to participate in a global economy?

Goal 2 states that "The high school graduation rate will increase to at least 90%." (U.S. Department of Education, n.d.) The data indicate that we have not reached this goal, and are far from achieving it. While there is some disagreement on the exact percentages, most researchers agree that we have not reached the goal of 90%. For example, Heckman and LaFontaine (2008) note regarding the graduation rates in the United States that the minority graduation rates are still substantially below the rates for non-Hispanic whites and the decline in high school graduation is greater for males than for females.

Goal 5 states that "Every adult American will be literate and will possess the knowledge and skills necessary to compete in a global economy and exercise the rights and responsibilities of citizenship" (U.S. Department of Education, n.d.). Educators have acknowledged that high school graduates get more satisfactory jobs, are happier in their job choices, and earn higher salaries than non-graduates. Heckman and LaFontaine (2008) note that the decline in high school graduation since 1970 (for cohorts born after 1950) has flattened growth in the skill level of the U.S. workforce. We must, at the very least, confront the drop-out problem to increase the skill levels of the future workforce. We must also consider how high schools that respond only to higher education demands may be ignoring the needs of the nation at large for a skilled workforce that can compete in a global market. Bridgeland, DiIulio, and Morrison (2006) found in a survey of dropouts that 47% reported that a major reason why they left school was that the classes were not interesting. We must consider that by simply preparing students to attend traditional 4-year institutions we may be ignoring their interests and desires, and thus alienating them.

Educational law and policy issues of NCLB and Individuals with Disabilities Educational Act-2004 are hot button topics in most schools of education. Each of the articles in this unit relates to the tension involved in conceiving how educational development should proceed in response to all the dramatic social and economic changes in society.

In the first article, Secretary of Education, Arne Duncan, responds to questions and lays out the rationale for the educational reform proposed by the Obama administration.

© The McGraw-Hill Companies, Inc/John Flournoy, photographer

These reforms are informed in part by his experiences as the CEO of the Chicago Public School system, and his firm belief that a quality education for all children is the civil rights issue of his generation. His goals are strikingly similar to the goals noted in *Goals 2000;* 1) preparing students for success in college and the workplace, 2) recruit, develop, retain, and reward effective teachers and principals, 3) build data systems that measure student success and inform teachers and principals how they can improve their practices, and 4) turn around low-performing schools. In the interview, he lays out several actions he believes will achieve these goals. However, he is not without detractors. In the article, *Duncan's strategy is flawed,* we can read the comments and concerns of educators across the country. As readers discuss these articles, perhaps a basic question to ask might be how will these reforms change the data presented in the paragraphs above under Goals 2 and 5 of *Goals 2000*?

On the other hand, the third and fourth articles in this unit present direct actions that may be taken to find and address a primary and devastating educational problem, struggling students who do not read well and are 80% of the students identified for special education. Response to Intervention (RTI) was introduced in the Public Law 108-446 (IDEA-2004) as a method to identify students with learning disability. Mesmer and Mesmer provide a straightforward explanation of the legislation with clear definitions and details supported with examples. All educational professionals will benefit from reading this article. In Responding to RTI, Allington expresses strong opinions about the use of RTI to achieve full literacy in our country by stating that RTI is possibly "our last, best hope", and that is just the beginning. He has much more to say about how we assess and teach reading in public schools, and in the end, he states we must ". . . ask the questions about what we are doing or not doing, rather than asking what is wrong with the child."

As we consider reformatting the educational system of the United States, we must engage in an intensively reflective and analytical effort. Further, we must give considerable contemplation and forethought to the consequences, because our actions will shape not only the students' futures, but also the future of our country, as a member of the global community. Prospective teachers are being encouraged to question their own individual educational experiences as they read the articles presented in this section. All of us must acknowledge that our values affect both our ideas about curriculum and what we believe is the purpose of educating others. This is vitally important while engaging in a dialog that will either help or hinder students' ability to meet graduation requirements and be successful in adult living and work settings. The economic and demographic changes in the last decade and those that will occur in the future necessitate a fundamental reconceptualization of how schools ought to respond to the many social and economic environments in which they are located. How can schools, for instance, reflect the needs of and respond to the diverse group of students they serve while meeting the needs of our democratic society?

References

Bridgeland, J. M., DiIulio, J. J., & Morrison, K. B. (2006). The Silent Epidemic: Perspectives of High School Dropouts. Bill & Melinda Gates Foundation. Retrieved on 28 May 2008 from www.gatesfoundation.org/Pages/home.aspx

Heckman, J. T. & LaFontaine, P. A. (2008). The Declining American High School Graduation Rate: Evidence, Sources, and Consequences: Research Summary 2008. National Bureau of Economic Research. Retrieved on 28 May 2008 from www.nber.org/reporter/2008number1/heckman.html

U.S. Department of Education. Summary of Goals 2000: Educate America Act. Author. Retrieved on 28 May 2008 from www.ed.gov/legislation/GOALS2000/TheAct/sec102.html

Article 1

'Quality Education Is Our Moon Shot'

An interview with Secretary of Education Arne Duncan.

JOAN RICHARDSON

KAPPAN: Whenever we embark on any project, we're always encouraged to "begin with the end in mind," so that's where I want to start this interview. The last Administration will be forever tagged with No Child Left Behind as its legacy. When Arne Duncan and Barack Obama leave Washington in four years or eight years, what do you hope folks will be saying about what you contributed to education?

DUNCAN: Well, the President has drawn a line in the sand. He has said that by 2020, we want to again have the largest percentage of college graduates in the world. We used to have that a couple of decades ago. We've lost our way. We've flat lined. Other countries have passed us by. That's our Moon shot.

But we have to get dramatically better to get there. That's the goal. We're going to push as hard as we can to hit that goal. The President and I both believe that we have to educate our way to a better economy. It's the only way we're going to get there.

Achieving a quality education for all children is the civil rights issue of our generation. We have to give children a chance to fulfill their potential and be successful. And the way to do that is by giving them quality educational opportunities.

Achieving a quality education for all children is the civil rights issue of our generation.

That means that we have to reduce the dropout rate significantly. We have to increase the graduation rate. We have to make sure that the students who graduate are prepared to go on to be successful in some form of higher education, whether it's a two-year college, a four-year university, vocational, or technical training.

We want to get dramatically better in every piece of the education continuum: early childhood, K-12, higher ed. as well. It's an ambitious agenda, but we think it's all critically important.

KAPPAN: Is there one phrase that you could use to describe what you just said?

DUNCAN: We want to become the most educated country in the world. That's the goal.

The Future of NCLB

KAPPAN: I want to talk about the reauthorization of ESEA (Elementary and Secondary Education Act). As you make plans to move ahead with that, I want to know how you think you can change No Child Left Behind from what many perceive to be a test-and-punish law to a law that is really focused on improving student learning?

DUNCAN: Let me start by telling you what I like about No Child Left Behind. I always try to give the previous Administration credit for its focus on the achievement gap and its use of disaggregating student data.

As a country, we used to sweep that conversation under the rug and not talk about the tremendous disparities in outcomes between white children and African-American and Latino children. Forever-more, we will keep that front and center.

I think that's an important conversation. It's sometimes uncomfortable. It's sometimes tough. But, as a country, we have a tremendous achievement gap that we have to continue to close. Having transparency around that and challenging ourselves to both raise the bar and close the gap is hugely important.

Having said that, there are things that need to change pretty fundamentally. The opportunity that we have is to be very pragmatic. If it worked, then let's keep it. If it didn't work, then let's blue sky it and think in very different ways.

First, as you know, No Child Left Behind was dramatically underfunded. We've put over $100 billion into education. While it's never enough, it's a huge investment.

Second, from a management standpoint, you have to figure out what you manage loose and what you manage tight. I think they got this one fundamentally backwards. NCLB was very, very loose on the goals. So there are 50 different goal posts, 50 different measurements at the state level.

And the vast majority of those got dummied down due to political pressure. In some states, including my state of Illinois,

3

The Four Reforms

Secretary Arne Duncan and President Barack Obama have pledged federal money to four central areas of reform that they believe will drive school improvement:

- Adopt internationally benchmarked standards and assessments that prepare students for success in college and the workplace;
- Recruit, develop, retain, and reward effective teachers and principals;
- Build data systems that measure student success and inform teachers and principals how they can improve their practices; and
- Turn around the lowest-performing schools.

Learn more about programs being supported by the American Recovery and Reinvestment Act and the Race to the Top funds.

www.ed.gov/policy/gen/leg/recovery/programs.html

we're actually lying to children. When you tell the parent that their child is meeting the 'state standard,' the logical assumption is that they're on track to be successful.

I would argue that, in many places, the standard has been dummied down so much that those children who are just meeting the standard are barely able to graduate from high school and absolutely inadequately prepared to go on to a competitive four-year university, much less graduate.

So, they were very loose on the goal but very prescriptive on how you get there. Very tight on that. I think that's backwards. I want to fundamentally flip that on its head.

We want common, career-ready, college-ready standards that would be internationally benchmarked. We would let people be creative and innovative about how they get to those standards, but we'd hold them accountable for results. Have people at the local level figure out the best way to get there.

I often joke that before I came to Washington, I didn't believe that all of the good ideas came out of Washington. Now that I'm in Washington, I *know* that all of the good ideas don't come out of Washington. The best ideas are always going to come at the local level.

So fundamentally, we want to be loose and tight. To become tight on the goals but to allow people to become much more entrepreneurial, much more creative, innovative to get there.

I also worry a lot about the narrowing of the curriculum under No Child Left Behind. Too many schools are focusing on just what's tested so there's a loss of P.E., music, art, the nontested subjects, even science in some places.

It's so important that all children at the early ages have exposure to those things. That's how children develop their skills and discover their passions. I worry particularly about disadvantaged children who don't have those opportunities in their homes or their communities. The only place they're going to have access to art or drama or music is in school. So how are we going to think differently about that? How are we going to make sure that we're giving all children a well-rounded education from the earliest ages on?

Then, finally, to your original starting point: No Child Left Behind did a lot of labeling of schools as failures. I'm much more interested in gain and growth than in absolute test scores. There were a lot of schools that were labeled as failures that were actually improving every year. That was wrong. That's tremendously demoralizing to staff and confusing to parents. That needs to be corrected.

No Child Left Behind is what I would call a blunt instrument. Schools that were improving got labeled as failures. Schools that were struggling didn't get the help that they needed. Schools at the bottom that need to be fundamentally and absolutely transformed got incremental help, which doesn't get us where we need to go.

If we have a much more finely tuned instrument that would understand those really important distinctions between schools, it would help us dramatically improve student outcomes. It would help us turn around schools that need dramatic, fundamental change and do it with a real sense of urgency.

Urban Districts

KAPPAN: You came into this job with dramatically different on-the-ground experience than most of your predecessors in this job. You had some demonstrated success in a very challenged urban district. What do you say to other urban superintendents about where they begin the hard work of improving student learning in those districts? How do you create systems of success? Where do you start?

DUNCAN: It's very complex, but it starts with real leadership at the top. You have to have strong, courageous leadership. You can't do anything without that. You have to rally the entire community behind these efforts. I've argued that if it's just the school system by itself trying to get better, you're not going to get there. You need the business community, the philanthropic community, the religious community; you need the not-for-profits, you need the parks and recreation, health and human services. This has to be a citywide effort. You cannot have a world-class city without a world-class school system.

> **You cannot have a world-class city without a world-class school system.**

You've seen a series of mayors—Mayor (Richard) Daley in Chicago, Mayor (Michael) Bloomberg in New York, Mayor (Adrian) Fenty here in Washington—provide real leadership at the top to rally an entire city, not just the school district by itself.

Leadership at the top, all hands on deck, everyone pushing hard in the right direction, and a commitment for the long haul. None of this is about an overnight success. You have to be willing to stick with it. But I can't imagine a more important activity for a city and one that a city can rally behind than dramatically improving the quality of public education.

It combines a real sense of self-interest. If you want to attract and retain jobs, you have to have an educated workforce. And the sense of altruism that our children deserve more than what we're giving them.

At the end of the day, it brings together a set of interests.

Mayoral Control

KAPPAN: I assume that all of the ideas that are in your plan, all of the ideas in the Obama plan for education, that all of those are driven by your belief that they will improve student learning.

DUNCAN: Yes, absolutely. That's what it's all about, driving student achievement. It's about closing the gap and raising the bar.

KAPPAN: Let's tick through some of those ideas and help me make the link between those ideas and improving student learning. You touched on mayoral control, so let's start there. What's the connection between mayoral control and improving student learning?

DUNCAN: It's not always the right answer. It's a piece of an answer. It's not a magic bullet. In some places, it might be the wrong answer. But I would argue that in large urban cities with a history of fairly dysfunctional school systems, the work is so hard and the challenges so intractable that you have to have strong leadership at the top to give you a chance to get there.

It doesn't guarantee success, but it puts you in the ball game. The problem is so large, the needs are so great that everyone in the city needs to rally around the effort.

The best person I can think of to rally all those different sectors together to achieve that is the mayor.

Charter Schools

KAPPAN: Same question related to charter schools. By the way, in the Gallup Poll, charter schools got a lot of support, even though people still seem to be confused by exactly what they are.

DUNCAN: I've always said I'm not a fan of charters, I'm a fan of good charters.

Three things have to happen for charter schools to be successful. First, you have to have a very high bar for entry. This is not "let a thousand flowers bloom." I would argue that there are far too many low-performing charters. We had a lot of charters in Chicago, but I closed three charter schools because they weren't performing.

This is not "let a thousand flowers bloom."

Arne Duncan

POSITION: U.S. Secretary of Education. Oversees a staff of 4,200 employees and a budget of $62.6 billion in regular FY 2009 discretionary appropriations and $96.8 billion in discretionary funding provided under the American Recovery and Reinvestment Act of 2009. Operates programs that touch every area and level of education—elementary and secondary programs annually serve nearly 14,000 school districts and about 56 million students attending some 98,000 public schools and 34,000 private schools. Department programs also provide grant, loan, and work-study assistance to more than 13 million postsecondary students.

AGE: 45

EDUCATION: Graduated magna cum laude from Harvard University with a bachelor's degree in sociology, 1987. Senior thesis: "The Values, Aspirations and Opportunities of the Urban Underclass" (unpublished) which he wrote after taking a year off and working at his mother's education center in Chicago. Attended University of Chicago Laboratory School, a private school that President Obama's children later attended.

PROFESSIONAL HISTORY: Played professional basketball with the Eastside Spectres in Australia, 1987 to 1991. Returned to Chicago in 1992 to run the Ariel Education Initiative, which helped fund a college education as part of the I Have a Dream program. Joined the Chicago Public Schools in 1998 as deputy chief of staff to then-CEO Paul Vallas. Replaced Vallas in 2001 and served as CEO for seven years. Became Secretary of Education in January 2009.

FAMILY: Wife, Karen, and two children (Claire, 7, Ryan, 4). Claire attends a public school in Northern Virginia. Mother, Sue Duncan, runs the Sue Duncan Children's Center (sueduncanchildrenscenter.org), an independent early-learning center on Chicago's South Side; father, the late Starkey Duncan Jr., was a psychology professor at the University of Chicago and a leading researcher in the study of nonverbal and verbal interactions.

PERSONAL: 6'5" tall. Plays basketball with the President. Grew up without a television at home.

The chance to educate our kids is like a sacred obligation. You really need to have a very clear vetting process so you're only allowing the best of the best to do that.

Once you've done that, two other things have to happen. You have to give these schools real autonomy. These are by definition educational entrepreneurs who have a different vision of education. You have to free them from the bureaucracy and give them the chance to innovate and create.

Third, you have to tie that autonomy to real accountability. We had five-year performance contracts. If they're not performing, you need to close them down.

When those three things happen, you can have remarkable, remarkable results for children. It's a piece of the answer. It's by no means the whole answer.

Merit Pay

KAPPAN: Another question that we asked in the Gallup Poll was about merit pay. We found that there was very high public support for merit pay. Are you surprised by that? Why do you think there was so much support? To the bigger question, why do you think that could be a lever for improving student learning?

DUNCAN: In education, we've been so scared to talk about excellence. I don't understand that. Great teachers and great principals make a tremendous difference in students' lives. Talent matters tremendously in education. Great teachers and great principals are the unsung heroes in our society. They perform miracles every day. They change student lives on a daily basis.

Somehow as a country, we've been scared to talk about that. In every other sector, in your world, in the media, business, sports, entertainment, music, excellence gets recognized. It gets rewarded. You learn from it. It gets replicated. In education, we're scared to do that. We have to do a much better job of identifying, rewarding, recognizing, spotlighting, and learning from excellence.

> **We have to do a much better job of identifying, rewarding, recognizing, spotlighting, and learning from excellence.**

Nobody goes into education to make a million dollars. People go into education for the most altruistic of reasons. They want to make a difference. It's a phenomenally committed group of folks. But there's no reason we can't provide some recognition for those who go beyond the call of duty every day and make a huge difference in students' lives. I don't think we can do enough of that. There's a lot that we can do, not just at the individual teacher level, but at the school level.

When I see a high-performing school, it's every adult in the building working together. It's not just the teachers and the principal, it's the custodians, the security guards, the social workers, the lunchroom attendants; they're all working hard and working together. We need to know who's doing a great job and shine a spotlight on them.

KAPPAN: Your proposal is to tie those pay increases into teacher evaluations and to testing data.

DUNCAN: Well, that's a piece of it. Teachers are concerned that that will be the only measure. I couldn't agree more. It should never be the only measure.

I'm fighting the reverse fight. I'm fighting the fight against those folks who say there should never be a tie between student achievement and teacher performance.

> **I'm fighting the fight against those folks who say there should never be a tie between student achievement and teacher performance.**

There are actually states that prohibit linking student data with teacher data. (Editor's note: California prohibits using its teacher-identification database for making decisions about teacher pay, promotion, evaluation, and other employment issues. New York prohibits using student achievement data in making tenure decisions.) That, to me, is stunning. That totally devalues the profession. It basically says that teaching doesn't matter, that anybody can do this. We know there's tremendous variation there. In those situations, everyone loses. Teachers who are successful don't get rewarded. Teachers who are struggling don't get the support that they need. Teachers who shouldn't be teaching don't get moved out. So every adult loses. And when the adults lose, guess what? The children lose, too. That doesn't make sense to me.

So we're creating significant incentives to encourage folks to think about this in a different way.

Grading the Public Schools

DUNCAN: Here's another Gallup result that I think is fascinating. This is the most remarkable finding. Everyone thinks their own school is good and that everybody else's school is bad. That's a constant theme.

KAPPAN: Why do you think that exists?

DUNCAN: Too many people don't understand how bad their own schools are. They always think it's somebody else's kid who's not being educated. They don't understand that it's their own kid who's being short-changed. That's part of our challenge. How do you awaken the public to believe that your own kid isn't getting what they need and you don't know it. If they would wake up, they could be part of the change. We need to wake them up.

Duncan and Sports

KAPPAN: OK, last question. This is the basketball question, but I'm not going to ask you whom you're playing, where you're playing, and who's winning. But talking about basketball is a required part of every interview with you, right?

DUNCAN: Absolutely.

KAPPAN: I'm assuming again that basketball, sports, played a big part in your life as you were growing up, or you wouldn't have gone on to do what you did, playing basketball at Harvard, playing professional basketball in Australia after graduation.

In this test-crazy environment where, as you noted, so many things are being lost at schools, what's the role of competitive athletics in schools today? What role do you think that ought to play in a kid's education?

DUNCAN: Sports can be a tremendous vehicle for teaching students really important life lessons. When you talk about student athletes, as long as that student piece is kept front and center, I think great things can happen. Too often, it gets flipped and becomes athlete first and student second. That has a very damaging impact on students. I worry about the skewed or warped sense of priorities and values there.

But when it's kept in perspective, the life lessons that you can learn on the court or the playing field—hard work, selflessness, teamwork, working for the greater good, not about yourself—those life lessons can be hugely important. I absolutely believe that I would not be doing what I'm doing today if I had not had a chance to learn those lessons. For me, that was on the basketball court.

With the proper coaching in the right context with a laser-like focus on academics first and sports being the carrot, the reward for good academic work, I think sports can have a huge and positive role.

What I worry about are adults living their own dreams through students and chasing a dream of going pro. When students don't focus academically, that ends up dooming a kid to academic failure.

It can be a tool for good or it can be really destructive to children, depending on the quality and character of the adults who are engaged with those children.

KAPPAN: And I won't ask you who wins when you play horse.

DUNCAN: (Laughs) I plead the fifth.

Assess Your Progress

1. List and explain the issues that Secretary of Education Duncan thinks make revision of the No Child Left Behind (NCLB) Act necessary. Your explanation should include a discussion of why these are important to you as a teacher.

2. Share the Duncan interview with a P-12 teacher. Engage the teacher in a conversation about the five strategies that are suggested to improve schools. Write a summary of your conversation to share with peers in class.

3. If you disagree with Secretary Duncan's four reform goals, what would be your top three goals for public education in the U.S.?

4. Secretary Duncan stated that "by 2020 we want to again have the largest percentage of college graduates in the world." Should this be the primary goal of our public schools? Provide a rationale for your answer.

JOAN RICHARDSON is editor-in-chief of *Phi Delta Kappan* magazine.

From *Phi Delta Kappan,* by Joan Richardson, September 2009, pp. 24–29. Reprinted with permission of Phi Delta Kappa International, www.pdkintl.org, 2009. All rights reserved.

Article 2

Duncan's Strategy Is Flawed

He's definitely racing somewhere, just maybe not to "The Top." That's what many of you seemed to be saying when asked if Arne Duncan is "on the right track" concerning his ambitious plan to reform the public schools. Just 16 percent said that the education secretary's plan is sound, compared with 26 percent who found it seriously flawed. The biggest group—48 percent—weighed in with "maybe," and 10 percent chose "none of the above."

Is this NCLB all over again? That thought scares Missouri board member Peggy Taylor.

"It appears we are selling out for big bucks, while compromising if not eroding local control," said Taylor, who is also president of the Missouri School Boards' Association. "Big bucks are owed to public education for all the broken promises over the years. The 'rush' to the race certainly guarantees another federal mess at a time we are challenged to survive with our budgets and save teaching positions. Secretary Duncan's enthusiasm for education is refreshing, but firing principals and 50 percent of the teachers is not the answer. Is this the preliminary test run for the new look of the replacement for NCLB? That is scary to me!"

More comments:

I believe he is on the right track, but I am not convinced he will be successful. To be successful, he will need many educational leaders to be willing to accept change that they have been unwilling to accept in the past. We need talented teachers to enter the classroom and better ways to evaluate their success. We need state governments to be prepared to uphold teacher quality and de-tenure teachers when it is warranted. We need to be willing to try to bring innovation back into schools by trying new things supported by research to determine when it works and when it does not work. This is all dependent on the willingness of current and future educators to be prepared to accept change. I hope Secretary Duncan can pull it off, and I am rooting for his side. —*Paul Herman, New Jersey*

Until they quit the procedure of "the whippings will continue until morale improves," they will continue to have issues. They need to treat educators as professionals and not the enemy. Most of the panels are made up of non-educators. Most educators now are working very hard to make sure that their students achieve; however, their opinions are not valued. Who will the experts get to put their plans and visions into action? Of course, the educators in the field. —*Ron Saunders, Superintendent, Georgia*

Duncan's desire to put mayors in control of public schools is a recipe for disaster. We need to talk about how money can matter when it is focused on specific academic interventions, tied to measureable outcomes, and embedded in a system with quality professional development and support. Just pouring more money into education won't solve our country's education problems. I'm waiting to hear a plan based on a foundation of local control, not Washington D.C., control. —*Fred Deutsch, Board Member, South Dakota*

There are so many endeavors that focus on "systemic change" in school reform. The one area that *always* engenders better results is when the students are blessed with a superb teacher. When the power of the teachers' unions is blunted, and poorly performing teachers can be removed more easily, then real reform will happen. The sad part is that these poor performers are probably only 5 percent of the profession. That is what we are protecting at such a great cost to kids. —*Paul Vranish, Superintendent, Texas*

The current system is functioning exactly as it was intended—play to the bell curve and prepare citizens for a life in an industrial world. Throwing money at a system that does not serve the needs of the current and future marketplace is insane. Substantive changes must occur in the way the education system is conceived. . . . Putting a high priority on teacher excellence is a good start and the subject of research by Battelle for Kids [a nonprofit focused on school improvement]. However, extending the school day and adding charter schools will do little to address the fundamental problem—outdated methods, buildings, and expectations. —*Anna Bucy, Board Member, Ohio*

Certainly the call for higher standards is warranted, and perhaps even [Duncan's] call for international standards. NAEP is just the latest "test" to come down the line. Until assessments are scored by third parties who truly are in the international arena, assessment will remain a political football. It is my hope that his insistence of tying performance to pay will make a difference. —*Michael R. Martin, Superintendent, Tennessee*

Assess Your Progress

1. Summarize the public responses to Duncan's suggested revision of NCLB.
2. Based on what you have read in this unit, your conversation with active teachers, and your own experiences as a public school student construct your own response to Duncan's plans to revise NCLB.

From *American School Board Journal*, February 2010, pp. 14–15. Copyright © 2010 by National School Boards Association. Reprinted by permission.

Article 3

Response to Intervention (RTI): What Teachers of Reading Need to Know

Clear definitions, details of relevant legislation, and examples of RTI in action help explain this approach to identifying and supporting learners who may be struggling.

ERIC M. MESMER AND HEIDI ANNE E. MESMER

In the most recent "What's hot, what's not for 2008?" *Reading Today* survey, 75% of prominent literacy researchers believed that Response to Intervention (RTI) was "very hot" and the same percentage believed that it should be "hot" (Cassidy & Cassidy, 2008). RTI is a new approach to identifying students with specific learning disabilities and represents a major change in special education law, the Individuals With Disabilities Act (IDEA). This change shifts the emphasis of the identification process toward providing support and intervention to struggling students early and is similarly reflected in the Reading First provisions of No Child Left Behind, which calls for proven methods of instruction to reduce the incidence of reading difficulties. RTI will alter the work of reading teachers because more than 80% of students identified for special education struggle with literacy (Lyon, 1995), and the law names "reading teachers" as qualified participants in the RTI process because of the International Reading Association's (IRA, 2007) lobbying efforts. However, RTI has only recently attracted the attention of the reading community (Bell, 2007), despite having roots in approaches such as prereferral intervention (Flugum & Reschly, 1994; Fuchs, Fuchs, & Bahr, 1990), curriculum-based measurement (Shinn, 1989), and Reading Recovery (Clay, 1987; Lyons & Beaver, 1995).

RTI in Theory
Background and Rationale
RTI was developed because of the many problems with the discrepancy model for identifying students with learning disabilities (e.g., Francis et al., 2005; O'Malley, Francis, Foorman, Fletcher, & Swank, 2002; Stanovich, 2005; Vellutino, Scanlon, & Lyon, 2000; Walmsley & Allington, 2007). In 1977, a learning disability was defined as "a severe discrepancy between achievement and intellectual ability" (U.S. Department of Education, 1977, p. G1082). In practice, this involves schools administering IQ tests and achievement tests and then examining scores for discrepancies between intellect and achievement to identify a learning disability (see Table 1). The discrepancy model has drawn four major criticisms. First, it requires that a learning problem becomes considerably acute in terms of an IQ/achievement discrepancy before a learner can receive additional support, a problem called "waiting to fail" (Vaughn & Fuchs, 2003, p. 139). Second, establishing a discrepancy is not necessary to improve outcomes for struggling readers, as students both with and without a discrepancy are qualitatively the same in their literacy instructional needs (Fuchs, Mock, Morgan, & Young, 2003; Vellutino et al., 2000). Third, the IQ/ achievement discrepancy has shifted focus away from understanding the impact of other possible factors, such as opportunities to learn (Walmsley & Allington, 2007). These factors need to be considered prior to determining that a learning disability exists. Fourth, under the discrepancy model, many districts and states have seen skyrocketing percentages of students identified as learning disabled, particularly minorities (IRA, 2007; Walmsley & Allington, 2007).

The Law
In 2004, IDEA, Public Law 108-446, introduced RTI language (U.S. Department of Education, 2006). In Table 2, the section entitled "Specific learning disabilities" (§ 300.307) asserts that states cannot be required to use the discrepancy model for identifying learning disabilities but may "permit the use of a process based on the child's response to scientific, research-based intervention." This is RTI, a process measuring whether a learner's academic performance improves when provided with well-defined, scientifically based interventions. In an RTI model, the "tests" of whether students possess learning disabilities are not standardized measures but students' measured responses to interventions. Within RTI, student potential (IQ) is replaced by a goal that allows for the evaluation of a performance relative to a defined academic standard (e.g., performance of other students

Table 1 Definitions of RTI Terms

Term	Definition
Discrepancy model	The standard for identifying students with learning disabilities based on the 1977 federal regulations. This process required that a significant difference be documented between a student's ability (IQ) and achievement in order for a learning disability to be identified. RTI models respond to the many problems identified with the discrepancy model.
Intervention	Targeted instruction provided in addition to the regular classroom program that addresses a student's documented instructional needs.
	Instruction that intends to prevent students who are struggling from falling farther behind their peers and intends to improve their future educational trajectory.
Level data	Information that reflects how students are performing in comparison to peers at a specific point in time.
	Slope data Information that reflects how a student is learning across time in comparison to his or her previous learning. These data capture rate of learning and can also be called growth rates. Slopes that are steeper show more growth over a smaller period of time than slopes that are flatter. Slope data are obtained by repeatedly measuring student performance in a particular area. They are displayed using a line graph.
Student progress monitoring	An assessment technique required by RTI regulations. Teachers administer quick assessments (1–5 minutes) frequently (weekly) to gauge the improvement of a student. The assessments provide information about the student's rate of learning and the effectiveness of a particular intervention (National Center on Student Progress Monitoring, 2007).
Literacy screening	The process of assessing the most basic and predictive literacy skills for all students in a school. The goal of screenings is to select learners whose reading achievement is significantly below standards. Literacy screenings are intended to identify students who require additional help so that further slippage and literacy failure can be prevented.

in the class or grade level). Students responding quickly and significantly to interventions are less likely to possess a disability than students responding more slowly or not at all. However, data showing a student's response to an intervention serves as only one source of information for determining whether a learning disability is present. Learning disabilities cannot be diagnosed when appropriate instruction, socioeconomic status, culture, sensory issues, emotional issues, or English as a second language may be of concern.

In the section entitled "Determining the existence of a specific learning disability" (§ 300.309), the law states that a learning disability may be present when a student's performance is not adequate to meet grade-level standards when provided with appropriate instruction and research-based interventions. The term *appropriate* refers to instruction in the classroom that matches a student's skill level. The descriptors *scientific* or *research-based* indicate that interventions should be based on practices that have produced verifiable results through research studies.

RTI Processes

The processes undergirding RTI have been used for evaluating the success of schoolwide supports, individualized interventions, and special education (O'Connor, Fulmer, Harty, & Bell, 2005; Powell-Smith & Ball, 2002; Taylor-Greene et al., 1997). However, in this article we focus on RTI as an initial referral and identification process for students suspected of having learning disabilities.

Step 1
Universal literacy practices are established. Prevention begins with universal literacy screenings to identify students who could be at risk (see Table 3). Any state receiving Reading First monies has identified a literacy screening in grades K–3. All students are screened on basic literacy skills approximately three times per year. Typically, student performance is compared with minimal benchmark scores and students not meeting benchmarks receive help.

Step 2
Scientifically valid interventions are implemented. When students do not meet benchmarks, they need additional instruction. Within most RTI models, interventions are first delivered to a small group and are intended to assist students in developing skills that will allow them to improve their reading skills.

Step 3
Progress of students receiving intervention instruction is monitored. RTI requires that progress-monitoring data are continuously collected as students receive interventions. Progress-monitoring assessments should address the skills that are being targeted for intervention and should indicate if the intervention is changing the student's reading. Also, the assessments should be administered repeatedly (weekly or biweekly) without introducing test-wise bias, which occurs when the results of an assessment reflect the testtaker's acquired knowledge about a test rather than true performance. In addition, the assessments

Table 2 Additional Procedures for Identifying Children with Specific Learning Disabilities

IDEA terminology	IDEA definition
§ 300.307 Specific learning disabilities.	A State must adopt, consistent with 34 CFR 300.309, criteria for determining whether a child has a specific learning disability as defined in 34 CFR 300.8(c)(10). In addition, the criteria adopted by the State: • Must not require the use of a severe discrepancy between intellectual ability and achievement for determining whether a child has a specific learning disability, as defined in 34 CFR 300.8(c)(10); • Must permit the use of a process based on the child's response to scientific, research-based intervention; and • May permit the use of other alternative research-based procedures for determining whether a child has a specific learning disability, as defined in 34 CFR 300.8(c)(10). A public agency must use the State criteria adopted pursuant to 34 CFR 300.307(a) in determining whether a child has a specific learning disability. [34 CFR 300.307] [20 U.S.C. 1221e-3; 1401(30); 1414(b)(6)]

§ 300.309 Determining the existence of a specific learning disability.	The group described in 34 CFR 300.306 may determine that a child has a specific learning disability, as defined in 34 CFR 300.8(c)(10), if:
	• The child does not achieve adequately for the child's age or to meet State-approved grade-level standards in one or more of the following areas, when provided with learning experiences and instruction appropriate for the child's age or State-approved grade–level standards:
	  • Oral expression.
	  • Listening comprehension.
	  • Written expression.
	  • Basic reading skills.
	  • Reading fluency skills.
	  • Reading comprehension.
	  • Mathematics calculation.
	  • Mathematics problem solving.
	• The child does not make sufficient progress to meet age or State-approved grade-level standards in one or more of the areas identified in 34 CFR 300.309(a)(1) when using a process based on the child's response to scientific, research-based intervention; or the child exhibits a pattern of strengths and weaknesses in performance, achievement, or both, relative to age, State-approved grade-level standards, or intellectual development, that is determined by the group to be relevant to the identification of a specific learning disability, using appropriate assessments, consistent with 34 CFR 300.304 and 300.305; and the group determines that its findings under 34 CFR 300.309(a)(1) and (2) are not primarily the result of:
	  • A visual, hearing, or motor disability;
	  • Mental retardation;
	  • Emotional disturbance;
	  • Cultural factors;
	  • Environmental or economic disadvantage; or
	  • Limited English proficiency.
	To ensure that underachievement in a child suspected of having a specific learning disability is not due to lack of appropriate instruction in reading or math, the group must consider, as part of the evaluation described in 34 CFR 300.304 through 300.306:
	• Data that demonstrate that prior to, or as a part of, the referral process, the child was provided appropriate instruction in regular education settings, delivered by qualified personnel; and
	• Data-based documentation of repeated assessments of achievement at reasonable intervals, reflecting formal assessment of student progress during instruction, which was provided to the child's parents.

Note. From U.S. Department of Education. (2006). *Assistance to states for the education of children with disabilities and preschool grants for children with disabilites* (Federal register 34 CFR Parts 300 and 301). Washington, DC: Author.

ANNUAL EDITIONS

Table 3 Examples of Literacy Screening Assessments

Screener	Authors
Dynamic Indicators of Basic Early Literacy Skills (DIBELS)	Good & Kaminski, 2002
Phonological Awareness Literacy Screening (PALS)	Invernizzi, Juel, Swank, & Meier, 2005
Texas Primary Reading Inventory (TPRI)	Texas Education Agency & University of Texas System, 2006
Illinois Snapshots of Early Literacy (ISEL)	Illinois State Board of Education, 2008

should be sufficiently sensitive to small changes in the student's reading performance (i.e., those that might occur within a few days) because it students are showing growth on the more sensitive, microlevel progress-monitoring measures, they will also be showing growth in the more comprehensive measures (Deno, Mirkin, & Chiang, 1982; Fuchs & Deno, 1981; Riedel, 2007). Finally, progress-monitoring measures must be reliable, valid, and brief (National Center on Student Progress Monitoring, 2007). For a list of tools for progress monitoring, see the National Center on Student Progress Monitoring website at www.studentprogress.org/chart/chart.asp.

Step 4

Individualize interventions for students who continue to struggle. Students who continue to struggle despite receiving initial intervention instruction will require more intense, targeted interventions. These interventions may require additional assessments to clarify the nature of the difficulty. The data generated from these additional assessments should be used collaboratively by teachers, reading specialists, school psychologists, and parents to develop more intensive intervention strategies. Upon implementation, the student's progress continues to be monitored.

Step 5

A decision-making process to determine eligibility for special education services occurs when necessary. In the last step, a team of school-based professionals and the student's parents review all data to determine whether the student is eligible for special education services. Special services may be indicated when the student has not responded to interventions that have been well implemented for a sufficient period of time. If the team suspects that the student's lack of response may be explained by some other factor (i.e., not explained by a learning disability), then it should request additional assessment of the student's social, behavioral, emotional, intellectual, and adaptive functioning.

RTI in Real Life: Making a Difference for Mark

To illustrate RTI processes, we use a vignette (with pseudonyms) based on our experiences in schools. This vignette shows how a team including Donisha, a reading teacher, Julie, a special educator, Carol, a second-grade teacher, and Sandra, a school psychologist, worked collaboratively (and sometimes painstakingly) within an RTI model to assist a student named Mark.

Step 1: Universal Literacy Practices Are Established

In September, Mark was administered the Phonological Awareness and Literacy Screening (PALS; Invernizzi, Juel, Swank, & Meier, 2005), an assessment that begins with two screening measures, the first-grade word list, given in the fall of grade 2, and a spelling assessment. From these measures, an entry benchmark score is formed. If the benchmark score does not meet the grade-level minimum, then additional diagnostics are administered (preprimer and primer lists, letter naming, letter sounds, concept of word, blending, and sound-to-letter). Students also read passages through which accuracy, reading rate, phrasing (a 3-point subjective scale), and comprehension scores are collected.

In the fall, Mark received a benchmark score of 22 (7/20 on the first-grade word list) and 15/20 on the spelling assessment. An expected benchmark score of 35, based on 15 words on the first-grade list, and 20 spelling feature points is expected for the beginning of second grade. Mark read instructionally at the primer level (1.1) with moderate phrasing and expression and answered five-sixths of the questions correctly. He read the 120 words in the primer story in 4 minutes and 20 seconds, a rate of about 28 words correct per minute (WCPM) and 20 words below the 50th percentile for second graders in the fall (Parker, Hasbrouck, & Tindal, 1992). When diagnostic assessments were administered, data showed that Mark had mastered alphabetic skills, such as phonemic awareness and letters. Carol described her initial analysis: "Mark seemed to have the basic building blocks for reading but needed more practice at his level." Initially, Mark received small-group classroom instruction, including reading daily in on-level materials and working with Carol on comprehension and decoding. In September, October, and November, Carol took running records on the books that Mark and the other students had been reading. Although the accuracy and book levels of other students were steadily increasing, Mark's accuracy was averaging 90% in less difficult books. Carol explained, "I felt like Mark needed more help, and we needed to act because I was concerned that he would continue to fall behind."

Step 2: Scientifically Valid Interventions Are Implemented

RTI requires that instructional interventions be scientifically valid, public, implemented with integrity, and systematically evaluated. Julie, who had recently attended the district's RTI workshop, explained that "The who, what, when, where, and how of interventions must be clear." The content of the intervention should be designated, the teacher responsible for implementing it identified, and the assessments determined. Often different team members plan, implement, or assess the intervention based on availability and expertise. For this reason, educators must collaborate and share information.

The team discussed Mark's needs and designed an intervention. Based upon its review of the data, the team determined that accurate, fluent reading in connected text seemed to be the problem. Mark could easily understand books above his reading level, but his progress was being impeded by word recognition. The group decided that an intervention increasing the amount of reading practice for Mark would build up his reading level. The designed intervention comprised the following components: modeling of fluent reading, repeated readings, error correction, comprehension questions, and self-monitoring. They decided that Donisha would implement the intervention with three other students in the classroom in 20-minute sessions, three times per week. In addition, Carol continued to work with Mark in the classroom during small-group instruction. Specifically, she had Mark read from the same materials used by Donisha to further increase practice opportunities, and she set a daily goal for Mark on comprehension questions. Mark checked his answers each day and provided the results to his teacher at the end of the reading block.

Step 3: Progress of Students Receiving Intervention Instruction Is Monitored

As the intervention was implemented, Sandra tracked Mark's accuracy and fluency in reading passages at the primer and second-grade levels, because the goal was to understand Mark's progress toward grade-level norms. She used a PDA device loaded with passages at different levels. As Mark read these passages weekly, Sandra kept track of his accuracy (percentage of words correct) and reading rate (WCPM). Figure 1 shows Mark's accuracy and Figure 2 shows his reading rate before and after implementing the intervention for six weeks. Mark demonstrated some gains in accuracy and fluency, but his progress was not increasing at a rate that would allow him to meet established second-grade goals.

As we have described RTI to this point, it sounds smooth and trouble free. But it was anything but that for the professionals involved. Donisha's first reaction to RTI was strong:

> At first, I felt like this group was shrinking reading down to something very simplistic. I had to advocate for comprehension questions to be included in the intervention. Even though Mark's comprehension was fine, we did not want him to believe that comprehension didn't matter. We also clarified that interventions are *additive* and by nature narrower because their power lies in solving specific problems. The comprehensive reading program is broad and multifaceted, and it keeps going on while a child is receiving an intervention. So Carol wasn't going to stop guided reading or doing the rest of her program.

We liken the intervention and the reading program to a balanced diet. The intervention is like an extra serving of milk, but it doesn't replace meat, fruits, or vegetables.

Donisha was also concerned that the intervention would be scripted. Scripts are directions to teachers that are read verbatim during instruction. Interventions are specific and systematic, but nothing in the law requires them to be scripted.

Carol also had concerns. "I was not used to people asking me specific questions about exactly what I was doing, and how often, and what my results were. At first, it felt invasive and suspicious." Given the frequency with which blame is placed on classroom teachers, Carol's reaction was understandable. However, the team members pointed out that the instruction was working well for almost all of the other students and acknowledged the time limitations and demands placed on Carol as a classroom teacher. Although she had felt it in the past, Carol did not feel as though fingers were being pointed at her. Sandra had faced equal frustration before:

> I come in because a teacher has a concern and when I start asking questions, I get tight responses and defensiveness. It's like asking questions is stepping on toes. I can't help others further understand the problem or contribute to a useful intervention if we can't talk nitty-gritty. Once I had a teacher tell me, "You're not a teacher. You won't be able to help." While I am not a teacher, I can contribute to the development of interventions, and I have particular skill in measuring effects.

In addition to reviewing Mark's progress during the six weeks of intervention instruction, Mark's midyear PALS scores were evaluated by the team. He was independent at the primer (1.1) level and barely instructional at the first-grade level with 14 errors and a reading rate of 42 WCPM. Despite his increase in instructional level and fluency, the team remained concerned about the lack of reduction in the number of errors that Mark was making. The team decided that these errors would ultimately become detrimental to Mark's fluency and comprehension, particularly as text increased in difficulty. The team determined that individualized intervention was warranted.

Step 4: Individualize Interventions for Students Who Continue to Struggle

Because they had no measure of decoding, the team decided to assess Mark using the Word Attack Test from the Woodcock Reading Mastery Test. Results from this assessment revealed that Mark was having difficulty decoding words with more than one syllable or those that contained difficult vowel patterns. This resulted in reduced accuracy and fluency. The team enhanced the intervention by adding practice with problem words. Mark practiced incorrectly read words, received instruction in how to analyze word parts, extended analytic skills to similar words, and practiced through word sorts. Following word sorts, Mark read each word within a sentence. Donisha implemented this individualized intervention for 10 minutes each day following the reading practice intervention (discussed earlier in the article).

Mark's reading accuracy and fluency continued to be monitored weekly by Sandra. The team determined that the intervention would be implemented for a minimum of 6 weeks, as this time frame would correspond with the end of the school year. However, the team recognized that interventions in early

ANNUAL EDITIONS

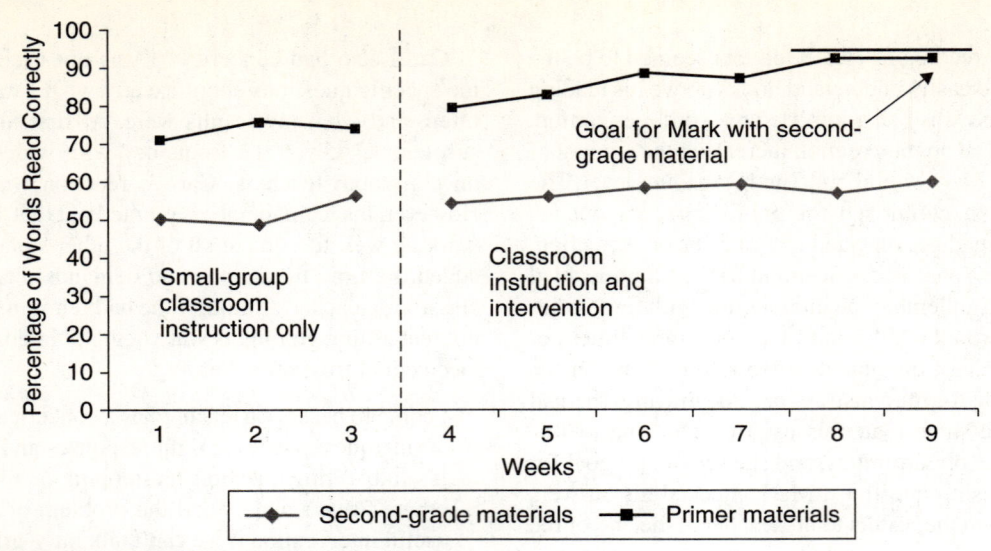

Figure 1 Mark's accuracy during intervention instruction.

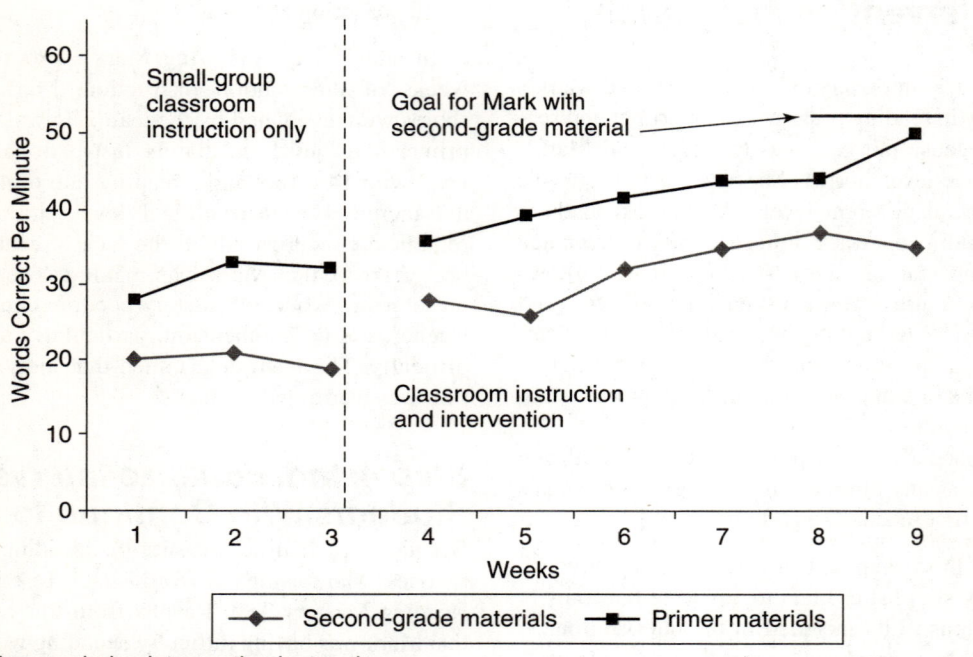

Figure 2 Mark's fluency during intervention instruction.

literacy often need to run longer, between 10 and 20 weeks, depending on factors such as the needs of the student and the intensity of the intervention (University of Texas Center for Reading and Language Arts, 2003; Wanzek & Vaughn, 2008). Moreover, Mark's progress was measured each week so that the intervention could be modified if he failed to make adequate gains. His response to the individualized reading intervention is provided in Figures 3 and 4. Figure 3 shows that Mark quickly responded to the word attack intervention. Data were collected once per week on the percentage of words read correctly from second-grade passages. Mark's response to the intervention contrasted dramatically with his performance reading unknown words prior to the intervention. By the sixth week, Mark correctly read 100% of words presented when prior to intervention he was only reading 55% to 60% accurately. Figure 4 shows that Mark improved in reading fluency as well. Prior to word attack intervention, the effects of the fluency intervention had leveled off. With the addition of the word attack intervention, Mark's fluency steadily improved until he met the second-grade goal. By the end of May, Mark met the PALS summed score benchmark. His end-of-the-year PALS (58 summer score) showed him meeting the benchmark, reading instructionally at second-grade level with comprehension, and reading at a rate of about 60 WCPM.

14

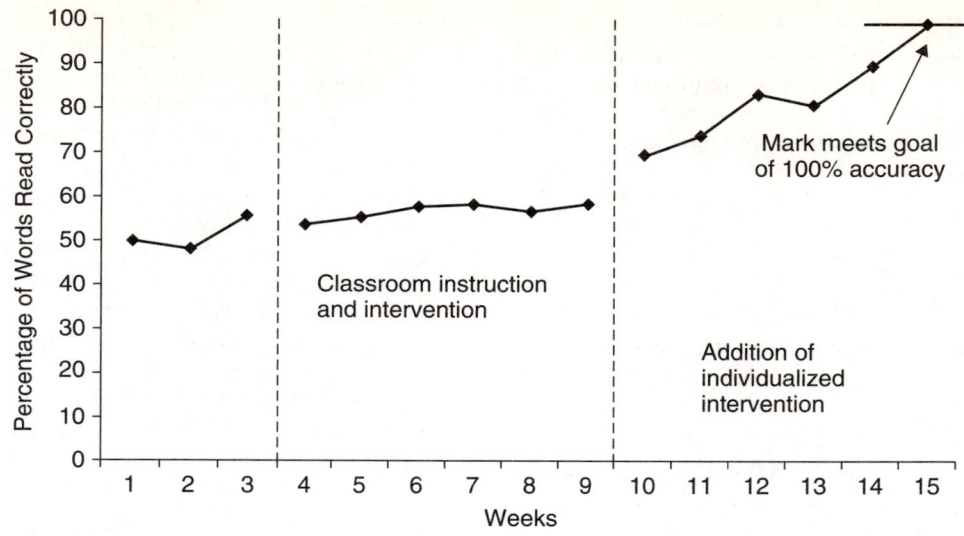

Figure 3 Mark's accuracy during individualized intervention.

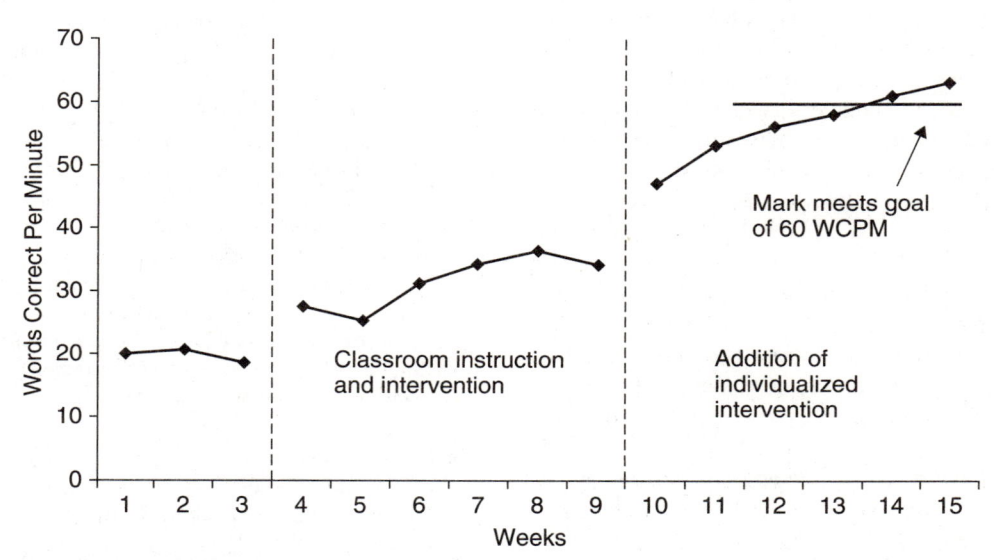

Figure 4 Mark's fluency during individualized intervention.

Step 5: Decision-Making Process to Determine Eligibility for Special Education Services

Despite falling below the second-grade benchmark in September, Mark demonstrated growth on accuracy, fluency, and decoding as a result of the efforts of school personnel. The team reviewed Mark's intervention data and determined that special education services were not necessary. However, Julie voiced concerns about Mark and the continued need for support:

> I could see that Mark had made great progress, but I knew that summer could potentially influence his starting point in the rail and that his progress was the result of substantive instruction *in addition* to the regular classroom. So I insisted that a meeting be scheduled for him in the fall to be proactive about his needs.

Mark's progress was significant relative to where his skills were at the beginning of the year. If the interventions had not met Mark's needs, the team would have been charged with determining whether the lack of response was indicative of a learning disability.

Why RTI?

As illustrated, RTI is a process that incorporates both assessment and intervention so that immediate benefits come to the student. Assessment data are used to inform interventions and determine the effectiveness of them. As a result of the intervention-focused nature of RTI, eligibility services shift toward a supportive rather than sorting function. A testing model that identifies and sorts students into programs or services is predicated upon the effectiveness of those services. Unfortunately, the effectiveness of special education, particularly placement of students in separate classrooms, has been variable at best (Bentum & Aaron, 2003; Kavale, 1990), even as an increasing percentage of students have been identified as learning disabled over the past 30 years (Gresham, 2002). Within the RTI model, instruction can at last be addressed.

Queries, Concerns, and Future Research

We have worked with state departments of education, school districts, schools, and teachers long enough to have questions about RTI. The first issue is that definitions of scientific research privilege experimental and quasi-experimental research (Eisenhart & Towne, 2003; Pressley, 2003). Experiments occur when subjects are randomly assigned to different conditions and the results measured, and they are the best way to know if a practice is causing a certain learning outcome. However, they depend on delivering an instructional treatment in a standardized way, often with study personnel. When teachers do participate in experiments, they often receive intensive support that may not be available when the strategy is widely implemented. The artifices of experiments can limit the degree to which the instructional treatment can be implemented in the real world (Pressley, 2003).

Second, if scientifically based interventions are to be implemented, then research findings must get to schools. We are concerned that the label *scientifically based* will be misused and will proliferate as publishers and companies slap it on everything they market to schools. The final issue is that diverse ways to screen in literacy are still emerging (Gersten & Dimino, 2006). Researchers note that phonologically based competencies, such as phoneme awareness, letter/sound knowledge, and decoding, contribute to part of what makes a student a successful reader (Gersten & Dimino, 2006; Paris, 2005; Scarborough, 2005). Readers must also have a deep knowledge of word meanings and be able to comprehend text. We know oral reading fluency is a good predictor of grade 1 comprehension (Riedel, 2007) but powerful, direct screenings in the areas of vocabulary and comprehension have yet to be developed for elementary learners. Nonetheless, intervening in these areas is important despite the fact that few screening tools exist.

Despite the challenges with RTI, we have seen this approach increase the quantity and quality of instruction for struggling readers. RTI is an initial attempt to provide an alternative to the dominant and damaging discrepancy model in which so much time is spent admiring the student's reading problem. By this we mean people discuss the problem, collect data on it, and write about it, months before they *do* anything about it. IDEA 2004 provides school districts with a choice to opt out of the discrepancy model.

References

Bell, M. (2007). *Reading teachers play key role in successful response to intervention approaches.* Retrieved May 31, 2007, from www.reading.org/downloads/resources/IDEA_RTI_teachers_role.pdf

Bentum, K.E., & Aaron, P.G. (2003). Does reading instruction in learning disability resource rooms really work?: A longitudinal study. *Reading Psychology, 24*(3–4), 361–382. doi:10.1080/02702710390227387

Cassidy, J., & Cassidy, D. (2008). What's hot, what's not for 2008? *Reading Today, 25*(4), 1, 10–11.

Clay, M.M. (1987). Learning to be learning disabled. *New Zealand Journal of Educational Studies, 22*(2), 155–173.

Deno, S.L., Mirkin, P.K., & Chiang, B. (1982). Identifying valid measures of reading. *Exceptional Children, 49*(1), 36–45.

Eisenhart, M., & Towne, L. (2003). Contestation and change in national policy on "scientifically based" education research. *Educational Researcher, 32*(7), 31–38. doi:10.3102/0013189X032007031

Flugum, K., & Reschly, D. (1994). Prereferral interventions: Quality indices and outcomes. *Journal of School Psychology, 32*(1), 1–14. doi:10.1016/0022-4405(94)90025-6

Francis, D.J., Fletcher, J.M., Stuebing, K.K., Lyon, G.R., Shaywitz, B.A., & Shaywitz, S.E. (2005). Psychometric approaches to the identification of LD: IQ and achievement scores are not sufficient. *Journal of Learning Disabilities, 38*(2), 98–108. doi:10.1177/00222194050380020101

Fuchs, D., Fuchs, L., & Bahr, M. (1990). Mainstream assistance teams: A scientific basis for the art of consultation. *Exceptional Children, 57*(2) 128–139.

Fuchs, D., Mock, D., Morgan, P.L., & Young, C.L. (2003). Responsiveness-to-intervention: Definitions, evidence, and implications for the learning disabilities construct. *Learning Disabilities: Research & Practice, 18*(3), 157–171. doi:10.1111/1540-5826.00072

Fuchs, L.S., & Deno, S.L. (1981). *The relationship between curriculum-based mastery measures and standardized achievement tests in reading* (Research Report No. 57). Minneapolis: University of Minnesota Institute for Research on Learning Disabilities. (ERIC Document Reproduction Service No. ED212662)

Gersten, R., & Dimino, J.A. (2006). RTI (Response to Intervention): Rethinking special education for students with reading difficulties (again). *Reading Research Quarterly, 41*(1), 99–108. doi:10.1598/RRQ.41.1.5

Good, R., & Kaminski, R. (2002). *DIBELS oral reading fluency passages for first through third grades* (Technical Report 10). Eugene: University of Oregon.

Gresham, F. (2002). Responsiveness to intervention: An alternative approach to the identification of learning disabilities. In R. Bradley, L. Danielson, & D. Hallahan (Eds.), *Identification of learning disabilities: Research to practice* (pp. 467–519). Mahwah, NJ: Erlbaum.

Illinois State Board of Education. (2008). *Illinois Snapshots of Early Literacy.* Retrieved June 5, 2007, from www.isbe.state.il.us/curriculum/reading/html/isel.htm

International Reading Association. (2007). *Implications for reading teachers in Response to Intervention (RTI).* Retrieved May 31, 2007, from www.reading.org/downloads/resources/rti0707_implications.pdf

Invernizzi, M., Juel, C., Swank, L., & Meier, J. (2005). *Phonological awareness literacy screening.* Virginia: The Rector and The Board of Visitors of the University of Virginia.

Kavale, K. (1990). Effectiveness of special education. In T.B. Gutkin & C.R. Reynolds (Eds.), *Handbook of school psychology* (2nd ed., pp. 868–898). New York: Wiley.

Lyon, G.R. (1995). Research initiatives in learning disabilities: Contributions from scientists supported by the National Institute of Child Health and Human Development. *Journal of Child Neurology, 10*(Suppl. 1), S120–S126.

Lyons, C., & Beaver, J. (1995). Reducing retention and learning disability placement through reading recovery: An educationally sound cost-effective choice. In R. Allington & S. Walmsley (Eds.), *No quick fix: Rethinking literacy programs in America's elementary schools* (pp. 116–136). New York: Teachers College Press.

National Center on Student Progress Monitoring. (2007). Common questions for progress monitoring. Retrieved May 20, 2007, from www.studentprogress.org/progresmon.asp#2

O'Connor, R.E., Fulmer, D., Harty, K.R., & Bell, K.M. (2005). Layers of reading intervention in kindergarten through third grade: Changes in teaching and student outcomes. *Journal of Learning Disabilities, 38*(5), 440–455. doi:10.1177/00222194050380050701

O'Malley, K., Francis, D.J., Foorman, B.R., Fletcher, J.M., & Swank, P.R. (2002). Growth in precursor and reading-related skills: Do low-achieving and IQ-discrepant readers develop differently? *Learning Disabilities Research & Practice, 17*(1), 19–34. doi:10.1111/1540-5826.00029

Paris, S.G. (2005). Reinterpreting the development of reading skills. *Reading Research Quarterly, 40*(2), 184–202. doi:10.1598/RRQ.40.2.3

Parker, R., Hasbrouck, J., & Tindal, G, (1992). Greater validity for oral reading fluency: Can miscues help? *The Journal of Special Education, 25*(4), 492–503.

Powell-Smith, K., & Ball, P. (2002). Best practices in reintegration and special education exit decisions. In A. Thomas & J. Grimes (Eds.), *Best practices in school psychology-IV* (pp. 541–557). Bethesda, MD: National Association of School Psychologists.

Pressley, M. (2003). A few things reading educators should know about instructional experiments. *The Reading Teacher, 57*(1), 64–71.

Riedel, B. (2007). The relation between DIBELS, reading comprehension, and vocabulary in urban first grade students. *Reading Research Quarterly, 42*(4), 546–567. doi:10.1598/RRQ.42.4.5

Scarborough, H. (2005). Developmental relationships between language and reading: Reconciling a beautiful hypothesis with some ugly facts. In H.W. Catts & A.G. Kamhi (Eds.), *The connections between language and reading disabilities* (pp. 3–24). Mahwah, NJ: Erlbaum.

Shinn, M, (1989). *Curriculum-based measurement: Assessing special children.* New York: Guilford.

Stanovich, K. (2005). The future of a mistake: Will discrepancy measurement continue to make the learning disabilities field a pseudoscience? *Learning Disability Quarterly, 28*(2), 103–106. doi:10.2307/1593604

Taylor-Greene, S., Brown, D., Nelson, L., Longton, J., Cohen, J., Swartz, J., et al. (1997). School-wide behavioral support: Starting the year off right. *Journal of Behavioral Education, 7*(1), 99–112. doi:10.1023/A:1022849722465

Texas Education Agency & University of Texas System. (2006). *Texas Primary Reading Inventory.* Retrieved from www.tpri.org/products/

University of Texas Center for Reading and Language Arts. (2003). *Three-tier reading model: Reducing reading difficulties for kindergarten through third grade students.* Austin, TX: Author.

U.S. Department of Education. (1977). *1977 code of federal regulations.* Washington, DC: Author.

U.S. Department of Education. (2006). *Assistance to states for the education of children with disabilities and preschools grants for children with disabilities, final rule.* Retrieved May 17, 2007, from eric.ed.gov/ERICDocs/data/ericdocs2sql/content_storage_01/0000019b/8011b/e9/95.pdf

Vaughn, S., & Fuchs, L.S. (2003). Redefining learning disabilities as inadequate response to instruction: The promise and potential problems. *Learning Disabilities Research & Practice, 18*(3), 137–146. doi:10.1111/1540-5826.00070

Vellutino, F.R., Scanlon, D.M., & Lyon, G.R. (2000). Differentiating between difficult-to-remediate and readily remediated poor readers: More evidence against the IQ-discrepancy definition of reading disability. *Journal of Learning Disabilities, 33*(3), 223–238. doi:10.1177/002221940003300302

Walmsley, S., & Allington, R. (2007). *No quick fix, the RTI edition: Rethinking literacy programs in America's elementary schools.* Newark, DE: International Reading Association.

Wanzek, J., & Vaughn, S. (2008). Response to varying amounts of time in reading intervention for students with low response to intervention. *Journal of Learning Disabilities, 41*(2), 126–142. doi:10.1177/0022219407313426

Assess Your Progress

1. Write a summary for each level of Response to Intervention.
2. Review the five steps used to implement RTI. Prepare a detailed outline of each step that would support your ability to implement the steps.
3. Outline a plan that uses RTI to meet the NCLB goals set by Secretary Duncan.
4. What do you believe are the critical issues of RTI for educators who will be implementing these procedures?

ERIC M. MESMER teaches at Radford University, Radford, Virginia, USA; e-mail emesmer@radford.edu. HEIDE ANNE E. MESMER teaches at Virginia Polytechnic Institute and State University, Blacksburg, USA; e-mail hamesmer@vt.edu.

Article 4

Responding to RTI

Early-reading expert Richard Allington believes response to intervention is possibly "our last, best hope" for achieving full literacy in the United States. So why does he sound so unhopeful?

Richard Allington, a professor of education at the University of Tennessee and the author of a number of prominent books on reading policy and instruction, is one of the country's most recognized experts on early literacy. A former president of the International Reading Association and the National Reading Council and co-editor of **No Quick Fix: Rethinking Literacy Programs in America's Elementary Schools** *(Teachers College Press, 1995), Allington has long advocated for intensifying instructional support for struggling readers, and he is often credited with helping lay the groundwork for the response to intervention concept. But while he believes RTI is "our last, best hope" for achieving full literacy in the United States, he is critical of the way it has been conceptualized and implemented in many schools. Allington's most recent book, tellingly, is titled* **What Really Matters in Response to Intervention** *(Allyn & Bacon, 2008).*

ANTHONY REBORA

In *No Quick Fix: The RTI Edition,* you describe response to intervention as an "old wine with a new label." What do you mean by that?

Well, I'm 62. And literally, since I entered the education field at 21 and became a reading specialist the following year, the promise has been held that we're going to teach all kids to read. The good news is that, in the past five or 10 years, we've had large-scale demonstrations that show that in fact we could do that if we wanted to. We have studies involving multiple school districts and hundreds or thousands of kids demonstrating that, with quality instruction and intervention, 98 percent of all kids can be reading at grade level by the end of 1st or 2nd grade.

So it's not a question that we don't know what to do. It's a question of having the will to develop full literacy in this country, and to organize schools and allocate money in ways that would allow us to do that. Instead, we've tended to come up with flim-flam excuses for why it's not possible.

So you see RTI as a way of building on the research that's been done on successful literacy instruction?

I'd like to think it could be. I've called it perhaps our "last, best hope."

Coming Soon: Education Week Teacher Book Club

Starting this Spring, *Teacher* will be hosting a series of **interactive book club discussions** featuring a prominent education author. Sign up for **book club notifications** and win a chance for a free book!

Why do you think it holds promise?

If for no other reason that, for the first time in many years, the federal government wrote a law that is not very prescriptive. It simply says: Take up to 15 percent of your current special education allocation and use that money instead to *prevent* the development of learning disabilities or reading disabilities. And do it in a way that, while there's no mention of specific intervention tiers, incorporates increasingly expert and increasingly intensive instruction. It's just telling schools to stop using money in ways that haven't worked over the past half-century and start investing at least some of that money in interventions that are designed to actually solve kids' reading problems.

So it's not so much the specific framework of RTI that you see as promising as the emphasis it puts on intensive reading instruction?

Yes. For me the most important part of the proverbial three tiers is the first one: regular classroom instruction. In my view, RTI works best if it's started in kindergarten and 1st grade—we know how to solve those problems. Unfortunately, we have good evidence that a lot of kindergarten and 1st grade teachers in this country are just not very skilled in teaching reading. They may offer solid social and emotional support, but when it comes to delivering high-quality academic instruction, they just don't do it. And a lot of them also assume that if a kid is struggling

18

and is way behind in reading, he must have some neurological problem, and therefore it's not their job to teach him.

So you can do a lot by strengthening instruction. The evidence is there in the research literature. We can reduce the number of kids who have trouble in the 1st grade by half just by improving the quality of kindergarten. And by 2nd grade, we can reduce the number of kids who are behind by another half just by improving the quality of 1st grade instruction.

How do you do that? I mean, if you were an administrator who was implementing RTI, what would you do in terms of professional development? How do you help teachers so they can deliver that high level of instruction?

I think it takes someone who knows what they're doing to start with, and virtually every school system already has those people on their staff. Again, we know from the research literature that, while a lot of kindergarten and 1st grade teachers might not be that strong in academic instruction, at least 25 percent of kindergarten and 1st grade teachers are in fact very skilled. So that 25 percent is out there whose expertise can be built on. The problem is they're just typically ignored.

But, yes, the most successful training models are those that involve teachers who are actually working with each other, where the teachers who don't know what to do in delivering reading instruction are given a few days each to observe a teacher who does know what to do. The skilled teacher, that is, becomes a mentor teacher who helps others acquire those types of skills.

And the effects of a little high-quality training can be significant. One of the studies on reading professional development that the [U.S. Department of Education's] What Works Clearinghouse has rated as having strong evidence—actually I think it's the only one—was done by my wife [University of Tennessee Professor **Anne McGill-Franzen**] in Philadelphia with kindergarten teachers. This program primarily involved using mentor teachers and some staff from an organization called the **Children's Literacy Initiative.** And it really only required about three days of work before the school year started and about three hours a month of professional development and, for some teachers, a little in-class support. But the difference in performance was dramatic: Students in the classes of the teachers who got the training ended the year in about the 45th percentile in reading, while those with teachers who didn't get the training ended the year at the 13th percentile.

And I'll tell you, I actually went down to help my wife with some of the debriefing interviews at the end of the year. We had veteran teachers—people my age—breaking down in the interview and starting to cry, saying, "Why didn't anyone ever teach us this before? Why have I been teaching for 30 years and never knew how to teach kids to read?"

What mistakes do schools commonly make in implementing RTI?

Letting the interventions be done by paraprofessionals or parent volunteers or special education teachers who have limited reading-instruction expertise. If you want a kid to remain illiterate and ultimately end up in special ed., send him out to work with someone who lacks expertise in teaching reading. If you want him to develop literacy, put him with someone with expertise in teaching kids at that age to read.

The idea behind RTI was for a district to actually take some of its special education budget to fund reading specialists, but in most cases, they haven't done that. In too many cases, they simply have paraprofessionals work with those kids. So the amount of expert reading instruction the kids are getting under RTI is typically very slight.

My question to superintendents is always, "Would you let me randomly select one of your paraprofessionals to be your assistant superintendent for finance, or to be the head football coach, or teach AP chemistry?" No, of course not, because those jobs require that you know something. But when you take people who are not reading experts and put them with the hardest kids to teach, and then blame the kids when they don't make progress, you penalize the children for the rest of their lives because of your decision.

You've been critical of the use of so-called packaged reading programs in schools. Why?

Well, the problem is that the concept of a packaged reading program doesn't have any scientific validity to start with, because we know that if you take 100 kids or even 10 kids, there are no prescribed programs that will work with all of them. What kids need are teachers who know how to teach and have multiple ways of addressing their individual needs. And the evidence that there's a packaged program that will make a teacher more expert is slim to none.

So the alternative would be to focus on building on teachers' expertise and knowledge?

Right. And one good example of how to do that is the much-criticized **Reading Recovery** program, which isn't a scripted program in the sense that most commercial programs are. Instead, it's a year long—or even life long—professional development plan. Of the 150 reading-intervention programs that the What Works Clearinghouse looked at, it was the only one determined to have strong evidence that it worked. And I've been telling principals for 20 years that the good thing about a program like Reading Recovery is that, if your district ever decides not to continue funding it, your teachers still have that expertise, and you can't take that away from them. You can take away the one-to-one tutoring that's part of the program, but even more important than that is the expertise of the teachers. Another example of a large-scale program that schools ought to be looking at is the **Interactive Strategies Approach,** developed by researchers F.R. Vellutino and Donna Scanlon. That is also a kind of extended PD plan.

When schools implement RTI, they often use digital screening and monitoring tools for assessment . . .

It's idiotic.

Those tools aren't effective?

No. We don't have any evidence that any computerized screening and monitoring tools are related to reading growth. It just doesn't exist. In fact, I think we have enough evidence in the opposite direction with the problems of Reading First.

So what do you advise schools to use to determine where a student is in his reading ability?

Well, I tell them, if the student is in kindergarten or 1st grade, to listen to the child read. And you have to have some sense of the difficulty level of the books, and you need to be expert enough to know what strategies students at different stages should be demonstrating in their reading.

OK, say I'm a principal, and I say to you, "Listen, I'm not sure my teachers have the expertise at this point to make those kinds of judgments without the help of available tools."

I'd say you're a principal who doesn't have a clue, and you probably need to go off and develop some expertise yourself. Or maybe find another job.

Look, the problem isn't that teachers don't know which students are in trouble and need help. I mean, you could try an experiment: Call 100 1st grade teachers around the country and ask them, "Do you have any kids who are in trouble in learning to read?" They're not going to say, "Gosh, I don't know. I haven't DIBEL'd them yet." Teachers know who needs help. If they don't know, they shouldn't be teaching.

But you just said that many teachers aren't skilled in teaching reading?

But that doesn't mean they don't know who's in trouble. They just don't know what to do with a kid who's in trouble. The point is we need to free teachers up from spending their time using an assessment program on kids every few weeks, or having reading or LD specialists going around doing it. Educators need to be working with kids and teaching them rather than continuing to document that they can't do something.

Do you have any guidelines for the amount of intervention time that should be provided for a struggling reader?

Well, let's talk about kindergarten and 1st grade. In kindergarten, amazingly, it takes as little as 15 to 20 minutes a day, working in a one-on-one or very small group setting with a child. That's it. In 1st grade, most of the studies have recommended either a half-hour or 45 minutes a day, five days a week, usually for a period of roughly 20 weeks, as an initial shot at it. At that point, some kids still may not be up to grade level. But if you give them another 20 weeks, you can be down to 2 percent of kids who aren't reading at grade level. And that 2 percent, according to the large-scale studies, are typically those students who are highly mobile and come in and out of the program, or are part of that very small portion of the school population who have very severe or profound cognitive disabilities. But you have to look around and ask, how many schools do we currently have that have any kind of intensive expert intervention in place in kindergarten, much less 30 or 45 minutes a day of one-to-one or one-to-three expert intervention for up to a year in the 1st grade? The answer is, there are virtually no schools like that in this country.

None?

None. And they'll say they don't have enough money to provide that kind of intervention. And I'm saying, wait a second, we're spending between $5,000 and $10,000 a year on every child who's identified as having a learning disability, and you don't have enough money to try to prevent that?

Can RTI work with older students or adolescents?

Well, we don't have a lot of research on how well it works with older children, but I certainly think it can. The problem is that you really have to ramp up instruction because, as they get older, the kids get further and further behind in the current setting. Let me give you an example: Let's say you have a 4th grader who's reading at the 2nd grade level. So you've got evidence that whatever you've been doing up to this point has produced about a half grade's growth per year. So even if you can provide something that will double his rate of growth, up to a year's growth per year, by the time he gets to 9th grade, he'll only be reading at a 7th grade level. Now, if we can triple his rate of growth—to a year and a half grade level per year—he'd be caught up by 9th grade. If we could quadruple it, he'd be caught up by 6th grade and in even better shape.

How do you do that?

I think you could do that, with a substantial amount of high-quality instruction—and that means, in effect, that his reading instruction has to take place all day long. In other words, if he's reading at a 2nd grade level in 4th grade, this child would need texts in social studies, science, and math that are written at the 2nd grade level but cover the 4th grade curriculum, so he has a book in his hands all day long that he can actually read. If we did that in addition to high-quality classroom reading instruction and then provided 45 minutes every day after school of one-on-one expert instruction, and maybe did something in the summer that wasn't as useless as what we usually see going on in summer school, we might be able to catch him up.

How realistic is that scenario?

I think it's pretty realistic, and it's not very expensive compared to what we're doing now to keep the child essentially illiterate. If you look at the research on the quality and quantity of reading instruction given to students in special education or Title I classes (some of which both my wife and I conducted), I mean, it's not a rosy scenario. Too often, no one gets worse or less instruction in reading than the kids who need it most. Did you know there are only 19 states that require special education teachers to take even one course in teaching reading? In other words, special education teachers often know less about teaching reading than the regular classroom teachers who turn to them for help.

When do you think a determination for special education should be made under an RTI framework?

I think if you've spent most of kindergarten and 1st grade giving a child expert, intensive instruction and he or she is still lagging way behind, it might be time. But I'd be awfully hesitant to classify any child given the lack of expectations for academic growth in special education. If we had evidence that special education programs were actually declassifying a third of their kids each year—in other words that two or three years of treatment in special education could get them caught up—I'd be more optimistic.

So, in most cases, you'd just continue the interventions and expert reading instruction?

Yes.

Even if a student failed to make it to grade level for several years running?

Yep. Now, you could define special education such that the whole point was that kids who go into it were getting more and better instruction every day, such that special education was likely to catch them up and perhaps lead to declassification. But I don't see any will in schools to do that. And I worry about RTI, in some states and schools, being run by special ed. personnel. Again, though it was created in a special education law and has potential bearing on how special education determinations are made, it's not intrinsically a spec. ed. program. It's about strengthening regular classroom instruction and general education interventions for students so they can stay out of special ed. But I'm afraid some schools just see it as a way to find more LD kids faster.

What advice would you have for a teacher who is in a school that is implementing RTI and wants to make it work?

Well, the best advice is to make sure you know what you're doing with struggling readers in your classroom, all day long. And then work to ensure that, when a student leaves your classroom for intervention, he or she is going out to work with someone who knows as much or even more than you do about what to do with that child.

Any particular resource or book you would recommend to start with?

I think one of the most powerful resources is a skinny little book called *Choice Words* by Peter Johnston. I think it's all of 68 pages long, and the subtitle is *How Our Language Affects Children's Learning*. It's simply a careful and close look at how effective teachers talk to their children and how less effective teachers talk to their children. How do you foster a child's sense of agency and identity? Think about it: By the end of 1st grade, most struggling readers already know they're terrible at reading and they think they're the problem. And at that point they start working very hard on any number of schemes to try to hide the fact that they can't read or aren't very good at it. And not surprisingly, they don't do much reading independently. This is a cycle that teachers need to and can break.

In the end it's us, educators, who really matter in the case of struggling readers. We have to understand that and ask the questions about what we are doing or not doing, rather than asking what is wrong with the child.

Assess Your Progress

1. Based on what you have read in these two articles, prepare an argument for or against implementation of RTI in your future classroom.
2. Do you believe that Allington's criticism of RTI implementation in public schools is valid? Prepare 2–3 reasons for your assessment with a rationale for each reason.

From *Teacher Magazine*, April 12, 2010, pp. 1–9. Copyright © 2010 by Editorial Projects in Education. Reprinted by permission.

UNIT 2
Preparing Teachers to Teach All Students in All Schools

Unit Selections

5. **Reluctant Teachers, Reluctant Learners,** Julie Landsman, Tiffany Moore, and Robert Simmons
6. **Musing: A Way to Inform and Inspire Pedagogy through Self-Reflection,** Jane Moore and Vickie Fields Whitfield
7. **All Our Students Thinking,** Nel Noddings
8. **Start Where Your Students Are,** Robyn R. Jackson
9. **Should Learning Be Its Own Reward?,** Daniel T. Willingham
10. **Learning to Love Assessment,** Carol Ann Tomlinson

Learning Outcomes

After reading this unit, you will be able to:

- Define the factors that may cause teachers to lose their motivation to teach all students.
- Summarize the actions teachers can take to improve motivation for both their teaching and students' learning.
- Discuss why teacher reflection is an effective way to improve instruction and student learning.
- Explain ways teachers can formally reflect on their teaching and student achievement.
- Explain how teachers can help students become lifelong learners.
- Defend the concept that teaching students to think critically will result in higher levels of achievement on end of year assessments than learning and memorizing facts.
- Determine how to find the appropriate classroom currency to motivate reluctant students.
- Share your rationale for or against using tangible rewards for learning.
- Prepare a plan for using rewards to motivate reluctant students to become lifelong learners.
- Define informative assessment and explain how it differs from what teachers generally think about assessment.
- Summarize the ten understandings that constitute informative assessment and lead to effective instruction and higher student achievement.
- Develop an instructional plan that synthesizes the information presented in this unit.

Student Website
www.mhhe.com/cls

Internet References

Mindsteps
www.mindstepsinc.com/resources.asp
Edutopia
www.edutopia.org
Teacher Magazine
www.edweek.org/ew/section/blogs/index.html

North Central Regional Educational Laboratory
www.ncrel.org/sdrs/areas/issues/methods/assment/as700.htm
Wrightslaw
www.wrightslaw.com/advoc/articles/tests_measurements.html

The task of preparing highly-qualified teachers with content area expertise is the responsibility of both colleges of education that prepare new teachers, and the school districts that provide professional staff development to their teachers. Just as internal considerations have an impact on career choices, so does a desire to make a difference in the lives of children inspire some to become teachers. There are also external pressures on the teaching profession today from a variety of public interest groups, which can make attracting and keeping excellent teachers difficult. Public perceptions of the teaching profession influence policy; changing demographics in the school population, and societal and family expectations may guide the choices teachers make. Therefore, teacher candidates must understand that our profession is dynamic and must be responsive to a changing world. What, then, constitutes those most defensible standards for assessing good teaching? The standards must be created with an understanding that the teaching profession is complex and must respond to changes in a society.

All of us who live the life of a teacher are aware of those features that we associate with the concept of a good teacher. In addition, we would do well to remember that the teacher/student relationship is both a tacit and an explicit one in which teachers' attitudes and emotional outreach are as important as students' responses to our instructional effort. The teacher/student bond in the teaching/learning process cannot be overemphasized. We must maintain an emotional link in the teacher/student relationship that will compel students to want to accept instruction and attain optimal learning.

To build their aspirations, as well as their self-confidence, teachers must be motivated to an even greater extent than they would be for professional growth. Teachers need support, appreciation, and respect. Creative, insightful persons who become teachers will usually find ways to network their interests and concerns with other teachers, and will create their own opportunities for innovative teaching, in spite of external assessment procedures. If peers in their school do not provide the support needed by the teachers, they look for support and opportunities for sharing elsewhere. The link to *Teacher Magazine* provided above will give you a place to find a blog or network suitable for your personal needs. Or do a Google search for other teacher blogs and read a few. By doing this you will be able to see how important it is to build a community of support for teachers. For many of the bloggers, their blogs are the journals they keep for self-reflection and problem solving. Teachers describe in detail their experiences in classrooms, ask for help regarding difficult issues, share their lesson plans, and sometimes develop support groups that meet off-line.

In this unit, we enter a dialogue about how to be an inspired teacher who uses networks and self-reflection to improve pedagogy. New teachers, whether just out of college or a second career educator, often state that teaching is the hardest job they ever had, and is certainly harder than their internship teaching with a mentor teacher. How do teachers keep their motivation for teaching and working with students who do not seem motivated? These are questions answered by Landsman, Moore, and Simmons. First, they discuss why teacher may be reluctant

© Getty Images/Blend Images

with reluctant learners. Next, they suggest building relationships with other teachers and with their own students. Finally, their suggestions are supported with examples that will help readers understand how to use these in any classroom across grades and content areas.

Moore and Whitfield suggest that teachers should reflect on their pedagogy to grow and defend their teaching practices. After describing three levels of reflection: reacting, elaborating, and contemplating, they offer questions to direct the reflection. As part of the reflection on practice as she developed her teaching skills, Tomlinson came to 10 understandings about the use of informative assessment, not as an end in itself, but as a beginning to better teaching. She shares those insights with us in a clear concise discussion of her evolution to seeing assessment as informing, teaching, and learning. So these two articles illustrate how self-reflection and informative assessment can help us be better teachers for better learners. In the third article, Noddings states that she is concerned about the intellectual development of all students, in particular, about their ability to think. She suggests that all teachers, regardless of their content area or grade level, can and should promote critical thinking in intellectually challenging ways. Teachers who model critical thinking about themselves and their students are better able to support such efforts in their students. Both reflections on teaching and informative assessment are critical in developing pedagogy to stimulate intellectual development of our students.

Do you long for students who sit quietly during independent work time, but have students who are hopping up to throw away paper or sharpen pencils and whispering to peers? How do you find a happy medium? Jackson asserts that each student has a personal currency, and conflict results when the currency desired by students is not used by the teacher. Jackson explains how to find the happy medium, while Willingham explains the complexities of using tangible rewards with children. The debate surrounding the use of rewards in school setting and for academic achievement has long been a stalemate between the "should" and "should not" advocates.

Perhaps this article will offer answer to your questions or give you more support as you struggle to make similar decision in your classrooms.

The articles in this unit were offered to facilitate discussion on complex issues of teaching. The most challenging task for teachers is to plan lessons, and structure the classrooms to meet the needs of all students. Obviously an effective teacher is one with expertise in his/her content areas, and can demonstrate the ability to convey that knowledge to students. But content knowledge is not enough in today's schools, especially in schools with multicultural student body. Today's teachers must be able to acknowledge the unique qualities that these students bring to the classroom and design educational experiences that meet their diverse learning needs.

Article 5

Reluctant Teachers, Reluctant Learners

The key to helping seemingly unmotivated students may be in the teacher's hands.

JULIE LANDSMAN, TIFFANY MOORE, AND ROBERT SIMMONS

How would students teach someone who doesn't want to learn? Here's what a few 9th graders we talked with at South High School in Minneapolis, Minnesota, had to say:

- "I don't believe that there are kids who 'don't want to learn.' I do believe though, that some kids have trouble learning or don't understand what the teacher is saying or teaching."
- "I think what motivates kids to learn is different for each individual student."
- "Well, first of all, I'd address the problem in a good way and find out the reason they don't want to learn."

By focusing on what we *can* do, we can reach many learners who appear to have given up.

As teachers, there are many things we can't control: district budgets, state legislatures' attitudes toward education and financing, No Child Left Behind and how it's interpreted, and inequality of wealth and educational privilege. But these 9th graders mentioned some things teachers can control. By focusing on what we *can* do, we can reach many learners who appear to have given up.

But first we need to reframe the problem.

Who Is Really Reluctant?

The discussion about reluctant learners seems to imply that students alone must become more involved in the schooling process. To reframe the conversation about the reluctant learner, we must also consider the "reluctant teacher."

Reluctant teachers often avoid students who do not look, act, or talk like them. They may categorize such students as being at risk, having behavior problems, or being unteachable. Ladson-Billings (2006) indicates that teachers who define students in such terms create a classroom environment that is no longer a place of learning and high expectations, but rather a place rooted in control and management. Such conditions will not help the reluctant learner become successful.

Just as all reluctant learners have the potential to become star students and contributors to our human family, all is not lost with the reluctant teacher. To succeed, the reluctant teacher must adopt attitudes and practices that reach every learner, particularly those who seem turned off to school.

Motivation in the Face of Difficulty

Those who become teachers want to make a difference in the world. They love and care about children. They also want a fulfilling job. Unfortunately, the reality of teaching today often does not match these expectations. Large class sizes, standardized testing, mandated curriculum, behavior issues, and school bureaucracy can make teaching more stressful than fulfilling. New teachers often comment that teaching is much more difficult than their training prepared them for Second-career teachers say that teaching is the hardest job they have ever had. One study found that around one-quarter of new hires leave teaching within five years. In schools that serve low-income urban areas, the retention rate dips to 50 percent within the first five years (Hare, Heap, & Raack, 2001).

How can teachers stay motivated when so many factors make teaching so difficult?

How can teachers stay motivated when so many factors make teaching so difficult? First, educators can create a network of peers to rely on when times are tough. They can eat lunch with supportive colleagues, take time out of a prep hour to chat with others, or go out and have fun with colleagues after work.

Second, teachers need to grab on to those small and all-too-rare expressions of gratitude they receive from students, parents, and administrators. All of us have experienced such welcome expressions as classroom teachers. Tiffany, for example, tucked away this note, left on her desk after she taught a unit on global warming to her social studies students at South High School in Minneapolis, Minnesota:

> Thank you for teaching me about how I can have an impact on my world. After you taught me about global warming, I went home and turned off all the lights we weren't using and rode my bike to the store rather than have my brother drive me in his car.

Tiffany had no idea the student had taken their class discussions to heart. That note reminded her of her influence on not only this one student, but also the entire planet.

Cultural Competence

For many learners, the school door represents a barrier that disconnects the classroom from their real life. The reluctant learner may feel isolated and turned off from school, be it because of family problems, cultural differences, language, dialect, or economic difficulties. His or her teachers often are more well off, speak differently, dress differently, and have a different color skin. Students who have had little prior exposure to the language and culture of schools can feel lost. Such students may resist the school environment and become apathetic, angry, restless, or disruptive, depending on their temperaments.

One avenue toward making the life of the classroom more accessible for students is for teachers to daily recognize the students' world outside the classroom. For example, posting a poem, quote, joke, song, or picture of a famous person from the students' culture demonstrates an awareness of and respect for students' backgrounds.

Becoming culturally competent means experiencing a culture that is not your own—and suspending judgment of that culture. Specifically, it may mean going to community meetings and shopping where students' families shop. It certainly means learning about the different basic facts, concepts, holidays, and economics of the cultures in your school.

Relationships with Students

Positive, caring relationships are vital for all students, especially those who seem hesitant. Students want teachers to understand that they have problems outside the classroom. They appreciate teachers who are willing to listen and guide them. Unfortunately, just as students can be disengaged from learning, many teachers can be disengaged from their students. This is not to say that they don't care about the students, but the students may not *feel* that caring (Kuykendall, 2004).

So how can teachers show students that they do care? They can begin by establishing a positive atmosphere on the first day of school. Some teachers may ask students to write pieces about themselves and share them with the class. Teachers can also have students guess the teacher's age or try to figure out where the teacher is from. This leads to lots of laughter and discussion about first impressions and stereotypes.

Teachers can maintain these positive relationships throughout the year by greeting students at the door and asking them how they are doing. These conversations only take a few minutes, and they ensure that, even in large classes, each student has been acknowledged in some way. This builds the trust that is vitally important for reaching reluctant students.

Many teachers, worrying about the curriculum they have to cover, don't want to lose instructional days by laying the groundwork for building community. Yet these relationships can actually make it easier to cover the curriculum efficiently because students feel invested in the classroom. The time required to develop relationships with students may be substantial. However, without this time, the reluctant learner may never become engaged in learning.

Connection to Families

Over the years, we have seen numerous teachers attempting to build relationships with students. Although many efforts have been sincere and well intentioned, too often they are disconnected from the students' families.

Robert discovered the value of connecting with families when, at the end of a long day, the father of one of his 8th grade science students at Elmdale Conservatory for the Visual and Performing Arts in Detroit, Michigan, stopped by to invite him to their home for dinner. Never one to turn down a home-cooked meal, Robert packed his things and headed to their home. This was not the first time that he had broken bread with a family, but it was the first time that he had dinner with *this* family. This student was in his 5th period class and was working with him on a science fair project, yet they had never connected beyond the usual good morning and afternoon.

During dinner, the parents commented on the number of times that Robert had called home to share positive information about their son. Their son was never a demonstrative student, so he appeared to Robert to be a reluctant learner. The parents believed that Roberts commitment to sharing good news fostered a sense of pride in their son. The student's participation in the science fair project was a by-product of Robert's proactive approach in contacting the parents.

Connection to Communities

Service learning projects give students an opportunity to connect what they learn in school with the communities in which they live. Several years ago, Robert and his 8th grade science students started a service learning project by discussing their Detroit community. The schools neighborhood had many vacant lots, burned-out homes, and trash on the streets and sidewalks.

The students and Robert developed a list of 10 problems they wanted to address. One student, Jamal, was adamant about placing mattresses on the list. A shy student who did not often participate, Jamal was alive with energy about this topic. Robert was unclear about why mattresses needed to be on the list, but service learning is about community needs, and this was Jamal's community.

In his service learning project, Jamal began a journey from reluctant learner to outspoken advocate for community awareness to award-winning science student. To support the science requirement for the project, Jamal cut out a piece of a mattress lying in a vacant lot and contacted a local company to help him analyze the contents. The bacteria and other particles contained in that small piece would turn anyone's stomach.

This project helped Jamal become much more engaged in class, and his grades began to improve. Projects in which students connect school with their communities can engage the most reluctant of learners.

Student Input

D. W., a South High 9th grader, offers this suggestion for teaching students who don't seem interested in. learning:

> I would simply ask them what their favorite things are and use these things as examples to teach these students.

Reluctant learners need to feel that they are heard, that *their* stories, *their* voices, *their* questions, and *their* contributions matter. The best teachers make student voices the center of the class. Sometimes they build whole themes and activities around student interests and concerns. One teacher, for example, created a science, history, music, and literary curriculum centered on hairstyles and the history of fashion (Delpit & Dowdy, 2002).

Reluctant learners need to feel that they are heard, that *their* stories, *their* voices, their questions, and *their* contributions matter.

Although No Child Left Behind may make such an imaginative approach difficult, teachers can modify subject and class assignments by incorporating such engaging activities as surveys, free-writing exercises, and storytelling. Small-group work, time before and after class to talk with teachers, or even organized after-school study sessions can also make reluctant learners feel connected.

The most important way to nurture students and keep them in school is to create opportunities for them to determine for themselves what will go on in the classroom. Contracts that give students choices, discussions or projects related to issues that pique students' interest, and classroom strategy meetings with students who seem to be drifting send a message to the young man who is sleeping in the back row or the young woman who has been skipping school: "Your voice, your thoughts, your concerns are important here."

Classroom Management

Nothing alienates students more than threatening them, and nothing creates more reluctant learners than force. Unfortunately, too many teachers begin their career without a tool kit full of strategies for managing student learning. Therefore, they end up disciplining students with force and threats.

A strong, well-planned lesson that has enough work to fill a class period from bell to bell can go a long way toward keeping students involved. The minute students walk into the classroom, there should be an activity to engage them: a warm-up journal topic; a crazy question about science (Do fish sleep?); or a puzzle to solve. Writing the learning objective and agenda for the class on the board each day—with specific directions—helps students transition from one activity to the next. Students also remain focused when they have a concrete outcome due at the end of the class period. If they have "until tomorrow" to finish an assignment, students will put off doing the work.

Another proactive strategy is to have a set of classroom guidelines and procedures that students (and parents) have agreed on. Once students know the rules and consequences and see that they will be enforced, they are less likely to argue. Creating a procedure and a place in the classroom for turning in work and for obtaining and storing supplies can add to the order of a classroom. Students who come from chaotic or disorganized homes or who feel intimidated by school generally welcome this predictability.

Even the teacher with the best relationship with students, the most organized classroom, and the best-planned lesson will face days when students do not want to participate. To keep students on task on such days, teachers must maintain an altitude of "with-it-ness," stopping to survey the class every couple of minutes. Students notice how "with-it" a teacher is and act accordingly.

When students are disruptive, the teacher can often simply "stop and stare" or move closer to the student who is misbehaving, giving no verbal attention to the problem. If this doesn't work, then the teacher should simply say the student's name and "please stop." If the student doesn't stop, the teacher may, if it's feasible, ask the student to move into the hall for a talk. Some teachers are brilliant at student hall talks. They speak quietly, get the student to tell what is happening, and then discuss what can be done. The calmer the teacher remains, the more students will respect the rules. This is especially true for students who need to feel they are being heard.

Self-Reflection

No matter how experienced, the best teachers are willing to change. Reflective teachers admit mistakes and create open conversations with students and colleagues in order to improve. They ask themselves whether their students are learning, and when they don't like the answer, they immediately change how they are teaching.

Some educators reflect and learn by writing down their thoughts and observations daily. Some attend workshops on areas where they need support. Others find a mentor to bounce ideas off of. Some learn from their students by giving surveys, asking students to write in a journal, or having an open class discussion about topics of teacher concern. Whatever their approach to learning, they remain open to new ideas and always seek new ways to ensure that all students are learning.

What We Can Do

Zoe, a South High 9th grader, says that teachers should "try to inspire [students]. Try to work with them, not against them. Try to make the class interesting."

Individual teachers can't control tax structures or national trends. We can't fix broken homes. We can't revamp our economic system to make things more equitable. However, we can do what Zoe suggests: We can inspire students with our own fire, motivation, research, and ideas. We can give students confidence in their ability and their future. And we can create classrooms that are so vibrant, so full of life and laughter, with such high expectations and such a clear connection to the world, that even the most reluctant learner will be tempted to join in.

The reluctant learner creates a thin veneer of resistance to cover his or her yearning. This veneer is penetrable by teachers who take the time—who themselves are not reluctant to teach and learn from all students.

References

Delpit, L., & Dowdy, J. K. (2002). *The skin that we speak.* New York: New Press.

Hare, D., Heap, J., & Raack, L. (2001). Teacher recruitment and retention strategies in the Midwest: Where are they and do they work? *NCREL Policy Issues, 8*, 1-8. Available: www.ncrel.org/policy/pubs/pdfs/pivol8.pdf

Kuykendall, C. (2004). *From rage to hope: Strategies for reclaiming black and Hispanic students* (2nd ed.). Bloomington, IN: National Educational Service.

Ladson-Billings, G. (2006). Yes, but how do we do it? Practicing culturally relevant pedagogy. In J. Landsman & C. Lewis (Eds.), *White teachers/Diverse classrooms: A guide to building inclusive schools, promoting higher expectations and eliminating racism* (pp. 29–42). Sterling, VA: Stylus.

Assess Your Progress

1. Define reluctant learners.
2. Why are the teachers in this article reluctant? What can you do to avoid becoming like these teachers?
3. Explain how you will incorporate at least two of the teaching strategies from this article into your future teaching to support reluctant learners.

JULIE LANDSMAN is a retired teacher; author of *A White Teacher Talks About Race* (Scarecrow, 2001); and coeditor of *White Teachers/Diverse Classrooms* (Stylus Press, 2006); jlandsman@goldengate.net. **TIFFANY MOORE** is a teacher mentor for Minneapolis Public Schools in Minnesota; tiffany.moore@mpls.k12.mn.us. **ROBERT SIMMONS** is Assistant Professor of Teacher Education at Eastern Michigan University, Ypsilanti; rsimmon6@emich.edu.

From *Educational Leadership*, March 2008, pp. 62–66. Copyright © 2008 by ASCD. Reprinted by permission. The Association for Supervision and Curriculum Development is a worldwide community of educators advocating sound policies and sharing best practices to achieve the success of each learner. To learn more, visit ASCD at www.ascd.org

Article 6

Musing: A Way to Inform and Inspire Pedagogy through Self-Reflection

JANE MOORE AND VICKIE FIELDS WHITFIELD

Teaching is a complex profession that involves grappling with a variety of management styles; federal, state, and local mandates; local policies and agendas; and informed curriculum practices that affect pedagogy. Teachers work in increasingly diverse schools, and they must be reflective practitioners to deal with the many social and educational issues that converge in such places. A reflective practitioner is better able to grow and defend teaching practices.

This is the time of year when teachers in many parts of the world begin to pack up their classrooms and prepare for a brief respite over the summer—only to begin anew in a few short months. It is the perfect time to create an atmosphere for and in support of reflection and learning so that, as teachers, we can unite to become professionals committed to perpetual growth—both personally and for those we teach.

Dewey (1933) introduced the idea of reflective thought to teachers. His basic assumption was that learning improves according to the degree of effort that comes out of the reflective process. Reflection is thinking over time by linking recent experiences to earlier ones in order to promote a more complex and interrelated mental schema. The thinking involves looking for commonalities, differences, and interrelations beyond superficial elements (Shermis, 1999).

To muse is a phrase that comes to mind when thinking about reflective thought. When looking up the word *muse* in a dictionary, it is defined as a verb, noun, and a proper noun. As a verb it means to ponder, to become absorbed in thought, or to meditate. As a noun, the word is described as the spirit or power of deep thought—the source of genius or inspiration. The proper noun definition leads to Greek mythology and the nine sister goddesses who presided over song and poetry and the arts and sciences.

In order to awaken self-reflection on our teaching practices, the following questions have been designed to assist teachers in reflecting on the skills and habits they have developed. By raising self-awareness of personal strengths and weaknesses, teachers can find and exploit the strengths of their students. Intrinsic, rather than extrinsic, motivation to reflect may produce better results. The nature of the stimulus to reflect will affect the quality of the reflection. Surbeck, Han, and Moyer (1991) identified three levels of reflection:

1. Reacting—commenting on feelings toward the learning experience, such as reacting with a personal concern(s) about an experience
2. Elaborating—comparing reactions with other events, such as referring to a general principle, theory, or a philosophical position
3. Contemplating—focusing on constructive personal insights or on problems or difficulties, such as education issues, training methods, future goals, attitudes, ethical matters, or moral concerns

The nature of the stimulus or directive initially provided, as well as the feedback received after initial reflection, will determine the extent to which one reaches the contemplative level of reflection. Dewey (1933) added that when teachers speculate, reason, and contemplate using open-mindedness, wholeheartedness, and responsibility, they will act with foresight and planning rather than base their actions on tradition, authority, or impulse.

In our November 2007 column, we focused on how each coach and mentor could reflect on his or her performance to enhance teacher productivity. In this column, we would like to invite the teacher to engage in the reflective process, thereby promoting a community of reflective thinking. The following list is not exhaustive but is designed to stimulate reflection on the pedagogy practiced, thus raising self-awareness and the ability to articulate these practices. The questions also may be used to reflect on skills developed and to assist in guiding personal development planning.

If we are truthful to ourselves during the reflective process, the results can become our muses—our source of inspiration and renewal. Honest self-examination helps us identify what motivates and inspires us. Forms of inspiration are vital to our happiness and important to sustain us in our work. The process can aid us in developing an acute awareness of what we teach, how we teach, and why we teach. Ultimately, that which inspires and directs our teaching may lead to student success.

The process is simple. Honestly mull over, ruminate, and spend time musing over any number of the questions offered in the following list. Self-reflection is for personal growth. If you are comfortable with your self-reflection, however, you might take it a step further and have a reflective conversation with a revered colleague, coach, mentor, or significant other.

Personal Growth
- What do you do with the feedback on your performance evaluations or annual evaluations?
- Have you created a specific development plan? How were your needs identified?
- When you have been made aware of, or have discovered for yourself, a problem in your work performance, what was your course of action? What did you learn?
- What makes learning difficult or easy for you?
- What are you concerned about? What do you look forward to?

Curriculum Decisions
- How diligent are you in the use of relevant, available data?
- What information do you take into account before coming to a conclusion?
- What do you reflect on at the end of the working day? Do you spend more time on what went well and why, or do you analyze any problems that may have occurred?
- Think about your favorite lesson. What made it work well? Can you apply this to other lessons?
- How are support services and interventions being implemented?

Flexibility
- Think about a time when priorities changed quickly. What did you do? What was the outcome?
- How do you handle interruptions?
- Are you facing new content or grade-level changes next year? What will you do to prepare?
- Are you amenable to criticism, advice, or suggestions?
- How flexible are you in meeting the differentiated needs of learners?

Professional Development
- What have you done to further your own professional development outside of your formal studies?

- How do you keep record of your achievements?
- What activities do you participate in to develop your skills?
- Do you readily seek opportunities to develop your skills and competencies?
- How often do you update a learning log or résumé?

Technology
- How do you think technological knowledge can support the planning, designing, or implementation of learning?
- How do you embrace the use of technology in your teaching?
- In what areas do you need more technological knowledge?
- How do you demonstrate your knowledge of technological advances and the impact of these on working practices and organizational strategies?
- Where do you find support to assist growth in this area?

Planning
- How do you typically plan your day to manage your time effectively?
- Describe how you are able to contribute to district or school goals. What are the goals or mission?
- Consider a time when you had to adopt a new approach or style to accomplish a task. How did you plan and manage the transition?
- How do you differentiate and prioritize short- and long-term needs?
- How does your classroom management augment your teaching?

Other Musings
- What inspires or drives you?
- What issue stands out as a focus for next year?

A Note to the Coach

Vygotsky (1934/1978) defined the Zone of Proximal Development as the distance between the actual developmental level and the level of potential development under adult guidance or collaboration with more capable peers. The role of the coach is enhanced when teachers can be led to reflection and then to form questions that assist in asking for resources, training, or mentoring. The actual development level and the potential level of the teacher's skills, strategies, and understandings remain constants. Training will no longer need to be reliant on group, grant, or management foci but rather to differentiate each teacher's growth and opportunity.

Article 6. Musing: A Way to Inform and Inspire Pedagogy through Self-Reflection

In Greek mythology, the muses were daughters of Zeus and Mnemosyne, the goddess of memory. For over 2,500 years and throughout Western civilization, artists of every sort have attributed most of their inspirations, creativity, and talent to the muses. Teaching is both art and science, so muse to become inspired, creative, and talented so that each child you touch may become successful.

References

Dewey, J. (1933). *How we think: A restatement of the relation of reflective thinking to the educative process.* Boston: D.C. Heath.

Shermis, S.S. (1999). Reflective thought, critical thinking. *ERIC Digest,* D143.

Surbeck, E., Han, E.P., & Moyer, J. (1991). Assessing reflective responses in journals. *Educational Leadership, 48*(6), 25–27.

Vygotsky, L.S. (1978). *Mind in society: The development of higher psychological processes* (M. Cole, V. John-Steiner, S. Scribner, & E. Souberman, Eds. & Trans.). Cambridge, MA: Harvard University Press. (Original work published 1934)

Assess Your Progress

1. Discuss why teacher reflection is an effective way to improve instruction and student learning.
2. Provide at least two examples for each of the three levels of reflection that teachers can use to formally reflect on their teaching and student achievement. Explain your choices.
3. Describe two ways that you as a student might reflect now, so that you can continue to use these as a teacher. Explain your choices.

JANE MOORE is a literacy coach for the Dallas Independent School District, Texas, USA; e-mail drjanemoore@gmail.com. **VICKIE FIELDS WHITFIELD** works for istation.com in curriculum development; e-mail vickiewhitfield7@gmail.com.

From *The Reading Teacher,* April 2008, pp. 586–588. Copyright © 2008 by International Reading Association. Reprinted by permission via Copyright Clearance Center.

# Article 7

All Our Students Thinking

Any subject—be it physics, art, or auto repair—can promote critical thinking as long as teachers teach in intellectually challenging ways.

NEL NODDINGS

One stated aim of almost all schools today is to promote critical thinking. But how do we teach critical thinking? What do we mean by *thinking*?

In an earlier issue on the whole child (September 2005), *Educational Leadership* made it clear that education is rightly considered a multipurpose enterprise. Schools should encourage the development of all aspects of whole persons: their intellectual, moral, social, aesthetic, emotional, physical, and spiritual capacities. In this issue, I am primarily concerned with intellectual development, in particular, with teaching students to think. However, as we address this important aim, we need to ask how it fits with other important aims, how our choice of specific goals and objectives may affect the aim of thinking, and whether current practices enhance or impede this aim.

Thinking and Intellect

Writers often distinguish among such thinking categories as critical thinking, reflective thinking, creative thinking, and higher-order thinking. Here, I consider thinking as the sort of mental activity that uses facts to plan, order, and work toward an end; seeks meaning or an explanation; is self-reflective; and uses reason to question claims and make judgments. This seems to be what most teachers have in mind when they talk about thinking.

For centuries, many people have assumed that the study of certain subjects—such as algebra, Latin, and physics—has a desirable effect on the development of intellect. These subjects, it was thought, develop the mind, much as physical activity develops the muscles. John Dewey (1933/1971) rejected this view, writing, "It is desirable to expel . . . the notion that some subjects are inherently 'intellectual,' and hence possessed of an almost magical power to train the faculty of thought". Dewey argued, on the contrary, that

> any subject, from Greek to cooking, and from drawing to mathematics, is intellectual, if intellectual at all, not in its fixed inner structure, but in its function—in its power to start and direct significant inquiry and reflection. What geometry does for one, the manipulation of laboratory apparatus, the mastery of a musical composition, or the conduct of a business affair, may do for another.

More recently, Mike Rose has shown convincingly not only that thinking is required in physical work (2005), but also that nonacademic subjects can be taught in intellectually challenging ways (1995). We do our students and society a disservice when we suppose that there is no intellectual worth in such subjects as homemaking, parenting, getting along with others, living with plants and animals, and understanding advertising and propaganda (Noddings, 2005, 2006). The point is to appreciate the topics that matter in real life and encourage thinking in each area. This is not accomplished by first teaching everyone algebra—thus developing mental muscle—and *then* applying that muscle to everyday matters.

Nor is it accomplished by simply adding thinking to the set of objectives for each disciplinary course. More than 20 years ago, educators and policymakers advocated greater emphasis on thinking as an aim of education. Commenting on this popular demand, Matthew Lipman (1991), one of the founders of the modern Philosophy for Children movement, remarked,

> School administrators are calling for ways of "infusing thinking into the curriculum," apparently on the understanding that thinking can be added to the existing courses of studies as easily as we add vitamins to our diet.

But thinking cannot be formulated as a lesson objective—as something to teach, learn, and evaluate on Thursday morning. How, then, do we go about it?

Learning as Exploration

A few years ago, I watched a teenager whom I'll call Margie struggle with courses that discouraged thinking. In her U.S. history course, students were required to learn a list of facts for each unit of study. Margie had to memorize a set of 40 responses (names, places, and dates) for the unit on the American Revolutionary War and the postwar period. Conscientiously, she memorized the material and got a good grade on the test. When I talked with her, however, it was clear that she had not been asked to think and would soon forget the memorized facts. None of it meant anything to her; passing the test was her only objective.

Suppose, instead, that the teacher had asked students to consider such questions as these:

- What happened to the Tories during and after the war?
- Why was Thomas Paine honored as a hero for his tract *Common Sense* but reviled for his book *The Age of Reason*?
- Why might we be surprised (and dismayed) that John Adams signed the Alien and Sedition Acts?

Such questions would encourage students to read, write, argue, and consider the implications for current political life—all important aims of education. How many Tories left the United States? Where did they go? Where do refugees go today? Discussing the question on Thomas Paine could lead to a critical discussion of both nationalism and religion centered on Paine's statement, "My country is the world; my religion is to do good." Who reviled Paine and why? After reading biographical material on John Adams, students might indeed be amazed that he signed the Alien and Sedition Acts. What lesson might we take from this story about the effects of fear and distrust on even highly intelligent people?

Algebra for Some

When I first met with Margie, she was taking algebra. Looking through her textbook, I thought the course would be wonderful. The textbook was loaded with real-world applications and exercises that invited genuine thinking. But the teacher did not assign even one of these exercises. Not one! The following year, in geometry, Margie was never asked to do a proof. These algebra and geometry classes were composed of kids who, had they had a choice in the matter, would not have chosen courses in academic mathematics. Today, in the name of equality of opportunity, we force nearly all students into courses called Algebra and Geometry, but the courses often do not deserve their names because they lack genuine intellectual content. This practice is little short of pedagogical fraud. Many of Margie's classmates (and Margie, too) would have been better served by good career and technical education courses that would challenge them to think about the world of work for which they were preparing.

I am not suggesting that we go back to a system in which students are tested, sorted, and assigned either to academic courses or dead-end tracks in which they are treated with neglect, sometimes even with contempt. But the present practice of forcing everyone into academic courses is not working well. We would do better to design excellent career and technical education courses—very like the job-oriented programs provided in two-year colleges—and allow students to choose their own course of study. Students should not be forced into or excluded from academic courses, but they should be able to choose a nonacademic program with pride and confidence. Such programs are available in many Western countries, such as Germany and the Scandinavian countries. Programs like these might offer courses to prepare machinists, film technicians, office managers, retail salespersons, food preparation and service workers, mechanics, and other skilled workers. Recent studies have shown that the United States actually has an oversupply of engineers and scientists but badly needs workers with high technical skills (Monastersky, 2007).

We can give students opportunities to think well in any course we offer, provided the students are interested in the subjects discussed. Algebra can be taught thoughtfully or stupidly. So can drafting, cooking, or parenting. The key is to give students opportunities to think and to make an effort to connect one subject area to other subject areas in the curriculum and to everyday life.

Consider the ongoing debate over popular science versus "real science." Many critics scorn popular science courses (for a powerful criticism of the critics, see Windschitl, 2006). They would prefer to enroll all students in science courses that would prepare them—through emphasis on vocabulary and abstract concepts—for the next science course. According to this view, practical or popular science has little value and should certainly not carry credits toward college preparation. But intelligent, well-educated nonscientists depend on popular (or popularized) science for a lifetime of essential information. Nonscientists like myself cannot run our own experiments and verify everything that comes through the science pipeline. Instead, we read widely and consider the credentials of those making various claims. High school courses should prepare not only future specialists but also all students for membership in this circle of thoughtful readers.

Deference to the formal disciplines sometimes actually impedes student thinking. A few years ago, it was recommended that math courses should teach students how to think like a mathematician. In science courses, they were to think like a scientist; in history, like a historian, and so on. But aside from the possibility that there may be more than one way to think like a mathematician, education efforts might better be aimed at showing students how to use mathematics to think about their own purposes. For example, carpenters don't need to think like mathematicians, but they do need to think about and use mathematics in their work.

Modeling Open-Ended Thinking

It may be useful, however, for students to see and hear their teachers thinking as mathematicians, historians, or artists. When I was studying for my master's degree in mathematics, I had one professor who frequently came to class unprepared. His fumbling about was often annoying; he wasted time. But sometimes his lack of preparedness led to eye-opening episodes. He would share aloud his thinking, working his way through a problem. Sometimes he would stop short and say, "This isn't going to work," and he'd explain why it wouldn't work. At other times, he'd say, "Ah, look, we're going great! What should we do next?" He modeled mathematical thinking for us, and I found it quite wonderful. The process was messy, uneven, time-consuming, and thrilling. That's the way real thinking is.

I am not recommending that teachers come to class unprepared, but we should at least occasionally tackle problems or ideas that we have not worked out beforehand. In doing so, we model thinking and demonstrate both the obstacles that we encounter and our successes.

Too often, we state beforehand exactly what we will teach and exactly what our students should know or do as a result. This is the right approach for some objectives. There is a place for automatic response in student learning; we do want students to carry out some operations automatically, without thinking. That sort of skill frees us to think about the real problems on which we should concentrate.

In today's schools, however, too much of what we teach is cast in terms of specific objectives or standards. Margie was told the 40 things she was expected to know about the American Revolutionary War. Some educators even argue that it is only fair to tell students exactly what they must know or do. But such full disclosure may foreclose learning to think. Thinking involves planning, ordering, creating structural outlines, deciding what is important, and reflecting on one's own activity. If all this is done for students—CliffsNotes for everything—they may pass tests on material they have memorized, but they will not learn to think, and they will quickly forget most of the memorized material.

Encouraging Teachers to Think

Our focus thus far has been on students. But what about teachers? Are they encouraged to think? Unfortunately, many teachers are told what topics to teach and how to teach them. In too many cases, they are even compelled to use scripted lessons. Ready-made lessons should be available for teachers who want to use them or for special purposes, but professional teachers should be allowed—even encouraged—to use their professional judgment in planning lessons and sequences of lessons.

If teachers want to teach students to think, they must think about what they themselves are doing. Critics both inside and outside the United States have characterized the U.S. curriculum as "a mile wide and an inch deep." The pressure to cover mandated material can lead to hasty and superficial instruction that favors correct responses to multiple-choice questions over thinking. Countless teachers have told me that they can't spend time on real-life applications of mathematics or the kinds of questions I suggested for Margie's history class. If they were to do so, they tell me, they wouldn't get through the required curriculum. But what is the point of getting through a huge body of material if students will soon forget it? How can we claim to educate our students if they do not acquire the intellectual habits of mind associated with thinking?

Teachers should also be willing to think critically about education theory and about what we might call education propaganda. Slogans are mouthed freely in education circles, and too few teachers challenge them (Noddings, 2007). For example, it is easy and politically correct to say, "All children can learn," but what does that mean? Can all children learn, say, algebra? If we answer a qualified *no* to this, are we demeaning the ability of some children (perhaps many), or might our answer be a respectful recognition that children differ and exhibit a wide range of talents and needs?

What Competing Really Means

Even if we believe that all children can learn algebra, we too seldom ask the question, Why should they? When we do ask it, the answer is usually that we live in an information age and that if students (and the United States) are to compete in a worldwide economy, they must know far more mathematics than previous generations did. We need, they say, more college-educated citizens.

Is this true? The information world is certainly growing, but in addition to its own growth, it has generated an enormous service world, and people in this world should also learn to think. The Bureau of Labor Statistics provides charts showing that, of the 10 occupations with the most openings in the next decade, only one or two require a college education. Occupations such as food preparation and service worker, retail salesperson, customer service representative, cashier, office clerk, and laborer and material mover will employ about five times more people than the computer/high-tech fields requiring a college education (see www.bls.gov/emp/home.htm for employment projections). No matter what we do in schools, most of our high school graduates will work at such jobs.

We live in an interdependent society, and one of our education aims is to prepare students for democratic citizenship. As part of that task, we should help students develop an appreciation for the wide range of essential work that must be done in our complex society. In the future, not everyone will need to have a traditional college education to experience occupational success, although postsecondary education or training will frequently enhance that success. Rather, occupational success will require flexibility, a willingness to continue learning, an ability to work in teams, patience and skill in problem solving, intellectual and personal honesty, and a well-developed capacity to think. Success in personal life requires many of the same qualities.

Even for those who go on to college and postgraduate education, the intellectual demands of the future are moving away from a narrow disciplinary emphasis. The biologist E. O. Wilson (2006) has commented on the new demands:

> The trajectory of world events suggests that educated people should be far better able than before to address the great issues courageously and analytically by undertaking a traverse of disciplines. We are into the age of synthesis, with a real empirical bite to it. Therefore, *sapere aude*. Dare to think on your own.

That's good advice for both teachers and students.

References

Dewey, J. (1933/1971). *How we think*. Chicago: Henry Regnery. (Original work published 1933)

Lipman, M. (1991). *Thinking in education*. Cambridge, UK: Cambridge University Press.

Monastersky, R. (2007, November 16). Researchers dispute notion that America lacks scientists and engineers. *The Chronicle of Higher Education, 54*(12), A14–15.

Noddings, N. (2005). *The challenge to care in schools* (2nd ed.). New York: Teachers College Press.

Noddings, N. (2006). *Critical lessons: What our schools should teach*. New York: Cambridge University Press.

Noddings, N. (2007). *When school reform goes wrong*. New York: Teachers College Press.

Rose, M. (1995). Possible lives: *The promise of public education in America*. Boston: Houghton Mifflin.

Rose, M. (2005). *The mind at work: Valuing the intelligence of the American worker*. New York: Penguin.

Wilson, E. O. (2006). *The creation: An appeal to save life on earth*. New York: Norton.

Windschitl, M. (2006). Why we can't talk to one another about science education reform. *Phi Delta Kappan, 87*(5), 348–355.

Assess Your Progress

1. Describe the attributes of a life long learner.
2. Did your teachers help you become lifelong learners, problem solvers, or critical thinkers? Share how they did that for you.
3. With a small group of peers from your class, prepare a poster presentation that summarizes and synthesizes the information in this unit's articles. The title of your presentation will be "From reluctant to lifelong learners: Teaching practices that work."

NEL NODDINGS is Lee L. Jacks Professor of Education, Emerita, at Stanford University, Stanford, California; noddings@stanford.edu.

From *Educational Leadership*, February 2008, pp. 9–13. Copyright © 2008 by ASCD. Reprinted by permission. The Association for Supervision and Curriculum Development is a worldwide community of educators advocating sound policies and sharing best practices to achieve the success of each learner. To learn more, visit ASCD at www.ascd.org

Article 8

Start Where Your Students Are

ROBYN R. JACKSON

Good grades. A quiet classroom. These are often what teachers value. But, what if students come to class looking for something else?

Cynthia quickly moved through the classroom, collecting the previous evening's homework assignment. While her back was to the door, Jason hurried in and slid into his seat. Without turning around, Cynthia said, "I saw that, Jason."

The class erupted in laughter as Jason blushed. "Take out your homework, and I'll be around in a second to deal with you," Cynthia instructed.

When Cynthia reached his chair and noticed that Jason did not have any work out, she moved past and finished collecting the other papers. She got the class started on a warm-up exercise and called Jason to her desk.

"Where's your homework?" she asked.

"I forgot to do it," Jason muttered.

"So you're not only late to class, but you also don't have your homework? Hmm, this is serious," Cynthia said. "Do you know what you owe me?"

"Detention?" Jason guessed.

Cynthia shook her head. "No indeed. You need to make things right with me. Tomorrow when you come to class, you need to be here early with your homework—*and* a Snickers bar. And it better be fresh!"

Jason looked up, startled, then smiled widely. He went back to his seat and got to work. The next morning, he arrived at Cynthia's class with not one but two Snickers bars and cheerfully handed in his missing homework assignment.

When Cynthia first told me this story, I have to admit that I was shocked. It seemed that she was letting Jason off the hook. "Cynthia, please tell me you aren't shaking kids down for candy," I mocked.

She laughed and then explained that too often, we make too big a deal of it when students make mistakes. We treat their mistakes as personal affronts and, as a result, kids are afraid to mess up—afraid that if they do, there is no road back. Over the years, Jason had adopted a cavalier attitude because he believed that once he made a mistake—and he made them all the time—he had ruined the entire school year. By having him give her a Snickers bar, Cynthia showed him a pathway to redemption.

"It isn't about the Snickers bar," she explained. "It's about giving kids a tangible way of redeeming themselves and recovering from their mistakes."

Cynthia is starting where her students are.

The Currency of the Classroom

Currency is a medium of exchange. Any behavior that students use to acquire the knowledge and skills important to your class functions as currency. For instance, if we teachers value student engagement, we take time and expend effort to make our lessons interesting to students. In exchange for our efforts, students give us their attention, curiosity, and participation. If students value adult approval, they work hard to abide by classroom rules and do well on assignments. In exchange for their efforts, we show them our approval in the form of praise, special classroom assignments, and attention.

But sometimes students come to school with currencies we find problematic. For instance, a student might use sarcasm as a way of earning the respect of his peers because it shows how clever and funny he is. However, teachers don't usually welcome sarcasm in their classrooms because they see it as a sign of disrespect; instead of gaining their admiration, it usually incurs their censure. If students don't feel that we understand or value their currencies, they often assume that there is no place for them in the classroom—and they opt out. What's worse, sometimes students *do* carry the preferred currency but resist spending it in the classroom because they resent the fact that it is the only currency we accept.

Currencies even influence the way students acquire the curriculum. The explicit curriculum is the stated objectives, content, and skills that students are expected to acquire. But to access that curriculum, students need to understand and possess certain underlying knowledge and skills.

For example, the explicit curriculum may require that students multiply fractions correctly or explain how geographic features affect migration patterns. But for students to do this, they need to have the right currencies. They need to know how to take effective notes, study from these notes, independently practice applying their skills, learn from their errors and self-correct, pay attention in class, monitor their comprehension, and ask for help when they do not understand.

To demonstrate that they have mastered the material, students need to understand how to write an essay or solve a certain number of math problems correctly under timed conditions. Many students struggle in school not because they can't learn the explicit curriculum, but because they don't have the currencies needed to access this curriculum.

These types of exchanges happen all the time in the classroom. As teachers, we communicate which currencies we require and accept in our classrooms; our students do their best to acquire and trade in our accepted form of currency. When they already possess—or can obtain and effectively use—our accepted form of currency, they thrive. When they can't, they flounder. In fact, most conflicts in the classroom are the result of a breakdown in the currency exchange.

A Winning Strategy

When we don't understand the concept of currencies, we often attempt to mitigate classroom problems by attempting to connect with our students through their interests or to backfill any learning gaps we discover. We may even try to reward students in ways that make sense to us but that are inconsistent with what they value. When we focus on superficial traits without also paying attention to students' currencies, we miss important information about what students can do and what they value—and even our noblest attempts to connect with them can backfire.

When I first started teaching advanced placement (AP) English, I attempted to get my students to sign up to take the AP exam by telling them how much it would help them in college. I explained the importance of having a capstone event that would really test how well they had achieved the course's objectives, and I showed them statistics on how much better students did in college after having taken the exam. I even broke down the economic advantages of having earned college credit in high school and the effect that doing so would have on their overall college costs.

Nothing worked. They didn't sign up for the test. It wasn't that they didn't see the benefit of taking the test. They knew it was important. But I realized that I wasn't starting where they were. I was trying to motivate them using *my* preferred currencies, not theirs.

So I changed my tack. I started a competition among my three AP classes to see which class would have the greatest percentage of test takers. All of a sudden, students were racing to sign up for the test. Within a week, 95 percent of my students had signed up. Although my students could intellectually see the value of taking the test, it wasn't until I connected signing up for the test to something they valued—in this case, it was competition and the camaraderie of affiliation with the "winning" class—that they actually signed up.

Starting where your students are goes beyond playing getting-to-know-you games to understand their likes and dislikes, their interests and hobbies. Such efforts can quickly become superficial. Can you really effectively get to know all 20–35 students in your classroom or make a personal connection with each one fast enough or deeply enough to help each student find a way to access the curriculum? Even if you could, can you really make logical connections between the curriculum and their lives every single lesson, every single day? Our students may be amused by our attempts to discuss with them hip-hop artist Jay Z's latest hit or the plot of an episode of the TV show *Gossip Girl*. However, will doing so really help them connect with the curriculum in a way that enables them to leverage their skills and talents to meet or exceed the objectives—especially when that curriculum is not always immediately relevant to their worlds or when we don't understand their worlds well enough to make a plausible connection?

Instead of forging superficial connections, starting where your students are is about showing kids how to learn in ways that work best for them. It's about creating spaces in the classroom where our students can feel comfortable being who they are rather than conforming to who we think they should be. It's about helping kids feel safe enough to bring with them their skills, strengths, culture, and background knowledge—and showing them how to use these to acquire the curriculum.

Getting Started

If we want to start where our students are, we have to understand how currencies are negotiated and traded in the classroom. The first step is to clarify the currencies we value. What do we consider to be a good student? How do we reward students for doing well? What do we think should motivate students?

When we understand our own currencies and recognize that they may be different from those our students value, we open ourselves to recognizing alternative currencies. For instance, earning good grades is a currency we may recognize. Maybe your students are not motivated by grades but really want the approval of their friends. When you recognize that being motivated by grades is really your preferred currency and that approval from friends isn't good or bad, that it's simply an alternate form of currency, you can find ways to leverage this currency to help students learn. Thus, you may stop trying so hard to get students to value grades and instead set up a classroom culture in which students push one another to do their very best. Understanding your currencies helps you withhold judgment and abandon the idea that your preferred currency is more valuable than those of your students.

Next, we need to unpack our curriculum so we have a better idea of the underlying skills—particularly the soft skills—that students need to be successful. For example, I once worked with a school whose students were struggling. The teachers complained that the students never did their homework. We sat down as a group and examined the homework assignments. One teacher assigned students to read a chapter of the textbook and take notes in preparation for a class discussion the following day. When we unpacked the assignment, we realized that to complete it, students would have to spend about two hours reading the densely written 19 pages, take 25 pages of notes using Cornell note-taking sheets, and look up 10 vocabulary words. Students would also have to organize their notes in such a way that they could refer to them quickly as support for any arguments they wanted to develop as they participated in the discussion. Now we understood why so many students were not completing their homework.

Once you understand the soft skills that are implied by the curriculum, the next step is to determine which of these soft skills your students already possess and which ones they will need to acquire. You can accomplish this through a quick pre-assessment or by observing how students interact with the material and with one another.

Or you can ask them directly. I often conduct focus groups with the students in the schools with which I work. I show them a list of the soft skills they will need to be successful in a particular class and ask them whether they know how to do these things. On the basis of their feedback, their teachers and I can determine what we need to preteach students to help them successfully tackle a particular lesson.

Our students often carry currencies that can help them learn, but we don't recognize that these currencies are valuable because they don't look like the ones we value. For instance, a student may have a different organizational system for his notebook that works better for the way he thinks, or a student may process information better by talking about it rather than writing about it, or a student may have a method for solving mathematical equations that differs drastically from the one you taught, but that is equally sound.

I once coached a teacher who was having difficulty with a student who interrupted her while she was teaching to ask questions and offer comments of his own. He wasn't intentionally being disrespectful, but it drove her crazy. After meeting with the student and his parents during parent/teacher conferences, she noticed that the family all talked at once. It was how they processed information. They thought aloud. At the same time. Loudly.

Once she recognized that his interruptions were not because he couldn't control himself, that they were just how he processed information, she no longer saw them as annoying, but as evidence that he was thinking and eager to share his thinking with the class. She then was able to figure out a way to help him process the information without disrupting the class. She showed him how to keep a journal during class discussions to write down his thoughts as they came to him and to select one or two comments to share. Eventually he learned how to participate in class discussions without the journal and to share his thinking appropriately.

Yes, But . . .

When I tell the Cynthia story in the workshops I give, many teachers become dismayed. Although they enjoy hearing about Cynthia's Snickers bar strategy it doesn't feel comfortable to them. It's a great story but what about those of us who are uncomfortable with forging a connection over candy?

I once coached a teacher who was having difficulty with her 6th graders. Whenever she gave them an assignment, they would spend the period talking to one another, finding any excuse to get out of their seats. No matter how often she threatened them, she couldn't keep them focused. I offered to observe her classroom and provide her with some feedback, but after being in her classroom for 30 minutes, I didn't see any gross misbehavior. The students were squirrelly but most of their talking was about the work. After school let out for the day, I met with her to discuss what I saw. Before I could begin, she said, "Do you see what I have to deal with? I'm exhausted. They just won't behave!"

"What would your class look like if your students were all well-behaved?" I asked.

"They'd all be in their seats quietly working," she said. "They'd raise their hands and ask permission before they got up to do anything, and they would also raise their hands before talking so that everyone can be heard."

I listened to her list and realized that she was talking about her currencies. She valued a quiet classroom and thought that was how students learned best. However, her students valued being able to discuss what they were learning with their classmates and getting up and moving once in a while. That was how they learned best. I explained to the teacher the concept of currency and then asked, "If you were sure that your students were talking about the lesson, would you allow them to talk quietly in class as they were working?"

She thought for a moment; I could tell she was uncomfortable with the idea. Finally she said, "I suppose so, but I'm afraid it might get out of hand."

We finally figured out a way for her to structure the students' conversations so that she could still feel that the class was orderly and productive. She decided to pause during the lesson and allow students time to turn to their neighbors and discuss the information before moving on in the lesson. That way, students had a chance to process the information during the lesson and were less likely to talk about it later on. She found a way to acknowledge their currencies while honoring her own.

Finding Common Ground

When you recognize and honor students' currencies, you don't abandon your own. Rather, you find a common currency that you both carry. This creates a safe place for both you and your students to be who you are. In Cynthia's case, she wanted Jason to acknowledge his mistake and correct it; Jason wanted a chance to do so without feeling like a failure or a bad person. The candy bar provided the common ground. Had Cynthia asked for an apology or demanded that Jason redeem himself by staying after school and repaying her the time he missed in class by being late, she might have alienated him. But by finding a common currency, she was able to quickly get Jason back on track.

For you, that common ground might be something less tangible. Maybe you are more comfortable lecturing, but your students are not good note takers. So you provide them with a note-taking sheet that helps them learn in the way that you are most comfortable teaching. Or perhaps you don't like lavishing verbal praise on your students, but verbal praise is their preferred form of currency. So you develop a set of code words you can use with students that signal to them that they have done a good job.

When you start where your students are, when you find that common currency you both carry, you communicate to students that it's OK to be exactly who they are. You create spaces for students to leverage who they are and what they know, to access the curriculum.

Assess Your Progress

1. Think back to your days in public school; pick any grade or content area. What was the primary currency that got you motivated to do well in that class?
2. Do you think the currency that worked for you will work with the students you are teaching? Support the reasons in your answer with information from the articles in this unit.

ROBYN R. JACKSON is President of Mindsteps and author of *Never Work Harder Than Your Students* and *Other Principles of Great Teaching* (ASCD, 2009); robyn@mindstepsinc.com.

Article 9

Should Learning Be Its Own Reward?

DANIEL T. WILLINGHAM

How does the mind work—and especially how does it learn? Teachers' instructional decisions are based on a mix of theories learned in teacher education, trial and error, craft knowledge, and gut instinct. Such gut knowledge often serves us well, but is there anything sturdier to rely on?

Cognitive science is an interdisciplinary field of researchers from psychology, neuroscience, linguistics, philosophy, computer science, and anthropology who seek to understand the mind. In this regular American Educator column, we consider findings from this field that are strong and clear enough to merit classroom application.

Question: In recent months, there's been a big uproar about students being paid to take standardized tests—and being paid even more if they do well. Can cognitive science shed any light on this debate? Is it harmful to students to reward them like this? What about more typical rewards like a piece of candy or five extra minutes of recess?

There has been much debate recently about boosting standardized test scores by paying students. Here are a few examples that I read about in the news. In Coshocton, Ohio, third- and sixth-graders are being paid up to $20 for earning high scores on standardized tests. In New York City, fourth-grade students will receive $5 for each standardized test they take throughout the year, and up to $25 for each perfect score. Seventh-graders will get twice those amounts. In Tucson, Ariz., high school juniors selected from low-income areas will be paid up to $25 each week for attendance. These and similar programs affect just a tiny fraction of students nationwide. But rewarding students with things like small gifts, extra recess time, stickers, certificates, class parties and the like is actually pretty common. Most teachers have the option of distributing rewards in the classroom, and many do. For example, in a recent survey of young adults, 70 percent said that their elementary school teachers had used candy as a reward (Davis, Winsler, and Middleton, 2006).

So whether or not your district offers cash rewards for standardized test scores or attendance, you've probably wondered if rewarding your students for their classwork is a good idea. Some authors promise doom if a teacher rewards students, with the predicted negative effects ranging from unmotivated pupils to a teacher's moral bankruptcy (e.g., Kohn, 1993). Others counter that rewards are harmless or even helpful (e.g., Cameron, Banko, and Pierce, 2001; Chance, 1993). Where does the truth lie? In the middle. There is some merit to the arguments on both sides. Concrete rewards can motivate students to attend class, to behave well, or to produce better work. But if you are not careful in choosing what you reward, they can prompt students to produce shoddy work—and worse, they can cause students to actually like school subjects less. The important guidelines are these: Don't use rewards unless you have to, use rewards for a specific reason, and use them for a limited time. Let's take a look at the research behind these guidelines.

Concrete rewards can motivate students to attend class, to behave well, or to produce better work. But if you are not careful in choosing what you reward, they can prompt students to produce shoddy work—and worse, they can cause students to actually like school subjects less.

Do Rewards Work?

Rewarding students is, from one perspective, an obvious idea. People do things because they find them rewarding, the reasoning goes, so if students don't find school naturally rewarding (that is, interesting and fun), make it rewarding by offering them something they do like, be it cash or candy.

In this simple sense, rewards usually work. If you offer students an appealing reward, the targeted behavior will generally increase (for reviews, see O'Leary and Drabman, 1971; Deci, Koestner, and Ryan, 1999). Teachers typically use rewards like candy, stickers, small prizes, or extra recess time. They use them to encourage student behaviors such as completing assignments, producing good work, and so on. In one example

(Hendy, Williams, and Camise, 2005) first-, second-, and fourth-graders were observed in the school cafeteria to see how often they ate fruits and vegetables. Once this baseline measure was taken, they were rewarded for eating one or the other. Students received a token for each day that they ate the assigned food, and tokens could be redeemed for small prizes at the end of the week. Not surprisingly, students ate more of what they were rewarded for eating.

But things don't always go so smoothly. If you mistakenly offer a reward that students don't care for, you'll see little result. Or, if you reward the wrong behavior, you'll see a result you don't care for. When I was in fourth grade, my class was offered a small prize for each book we read. Many of us quickly developed a love for short books with large print, certainly not the teacher's intent. In the same way, if you reward people to come up with ideas, but don't stipulate that they must be good ideas, people will generate lots of ideas in order to gain lots of rewards, but the ideas may not be especially good (Ward, Kogan, and Pankove, 1972). It's often possible to correct mistakes such as these. Unappealing rewards can be replaced by valued rewards. The target behavior can be changed. My fourth-grade teacher stipulated that books had to be grade-appropriate and of some minimum length.

Because rewards are generally effective, people's objection to them in the classroom is seldom that they won't work. The op-ed newspaper articles I have seen about the student payment plans described above don't claim that you can't get students to go to school by paying them (e.g., Carlton, 2007; Schwartz, 2007). They raise other objections.

The common arguments against rewards fall into three categories. Let me state each one in rather extreme terms to give you the idea, and then I'll consider the merits of each in more detail. The first objection is that using rewards is immoral. You might toss your dog a treat when he shakes hands, but that is no way to treat children. Classrooms should be a caring community in which students help one another, not a circus in which the teacher serves as ringmaster. The second objection is that offering rewards is unrealistic. Rewards can't last forever, so what happens when they stop? Those who make this argument think it's better to help students appreciate the subtle, but real rewards that the world offers for things like hard work and politeness. After all, adults don't expect that someone will toss them a candy bar every time they listen politely, push their chair under a table, or complete a report on time. The third objection is that offering rewards can actually decrease motivation. Cognitive science has found that this is true, but only under certain conditions. For example, if you initially enjoy reading and I reward you for each book you finish, the rewards will make you like reading less. Below, I'll explain how and why that happens. Let's consider each of these arguments in turn.

Are Rewards Immoral?

Don't rewards control students? Aren't rewards dehumanizing? Wouldn't it be better to create a classroom atmosphere in which students wanted to learn, rather than one in which they reluctantly slogged through assignments, doing the minimal work they thought would still earn the promised reward? Cognitive science cannot answer moral questions. They are outside its purview. But cognitive science can provide some factual background that may help teachers as they consider these questions.

It is absolutely the case that trying to control students is destructive to their motivation and their performance. People like autonomy, and using rewards to control people definitely reduces motivation. Even if the task is one students generally like, if they sense that you're trying to coerce them, they will be less likely to do it (e.g., Ryan, Mims, and Koestner, 1983). It is worth pointing out, however, that rewards themselves are not inherently controlling. If students are truly offered a choice—do this and get a reward, don't do it and get no reward—then the student maintains control. Within behavioral science, it is accepted that rewards themselves are coercive if they are excessive (e.g., National Commission for the Protection of Human Subjects of Biomedical and Behavioral Research, 1978). In other words, if I offer you $200 to take a brief survey, it's hard to know that you're freely choosing to take the survey.

Rewards in classrooms are typically not excessive, and so are not, themselves, controlling. Rather, rewards might be an occasion for control if the teacher makes it quite clear that the student is expected to do the required work and collect his or her reward. That is, the teacher uses social coercion. So too, we've all known people we would call "manipulative," and those people seldom manipulate us via rewards. They use social means. In sum, the caution against controlling students is well-founded, but rewards are not inherently controlling.

Are rewards dehumanizing? Again, it seems to me that the answer depends on how the student construes the reward. If a teacher dangles stickers before students like fish before a seal, most observers will likely wince. But if a teacher emphasizes that rewards are a gesture of appreciation for a job well done, that probably would not appear dehumanizing to most observers.[1] Even so, rather than offer rewards, shouldn't teachers create classrooms in which students love learning? It is difficult not to respond to this objection by saying "Well, duh." I can't imagine there are many teachers who would rather give out candy than have a classroom full of students who are naturally interested and eager to learn. The question to ask is not "Why would you use rewards instead of making the material interesting?" Rather, it is "After you've wracked your brain for a way to make the material interesting for students and you still can't do it, then what?" Sanctimonious advice on the evils of rewards won't get chronically failing students to have one more go at learning to read. I think it unwise to discourage teachers from using any techniques in the absolute; rather, teachers need to know what research says about the benefits and drawbacks of the techniques, so that they can draw their own conclusions about whether and when to use them. Considering the merits of the two other objections will get us further into that research.

> Sanctimonious advice on the evils of rewards won't get chronically failing students to have one more go at learning to read. I think it unwise to discourage teachers from using any techniques in the absolute; rather, teachers need to know what research says about the benefits and drawbacks of the techniques.

What Happens When Rewards Stop?

This objection is easy to appreciate. If I'm working math problems because you're paying me, what's going to happen once you stop paying me? Your intuition probably tells you that I will stop doing problems, and you're right. In the fruits and vegetables study described earlier, students stopped eating fruits and vegetables soon after the reward program stopped.

Although it might seem obvious that this would happen, psychologists initially thought that there was a way around this problem. Many studies were conducted during the 1960s using token economies. A token economy is a system by which rewards are administered in an effort to change behavior. There are many variants but the basic idea is that every time the student exhibits a targeted behavior (e.g., gets ready to work quickly in the morning), he or she gets a token (e.g., a plastic chip). Students accumulate tokens and later trade them for rewards (e.g., small prizes). Token economies have some positive effects, and have been used not only in classrooms, but in clinical settings (e.g., Dickerson, Tenhula, and Green-Paden, 2005).

When the idea of a token economy was developed, the plan was that the rewards would be phased out. Once the desired behavior was occurring frequently, you would not give the reward every time, but give it randomly, averaging 75 percent of the time, then 50 percent of the time, and so on. Thus, the student would slowly learn to do the behavior without the external reward. That works with animals, but normally not with humans. Once the rewards stop, people go back to behaving as they did before (Kazdin, 1982; O'Leary and Drabman, 1971).[2]

Well, one might counter, it may be true that students won't spontaneously work math problems once we stop rewarding them, but at least they will have worked more than they otherwise would have! Unfortunately, there is another, more insidious consequence of rewards that we need to consider: Under certain circumstances, they can actually decrease motivation.

How Can Rewards Decrease Motivation?

The previous section made it sound like rewards boost desired behavior so long as they are present, and when they are removed behavior falls back to where it started. That's true sometimes, but not always. If the task is one that students like, rewards will, as usual, make it more likely they'll do the task. But after the rewards stop, students will actually perform the previously likable task *less* than they did when rewards were first offered.

A classic study on this phenomenon (Lepper, Greene, and Nisbett, 1973) provides a good illustration. Children (aged 3 to 5 years old) were surreptitiously observed in a classroom with lots of different activities available. The experimenters noted how much time each child spent drawing with markers. The markers were then unavailable to students for two weeks. At the end of the two weeks, students were broken into three groups. Each student in the first group was taken to a separate room and was told that he or she could win an attractive "Good Player" certificate by drawing a picture with the markers. Each was eager to get the certificate and drew a picture. One-by-one, students in a second group were also brought to a separate room, encouraged to draw, and then given a certificate, but the certificate came as a surprise; when they started drawing, they didn't know that they would get the certificate. A third group of students served as a control group. They had been observed in the first session, but didn't draw or get a certificate in this second session. After another delay of about two weeks, the markers again appeared in the classroom, and experimenters observed how much children used them. The students in the first group—those who were promised the certificate for drawing—used the markers about half as much as students in the other two groups. Promising and then giving a reward made children like the markers less. But giving the reward as a surprise (as with the second group of students) had no effect.

This has been replicated scores of times with students of different ages, using different types of rewards, and in realistic classroom situations (see Deci et al., 1999 for a review). What is going on? How can getting a reward reduce your motivation to do something? The answer lies in the students' interpretation of why they chose to use the markers. For students who either didn't get a reward or who didn't expect a reward, it's obvious that they weren't drawing for the sake of the reward; they drew pictures because they liked drawing. But for the children who were promised a reward, the reason is less clear. A student might not remember that he drew because he wanted to draw, but rather he remembered really wanting the certificate. So when the markers were available again but no certificate was promised, the student may well have thought "I drew because I wanted that certificate; why should I draw now for nothing?"

The analogy to the classroom is clear. Teachers seek to create lifelong learners. We don't just want children to read, we want children to learn to love reading. So if, in an effort to get children to read more, we promise to reward them for doing so, we might actually make them like reading less! They will read more in order to get the pizza party or the stickers, but once the teacher is no longer there to give out the rewards, the student will say "Why should I read? I'm not getting anything for it."

The key factor to keep in mind is that rewards only decrease motivation for tasks that students initially like. If the task is dull, motivation might drop back down to its original level once the rewards stop, but it will not drop below its original level.

Why does the appeal of the task make a difference? As I mentioned, rewards hurt motivation because of the way students construe the situation: "I drew with markers in order to get a certificate," instead of "I drew with markers because I like to draw with markers." But if the task is dull, students won't make that mistaken interpretation. They never liked the task in the first place. That hypothesis has been confirmed in a number of studies showing that once the reward is no longer being offered, having received a reward in the past harms the motivation for an interesting task, but not for a dull task (e.g., Daniel and Esser, 1980; Loveland and Olley, 1979; Newman and Layton, 1984).

The key factor to keep in mind is that rewards only decrease motivation for tasks that students initially like. If the task is dull, motivation might drop back down to its original level once the rewards stop, but it will not drop below its original level.

This finding might make one wonder whether rewards, in the form of grades, are behind students' lack of interest in schoolwork; by issuing grades, we're making students like school less (Kohn, 1993). It is true that students like school less and less as they get older. But it is wise to remember that motivation is a product of many factors. Researchers often distinguish between extrinsic motivators (e.g., concrete rewards or grades that are external to you) and intrinsic motivators (things that are internal to you such as your interest in a task). The effect described above can be succinctly summarized: Extrinsic rewards can decrease intrinsic motivation. We would thus expect that intrinsic and extrinsic motivation would be negatively correlated. That is, if you work mostly for the sake of getting good grades and other rewards, then you aren't very intrinsically motivated, and if you are highly intrinsically motivated, that must mean you don't care much about rewards. That's true to some extent, but the relationship is far from perfect. College students whose intrinsic and extrinsic motivation have been measured usually show a modest negative correlation, around -.25[3] (Lepper, Corpus, and Iyengar, 2005). This seems reasonable since motivation is actually pretty complex—we rarely do things for just one reason.

What Makes Rewards More or Less Effective?

If you decide to use rewards in the classroom, how can you maximize the chances that they will work? Three principles are especially important. Rewards should be desirable, certain, and prompt.

The importance of desirability is obvious. People will work for rewards that appeal to them, and will work less hard or not at all for rewards that are not appealing.[4] That is self-evident, and teachers likely know which rewards would appeal to their students and which would mean little to them.

If you decide to use rewards in the classroom, how can you maximize the chances that they will work? Three principles are especially important. Rewards should be desirable, certain, and prompt.

Less obvious is the importance of the certainty of a reward, by which I mean the probability that a student will get a reward if he or she attempts to do the target behavior. What if you've set a target that seems too difficult to the student, and he won't even try? Or what if the target seems achievable to the student, he makes an attempt and does his best, but still fails? Either reduces the likelihood that the student will try again. Both problems can be avoided if the reward is contingent on the student trying his best, and not on what he achieves. But that has its drawbacks, as well. It means that you must make a judgment call as to whether he tried his best. (And you must make that judgment separately for each student.) It is all too likely that some students will have an inflated view of their efforts, and your differing assessment will lead to mistrust. Ideally, the teacher will select specific behaviors for each student as targets, with the target titrated to each student's current level of ability.

A corollary of rewards being desirable is that they be prompt. A reward that is delayed has less appeal than the same reward delivered immediately. For example, suppose I gave you this choice: "You can have $10 tomorrow, or $10 a week from tomorrow." You'd take the $10 tomorrow, right? Rewards have more "oomph"—that is, more power to motivate—when you are going to get them soon. That's why, when my wife calls me from the grocery store, it's easy for me to say "Don't buy ice cream. I'm trying to lose weight." But when I'm at home it's difficult for me to resist ice cream that's in the freezer. In the first situation, I'm denying myself ice cream sometime in the distant future, but in the second I would be denying myself ice cream right at that moment. The promise of ice cream two minutes from now has higher value for me than the promise of ice cream hours from now.

It is possible to measure how much more desirable a reward is when given sooner rather than later. In one type of experiment, subjects participate in an auction and offer sealed bids for money that will be delivered to them later. Thus, each subject might be asked "What is the maximum you would pay right now for a reward of $10, to be delivered tomorrow?"[5] Subjects are asked to make bids for a variety of rewards to be delivered at delays varying from one to 30 days. Then, researchers use subjects' bids to derive a relationship between the amount of time that the reward is delayed and how much people value the delayed reward. Subjects typically show a steep drop off in how much they value the reward—with a one-day delay, $20 is worth about $18 to most subjects, and with a one-week delay, the value is more like $15 (e.g., Kirby, 1997). In other words, there is a significant cost to the reward value for even a brief delay. Other studies show that the cost

> ## What is the Difference between Rewards and Praise?
>
> You may have noticed that I have limited my discussion to the effects of concrete rewards—candy, cash, and so on. Isn't praise a reward as well? It can be, but praise as it's usually administered has some important differences. The most important is that praise is usually given unpredictably. The student doesn't think to himself, "If I get 90 percent or better on this spelling test, the teacher will say 'Good job, Dan!'" Rewards are different. There is usually an explicit bargain in the classroom, with the understanding that a particular behavior (e.g., 90 percent or better on a spelling test) merits a reward. As described in the main article, the decrease in motivation for a task only occurs if the reward was expected (and if the students enjoy the task). Since praise is not expected, it does not lead to an immediate decrement to motivation.
>
> Another important difference between praise and concrete rewards is that the former is often taken as a more personal comment on one's abilities. Rewards typically don't impart information to the student. But praise can carry quite a bit of meaning. For starters, it tells the student that she did something noteworthy enough to merit praise. Then too, the student learns what the teacher considers important by listening to what she praises. A student may be told that she's smart, or that she tried hard, or that she's improving. In the short run, sincere praise will provide a boost to motivation (Deci et al., 1999), but in the long run, the content of praise can have quite different effects on the students' self-concept and on future efforts (e.g., Henderlong and Lepper, 2002; Mueller and Dweck, 1998). The key is in what type of praise is given. When faced with a difficult task, a child who has been praised in the past for her *effort* is likely to believe that intelligence increases as knowledge increases and, therefore, will work harder and seek more experiences from which she can learn. In contrast, a student who has been praised for her *ability* will likely believe that intelligence is fixed (e.g., is genetically determined) and will seek to maintain the "intelligent" label by trying to look good, even if that means sticking to easy tasks rather than more challenging tasks from which more can be learned.
>
> A final difference between praise and rewards lies in students' expectations of encountering either in school. At least in the U.S., praise is part of everyday social interaction. If someone displays unusual skill or determination or kindness, or any other attribute that we esteem, it is not unusual to offer praise. In fact, a teacher who never praised her students might strike them as cold, or uncaring. No such expectation exists for rewards, however. It is hard to imagine teaching students without ever praising them. It is easy to imagine teaching students without ever offering them a concrete reward.
>
> For more on praise and its effects, see "Ask the Cognitive Scientist," *American Educator,* Winter 2005–2006, available at www.aft.org/pubs-reports/american_educator/issues/winter05-06/cogsci.htm.
>
> —D.W.

is greater for elementary school students than college students (e.g., Green, Fry and Myerson, 1994). That finding probably matches your intuition: As we get older, we get better at delaying gratification. Distant rewards become more similar to immediate rewards.

In this section I've summarized data showing that rewards should be desirable, certain, and prompt if they are to be effective. These three factors provide some insight into the extrinsic (but non-tangible) rewards that almost all schools offer: grades and graduation. Grades are not as rewarding as we might guess because they are seldom administered right after the required behavior (studying), and the reward of a diploma is, of course, even more distant. Then too, low-achieving students likely perceive these rewards as highly uncertain. That is, hard work does not guarantee that they will receive the reward.

Putting It All Together: Are Rewards Worth It?

When all is said and done, are rewards worth it? I liken using rewards to taking out a loan. You get an immediate benefit, but you know that you will eventually have to pay up, with interest. As with loans, I suggest three guidelines to the use of rewards: 1) try to find an alternative; 2) use them for a specific reason, not as a general strategy; and 3) plan for the ending.

Try to Find an Alternative

It is very difficult to implement rewards without incurring some cost. If the reward system is the same for all class members, it won't work as well as an individualized approach and you will likely reward some students for tasks they already like. If you tailor the rewards to individual students, you vastly increase your workload, and you increase the risk of students perceiving the program as unfair.

The size of the costs to motivation, although real, should not be overstated. As mentioned earlier, there are many contributors to motivation, and putting a smiley sticker on a spelling test will probably not rank high among them. Still, why incur the cost at all, if an alternative is available? The obvious alternative is to make the material intrinsically interesting. Indeed, if you follow that precept, you will never offer an extrinsic reward for an intrinsically interesting task, which is when the trouble with motivation really starts.

It is also worth considering whether student motivation is the real reason you use rewards. Do you put stickers on test papers in the hopes that students will work harder to earn them, or just for a bit of fun, a colorful diversion? Do you throw a class pizza party to motivate students, or to increase the class's sense of community? You might still distribute stickers and throw the party, but not make them explicitly contingent on performance beforehand. Announce to the class that they have done such a good job on the most recent unit that a party seems in order. Thus, the party is still an acknowledgement of good work and still might contribute to a positive class atmosphere, but it is not offered as a reward contingent on performance.

Use Rewards for a Specific Reason

A wise investor understands that taking out a loan, although it incurs a cost, might be strategic in the long run. So too, although a rewards program may incur some cost to motivation, there are times when the cost might be worth it. One example is when students must learn or practice a task that is rather dull, but that, once mastered, leads to opportunities for greater interest and motivation. For example, learning the times tables might be dull, but if students can get over that hump of boredom, they are ready to take on more interesting work. Rewards might also be useful when a student has lost confidence in himself to the point that he is no longer willing to try. If he'll attempt academic work to gain a desirable extrinsic reward and succeeds, his perception of himself and his abilities may change from self-doubt to recognition that he is capable of academic work (Greene and Lepper, 1974). Thereafter, the student may be motivated by his sense of accomplishment and his expectation that he will continue to do well.

> **Although a rewards program may incur some cost to motivation, there are times that the cost might be worth it. For example, learning the times tables might be dull, but if students can get over that hump of boredom, they are ready to take on more interesting work.**

Use Rewards for a Limited Time

No one wants to live with chronic debt, and no one should make rewards a long-term habit. Although the cost of using rewards may not be large, that cost likely increases as rewards are used for a longer time. In addition, there would seem to be an advantage to the program having a natural ending point. For example, students are rewarded for learning their times tables, and once they are learned, the rewards end. The advantage is that any decrease in motivation might stick to the task. In other words, students will think "times tables are boring, and we need to be rewarded to learn them" rather than "math is boring, and we need to be rewarded to learn it." In addition, if students are told at the start of the program when it will end, there may be fewer complaints when the goodies are no longer available.

Notes

1. Such positive framing of rewards does not reverse the negative impact of rewards on motivation, but telling students that rewards signal acknowledgement of good work, rather than the closing of a bargain, seems more in keeping with the spirit of education.

2. Readers who are familiar with interventions to reduce students' aggressive or antiscoial behavior may be surprised at this finding. Such interventions do often use rewards and then phase them out. But keep in mind that the rewards are just one part of a complex intervention and that in order to be effective, such interventions must be implemented in full. To learn more about the use of rewards in such an intervention, see "Heading Off Disruption: How Early Intervention Can Reduce Defiant Behavior—and Win Back Teaching Time," *American Educator*, Winter 2003–2004, available at www.aft.org/pubs-reports/american_educator/winter03-04/index.html.

3. A correlation of zero would indicate that they were unrelated, and a correlation of -1.0 would indicate that they were perfectly related.

4. There are exceptions to this generalization, notably in the social realm. People will work hard without reward as part of a social transaction. In such situations a small reward will actually make people less likely to work (e.g., Heyman and Ariely, 2004). For example, if an acquaintance asks you to help her move a sofa, you would assume that she's asking a favor as a friend, and you might well help. But if she offers you $5 to move the sofa you think of the request as a business transaction, and $5 may not seem like enough money. These social concerns could apply to the classroom; some students might work to please the teacher. But such social transactions rest on reciprocity. If your friend with the poorly placed sofa never helps you out, you will get tired of her requests. It would be difficult to set up a classroom relationship that used social reciprocity between teachers and students.

5. The procedure is actually what researchers call a second-bid auction; the highest bidder wins the auction, but pays the price of the second highest bid. This procedure is meant to ensure that people bid exactly what the item is worth to them. The workings of the auction are explained in detail to subjects.

Assess Your Progress

1. Is giving rewards for academic work or appropriate classroom behavior an effective practice for teachers to use? Defend your response with evidence from the articles you have read here.

2. Why can rewards decrease motivation? Can you retell a time when this happened to you or that you observed happening in a classroom? How might you have changed that situation if you were the teacher?

3. How can using appropriate rewards or classroom currency help your students be lifelong learners, problem solvers, or critical thinkers? Cite evidence from the article in this unit for each of your reasons.

DANIEL T. WILLINGHAM is professor of cognitive psychology at the University of Virginia and author of *Cognition: The Thinking Animal*. His research focuses on the role of consciousness in learning. Readers can pose specific questions to "Ask the Cognitive Scientist," American Educator, 555 New Jersey Ave. N.W., Washington, DC 20001, or to amered@aft.org. Future columns will try to address readers' questions.

From *American Educator*, Winter 2007–2008, pp. 29–35. Copyright © 2008 by Daniel T. Willingham. Reprinted with permission of the American Educator, the quarterly journal of the American Federation of Teachers, AFL-CIO, and reprinted with permission of Daniel T. Willingham.

Article 10

Learning to Love Assessment

From judging performance to guiding students to shaping instruction to informing learning, coming to grips with informative assessment is one insightful journey.

CAROL ANN TOMLINSON

When I was a young teacher—young both in years and in understanding of the profession I had entered—I nonetheless went about my work as though I comprehended its various elements. I immediately set out to arrange furniture, put up bulletin boards, make lesson plans, assign homework, give tests, compute grades, and distribute report cards as though I knew what I was doing.

I had not set out to be a teacher, and so I had not really studied education in any meaningful way. I had not student taught. Had I done those things, however, I am not convinced that my evolution as a teacher would have been remarkably different. In either case, my long apprenticeship as a student (Lortie, 1975) would likely have dominated any more recent knowledge I might have acquired about what it means to be a teacher. I simply "played school" in the same way that young children "play house"—by mimicking what we think the adults around us do.

The one element I knew I was unprepared to confront was classroom management. Consequently, that's the element that garnered most of my attention during my early teaching years. The element to which I gave least attention was assessment. In truth, I didn't even know the word *assessment* for a good number of years. I simply knew I was supposed to give tests and grades. I didn't much like tests in those years. It was difficult for me to move beyond their judgmental aspect. They made kids nervous. They made me nervous. With no understanding of the role of assessment in a dynamic and success-oriented classroom, I initially ignored assessment when I could and did it when I had to.

Now, more than three decades into the teaching career I never intended to have, it's difficult for me to remember exactly when I had the legion of insights that have contributed to my growth as an educator. I do know, however, that those insights are the milestones that mark my evolution from seeing teaching as a job to seeing teaching as a science-informed art that has become a passion.

Following are 10 understandings about classroom assessment that sometimes gradually and sometimes suddenly illuminated my work. I am not finished with the insights yet because I am not finished with my work as a teacher or learner. I present the understandings in something like the order they unfolded in my thinking.

The formulation of one insight generally prepared the way for the next. Now, of course, they are seamless, interconnected, and interdependent. But they did not come to me that way. Over time and taken together, the understandings make me an advocate of *informative assessment*—a concept that initially played no conscious role in my work as a teacher.

Understanding 1. Informative assessment isn't just about tests.
Initially I thought about assessment as test giving. Over time, I became aware of students who did poorly on tests but who showed other evidence of learning. They solved problems well, contributed to discussions, generated rich ideas, drew sketches to illustrate, and role-played. When they wanted to communicate, they always found a way. I began to realize that when I gave students multiple ways to express learning or gave them a say in how they could show what they knew, more students were engaged. More to the point, more students were learning.

Although I still had a shallow sense of the possibilities of assessment, I did at least begin to try in multiple ways to let kids show what they knew. I used more authentic products as well as tests to gain a sense of student understanding. I began to realize that when one form of assessment was ineffective for a student, it did not necessarily indicate a lack of student success but could, in fact, represent a poor fit between the student and the method through which I was trying to make the student communicate. I studied students to see what forms of assessment worked for them and to be sure I never settled for a single assessment as an adequate representation of what a student knew.

Understanding 2. Informative assessment really isn't about the grade book.
At about the same time that Understanding 1 emerged in my thinking, I began to sense that filling a grade book was both less interesting and less useful than trying to figure out what individual students knew, understood, or could do. My thinking was shifting from assessment as judging students to assessment as guiding students. I was beginning to think about student accomplishment more than about student ranking (Wiggins, 1993).

Giving students feedback seemed to be more productive than giving them grades. If I carefully and consistently gave them feedback about their work, I felt more like a teacher than a warden. I felt more respectful of the students and their possibilities (Wiggins, 1993). I began to understand the difference between teaching for success and "gotcha" teaching and to sense the crucial role of informative assessment in the former.

Understanding 3. Informative assessment isn't always formal.
I also became conscious of the fact that some of the most valuable insights I gleaned about students came from moments or events that I'd never associated with assessment. When I read in a student's journal that his parents were divorcing, I understood why he was disengaged in class. I got a clear picture of one student's misunderstanding when I walked around as students worked and saw a diagram she made to represent how she understood the concept we were discussing. I could figure out how to help a student be more successful in small groups when I took the time to study systematically, but from a distance, what he did to make groups grow impatient with him.

Assessment, then, was more than "tests plus other formats." Informative assessment could occur any time I went in search of information about a student. In fact, it could occur when I was not actively searching but was merely conscious of what was happening around me.

I began to talk in more purposeful ways with students as they entered and left the classroom. I began to carry around a clipboard on which I took notes about students. I developed a filing system that enabled me to easily store and retrieve information about students as individuals and learners. I was more focused in moving around the room to spot-check student work in progress for particular proficiencies. I began to sense that virtually all student products and interactions can serve as informative assessment because I, as a teacher, have the power to use them that way.

Understanding 4. Informative assessment isn't separate from the curriculum.
Early in my teaching, I made lesson plans. Later on, I made unit plans. In neither time frame did I see assessment as a part of the curriculum design process. As is the case with many teachers, I planned what I would teach, taught it, and then created assessments. The assessments were largely derived from what had transpired during a segment of lessons and ultimately what had transpired during a unit of study. It was a while before I understood what Wiggins and McTighe (1998) call *backward design*.

That evolution came in three stages for me. First, I began to understand the imperative of laying out precisely what mattered most for students to know and be able to do—but also what they should understand—as a result of our work together. Then I began to discover that many of my lessons had been only loosely coupled to learning goals. I'd sometimes (often?) been teaching in response to what my students liked rather than in response to crucial learning goals. I understood the need to make certain that my teaching was a consistent match for what students needed to know, understand, and be able to do at the end of a unit. Finally, I began to realize that if I wanted to teach for success, my assessments had to be absolutely aligned with the knowledge, understanding, and skill I'd designated as essential learning outcomes. There was a glimmer of recognition in my work that assessment was a part of—not apart from—curriculum design.

Understanding 5. Informative assessment isn't about "after."
I came to understand that assessments that came at the end of a unit—although important manifestations of student knowledge, understanding, and skill—were less useful to me as a teacher than were assessments that occurred during a unit of study. By the time I gave and graded a final assessment, we were already moving on to a new topic or unit. There was only a limited amount I could do at that stage with information that revealed to me that some students fell short of mastering essential outcomes—or that others had likely been bored senseless by instruction that focused on outcomes they had mastered long before the unit had begun. When I studied student work in the course of a unit, however, I could do many things to support or extend student learning. I began to be a devotee of *formative assessment*, although I did not know that term for many years.

It took time before I understood the crucial role of preassessment or diagnostic assessment in teaching. Likely the insight was the product of the embarrassment of realizing that a student had no idea what I was talking about because he or she lacked vocabulary I assumed every 7th grader knew or of having a student answer a question in class early in a unit that made it clear he already knew more about the topic at hand than I was planning to teach. At that point, I began to check early in the year to see whether students could read the textbook, how well they could produce expository writing, what their spelling level was, and so on. I began systematically to use preassessments before a unit started to see where students stood in regard to prerequisite and upcoming knowledge, understanding, and skills.

Understanding 6. Informative assessment isn't an end in itself.
I slowly came to realize that the most useful assessment practices would shape how I taught. I began to explore and appreciate two potent principles of informative assessment. First, the greatest power of assessment information lies in its capacity to help me see how to be a better teacher. If I know what students are and are not grasping at a given moment in a sequence of study, I know how to plan our time better. I know when to reteach, when to move ahead, and when to explain or demonstrate something in another way. Informative assessment is not an end in itself, but the beginning of better instruction.

Understanding 7. Informative assessment isn't separate from instruction.
A second and related understanding hovered around my sense that assessment should teach me how to be a better teacher. Whether I liked it or not, informative assessment always demonstrated to me that my students' knowledge, understanding, and skill were emerging along different time continuums and at different depths. It became excruciatingly clear that my brilliant teaching was not equally brilliant for everyone in my classes. In other words, informative assessment helped me solidify a need for differentiation. As Lorna Earl (2003) notes, if teachers know

a precise learning destination and consistently check to see where students are relative to that destination, differentiation isn't just an option; it's the logical next step in teaching. Informative assessment made it clear—at first, painfully so—that if I meant for every student to succeed, I was going to have to teach with both singular and group needs in mind.

> **If I meant for every student to succeed, I was going to have to teach with both singular and group needs in mind.**

Understanding 8. Informative assessment isn't just about student readiness.

Initially, my emergent sense of the power of assessment to improve my teaching focused on student readiness. At the time, I was teaching in a school with a bimodal population—lots of students were three or more years behind grade level or three or more years above grade level, with almost no students in between. Addressing that expansive gap in student readiness was a daily challenge. I was coming to realize the role of informative assessment in ensuring that students worked as often as possible at appropriate levels of challenge (Earl, 2003).

Only later was I aware of the potential role of assessment in determining what students cared about and how they learned. When I could attach what I was teaching to what students cared about, they learned more readily and more durably. When I could give them options about how to learn and express what they knew, learning improved. I realized I could pursue insights about student interests and preferred modes of learning, just as I had about their readiness needs.

I began to use surveys to determine student interests, hunt for clues about their individual and shared passions, and take notes on who learned better alone and who learned better in small groups. I began to ask students to write to me about which instructional approaches were working for them and which were not. I was coming to understand that learning is multidimensional and that assessment could help me understand learners as multidimensional as well.

Understanding 9. Informative assessment isn't just about finding weaknesses.

As my sense of the elasticity of assessment developed, so did my sense of the wisdom of using assessment to accentuate student positives rather than negatives. With readiness-based assessments, I had most often been on the hunt for what students didn't know, couldn't do, or didn't understand. Using assessment to focus on student interests and learning preferences illustrated for me the power of emphasizing what works for students.

When I saw "positive space" in students and reflected that to them, the results were stunningly different from when I reported on their "negative space." It gave students something to build on—a sense of possibility. I began to spend at least as much time gathering assessment information on what students *could* do as on what they couldn't. That, in turn, helped me develop a conviction that each student in my classes brought strengths to our work and that it was my job to bring those strengths to the surface so that all of us could benefit.

Understanding 10. Informative assessment isn't just for the teacher.

Up to this point, much of my thinking was about the teacher—about me, my class, my work, my growth. The first nine understandings about assessment were, in fact, crucial to my development. But it was the 10th understanding that revolutionized what happened in the classrooms I shared with my students. I finally began to grasp that teaching requires a plural pronoun. The best teaching is never so much about *me* as about *us*. I began to see my students as full partners in their success.

> **Informative assessment is not an end in itself, but the beginning of better instruction.**

My sense of the role of assessment necessarily shifted. I was a better teacher—but more to the point, my students were better learners—when assessment helped all of us push learning forward (Earl, 2003). When students clearly understood our learning objectives, knew precisely what success would look like, understood how each assignment contributed to their success, could articulate the role of assessment in ensuring their success, and understood that their work correlated with their needs, they developed a sense of self-efficacy that was powerful in their lives as learners. Over time, as I developed, my students got better at self-monitoring, self-managing, and self-modifying (Costa & Kallick, 2004). They developed an internal locus of control that caused them to work hard rather than to rely on luck or the teacher's good will (Stiggins, 2000).

Assessing Wisely

Lorna Earl (2003) distinguishes between assessment *of* learning, assessment *for* learning, and assessment *as* learning. In many ways, my growth as a teacher slowly and imperfectly followed that progression. I began by seeing assessment as judging performance, then as informing teaching, and finally as informing learning. In reality, all those perspectives play a role in effective teaching. The key is where we place the emphasis.

Certainly a teacher and his or her students need to know who reaches (and exceeds) important learning targets—thus summative assessment, or assessment *of* learning, has a place in teaching. Robust learning generally requires robust teaching, and both diagnostic and formative assessments, or assessments *for* learning, are catalysts for better teaching. In the end, however, when assessment is seen *as* learning—for students as well as for teachers—it becomes most informative and generative for students and teachers alike.

References

Costa, A., & Kallick, B. (2004). *Assessment strategies for self-directed learning*. Thousand Oaks, CA: Corwin.

Earl, L. (2003). Assessment as learning: Using classroom assessment to maximize student learning. Thousand Oaks, CA: Corwin.

Lortie, D. (1975). *Schoolteacher: A sociological study*. Chicago: University of Chicago Press.

Stiggins, R. (2000). *Student-involved classroom assessment* (3rd ed.). Upper Saddle River, NJ: Prentice-Hall.

Wiggins, G. (1993). Assessing student performance: Exploring the purpose and limits of testing. San Francisco: Jossey-Bass.

Wiggins, G., & McTighe, J. (1998). *Understanding by design*. Alexandria, VA: Association for Supervision and Curriculum Development.

Assess Your Progress

1. As you read the 10 "Understandings" in the Tomlinson article, write a new phrase to use as a title for each. Be creative, but keep the meaning.
2. Why is learning to love assessment essential to effective teaching practices?

CAROL ANN TOMLINSON is Professor of Educational Leadership, Foundation, and Policy at the University of Virginia in Charlottesville; cat3y@virginia.edu.

From *Educational Leadership*, December 2008, pp. 8–13. Copyright © 2008 by ASCD. Reprinted by permission. The Association for Supervision and Curriculum Development is a worldwide community of educators advocating sound policies and sharing best practices to achieve the success of each learner. To learn more, visit ASCD at www.ascd.org

UNIT 3

Cornerstones to Learning: Reading and Math

Unit Selections

11. **Print Referencing during Read-Alouds: A Technique for Increasing Emergent Readers' Print Knowledge,** Tricia A. Zucker, Allison E. Ward, and Laura M. Justice
12. **You Gotta See It to Believe It: Teaching Visual Literacy in the English Classroom,** Robyn Seglem and Shelbie Witte
13. **You Should Read This Book!,** Jennifer Hartley
14. **Do Girls Learn Math Fear from Teachers?,** *Teacher Magazine*
15. **How Mathematics Counts,** Lynn Arthur Steen
16. **Textbook Scripts, Student Lives,** Jana Dean

Learning Outcomes

After reading this unit, you will be able to:

- Define *print referencing*.
- Explain the importance of *print referencing* to reading achievement of emergent readers.
- Demonstrate your ability to select appropriate books for teaching print referencing.
- Define *visual literacy*.
- Explain the importance of *visual literacy* to reading and mathematics achievement.
- Plan an activity to teach visual literacy in your content area.
- Discuss the value of silent reading across the curriculum.
- Outline a process to develop a silent reading program in your classroom or content area.
- Explain why and how students learn to fear a subject from their teachers.
- Generate ideas to avoid transferring gender and personal bias about subject matter to students.
- Provide justification to P-12 students the need for mathematics in adult life.
- Describe the problems related to using teacher manuals provided by the publisher of mathematics textbooks.
- Evaluate the scripts and pacing guides provided by publishers of mathematics textbooks.

Student Website
www.mhhe.com/cls

Internet References

The National Council of Teachers of English (NCTE)
www.ncte.org/search?q=teaching+ELL

National Council of Teachers of Mathematics
www.nctm.org

International Association of Reading
www.reading.org/General/Default.aspx

Visible Thinking
www.pzweb.harvard.edu/vt/index.html

Jim Trelease's Read-aloud Home Page
www.trelease-on-reading.com

Literature Circles Resource Center
www.litcircles.org

Read, Write, Think
www.readwritethink.org

National Library of Virtual Manipulatives
www.nlvm.usu.edu/en/nav/vlibrary.html

In this unit of the Annual Edition we focus on core skills that are taught in all public schools: reading and math. We have selected this topic because these skills are fundamental skills acquired from printed materials that are a primary source of knowledge. Additionally, being able to read and calculate are fundamental rights of all citizens in a democratic society. Many of us who read for both learning and pleasure cannot imagine a life without reading. Just as reading is an essential skill for learning and living a successful life, so are math skills. Imagine not being able to balance your checking, keep a budget, or understand and check the deductions on your paycheck. Good math skills are even more important when you try to read the fine print on a car and home mortgage loans or credit card bills. These issues are a reality for persons who lack basic math skills. In school, students may have the intellectual ability to attend college, but cannot pass those higher level math classes required in college prep programs. Thus, we are adding several articles about math to this section on cornerstones to learning.

The first two articles in the unit ask us to think about the teaching of reading in new ways: print referencing, and visual literacy. The articles were chosen because they offer us ways of looking at and thinking about reading books with children. Most of us have fond memories of sitting on a rug in a classroom, listening to our happy teacher read a story to us. She (most early childhood teachers are women) spoke in a lilting voice and pointed to the pictures to call attention to important characters or environmental elements. But did she help us learn print-related skills? According to Zucker, Ward, and Justice during story time children spend very little time in actually looking at the print in the book if teachers do not call specific attention to the print. Referencing Vygotskian theory, the authors emphasize the importance for increasing children's interest in and knowledge of print through meaningful social interactions. After defining this important set of skills, the authors give us a clear scientific basis and suggestions for print referencing, followed by examples of teaching techniques, a list of books containing print salient features, and the three steps to beginning print referencing. To continue the conversation about teaching and reading, Seglem and Witte assert that reading is more than text; it is about visual literacy as well, as we move from picture books to chapter books, visuals disappear from our books and the reader is called upon to make their own pictures. In fact, the authors note that creating mind movies is an essential element for engaging with, comprehending, and reflecting on the text. As the title of the article suggests, visual literacy should be taught to ensure that all student are able to use this important skill throughout their lives. After defining terms, the authors have a detailed description of how they teach visual literacy in their ninth-grade English classes using tattoos, collages, paintings, and poetry comics.

As readers and teachers, we understand that fluency is a key to reading well and with pleasure. But even if they are fluent, some readers resist silent reading activities in school. Hartley shares the story of her repeated efforts to engage urban students in sustained silent reading. Her realization that she needed to

© Getty Images/PhotoAlto

give up control and that her students needed to make their own choices on what to read was a breakthrough moment. In yet another urban setting, Teale and others worked to get students into books. Their efforts yielded results when students engaged themselves in authentic reading, writing, and thinking. These two articles illustrate that students read when given choices and authentic learning tasks.

The article from *Teacher Magazine* may spark an interesting debate. Do female educators transfer their fear about math to your children? Does this lead to poor math skills in young girls that perpetuate math fear in older girls? Does all of this lead to more female teachers who do poorly in college math classes? A quick poll might be an interesting class activity. However, we can no longer allow students to go through grade after grade without understanding the manipulation of numbers, because mathematics counts in today's schools. According to Steen, almost all high schools require Algebra II in order to graduate because the U.S. workforce needs workers with technical skills and college degrees require at least one college-level algebra course. It has become imperative that we graduate students who are not flummoxed by math problems that require more than simple fractions. Steen suggests that one reason students do not see the relevance for studying mathematics is that the only people they see use mathematics are math teachers. His answer is for schools to emphasize three important ingredients: communication, connections, and contexts. For one teacher it is the context that is missing from most mathematics textbooks. As Dean states, ". . . the problems do not invite students to apply mathematics to analyze the institutions and social and environmental issues that matter in local communities." Further, she notes that many students do not see their lives reflected in mathematics curriculum. What follows this list of concerns is her compelling journey to find balance between the required text with prescribed curricular objectives and the lives of her students.

This collection of articles is presented to stimulate your thinking about ways to help your students (or prospective students) become lifelong readers and competent users of math.

Print Referencing during Read-Alouds: A Technique for Increasing Emergent Readers' Print Knowledge

Daily classroom read-alouds provide an important context for supporting children's emergent literacy skills.

TRICIA A. ZUCKER, ALLISON E. WARD, AND LAURA M. JUSTICE

Daily classroom read-alouds provide a versatile context for supporting a range of emergent literacy skills. Yet most adults view read-alouds as a time to discuss story meaning or comprehension skills and rarely take advantage of opportunities to talk about print-related skills (Ezell & Justice, 2000). This article describes how early childhood educators can readily increase emergent readers' print knowledge by using an evidence-based technique called *print referencing* to ensure that classroom read-alouds include not only a focus on comprehension and meaning but also a complementary focus on print. Chief motivations for using print referencing with young readers include the following:

- Increasing children's print knowledge
- Developing children's metalinguistic understanding of print
- Fostering children's interest in print during a familiar and highly contextualized social activity

Print referencing is a technique that is integrated with one's existing language arts program and that provides a developmentally appropriate means for achieving curriculum and state standards that specify the importance of systematically addressing children's development of print knowledge.

This article describes how classroom teachers and reading specialists can effectively employ this technique. Because of the strong research base supporting use of print referencing, it was described in *The Reading Teacher* as one of three "particularly compelling approaches to reading aloud" (Lane & Wright, 2007, p. 670). This claim is well supported (see What Works Clearinghouse, Institute of Education Sciences, 2007); nonetheless, research makes a strong contribution to evidence-based practice when findings are put in a useable form and translated for end users (Teale, 2003). In what follows, we provide explicit guidance on translating use of print referencing to the classroom environment by defining print referencing, outlining evidence on the efficacy of print referencing, and providing suggestions for reading teachers and classroom teachers to successfully implement print referencing.

What Is Print Referencing?

Print referencing refers to techniques educators use to increase emergent readers' knowledge about and interest in print by highlighting the forms, functions, and features of print during read-alouds (see Justice & Ezell, 2002, 2004; Justice, Kaderavek, Fan, Sofka, & Hunt, 2009). To implement print referencing, educators call children's attention to print with verbal and nonverbal referencing techniques that include the following:

Questions
- How many words are on this page?
- There are words in the wolf's speech bubble; what do you think they say?

Requests
- Show me where I would start reading on this page.
- Point to a letter that's in your name.

Comments
- The illustrator wrote the word *bus* on this yellow school bus.
- These words are exactly the same.

Nonverbal techniques
- Track print from left to right while reading.
- Point to print.

For many years, researchers have argued that adults play an essential role in actively mediating children's attention to print during book reading (Adams, 1990; Snow & Ninio, 1986). Indeed, eye-gaze studies confirm that children spend very little time looking at print when adults do not use specific behaviors, like questioning about print and pointing to print, that elicit attention to print during read-alouds (Evans & Saint-Aubin, 2005; Justice, Pullen, & Pence, 2008). It is likely no surprise to teachers that pictures grab children's attention more often than the printed words; in fact, unless adults strategically and deliberately highlight print, young children spend less than 6% of read-aloud time looking at print (Evans, Williamson, & Pursoo, 2008). However, estimates suggest that when preschool-age children are read to with a print-referencing style every day for 10 minutes they may fixate on print 20,000 times more often than children who are read to in a way that does not draw their attention to print (Justice et al., 2008). As stipulated by Vygotskian theory, these studies indicate the importance of teachers for increasing children's interest in and knowledge about print through meaningful social interactions (Vygotsky, 1978).

What Aspects of Print Knowledge Are Taught?

The print-referencing technique is used primarily to develop children's emergent literacy skills and knowledge within the domain of print knowledge. Emergent literacy can be defined as the time before conventional reading and writing begins, including the skills, knowledge, attitudes, and experiences within a literate culture that precede conventional literacy (Sulzby & Teale, 1996). Marie Clay is credited as the leader of the movement toward viewing emergent literacy as an important and observable period of reading development (see Clay, 2000). As discussed by Clay and others, children progress through a series of developmental stages as they acquire literacy; from ages 3 to 5 years, typically, children are in the emergent stage of reading (Chall, 1996). The emergent reader is developing important knowledge about the forms and functions of print that, coupled with developing skills in oral language and phonological awareness, will serve as a foundation for later achievements in word recognition and reading comprehension.

Regarding print knowledge, specifically, children learn concepts such as book handling and print conventions or that letters and words convey a message (see Clay, 2000). The following four broad domains of print knowledge may be addressed using print referencing (Justice & Ezell, 2000, 2002, 2004):

1. Print as an object of meaning
2. Book organization and print conventions
3. Alphabet knowledge
4. Concept of word

Although not a lockstep hierarchy, children typically understand early developing concepts, such as print conventions and functions of print, before later developing concepts, such as learning to recognize letters and words (Justice & Ezell, 2004; Lomax & McGee, 1987). Adults use print referencing to target different aspects of print knowledge according to children's level of understanding so that instruction occurs within the child's zone of proximal development (ZPD; Vygotsky, 1978), including increasing the complexity of talk about print as children's understanding of print increases. The four broad domains of print knowledge encompass 15 specific *print targets* (Justice, Sofka, Sutton, & Zucker, 2006). Table 1 provides a definition of each print target followed by specific examples that are ordered in the hypothetical progression of the four broad print knowledge domains.

A central goal of print referencing is to engage emergent readers in conversations about print that foster metalinguistic awareness. Metalinguistic awareness is one's ability to consider language—whether spoken or written—as an object of attention. When adults use print referencing in read-alouds, they promote children's metalinguistic awareness by encouraging children to consider written language (i.e., print) as an object of attention while also modeling specific words one may use to talk about and negotiate the forms and functions of written language. This vocabulary provides a "functional 'tool'" (Vygotsky, 1934/1986, p. 107) that may further support children's interests in and conversations about print as they internalize words describing written language (e.g., *read, write, story, word, page, book, letter, capital, spell*). Children who enter formal reading instruction with limited vocabulary concerning print may be at risk for reading difficulties because this vocabulary is entrenched in formal reading instruction (van Kleeck, 1990).

What Is the Scientific Basis for Print Referencing?

A large body of empirical work provides evidence for the potential value of print referencing, making it an appropriate technique for reading teachers seeking to use evidence-based practices. These studies have provided rich qualitative descriptions of the ways adults may mediate children's interactions with print (Clay, 1991; Snow & Ninio, 1986) plus experimental investigations of how specific adult behaviors influence the amount of time children spend looking at print in books (Evans et al., 2008) or the frequency of children's responses about print (Girolametto, Weitzman, Lefebvre, & Greenberg, 2007). Studies have also used survey data to show that parental reports of how often they explicitly teach their children about print during literacy activities, including readalouds, is positively associated with their children's emergent literacy skills (Sénéchal, LeFevre, Thomas, & Daley, 1998).

Convincing evidence for the positive impact of print referencing comes from several recent studies that have sought to explicitly test whether print referencing improves children's print knowledge using experimental methods in which one group of children receives print referencing and others do not. Experimental methods that feature random assignment provide strong evidence of the causal impacts of a particular instructional approach (in this case, children's exposure to print referencing) and associated changes in child outcomes (in this case, children's print knowledge growth over time). We provide an overview of these studies, and encourage readers to review the original works for specific details.

In an initial study of print referencing, published in 2000 by Justice and Ezell, researchers randomly assigned 28 parent–child pairs (14 in an experimental group, 14 in a control group) to implement a 16-session book reading program in their homes over a four-week period. The children were 4 years old and had typically developing language ability as assessed through standardized testing. Parents received one new book per week to use in their home reading sessions. Prior to the home reading program parents in the experimental group viewed a 10-minute video that modeled for them how to integrate verbal and nonverbal references to print into reading sessions. Parents in the control group were told only to read the books as they normally would with their children. Comparison of children's gains on an emergent literacy assessment battery conducted before and after their four-week reading programs showed that children in the experimental group exhibited significantly greater growth on measures of print concepts, concept of word, and word identification.

In a related study, Justice and Ezell (2002) randomly assigned 30 children (15 in an experimental group, 15 in a control group) to complete a 24-session book reading program held over eight weeks in a preschool center. The children ranged in age from 3 to 5 years, had typically developing language ability, and were from lower income households. Each child completed small-group reading sessions, and a total of eight book titles were rotated through the reading sessions. The single difference between the reading program for the children in the experimental group and those in the control group was that the former included nine references to print in each reading session whereas the latter included nine references to pictures. Children in the experimental group showed significantly greater growth from pretest to posttest on measures of alphabet knowledge, concept of word, and word identification.

Table 1 Print Targets Addressed Through Print-Referencing Read-Alouds in Early Childhood Settings

Print Targets	Definition/Examples
Print Meaning Domain	
Print Function	The function of print is to carry meaning; some special typefaces convey meaning. Sometimes print appears in illustrations (e.g., visible sound). <ul><li>"These are fox's words—he's talking."</li><li>"These words are red because he's angry."</li></ul>
Environmental Print	Words present in the environment are portrayed in illustrations (e.g., signs, labels, lists, calendars, recipes, etc.). <ul><li>"This jar has the word *Cookies* on it."</li><li>"Let's read these traffic signs."</li></ul>
Concept of Reading	The function of reading is to convey information or tell a story. There are many things we do when we read. <ul><li>"If I want to find out how they solve this problem I will have to keep reading."</li><li>"Who can tell me some things we do when we read?"</li></ul>
Book & Print Organization Domain	
Page Order	The order in which book pages are read (i.e., the physical act of manipulating a book). <ul><li>"I read this page first and this page next."</li><li>"Where is the front of the book?"</li></ul>
Title of Book	The role of the title as a label and to convey meaning. <ul><li>"This is the half title page. It tells us the name of the book again."</li><li>"The title page tells us this was published in New York."</li></ul>
Top and Bottom of Page	Reading in English occurs from top of the page to the bottom of the page. <ul><li>"This is the top of the page. The writing starts here."</li><li>(move finger down page) "I will read this top line, then this line, and then this last line."</li></ul>
Print Direction	Reading in English must occur from left to right. Some text is printed with unusual orientations or shapes to convey meaning. <ul><li>(sweep finger under print) "When I read I go this way."</li><li>"These words are printed at an angle so they'll look like they're splashing into the water."</li></ul>
Author's Role	The role of the author(s)/illustrator(s). <ul><li>"The author is the person who wrote the words in this book."</li><li>"The author wrote a dedication to his mother."</li></ul>
Letters Domain	
Names of Letters	There are names for all 26 letters. <ul><li>"I see a word on this page that starts with an *R!*"</li><li>"Who can find a letter *S*?"</li></ul>
Concept of Letter	The purpose of letters in forming words. The same letters can be used in many ways. <ul><li>"I see the same letter in these two words."</li><li>"There are three letters in the word *cat*."</li></ul>
Upper and Lower Case Letters	Letters come in two forms. <ul><li>"This is a capital *D*. Damian has a capital *D* in his name."</li><li>"Uppercase *S* is the same shape as lowercase *s*."</li></ul>
Words Domain	
Concept of Word in Print	Words are distinct units of print and are different from letters. <ul><li>"Let's count the words on this page."</li><li>"Who can show me just one word?"</li></ul>
Words Domain	
Short vs. Long Words	Words have different structures. Some words are short, others are long. <ul><li>"*Dinosaur* is a long word. It has lots of letters."</li><li>"Which word is longer—*vegetable* or *soup*?"</li></ul>

(continued)

Table 1 Print Targets Addressed Through Print-Referencing Read-Alouds in Early Childhood Settings *(continued)*

Print Targets	Definition/Examples
Letters vs. Words	Letters make up words. • "This is the letter *G*. It is in the word *grow* and *garden*." • "This is the word *sun*. S-u-n spells sun."
Word Identification	Some familiar or meaningful words can be identified. • "This is a picture of a tomato. The word *tomato* is written beside it." • "This is the word *the*. It's in this book a lot!"

Adapted from Justice, Sofka, Sutton, & Zucker. (2006). Adapted with permission.

Of particular relevance to the present audience, a recent replication involved testing the impact of print referencing when implemented by preschool teachers during whole-group, classroom read-alouds over an entire academic year. This large scale multistate study is called Project STAR (Sit Together and Read) and will ultimately involve replication tests in 90 early childhood classrooms and 90 early childhood special education classrooms. Results from an initial cohort involving 106 4-year-old children randomly sampled from 23 need-based Project STAR classrooms indicated that children who experienced daily whole-group read-alouds in which teachers used print referencing showed significantly greater gains on three measures of print knowledge (name-writing ability, alphabet knowledge, print concepts) from fall to spring compared with children who received "business-as-usual" read-alouds with the same set of books and the same schedule of reading (see Justice et al., 2009). The major difference between this study and previous experimental studies of print referencing is that this study involved implementation of print referencing by classroom teachers for an entire academic year in their whole-group read-alouds; additionally, the 106 children studied showed more diversity than prior samples with respect to cultural backgrounds and level of achievement.

Other researchers have found similar positive effects for print referencing. Notably, Lovelace and Stewart (2007) studied the effectiveness of using non-evocative print-referencing (i.e., commenting, tracking, and pointing) with preschoolers with language impairment. This study involved a single-subject research design and five 4- to 5-year-old children who participated in regular one-on-one read-alouds conducted in the classroom setting by research personnel. Children in this study made significant growth in knowledge of print concepts over the intervention period. Taken together, the convergent findings across research studies involving various implementers (e.g., parents, teachers, research personnel), various recipients (e.g., children who are developing typically, children who have developmental disabilities), and various settings (e.g., classrooms, homes, clinics) provide strong and consistent evidence that use of print referencing within the familiar contexts of read-alouds is a useful method for improving emergent readers' knowledge about print.

Suggestions for Print Referencing

Thus far we have explained the "what" and the "why" behind print referencing; that is, we have defined what techniques adults can use to reference 15 print targets (see Table 1) and we have summarized several research studies demonstrating the effectiveness of print referencing for increasing emergent readers' print knowledge. Now we turn to important questions about when, how, and with what texts print referencing should be used to derive suggestions for reading teachers and classroom teachers to effectively integrate print referencing into their larger curriculum. We offer suggestions from previous research and from our own study of transcripts of teachers who have strategically encouraged their 4-year-old students to engage with print during Project STAR read-alouds (Justice et al., 2009).

When and How Do Teachers Integrate Print Referencing?

Instructional time is a precious commodity in classrooms; accordingly, teachers want to know how to make the most of every minute. Thus, teachers may wonder how often they ought to reference print when reading. As a general guideline, our suggestion is that print referencing should be used when it seems to add value to a read-aloud experience in terms of furthering children's print knowledge. What this means is that when teachers are reading books with children with the intent of promoting their literacy development, print referencing can be incorporated. For instance, many preschool classrooms start their day with a group read-aloud that serves explicit instructional purposes relevant to the classroom curriculum or state learning standards. In such cases, this read-aloud provides an exemplary opportunity to incorporate print referencing as a means to heighten children's attention to and learning about print. Most of the available work on benefits attributable to adult use of print referencing has featured children's participation in only one read-aloud per day for three or four days per week (e.g., Justice & Ezell, 2002; Lovelace & Stewart, 2007). Consequently, it seems that in the typical preschool classroom, if children could participate in one small- or large-group read-aloud per day that involves opportunities to learn and talk about print, benefits to their print knowledge would be apparent.

Within these read-alouds, it is reasonable to ask how much attention, exactly, the teacher should direct to print. Generally, teachers must be strategic in considering how much attention to print should occur to promote children's learning about the forms and functions of print while not detracting from the reading experience or other benefits that might be gained from that experience (e.g., learning new vocabulary words, developing content knowledge). In Project STAR, teachers deliberately highlighted two specific print targets during a read-aloud (e.g., print function, page order) and addressed these using varying combinations of techniques to highlight print (e.g., commenting, tracking) and varying amounts of scaffolding to differentiate for individual students' understandings of the print target. In instances when it seems that children just do not want to talk about print, teachers can rely on nonverbal techniques to draw children's attention to interesting aspects of print within texts because adults' verbal references to print (i.e., questions and comments) and nonverbal references to print (i.e., tracking print) both increase the amount of time children spend looking at print during read-alouds (Justice et al., 2008).

Let's look at an excerpt from a read-aloud of *The Way I Feel* (Cain, 2000) that shows how a teacher leverages a combination of print referencing techniques to evoke children's attention to and consideration of print in the book. The teacher is discussing the heading on a page about feeling shy; the word *shy* is printed in a thin, pink typeface against a pastel background.

Teacher: Now you can barely see the **word** *shy*. It's in light pink. You see it right there? (Points to word)

Child: Yeah.

Teacher: (Tracks letters as she spells) **S-H-Y.** It's hiding in the page, because even the **word** is shy. (She hides her face behind the book as if she is shy.) Shy is an interesting word that we should talk about. We read a book about a shy character last week. Do you remember what we said *shy* means?

This excerpt is useful for consideration, as it illustrates how print referencing can be used alongside other techniques that can promote children's language growth within the read-aloud. There is tremendous value in read-alouds that focus on narrative events or vocabulary in the book (Sipe, 2008; Teale, 2003); teachers should ensure that inclusion of a focus on print does not preclude other opportunities for talking about interesting words, text structures, or story content.

Print referencing can be used alongside other techniques that can promote children's language growth within the read-aloud.

How Can Teachers Fully Engage Children When Using Print Referencing?

Print referencing read-alouds require teachers to pay careful attention to individual characteristics of children, including their orientation toward literacy and their desire and need for active engagement in interactions with teachers. Particularly for those at-risk for later reading difficulties, it is important to use social activities like read-alouds to foster a positive orientation to literacy. When adults embed print references into book reading, lively discussions about print unfold because young children typically find print as interesting as other text stimuli, such as illustrations; this can promote children's positive orientation toward literacy. Project STAR teachers used a variety of methods to make discussions exciting and fun. Many teachers, for example, linked the printed text to meaningful print in the children's lives. In this excerpt from a discussion of *Rumble in the Jungle* (Andreae, 1996), the teacher points to the word *tiger* and connects the print to children's own names (all names are pseudonyms).

Teacher: Look at this **word** boys and girls. This **word** begins with a **T,** like Tim's name begins with a **T.** Can you think of any other **words** that begin with **T**—like *Tim* and *tiger*?

Research has indicated that children's names constitute a unit of print that is of great interest to young children (Clay, 2000; Treiman & Broderick, 1998).

In other sections of this read-aloud this teacher demonstrates sensitivity to students' attentional focus by finding creative ways to actively engage students with print. She encouraged a kinesthetic response to print by asking students to "skywrite" the letter Z during *Rumble in the Jungle* (Andreae, 1996).

Teacher: Now who do we have?

Children: Zebras!

Teacher: The zebras. That's right. Look, here's the **letter Z.** Put your finger up and let's make the **letter Z.** (Teacher and children point their index finger in air and move their arms together, the teacher with her back to the children so as to not confuse the orientation of the letter.) Across, slant down, and then back across.

In addition, Project STAR teachers asked children to come forward and point to print or turn pages during reading, thereby actively involving children with print.

Young children will comment on or ask questions about print, particularly when print is made salient through features like speech bubbles or as environmental print embedded in illustrations (Smolkin, Conlon, & Yaden, 1988). Teachers should encourage children's spontaneous comments about print during read-alouds by spending time following a child's lead when print is discussed; this communicates that the child's point of view is valuable.

What Are Appropriate Texts for Print Referencing?

As we turn to the question of which texts are best suited to print referencing, it is important to take a step back and consider why the print itself is worthy of our attention. Sipe (2008) explained that children's picture books provide a sophisticated visual aesthetic experience that in many ways is like an art form in which print is a key aspect:

> Navigating picturebooks requires that we pay attention to every feature, from the front cover and the dust jacket to the back cover . . . We should speculate (along with children) on why the illustrator, designer, or editor made these choices, communicating to children that every single detail of the book—down to the typefaces, the size and shape of the book, and the placement of the illustrations on the pages—is the result of somebody's calculated decision.

As Sipe pointed out, all elements of a book's design communicate meaning and warrant attention for reasons beyond learning how to handle a book or name its parts; there is interdependence between the printed text and the pictures in creating the full story. When considering features of print within children's books, it is often possible to see how the illustrator or author use a visual "language" through such features of typeface as colors (e.g., bright colors suggest happiness/optimism), lines (e.g., jagged fonts suggest anxiety/pressure), and orientations (e.g., horizontal is stable, whereas diagonal words suggest motion). In high print salience books, a term which describes children's books with a high frequency of interesting print features, texts and pictures are completely interdependent because print is embedded in illustrations through speech balloons, visible sounds, or environmental print labeling objects in illustrations (e.g., the word *honey* on a jar). Print salient books are particularly amenable to creating a context in which print referencing is a natural fit to the read-aloud experience.

Table 2 Print Salient Features

Print in Illustrations					Print in Body of Text	
Labels	**Environmental Print**	**Visible Speech**	**Visible Sound**	**Letters in Isolation**	**Font Changes**	**Bold or Unique Fonts**
Diagrams, figures, or photos contain a print label.	Object has a label, word, or letter on it, often on everyday objects (e.g., jar labeled "Cookies" or "Stop" sign).	Character has words or speech balloons nearby indicating it is speaking.	Character or object has a sound written nearby (e.g., /grrr/ near a tiger, "clunk" near a wheel).	Letters are printed in isolation, as may occur in an alphabet book.	Changes to font color/size/orientation (e.g., words are written at an angle or in an arc or swirl instead of standard horizontal).	Font changes (e.g., from **serif** to **block** or artistic) including bold, italics, or underlining.

In this transcript, the teacher discusses how two different typefaces in *The Way I Feel* (Cain, 2000) carry noteworthy meaning. She discusses the heading word *silly* that is written in a rainbow of colors with a curly font that follows a wavelike orientation. The *S* and the dot of the lowercase *I* have small eyes drawn within so that they appear cross-eyed.

Teacher: Look at that **word** *Silly*. How does that **word** look?

Several children: Silly

Teacher: It looks silly! (Points to plainer typeface below) Do those **words** look the same?

Children: No.

Teacher: (Points to silly again) What do they have on these **letters**?

Children: Eyes!

Teacher: Eyes!

Child: Eyes in S.

Teacher: So the **letters** look like the **words** feel in this book . . . They look silly. That's the word *silly*.

Child: The word's silly?

Teacher: Yes, and that's the way he feels on this page.

Teachers should use print referencing with high print salience texts as well as with texts that do not have particularly interesting print features. Nonetheless, high print salience texts, like the one in this example, can provide a natural springboard for talking about print targets such as how print carries meaning or functions in the environment (Zucker, Justice, & Piasta, in press). There are many examples of high-quality children's literature that contain print salient visual aesthetic elements, including popular titles and classics; and print salient texts extend beyond the genre of alphabet books, which are also known to promote talk about print (e.g., Bradley & Jones, 2007). Table 2 provides a simplified version of a rubric we have used to analyze the occurrence of print salient features in texts, and Table 3 lists some high print salience texts coded on this rubric. It is likely that analyzing your

Table 3 Texts Containing Print Salient Features

Text (Author)	Illustrations					Text	
	Labels	Environmental Print	Visible Speech	Visible Sound	Letters in Isolation	Font Changes	Bold or Unique Fonts
Big Plans (Shea & Smith, 2008)		+				+	+
Bunny Cakes (Wells, 2000)		+				+	+
Fancy Nancy (O'Connor, 2006)		+				+	
Growing Vegetable Soup (Ehlert, 1993)	+	+					+
I Stink (McMullan, 2002)			+	+	+	+	+
Miss Bindergarten Gets Ready for Kindergarten (Slate, 1996)		+			+	+	+
The Noisy Airplane Ride (Downs, 2005)	+			+		+	+
Rumble in the Jungle (Andreae, 1996)				+		+	+
Truck (Crews, 1997)		+					
The Way I Feel (Cain, 2000)	+					+	+

library collection with an eye toward the important ways that print carries meaning will produce several titles through which meaningful discussions about print can occur.

Get More From a Read-Aloud

Daily classroom read-alouds provide an important context for supporting children's emergent literacy skills, particularly children's developing knowledge of print forms and functions. Although read-alouds are a fairly commonplace activity within most early childhood classrooms, evidence suggests that this activity is most often used as a time to discuss story meaning or comprehension skills; too often, educators do not take advantage of this activity as an opportunity to develop children's print-related skills. This article provides guidance to educators, including reading specialists, regarding how print referencing may be used to increase children's knowledge about print, and, as importantly, to support children's development of an interest in print as a salient feature of many texts.

In the present educational climate, educators are being pressed to use instructional techniques that do many things at once. Regarding emergent literacy instruction, educators are asked to use techniques that are linked to state standards of learning and that have scientific support with respect to demonstrated increases in students' learning, while simultaneously ensuring that these techniques are developmentally appropriate, engaging and motivating, and sensitive to the diverse needs of their students. These are indeed tall orders! In the present article, we discussed a simple, inexpensive, and likely high-yield technique that early educators may easily implement and that we believe achieves all of these aims. Educators can take a few small steps such as the following to get started tomorrow on making print referencing a systematic component of their literacy instruction.

- **Determine which read-aloud within your classroom will regularly involve your use of print referencing techniques.** These may be large-group or small-group sessions. Just be sure that every child in the classroom is involved!
- **Examine the 15 targets presented in Table 1. Order these over the remaining weeks of school so that one or two targets are addressed in each reading session.** There are many ways to organize the targets: you might rotate these daily (a different target each day) or by week. It's up to you—the important thing is to ensure that all of the targets receive attention during an academic year and that you revisit print targets as necessary to ensure children's understanding of print.
- **Examine your classroom library or school library to select books that feature a high level of print salience.** You might use the rubric in Table 2. Try to secure a collection of 20 or 30 books that you can read aloud repeatedly over the year to address your selected targets. You might rotate books daily or use one book for a week. Regardless, be sure that children have multiple opportunities to hear each book, as this seems an important component of most print referencing studies to date.

Note

This research was supported by Grant R305F050124 from the U.S. Department of Education, Institute of Education Sciences.

References

Adams, M.J. (1990). *Beginning to read: Thinking and learning about print.* Cambridge, MA: MIT Press.

Bradley, B.A., & Jones, J. (2007). Sharing alphabet books in early childhood classrooms. *The Reading Teacher, 60*(5), 452–463. doi:10.1598/RT.60.5.5

Chall, J.S. (1996). *Stages of reading development* (2nd ed.). Fort Worth, TX: Harcourt Brace.

Clay, M. (2000). *Concepts about print: What have children learned about the way we print language?* Portsmouth, NH: Heinemann.

Clay, M.M. (1991). Introducing a new storybook to young readers. *The Reading Teacher, 45*(4), 264–273. doi:10.1598/RT.45.4.2

Evans, M.A., & Saint-Aubin, J. (2005). What children are looking at during shared storybook reading: Evidence from eye movement monitoring. *American Psychological Society, 16*(11), 913–920.

Evans, M.A., Williamson, K., & Pursoo, T. (2008). Preschoolers' attention to print during shared book reading. *Scientific Studies of Reading, 12*(1), 106–129. doi:10.1080/10888430701773884

Ezell, H.K., & Justice, L.M. (2000). Increasing the print focus of adult-child shared book reading through observational learning. *American Journal of Speech-Language Pathology, 9*(1), 36–47.

Girolametto, L., Weitzman, E., Lefebvre, P., & Greenberg, J. (2007). The effects of in-service education to promote emergent literacy in child care centers: A feasibility study. *Language, Speech, and Hearing Services in Schools, 38*(1), 72–83. doi:10.1044/01611461(2007/007)

Justice, L.M., & Ezell, H.K. (2000). Enhancing children's print and word awareness through home-based parent intervention. *American Journal of Speech-Language Pathology, 9*(3), 257–269.

Justice, L.M., & Ezell, H.K. (2002). Use of storybook reading to increase print awareness in at-risk children. *American Journal of Speech-Language Pathology,* 1 (1), 17–29. doi:10.1044/10580360(2002/003)

Justice, L.M., & Ezell, H.K. (2004). Print referencing: An emergent literacy enhancement strategy and its clinical applications. *Language, Speech, and Hearing Services in Schools, 35*(2), 185–193. doi:10.1044/0161-1461(2004/018)

Justice, L.M., Kaderavek, J.N., Fan, X., Sofka, A., & Hunt, A. (2009). Accelerating preschoolers' early literacy development through classroom-based teacher–child storybook reading and explicit print referencing. *Language, Speech, and Hearing Services in Schools, 40*(1), 67–85. doi:10.1044/0161-1461(2008/07-0098)

Justice, L.M., Pullen, P.C., & Pence, K. (2008). Influence of verbal and nonverbal references to print on preschoolers' visual attention to print during storybook reading. *Developmental Psychology, 44*(3), 855–866. doi:10.1037/0012-1649.44.3.855

Justice, L.M., Sofka, A.E., Sutton, M., & Zucker, T.A. (2006). *Project STAR: Fidelity coding checklist.* Charlottesville: Preschool Language and Literacy Lab, University of Virginia.

Lane, H.B., & Wright, T.L. (2007). Maximizing the effectiveness of reading aloud. *The Reading Teacher, 60*(7), 668–675. doi:10.1598/RT.60.7.7

Lomax, R.G., & McGee, L.M. (1987). Young children's concepts about print and reading: Toward a model of word reading acquisition. *Reading Research Quarterly, 22*(2), 237–256. doi:10.2307/747667

Lovelace, S., & Stewart, S.R. (2007). Increasing print awareness in preschoolers with language impairment using non-evocative print referencing. *Language, Speech, and Hearing Services in Schools, 38*(1), 16–30. doi:10.1044/0161-1461(2007/003)

Sénéchal, M., LeFevre, J., Thomas, E.M., & Daley, K.E. (1998). Differential effects of home literacy experiences on the development of oral and written language. *Reading Research Quarterly, 33*(1), 96–116. doi:10.1598/RRQ.33.1.5

Sipe, L.R. (2008). *Storytime: Young children's literary understanding in the classroom.* New York: Teachers College Press.

Smolkin, L.B., Conlon, A., & Yaden, D.B. (1988). Print salient illustrations in children's picture books: The emergence of written language awareness. In J.E. Readence & R.S. Baldwin (Eds.), *Dialogues in literacy research* (37th yearbook of the National Reading Conference, pp. 59–68). Chicago, IL: National Reading Conference.

Snow, C.E., & Ninio, A. (1986). The contracts of literacy: What children learn from learning to read books. In W.H. Teale & E. Sulzby (Eds.), *Emergent literacy: Writing and reading* (pp. 116–137). Norwood, NJ: Ablex.

Sulzby, E., & Teale, W. (1996). Emergent literacy. In R. Barr, M.L. Kamil, P.B. Mosenthal, & P.D. Pearson (Eds.), *Handbook of reading research* (Vol. 2, pp. 727–757). Mahwah, NJ: Erlbaum.

Teale, W.H. (2003). Reading aloud to children as a classroom instructional activity: Insights from research to practice. In A. van Kleeck, A.A. Stahl, & E.B. Bauer (Eds.), *On reading books to children: Parents and teachers* (pp. 109–133). Mahwah, NJ: Erlbaum.

Treiman, R., & Broderick, V. (1998). What's in a name: Children's knowledge about the letters in their own names. *Journal of Experimental Child Psychology, 70*(2), 97–116. doi:10.1006/jecp.1998.2448

van Kleeck, A. (1990). Emergent literacy: Learning about print before learning to read. *Topics in Language Disorders, 10*(2), 25–45.

Vygotsky, L.S. (1978). *Mind in society: The development of higher psychological processes* (M. Cole, V. John-Steiner, S. Scribner, & E. Souberman, Eds. & Trans.). Cambridge, MA: Harvard University Press.

Vygotsky, L. S. (1986). *Thought and language* (A. Kozulin, Trans.). Cambridge, MA: MIT Press. (Original work published 1934)

What Works Clearinghouse, Institute of Education Sciences. (2007, January). *Interactive shared book reading.* Retrieved June 20, 2008, from http://ies.ed.gov/ncee/wwc/pdf/WWC_ISBR_011807.pdf

Zucker, T.A., Justice, L.M., & Piasta, S.B. (in press). Prekindergarten teachers' verbal references to print during classroom-based large-group shared reading. *Language, Speech, and Hearing Services in Schools.*

Children's Literature Cited

Andreae, D. (1996). *Rumble in the jungle.* London: Little Tiger Press.
Cain, J. (2000). *The way I feel.* Seattle, WA: Parenting Press.
Crews, D. (1997). *Truck.* New York: HarperCollins.
Downs, M. (2005). *The noisy airplane ride.* Berkeley, CA: Tricycle Press.
Ehlert, L. (1993). *Growing vegetable soup.* San Diego: Harcourt.
McMullan, K. (2002). *I stink!* New York: HarperCollins.
O'Connor, J. (2006). *Fancy Nancy.* New York: HarperCollins.
Shea, B., & Smith, L. (2008). *Big plans.* New York: Hyperion.
Slate, J. (1996). *Miss Bindergarten gets ready for kindergarten.* New York: Dutton.
Wells, R. (2000). *Bunny cakes.* New York: Puffin.

Assess Your Progress

1. You have been asked to present a brief description of print referencing for parents at the Back-to-School Night. Prepare a 5 minute presentation or demonstration.

2. Find three books *not* listed by Zucker, Ward, & Justice that you could recommend to parents during your presentation at the Back-to-School Night. Prepare a table to illustrate why your selected books are appropriate for teaching print referencing.

ZUCKER is a postdoctoral research fellow at the University of Texas Health Science Center—Houston, USA; e-mail tricia.zucker@uth.tmc.edu. WARD is a doctoral student at the University of Virginia, Charlottesville, USA; e-mail aew9b@virginia.edu. JUSTICE teaches at The Ohio State University, Columbus, USA; e-mail ljustice@ehe.osu.edu.

Article 12

You Gotta See It to Believe It: Teaching Visual Literacy in the English Classroom

By teaching students how to read and view all texts critically, not just the traditional print texts, teachers can build upon the skills students need to read and write, increasing their literacy levels in all areas.

ROBYN SEGLEM AND SHELBIE WITTE

Clarisse: What do the instructions mean when they ask "what the painting says"?

Daniel: You've got to be able to read the picture.

Clarisse: Easy. It says "Lift Thine Eyes."

Daniel: Duh. Not just the words, you gotta be able to read the entire picture, like it has words on it. Like, look at all the people looking down. What do you think that means or what it's sayin'?

Clarisse: That people aren't paying attention?

Daniel: Right, that people are too caught up in their lives to see what's happening.

Clarisse: To stop and smell the roses? Whatever that means, I've heard my mom say it.

Daniel: Yeah, I think that's right. That sometimes we don't pay attention to life and it just goes on without us.

This discussion of Norman Rockwell's painting "Lift Up Thine Eyes" illustrates a student's discovery of a different way of reading (all student names used are pseudonyms). More than ever in the history of education, the demands placed upon students in the realm of literacy are becoming more stringent. No longer are the abilities to read and write in a linear, left-to-right fashion the sole indicators of successful communications. Rather, the world is made up of visual symbols that require more complex thinking skills than traditional literacy requires.

Today, the concept of literacy has ceased to be narrowly defined. Literacy is now a fluid concept determined by cultural context (Williams, 2004). From this necessity and with this fluidity in mind, students need instruction in analyzing and creating a variety of texts in new ways (Alvermann, 2002). If educators want students to perform well in both the world and on new assessments, students need a critical understanding of print and nonprint texts in relationship to themselves as readers and viewers within different social, cultural, and historical contexts (Alvermann & Hagood, 2000). Incorporating visual literacy into the curriculum is vital for student success.

Why Visual Literacy?

While many agree that visual literacy should be included in the educational arena, there has been great debate among researchers as to what the term actually encompasses. Visual literacy was originally recognized as the ability for someone to discriminate and interpret the visuals encountered in the environment as fundamental to learning (Debes, 1969). Critics of that original interpretation of visual literacy feel it is too broadly stated, failing to narrow the concept to what visual literacy allows people to do or how symbols work within its context (Avgerinou & Ericson, 1997). During the 1980s and early 1990s, three major categories emerged to refer to visual literacy: human abilities, the promotion of ideas, and teaching strategies (Avgerinou & Ericson, 1997). With these three categories in mind, perhaps the best definition for visual literacy is a simple one, such as the one Braden and Hortin (1982) proposed: "Visual literacy is the ability to understand and use images, including the ability to think, learn and express oneself in terms of images".

Because using visuals is a powerful instructional tool, and because students receive information in a variety of formats, literacy must be expanded beyond traditional reading and writing to include the visual arts as one of the ways in which we communicate (Flood & Lapp, 1997/1998). According to Flood and Lapp (1997/1998), the best reason most teachers give for not including visual arts within the classroom is their fear that it would take time away from traditional reading and writing skills. Their view, while legitimate, denies students the experience of the layered information in the real world and reflects the unsupported view that traditional literacy is the only literacy. This article seeks to explore the issues encompassing visual literacies as well as to provide ideas for teachers on how to begin working with them in the classroom.

Visual Literacy at Work

Including visualization in the classroom cannot be a one-shot activity. Rather, it must be woven into the regular classroom curriculum. Following Eisner's (1992) philosophy that imagination and reading ability are closely interwoven, it is important to understand the diverse ways in which students imagine or visualize. Instantaneously, students can receive imagery and information from television shows and movies, cartoons, websites, and advertisements. Helping students to understand the diversity of print and non-print texts as well as the visual connections that can be made between them is a practical way to connect the concrete and abstract thinking of students who struggle to make meaning from text. While many students automatically interpret print text into nonprint visual images, some students struggle with making the leap from words to images.

Visualization—the ability to build mental pictures or images while reading—partnered with a reader's prior background knowledge and level of engagement in the reading topic greatly affects the reader's understanding of the text (Keene & Zimmermann, 1997). Visualization allows students the ability to become more engaged in their reading and use their imagery to draw conclusions, create interpretations of the text, and recall details and elements from the text (Keene & Zimmermann, 1997). Struggling students' ability to monitor and evaluate their own comprehension is enhanced by mental imagery (Gambrell & Bales, 1986). When a breakdown in comprehension occurs, and a mental image cannot be visualized, students will become aware of the need for a corrective strategy.

Creating visual images or mind movies while one reads is an essential element of engagement with the text, comprehension, and reflection (Wilhelm, 2004). Visualization and the creation of visuals allow students ways to read, respond, analyze, organize, and represent the learning that is taking place. Visualization strategies (Gambrell & Koskinen, 2002; Keene & Zimmermann, 1997; Wilhelm, 1995) can do the following:

- Heighten motivation, engagement, and enjoyment of reading
- Immerse students in rich details of the text
- Improve literal comprehension of texts
- Build background knowledge
- Aid in identifying important details to form inferences, elaborations, and patterns across multiple texts
- Help in solving spatial and verbal problems
- Improve a reader's ability to share, critique, and revise what has been learned with others

Through emphasizing and modeling visualization with students, teachers show how effortlessly connections between text and media can be made. Bridging visualization to the world of multiliteracies allows students to compose and explore ideas through "democratic avenues of meaning making" (Wilhelm, 2004).

Tattoos

Visual media are not confined to glossy pages or computer screens. Perhaps one of the most fascinating forms to today's youth are the colorful images that span the bicep or peek over the top of a sock. Like a modern-day coat-of-arms, tattoos have burst into the popular culture of the United States in a powerful way. Tattoos, once viewed as taboo, are seen in a variety of environments. Celebrities such as Angelina Jolie famously bare their tattoos for tabloids, while networks develop reality shows depicting the journeys of tattoo artists, shops, and the background stories about the individuals who patronize them (e.g., *Inked, Miami Ink, L.A. Ink*). This fascination can be translated into an introduction to visual media.

To accomplish this, we introduced our ninth-grade students to the Norman Rockwell painting "Tattoo Artist." Rockwell illustrates a scene in which a Navy sailor chooses to have a tattoo applied, signaling his newest relationship with Betty, while above the chosen spot, viewers can see that this arm has chronicled all his past relationships, a single line struck through each name to signify the end of the relationship. Typically, the students picked up on the irony of the painting immediately and make the connection to their own relationship pasts. Many students cringed when thinking what their arms might look like had they tattooed each former flame on their arms.

To encourage students to move beyond their initial reactions, we also prompted them to think of Rockwell's painting as a scene from a movie, predicting what each character is thinking in this snapshot of a scene. This required students to pay close attention to the details presented in the painting. They had to read every nuance to frame a narrative that explores each character's motivation and reactions. This attention to detail also highlights that the growing list of names, like tattoos, cannot be undone with a simple change of mind.

Once students realized the permanence of tattoos as depicted in Rockwell's painting, we provided articles related to the health risks and issues surrounding tattoos. We then asked students to design personal tattoos that symbolized an important life event. Although the tattoo designs were not applied as actual tattoos, designing hypothetical personal tattoos gave students the opportunity to express themselves and their experiences through color and images. Knowing that tattoos are essentially permanent, the students were asked to keep this permanence in mind as they designed their tattoos.

Megan, a student reluctant to write in class, created a tree tattoo to symbolize her complicated family history. Because we asked students to write about the tattoo's symbolism Megan wrote at length about the impact of her family history on her life:

> My family tree is complicated, so complicated that to explain it at length wouldn't really matter. What matters is my life is a tree unlike any other . . . not straight and tall like a redwood or well-rounded and full like an evergreen. My tree is broken and jagged and yet, it springs a newness when I least expect it.

Megan was also able to verbalize the impact that this visual image would have on others as they view it. "When others see my tattoo, I don't want them to feel sorry for me or focus on all of the dead branches. I want them to focus on the hope that there will be more leaves if I'm given the chance."

Once students had an opportunity to explore how their own histories would shape their tattoos, they were then asked to apply the tattoo activity to a character from Shakespeare's *Romeo and Juliet*. Creating a tattoo to represent the character traits of one of Shakespeare's memorable characters allowed the students to better examine the play as well as understand how precisely a visual image can be used to represent their comprehension. Kevin chose to create a tattoo for the character of Friar Lawrence. In his explanation of the tattoo, Kevin wrote about the importance of Friar Lawrence:

> Some people think that Friar Lawrence wasn't an important character in the play, but I disagree. I think that he was really important because not only does he marry Romeo and Juliet in secret, but he also spends the rest of the play trying to cover up his mistakes as they snowball. The scales for the Montague and Capulet families represent his efforts to balance the destruction that will follow.

Kevin went on to analyze the ethical repercussions of Friar Lawrence's actions, explaining that "the serpent in the tattoo represents the sin that rears its head in his actions and intertwines itself so closely to him that he has difficulty determining the difference between right and wrong."

More than an art activity, creating tattoos to represent literary characters challenges students to think beyond the written text. By representing their personal journeys as well as fictional characters in texts, students weave together their exposure to print and nonprint texts through a layering of mental, emotional, and physical learning activities (Bloom, 1969; Krathwohl, Bloom, & Masia, 1964; Simpson, 1972).

Collages

Including visuals is sometimes as simple as reexamining how we accomplish routine classroom assignments. Take research, for example. The traditional approach to teaching students how to research and paraphrase sources tends to be rather linear. Students find information on their topics, write down their sources, and then attempt to put what they found in their own words. Unfortunately, this often leads to hours of frustration as teachers discover paper after paper that simply lifted information from the original sources. Angered, the teacher returns to the classroom, scolding the class for their laziness. Then, when the next group of papers comes in, the process repeats itself, leaving the teacher even more upset. Plagiarism is an issue that English teachers across the country battle on a regular basis, particularly with the advent of the Internet. Some students very consciously choose to follow that easy route, anxious to get their papers turned in and out of the way. But for others, plagiarism occurs because they cannot figure out how to avoid doing it. For these students, the linear path leads to a direct transfer of information, resulting in papers that sound almost identical to the original sources.

Brock was one such student. When we asked him to research his idol, Jackie Robinson, Brock followed the traditional research route. He combed the Internet looking for sources and even brought in a book from home. And when the time came for him to turn in his paper, it reflected none of Brock's admiration. Rather, the paper was a re-creation of his three sources, albeit rearranged with words changed here and there. When we approached him, it became obvious that Brock had not purposefully cheated on the assignment. Tears filled his eyes as he promised he had not cheated. He had, he said, simply read through the information and then written it down on his note cards. Brock had such a memory for written text that even when he was not looking at the screen, he recalled most of what he had read, and because he knew he needed to get the information down, he wrote what he remembered. Brock needed something to break the linear path. Fortunately, incorporating visuals into the research process can do just that.

As one way to break the linear path and to incorporate visuals into the research process, we asked students to select a topic, searching for information just as they had always done. Instead of taking notes on the information they discovered, however, students began flipping through magazines, seeking out images to represent the key facts. This forced students to activate their background knowledge as they worked to build connections between the images in the magazines and the information they needed to convey. More often than not, students had to be creative in their illustrations because the likelihood of finding a picture of Jackie Robinson playing baseball or a Holocaust victim working behind barbed wire was slim. Then, on note cards or half sheets of paper, they would affix their pictures. Each collage represented a single idea or fact. After creating the collage, our students turned their papers over, and, using the images as a guide, they wrote one to two sentences explaining the images and citing the original source. The process required them to focus on the ideas and facts represented in their sources and not on a word-for-word replay. Most important, it broke the linear path between the written text in their sources and the written text of their papers. By taking the time to work with the information in a visual format, students were able to separate themselves from the language of the source, which resulted in language of their own. By the time they finished with the process, they had a collection of images they could arrange and rearrange as they began organizing their ideas for their papers.

Paintings

While creating collages provides an effective avenue for teaching students to paraphrase by using visual images, it can still be a challenge to some students. So what other forms can visualizing take? Anyone wandering into our classrooms might find students sketching out their preliminary ideas or sweeping broad strokes of color onto white canvasses. In fact, outsiders might mistake our English class for an art class as students work to create symbolic representations of novels in the form of 11" × 14" paintings. For some, this task provides an avenue to explore their ideas and interpretations in a creative way or allows them to showcase their artistic talents in a forum that usually focuses on written language. For others, just getting started is a struggle because the novel's meaning and messages continue to elude them. Take Jake, for example. A sophomore, Jake simply did not see himself as a successful student. He struggled to keep up with reading expectations and rarely completed a writing assignment. When asked to visualize what he read, his first reaction was to throw up his hands in defeat. He simply did not know how to complete this task. Yet, he wanted to. All around him, he watched his classmates laughing as they set to work, stopping from time to time to ask their peers to read their pictures or to share their visions with us. This, he recognized, was not the typical English assignment, and he wanted to experience it just like everyone else.

To begin the assignment, we asked the class to free write on a series of guiding questions: When you think of your book, what is the overall feeling you walk away with? Which scenes in the book are attributed to this feeling? What is the overall theme or message of the book? We talked about symbolism and how to use concrete symbols to represent the abstract ideas presented in the books. The students spent an entire class period writing and sketching their ideas. When Jake left the classroom that day, his page was blank. Although he had completed his book, *I Know What You Did Last Summer* by Lois Duncan, he could not see how our class discussions could apply to this teen suspense novel. His understanding of the book was superficial. He could recite the basics of the plot but could not move his comprehension to a deeper thinking level. Thus began a series of conversations between us.

We started with what Jake did know. The book, he explained, was about four teens who had been involved in an accident the previous summer, which resulted in the death of a young boy. Months later, each of the teens was reminded of this crime as an unknown figure stalked them, sending them alarming messages. We talked about the setting of the book, pointing out that while the bulk of the book takes place during the time of the stalking, the past has a significant impact on its events. We talked about how the characters felt about what they had done, as well as about what was happening to them. We talked about the significant objects in the book that helped relay the tone and message in the book. And then we gave Jake time to think, to imagine how these elements could all come together in a single visual image. While a cohesive picture did not emerge all at once, Jake had progressed at each check. The first image he settled on became the centerpiece of his entire painting. On a sheet of paper, he had sketched a large rectangle across the top third of the page. This, he explained, was a rearview mirror. It represented the actual accident because it had been a hit-and-run, but he chose the mirror rather than another part of the car because the characters were being forced to look back on what they had done. Already, Jake was demonstrating that he had moved to a deeper understanding of the book.

His face lit up when praised about his progress, and he eagerly turned back to his sketch when presented with more questions to consider. We repeated this process as Jake worked on his confidence as a reader. By the time he had completed his painting, he had obviously made great progress in his visualization skills, resulting in a deeper understanding of the book itself. The rearview mirror reflected details like a noose, signaling the threats of the stalker, next to a set of child's clothing hanging on a clothesline. From the mirror hung the traditional evergreen air freshener, but this one was covered in blood, symbolizing how sour everything had gone, Jake explained. Through the process, Jake had learned to use the details from the book, as well as his own detailed interpretations, leaving him with a much stronger understanding of what he had read than he had possessed before.

Persuasive Narratives: J. Peterman Catalog

As big fans of *Seinfeld* in the 1990s, we believed the J. Peterman Company featured on the show was fictional. Elaine, one of the show's main characters, worked at J. Peterman in a variety of capacities; most memorably, she wrote advertisements for the catalog's eclectic collection of clothing and accessories. The persuasive advertisements were long passages of description embedded within narrative, intended to bring the item to life through an adventurous story. We were thrilled to discover that the company actually existed, and we quickly ordered the catalog to use in our classrooms as examples of how writing can create visual images in a real-world medium.

To begin the activity, we showed a series of short clips from *Seinfeld* in which J. Peterman was depicted or in which the characters were working on the catalog. Although several of our students had seen *Seinfeld* in syndication, we felt it was important for all of the students to see how stories about the merchandise were developed and depicted in popular culture. Also, to help our students understand what made the catalog so unique, we surveyed a variety of catalogs from department stores to discover the ways in which items were displayed and described. Students quickly noted the differences in catalogs and the unique characteristics of J. Peterman's catalog.

To practice using the detailed narrative style, students cut out pictures of clothing and accessories from fashion and sports magazines to create parody advertisements in the J. Peterman style. Clarisse, a fashionista at heart, took great care to describe the boots in her parody ad:

> Life gets hard on the road, but that's not an excuse to not look my best. Confident and determined, I travel from city to city, state to state, meeting to meeting, with a strong walk and an even stronger mind. It's all about the impression you give, my dad would say. I'm proud to be following in his footsteps, his bootsteps. I wouldn't travel anywhere without my suede leather boots, No. 5446, in sizes 6–10, colors brown, black, and purple. $599.00.

Daniel, an unlikely catalog or mall shopper, was also inspired by the assignment and wanted to write about his mother's U.S. Army uniform:

This uniform is not for the timid or meek, nor is it for the lazy or those known to be cowards. This uniform is for those who sacrifice their lives in more ways than one. It is not a costume for your Halloween party, nor is it a piece of clothing that should be put on as carelessly as a white t-shirt while running to the store. This uniform deserves your respect. It is bravery, pride, and tradition. It is freedom. Army Dress Uniform, No. 111, in sizes 2–14, standard issue color. PRICELESS.

Clarisse and Daniel wove their narrative storylines into persuasive advertisements, including the description of the items, targeting specific audiences. This activity also prepared the students to think about objects in a personified way and to think about purpose and audience in their writing.

Our next step in the activity transitioned to writing about iconic symbols in young adult literature. Students worked collaboratively to create J. Peterman catalogs for the texts they were reading in their literature circle/book study groups. Students created catalogs for Laurie Halse Anderson's *Speak*, Walter Dean Myers's *Monster,* and Ben Mikaelsen's *Touching Spirit Bear.* The *Touching Spirit Bear* book club created an advertisement for many important objects and events in the text, most notably, the Ancestor Rock:

In a place where cold, salty water sweeps onto the rocky shore of a long forgotten island, Tlingit elders chisel away at a mountainside, freeing away tools for their tribal rituals. The Ancestor Rock is more than rock; it is truth, introspection, and justice. While pushing it up steep hillsides, the Ancestor Rock serves as a mentor and protector. And yet, when it is let go, to fall quickly down the hill it had recently climbed, it is forgiveness. Ancestor Rock, No. 232, One size fits all, Colors will vary. $199.00

Not only did the activity emphasize purpose and audience in writing, but it also demonstrated how written texts do not always need to be created in isolation. Persuasive, descriptive, and narrative texts can be interwoven to create a powerful companion to visual images. Through the development of their book club catalogs, the students touched on the important themes of each novel as well as described specific setting details and character traits of important characters. Collaboratively, the students created meaning from the text and worked together to create a project with print and non-print texts that symbolized their collective understanding of the novel.

Gee (2000) stated that when creating meaning from texts, the human mind is social. Additionally, as the mind engages in thinking, it distributes information "across other people and various symbols, tools, objects and technologies" (para. 6). If the culture teens are immersed in revolves around the visual and the media, their minds recognize the patterns created by these images, creating a persuasive argument for incorporating these patterns within the classroom. Gee wrote that "Thinking and using language is an active matter of assembling the situated meanings that you need for action in the world" (para. 12). Taking these meanings and showing students how to apply them both inside and outside the classroom can be an effective instructional tool.

> **If the culture teens are immersed in revolves around the visual and the media, their minds recognize the patterns created by these images, creating a persuasive argument for incorporating these patterns within the classroom.**

A study by Pompe (1996) about popular culture's influence on young consumers upheld her convictions as to why it is so influential on students. She found that the pleasures provided by these visually oriented texts were deep in nature, rather than superficial; that consumers' desires were powerful influences on what the popular media produced; that viewers and listeners of audiovisual texts just as actively made meaning as readers of print text; and that teachers and students could satisfy their own desires while they were learning about the desires of others. It is this powerful influence that makes popular media texts important additions to the classroom. By including elements of popular culture, teachers can tap into the patterns students' minds already recognize, which makes transitioning them to more traditional texts much more effective.

Poetry Comics

Graphic novels are more popular in our culture than ever before. Whether they are in the form of the traditional Japanese art (manga) or the more popular Americanized version of graphic illustrations such as the *Bone* novels by Jeff Smith, these books often sit atop a pile of students' chosen books. Canon classics and new young adult literature are even being reformatted to appeal to a new generation of graphic novel readers. Much more than comic strips, today's graphic novels are complex and mature, capturing an intellectual readership looking for more visual stimulation from their reading experiences.

There are two reasons teachers should be drawn to the manga genre: first, the popularity of the genre, measured by sales and distribution, and second, the unique multimodal reading that manga demands (Schwartz & Rubinstein-Ávila, 2006). Fortunately, it is possible to marry students' outside interests with those of traditional academia. An example of this would be tackling complicated texts in the classroom using poetry comics. Poetry comics illustrate poetry in the form of a comic strip. The text of the comic strip is the text of the poem, with illustrations inspired by the text. To begin this activity with our eighth-grade students, we introduced Langston Hughes's "A Dream Deferred," and after reading it as a class, we presented a poetry comic based on Hughes's poem (see Morice, 2002). A comparison of the two emphasizes the ways in which poetry can be interpreted and illustrated differently by each reader.

Once students had a clear understanding of poetry comics, we asked them to read two complex poems, Walt Whitman's "O Captain! My Captain" and T.S. Eliot's "The Naming of Cats," and demonstrate their understanding through poetry comics. Jasmine tackled Eliot and illustrated the poem with her understanding of the text. Ordered in a traditional comic strip format, Jasmine also added personalized touches outside of the borders. Jasmine incorporated the entire poem in its traditional form, while giving the narrator a cat personality.

Kaitlin approached Whitman in a different comic format. Instead of the traditional squares in a linear sequence, Kaitlin opted for ships to anchor each stanza, with characters quoting lines from the poem. Kaitlin understood the poem to be about President Abraham Lincoln's death and chose to depict the country metaphorically as the ship Whitman speaks of in the poem.

Much more than a superficial illustration of poetry, these poetry comics allow for students to experiment with narrator voice, setting, and literal and metaphorical meanings. Layering complex literary analysis skills with visual representations allows students to practice visualizing the texts that they read. Graphic representations of popular texts provide a contemporary canvas for authors to share their stories using a fresh, relevant approach. Educators, librarians, and bookstores that have embraced this new genre of literature have difficulty keeping titles on their shelves. Further, they are pleased to see more young people choosing books at a time when video games and the Internet seem to take up so much attention. With the growing demand for and popularity of graphic novels, the integration of the genre with traditional English language arts practices should continue to be explored (Schwartz & Rubinstein-Ávila, 2006).

Final Thoughts

Just as the classrooms and students of the 21st century look very different than those of centuries before, so too must the curriculum change. Teachers can prepare students for today's changing world by introducing texts of all types into the learning environment.

By teaching students how to critically read and view all texts, not just the traditional print texts, teachers can build upon the skills needed to read and write, increasing students' literacy levels in all areas. And perhaps even more important, as O'Brien (2001) pointed out, the study of visual symbols can reach those students who have been burned by print. Ultimately, however, visual literacy must be included within all school curricula if teachers want to adequately prepare students for a world that is surrounded by and driven by images.

References

Alvermann, D.E. (2002). Effective literacy instruction for adolescents. *Journal of Literacy Research, 34*(2), 189–208. doi:10.1207/s15548430jlr3402_4

Alvermann, D.E., & Hagood, M.C. (2000). Critical media literacy: Research, theory, and the practice in "new times." *The Journal of Educational Research, 93*(3), 193–206.

Avgerinou, M., & Ericson, J. (1997). A review of the concept of visual literacy. *British Journal of Educational Technology, 28*(4), 280–291. doi:10.1111/1467-8535.00035

Bloom, B.S. (Ed.). (1969). *Taxonomy of educational objectives: The classification of educational goals* (Handbook I: The cognitive domain). New York: David McKay.

Braden, R.A., & Hortin, J.A. (1982). Identifying the theoretical foundations of visual literacy. *Journal of Visual/Verbal Languaging, 2*(2), 37–42.

Debes, J.L. (1969). The loom of visual literacy—An overview. *Audio Visual Instruction, 14*(8), 25–27.

Eisner, E.W. (1992). The misunderstood role of the arts in human development. *Phi Delta Kappan, 73*(8), 591–595.

Flood, J., & Lapp, D. (1997/1998). Broadening conceptualizations of literacy: The visual and communicative arts. *The Reading Teacher, 51*(4), 342–344.

Gambrell, L.B., & Bales, R.J. (1986). Mental imagery and the comprehension-monitoring performance of fourth- and fifth-grade poor readers. *Reading Research Quarterly, 21*(4), 454–464. doi:10.2307/747616

Gambrell, L.B., & Koskinen, P.S. (2002). Imagery: A strategy for enhancing comprehension. In C.C. Block & M. Pressley (Eds.), *Comprehension instruction: Research-based best practices* (pp. 305–318). New York: Guilford.

Gee, J.P. (2000, September). Discourse and sociocultural studies in reading. *Reading Online, 4*(3). Retrieved October 18, 2008, from www.readingonline.org/articles/art_index.asp?HREF=/articles/handbook/gee/index.html

Keene, E.O., & Zimmermann, S. (1997). *Mosaic of thought: Teaching comprehension in a reader's workshop.* Portsmouth, NH: Heinemann.

Krathwohl, D.R., Bloom, B.S., & Masia, B.B. (1964). *Taxonomy of educational objectives: The classification of educational goals* (Handbook II: Affective domain). New York: David McKay.

Morice, D. (2002). *Poetry comics: An animated anthology.* New York: T&W Books.

O'Brien, D. (2001, June). "At-risk" adolescents: Redefining competence through the multiliteracies of intermediality, visual arts, and representation. *Reading Online, 4*(11). Available: www.readingonline.org/newliteracies/lit_index.asp?HREF=/newliteracies/obrien/index.html

Pompe, C. (1996). "But they're pink!"—"Who cares!" Popular culture in the primary years. In M. Hilton (Ed.), *Potent fictions: Children's literacy and the challenge of popular culture* (pp. 92–125). London: Routledge.

Schwartz, A., & Rubinstein-Ávila, E. (2006). Understanding the manga hype: Uncovering the multimodality of comic-book literacies. *Journal of Adolescent & Adult Literacy, 50*(1), 40–49. doi:10.1598/JAAL.50.1.5

Simpson, E.J. (1972). *The classification of educational objectives in the psychomotor domain.* Washington, DC: Gryphon House.

Wilhelm, J.D. (1995). Reading is seeing: Using visual response to improve the literary reading of reluctant readers. *Journal of Reading Behavior, 27*(4), 467–503.

Wilhelm, J. (2004). *Reading is seeing: Learning to visualize scenes, characters, ideas, and text worlds to improve comprehension and reflective reading.* New York: Scholastic.

ANNUAL EDITIONS

Williams, B.T. (2004). "A puzzle to the rest of us": Who is a "reader" anyway? *Journal of Adolescent & Adult Literacy, 47*(8). Retrieved October 18, 2008, from www.readingonline.org/newliteracies/lit_index.asp?HREF=/newliteracies/jaal/5-04_column_lit/index.html

Assess Your Progress

1. Make a table or graphic organizer to compare and contrast visual literacy and print referencing.
2. Tell why visual literacy could be important to the grade or content you will teach.
3. Provide examples of visuals you might use to enrich students' ability to learn your subject matter.

SEGLEM is a National Board Certified Teacher and an assistant professor at Illinois State University, Normal, USA; e-mail rseglem@ilstu.edu. WITTE is a National Board Certified Teacher and an assistant professor at Florida State University, Tallahassee, USA; e-mail switte@fsu.edu.

From *Journal of Adolescent & Adult Literacy,* November 2009, pp. 216–226. Copyright © 2009 by International Reading Association. Reprinted by permission via Copyright Clearance Center.

Article 13

You Should Read This Book!

Sustained silent reading was the breakthrough for these urban learners—but only because their teacher tried and tried again.

JENNIFER HARTLEY

One Monday, my 5th grade students were, as usual, visiting the classroom library, returning and checking out books. One of my boys pulled a bookmark out from about 10 pages into his book. When I asked why he was returning his book, he said, "Because I'm finished." When I questioned him about the story, he could only give details about the very beginning. He checked out another book and went on his way. Although my kids always had a book available to read after they finished their class work, I began to notice the pattern: Many students turned books in whether they were finished with them or not. Perhaps my students were not reading as much as I had thought.

I teach in an urban elementary school; 98 percent of my students are economically disadvantaged. My 5th grade class that year consisted of 20 black students, 11 boys and 9 girls. Their reading abilities ranged from a low 1st grade level to a middle school level. To begin gathering information about their reading habits, I surveyed students' parents about their children's reading behaviors at home. Most of my students were not reading outside of school, and many parents indicated that they wished their child could and would read more. Although we had shared and guided reading daily, my students were only reading assigned materials at assigned times. True, I gave them choices, but their choices came from a list of *my* choices. The truth was, my students were not getting enough time to sit and really read what *they* wanted to read.

After discovering Pilgreen's (2000) research about making independent reading a success, I committed to changing my book selections, my classroom's appearance, and my instruction. Sustained silent reading is a time when everyone, including the teacher, reads silently for a given length of time (Butler & Turbill, 1987). To get essential information from my students about what they enjoyed and did not enjoy about reading, I gave each student a short reading survey. The results revealed that most of my students were not motivated to read—especially the boys, many of whom claimed they did not like to read at all.

Ready, Set—Chaos!

Clearly, I had to begin updating my classroom library. I started by ordering *Sports Illustrated Kids and National Geographic for Kids*. Right away I noticed that the boys, and many of the girls, gravitated toward the magazine section. My next step was to get the students involved in choosing books for our classroom library. During our book fair, when boys got to pick two books apiece to add to our collection, they came up with graphic novels featuring Batman and Spiderman, as well as the Goosebumps graphic novel series. They also selected multiple nonfiction books, of which we had few to start with, centered on science, sports heroes, and world records. Girls also picked for the library, choosing mostly fiction that highlighted female characters and books based on TV shows.

My next step was to change the class library's appearance. I needed a shelf that screamed, "Choose me!" On our new display shelf, books face forward with their covers visible; the shelf reads "Excellent 5th Grade Reads." At Wal-Mart, I found cushions, chairs, mats, and beanbags for reading comfort.

My final step was to incorporate silent reading into our daily classroom routine. I knew my students would initially be reluctant, but I was hoping the added books and comfy seating arrangement would make the transition easier for them.

The first day of our new sustained silent reading trial, students decorated their own folders and picked out books they wanted to read. They could sit anywhere they wanted. I was hoping that finding a comfortable reading position would help motivate them to read.

What I got was chaos! Students ran around the room fighting over the cushions or a place to read on the carpet. Some chose reading materials that were too difficult for them, and some chose books they could finish in two minutes. Needless to say, we did not get a lot of reading done that day. I was disheartened and frustrated. How was I going to get students to love reading?

Setting up Supports

Instead of scrapping the whole idea, I hit the computer to do a little research on the best way to implement sustained silent reading in my classroom. Steve Gardiner (2005) discussed how he models for his classes what good adult readers do. I began working with my students on how to choose appropriate reading materials at their ability levels by evaluating books through the "five-finger test." Students determine whether a book is too hard for them by skimming a page and raising a finger every time they come to a word they do not understand. If they raise all five fingers, the book is too difficult to read without help. We talked about different physical places where a reader might feel comfortable reading. Students described situations that might distract them when they read, giving them a way to determine whether their reading location was appropriate for focusing on reading.

We discussed different ways students could monitor and support their own reading using strategies like predicting, asking questions, rereading for meaning, and making connections. Students decided to use reading logs to track what they were reading, how much they were reading, and when they finished a book. Because they wanted to share what they read with other students, I downloaded from the Internet (at www.abcteach.com/free/f/form_bookrecommendation.pdf) a form we could use titled "You Should Read This Book!" The form gives readers the opportunity to share their favorite parts of each text and articulate why they would recommend favored books to their peers.

I also modeled ways students could set personal reading goals. Goals included such achievements as completing one to three pages every five minutes (for my lowest-achieving readers); choosing harder and longer books; or focusing on a particular comprehension strategy, such as summarizing or questioning. Students let me know how many books they wanted to read each week and month. We discussed their reading levels and book choices and made goals together depending on the types of books each student decided to read.

We had two rules for sustained silent reading, adapted from Kelley and Clausen-Grace (2006):

- Students must have self-selected reading materials in their desks before the reading period begins. If a student forgets to bring something to read, the teacher gives the reader a book, selecting something he or she might like.
- No one moves around during the reading period.

Success!

The second time we tried silent reading, students came in after lunch, pulled out their reading folders, and began to read at their desks. After a couple of minutes, I announced that students should choose a reading spot somewhere around the room. Each reader could pick his or her own place, but if the reader was distracted—or distracting—in that spot, I would suggest a better location. Some pulled out beanbags, some settled under their desks on mats and pillows, and one tucked up underneath the computer tables. Contrary to the second s in *sustained silent reading*, my classroom was not completely quiet. You could hear whisper-reading and hushed talking throughout the room and the occasional burst of laughter when someone read something funny.

The class worked up from reading 5 minutes to 25 minutes each day. It wasn't long before students were begging me to let them share what they were reading with their peers. The reading by itself was not satisfying enough, and they wanted to go beyond filling out the "You Should Read This Book!" form.

So we instituted partner sharing. After each reading stretch, students returned to their desks and turned to a partner to share what they were reading. This practice actually helped with accountability; unfocused readers now had a motivating reason to delve into their books. Occasionally, students asked to share with the whole class. These presentations gave students ideas for books they wanted to read and initiated some excellent book discussions.

Eventually, we combined the partner and whole-group sharing through a strategy called "Rap" (Kelley & Clausen-Grace, 2006). After one partner shared what he or she had experienced in a book, the other partner would turn around and pass on what he or she had heard to the rest of the class. This technique helped my students become better listeners and improved their retelling skills, which standardized tests in our district evaluate. One unexpected outcome of this method of operating was that my classroom blossomed into a learning community

Worth All the Work

After nine weeks of this daily reading, students again filled out the reading survey they took at the beginning. The results were astounding: Surveys showed a major increase in students' motivation to read. Students read more at home, embraced more variety in their reading selections, and were more likely to finish their books. Many students reported that they enjoyed the peer sharing and the quiet atmosphere, which they didn't have at home. Throughout the year, I assessed students using the ThinkLink test, Rigby Running Records, and the DIBELS assessment. Students' scores on all assessments improved as we continued to do sustained silent reading. All but one of my students were eager to continue the program, and my readers made comments like, "Sustained silent reading gives you more time to communicate with books. You get the feeling you want to read all the way through the book, and you get to know the characters."

Although introducing silent reading into my classroom took a lot of hard work and multiple adjustments, it was a success that will contribute to these students' future learning. They grew to love reading, and they used books to expand their knowledge both at school and at home. Now, whenever we miss a day of silent reading, my students beg me to let them read.

References

Butler, A., & Turbill, J. (1987). *Towards a reading-writing classroom.* Portsmouth, NH: Heinemann.

Gardiner, S. (2005). A skill for life. *Educational Leadership, 63*(2), 67–70.

Kelley, M., & Clausen-Grace, N. (2006). R5: The sustained silent reading makeover that transformed readers. *The Reading Teacher, 60*(2), 148–156.

Pilgreen, J. (2000). *The SSR handbook: How to organize and manage a sustained silent reading program.* Portsmouth, NH: Heinemann.

Assess Your Progress

1. What lessons did you learn from this article about developing a silent reading time in your classroom?
2. Why should teachers be concerned that students read for pleasure? Provide rationale from the articles in this unit.
3. Construct an annotated bibliography of at least five books that you would like to have in your class library. Explain how or why these books would be appropriate for your content area and age of your future students.

JENNIFER HARTLEY teaches 5th grade at Hardy Elementary School in Chattanooga, Tennessee; jhartley@comcast.net.

From *Educational Leadership,* March, 2008, pp. 73–75. Copyright © 2008 by ASCD. Reprinted by permission. The Association for Supervision and Curriculum Development is a worldwide community of educators advocating sound policies and sharing best practices to achieve the success of each learner. To learn more, visit ASCD at www.ascd.org

Article 14

Do Girls Learn Math Fear From Teachers?

Washington (AP)—Little girls may learn to fear math from the women who are their earliest teachers.

Despite gains in recent years, women still trail men in some areas of math achievement, and the question of why has provoked controversy. Now, a study of first- and second-graders suggests what may be part of the answer: Female elementary school teachers who are concerned about their own math skills could be passing that along to the little girls they teach.

Young students tend to model themselves after adults of the same sex, and having a female teacher who is anxious about math may reinforce the stereotype that boys are better at math than girls, explained Sian L. Beilock, an associate professor in psychology at the University of Chicago.

Beilock and colleagues studied 52 boys and 65 girls in classes taught by 17 different teachers. Ninety percent of U.S. elementary school teachers are women, as were all of those in this study.

Student math ability was not related to teacher math anxiety at the start of the school year, the researchers report in today's edition of Proceedings of the National Academy of Sciences.

But by the end of the year, the more anxious teachers were about their own math skills, the more likely their female students—but not the boys—were to agree that "boys are good at math and girls are good at reading."

In addition, the girls who answered that way scored lower on math tests than either the classes' boys or the girls who had not developed a belief in the stereotype, the researchers found.

"It's actually surprising in a way, and not. People have had a hunch that teachers could impact the students in this way, but didn't know how it might do so in gender-specific fashion," Beilock said in a telephone interview.

Beilock, who studies how anxieties and stress can affect people's performance, noted that other research has indicated that elementary education majors at the college level have the highest levels of math anxiety of any college major.

"We wanted to see how that impacted their performance," she said.

After seeing the results, the researchers recommended that the math requirements for obtaining an elementary education teaching degree be rethought.

"If the next generation of teachers—especially elementary school teachers—is going to teach their students effectively, more care needs to be taken to develop both strong math skills and positive math attitudes in these educators," the researchers wrote.

Janet S. Hyde, a professor in the Department of Psychology at the University of Wisconsin-Madison, called the study a "great paper, very clever research."

"It squares with an impression I've had for a long time," said Hyde, who was not part of the research team.

Hyde was lead author of a 2008 study showing women gaining on men in math skills but still lagging significantly in areas such as physics and engineering.

Girls who grow up believing females lack math skills wind up avoiding harder math classes, Hyde noted.

"It keeps girls and women out of a lot of careers, particularly high-prestige, lucrative careers in science and technology," she said.

Beilock did note that not all of the girls in classrooms with math-anxious teachers fell prey to the stereotype, but "teachers are one source," she said.

Teacher math anxiety was measured on a 25-question test about situations that made them anxious, such as reading a cash register receipt or studying for a math test. A separate test checked the math skills of the teachers, who worked in a large Midwestern urban school district.

Student math skills were tested in the first three months of the school year and again in the last two months of the year.

The research was funded by the National Science Foundation.

Assess Your Progress

1. Where did you learn to love or fear mathematics? Describe what the teacher or other person did to cause this love/fear.
2. With a small group of peers, make a list of ways that teachers can encourage all students to love and learn math.

From *Teacher Magazine*, January 26, 2010, pp. 1–2. Copyright © 2010 by Associated Press. Reprinted by permission.

Article 15

How Mathematics Counts

Fractions and algebra represent the most subtle, powerful, and mind-twisting elements of school mathematics. But how can we teach them, so that students understand?

LYNN ARTHUR STEEN

Much to the surprise of those who care about such things, mathematics has become the 600-pound gorilla in U.S. schools. High-stakes testing has forced schools to push aside subjects like history, science, music, and art in a scramble to avoid the embarrassing consequences of not making "adequate yearly progress" in mathematics. Reverberations of the math wars of the 1990s, roil parents and teachers as they seek firm footing in today's turbulent debates about mathematics education.

Much contention occurs near the ends of elementary and secondary education, where students encounter topics that many find difficult and some find incomprehensible. In earlier decades, schools simply left students in the latter category behind. Today, that option is neither politically nor legally acceptable. Two topics—fractions and algebra, especially Algebra II—are particularly troublesome. Many adults, including some teachers, live their entire lives flummoxed by problems requiring any but the simplest of fractions or algebraic formulas. It is easy to see why these topics are especially nettlesome in today's school environment. They are exemplars of why mathematics counts and why the subject is so controversial.

Confounded by Fractions

What is the approximate value, to the nearest whole number, of the sum 19/20 + 23/25? Given the choices of 1, 2, 42, or 45 on an international test, more than half of U.S. 8th graders chose 42 or 45. Those responses are akin to decoding and pronouncing the word *elephant* but having no idea of what animal the word represents. These students had no idea, of that 19/20 is a number close to 1, as is 23/25.

Neither, it is likely, did their parents. Few adults understand fractions well enough to use them fluently. Because people avoid fractions in their own lives, some question why schools (and now entire states) should insist that all students know, for instance, how to add uncommon combinations like 2/7 + 9/13 or how to divide 1 3/4 by 2/3. When, skeptics ask, is the last time any typical adult encountered problems of this sort? Even mathematics teachers have a hard time imagining authentic problems that require these exotic calculations (Ma, 1999).

Moreover, many people cannot properly express in correct English the fractions and proportions that *do* commonly occur, for instance, in ordinary tables of data. A simple example illustrates this difficulty (Schield, 2002). Even though most people know that 20 percent means 1/5 of something, many cannot figure out what the something is when confronted with an actual example, such as the table in Figure 1. Although calculators can help the innumerate cope with such exotica as 2/7 + 9/13 and 1 3/4 ÷ 2/3, they are of no help to someone who has trouble reading tables and expressing those relationships in clear English.

These examples illustrate two very different aspects of mathematics that apply throughout the discipline. On the one hand is calculation; on the other, interpretation. The one reasons *with* numbers to produce an answer; the other reasons *about* numbers to produce understanding. Generally, school mathematics focuses on the former, natural and social sciences on the latter. For lots of reasons—psychological, pedagogical, logical, motivational—students will learn best when teachers combine these two approaches.

> **On the one hand is calculation; on the other, interpretation. The one reasons *with* numbers to produce an answer; the other reasons *about* numbers to produce understanding.**

There may be good reasons that so many children and adults have difficulty with fractions. It turns out that even mathematicians cannot agree on a single proper definition. One camp argues that fractions are just names for certain points on the number line (Wu, 2005), whereas others say that it's better to think of them as multiples of basic unit fractions such as 1/3, 1/4, and 1/5 (Tucker, 2006). Textbooks for prospective elementary school teachers exhibit an even broader and more confusing array of approaches (McCrory, 2006).

Instead of beginning with formal definitions, when ordinary people speak of fractions they tend to emphasize contextual

Figure 1 The Challenge of Expressing Numerical Data in Ordinary Language

	Percentage Who Are Runners		
	Nonsmoker	**Smoker**	**Total**
Female	50%	(20%)	40%
Male	25%	10%	20%
Total	37%	15%	30%

Source: From *Schield Statistical Literacy Inventory: Reading and Interpreting Tables and Graphs Involving Rates and Percentages*, by M. Schield, 2002. Minneapolis. MN: Augsburg College, W. M. Keck Statistical Literacy Project. Copyright 2002 by M. Schield. Available: http://web.augsburg.edu/~schield/MiloPapers/StatLitKnowledge2r.pdf. Reprinted with permission.

Which of the following correctly describes the 20% circled in the table above?

a. 20% of runners are female smokers.
b. 20% of females are runners who smoke.
c. 20% of female smokers are runners.
d. 20% of smokers are females who run.

meaning. Fractions (like all numbers) are human constructs that arise in particular social and scientific contexts. They represent the magnitude of social problems (for example, the percentage of drug addiction in a given population); the strength of public opinion (for example, the percentage of the population that supports school vouchers); and the consequences of government policies (for example, the unemployment rate). Every number is the product of human activity and is selected to serve human purposes (Best, 2001, 2007).

Fractions, ratios, proportions, and other numbers convey quantity; words convey meaning. For mathematics to make sense to students as something other than a purely mental exercise, teachers need to focus on the interplay of numbers and words, especially on expressing quantitative relationships in meaningful sentences. For users of mathematics, calculation takes a backseat to meaning. And to make mathematics meaningful, the three *Rs* must be well blended in each student's mind.

Algebra for All?

Conventional wisdom holds that in Thomas Friedman's metaphorically flat world, all students, no matter their talents or proclivities, should leave high school prepared for both college and high-tech work (American Diploma Project, 2004). This implies, for example, that all students should master Algebra II, a course originally designed as an elective for the mathematically inclined. Indeed, more than half of U.S. states now require Algebra 11 for almost all high school graduates (Zinth, 2006).

Advocates of algebra advance several arguments for this dramatic change in education policy:

- Workforce projections suggest a growing shortage of U.S. citizens having the kinds of technical skills that build on such courses as Algebra II (Committee on Science, Engineering, and Public Policy, 2007).
- Employment and education data show that Algebra II is a "threshold course" for high-paying jobs. In particular, five in six young people in the top quarter of the income distribution have completed Algebra II (Carnevale & Desrochers, 2003).
- Algebra II is a prerequisite for College Algebra, the mathematics course most commonly required for post-secondary degrees. Virtually all college students who have not taken Algebra II will need to take remedial mathematics.
- Students most likely to opt out of algebra when it is not required are those whose parents are least engaged in their children's education. The result is an education system that magnifies inequities and perpetuates socioeconomic differences from one generation to the next (Haycock, 2007).

Skeptics of Algebra II requirements note that other areas of mathematics, such as data analysis, statistics, and probability, are in equally short supply among high school graduates and are generally more useful for employment and daily life. They point out that the historic association of Algebra II with economic success may say more about common causes (for example, family background and peer support) than about the usefulness of Algebra II skills. And they note that many students who complete Algebra II also wind up taking remedial mathematics in college.

Indeed, difficulties quickly surfaced as soon as schools tried to implement this new agenda for mathematics education. Shortly after standards, courses, and tests were developed to enforce a protocol of "Algebra II for all," it became clear that many schools were unable to achieve this goal. The reasons included, in varying degrees, inadequacies in preparation, funding, motivation, ability, and instructional quality. The result has been a proliferation of "fake" mathematics courses and lowered proficiency standards that enable districts and states to pay lip service to this goal without making the extraordinary investment of resources required to actually accomplish it (Noddings, 2007).

Several strands of evidence question the unarticulated assumption that additional instruction in algebra would necessarily yield increased learning. Although this may be true in some subjects, it is far less clear for subjects such as Algebra II that are beset by student indifference, teacher shortages, and unclear purpose. For many of the reasons given, enrollments in Algebra II have approximately doubled during the last two decades (National Center for Education Statistics [NCES], 2005a). Yet during that same period, college enrollments in remedial mathematics and mathematics scores on the 12th grade National Assessment of Educational Progress (NAEP) have hardly changed at all (NCES, 2005b; Lutzer, Maxwell, & Rodi, 2007). Something is clearly wrong.

Although we cannot conduct a randomized controlled study of school mathematics, with some students receiving a treatment and others a placebo, we can examine the effects of the current curriculum on those who go through it. Here we find more disturbing evidence:

- One in three students who enter 9th grade fails to graduate with his or her class, leaving the United States with the highest secondary school dropout rate among industrialized nations (Barton, 2005). Moreover, approximately half of all blacks, Hispanics, and American Indians fail to graduate with their class (Swanson, 2004). Although mathematics is not uniquely to blame for this shameful record, it is the academic subject that students most often fail.
- One in three students who enter college must remediate major parts of high school mathematics as a prerequisite to taking such courses as College Algebra or Elementary Statistics (Greene & Winters, 2005).
- In one study of student writing, one in three students at a highly selective college failed to use any quantitative reasoning when writing about subjects in which quantitative evidence should have played a central role (Lutsky, 2006).
- College students in the natural and social sciences consistently have trouble expressing in precise English the meaning of data presented in tables or graphs (Schield, 2006).

One explanation for these discouraging results is that the trajectory of school mathematics moves from the concrete and functional (for example, measuring and counting) in lower grades to the abstract and apparently nonfunctional (for example, factoring and simplifying) in high school. As many observers have noted ruefully, high school mathematics is the ultimate exercise in deferred gratification. Its payoff comes years later, and then only for the minority who struggle through it.

High school mathematics is the ultimate exercise in deferred gratification. Its payoff comes years later, and then only for the minority who struggle through it.

In the past, schools offered this abstract and ultimately powerful mainstream mathematics curriculum to approximately half their students—those headed for college—and little if anything worthwhile to the other half. The conviction that has emerged in the last two decades that all students should be offered useful and powerful mathematics is long overdue. However, it is not yet clear whether the best option for all is the historic algebra-based mainstream that is animated primarily by the power of increasing abstraction.

Mastering Mathematics

Fractions and algebra may be among the most difficult parts of school mathematics, but they are not the only areas to cause students trouble. Experience shows that many students fail to master important mathematical topics. What's missing from traditional instruction is sufficient emphasis on three important ingredients: communication, connections, and contexts.

Communication

Colleges expect students to communicate effectively with people from different backgrounds and with different expertise and to synthesize skills from multiple areas. Employers seek the same things. They emphasize that formal knowledge is not, by itself, sufficient to deal with todays challenges. Instead of looking primarily for technical skills, today's business leaders talk more about teamwork and adaptability. Interviewers examine candidates' ability to synthesize information, make sound assumptions, capitalize on ambiguity, and explain their reasoning. They seek graduates who can interpret data as well as calculate with it and who can communicate effectively about quantitative topics (Taylor, 2007).

To meet these demands of college and work, K–12 students need extensive practice expressing verbally the quantitative meanings of both problems and solutions. They need to be able to write fluently in complete sentences and coherent paragraphs; to explain the meaning of data, tables, graphs, and formulas; and to express the relationships among these different representations. For example, science students could use data on global warming to write a letter to the editor about carbon taxes; civics students could use data from a recent election to write op-ed columns advocating for or against an alternative voting system; economics students could examine tables of data concerning the national debt and write letters to their representatives about limiting the debt being transferred to the next generation.

We used to believe that if mathematics teachers taught students how to calculate and English teachers taught students how to write, then students would naturally blend these skills to write clearly about quantitative ideas. Data and years of frustrating experience show just how naïve this belief is. If we want students to be able to communicate mathematically, we need to ensure that they both practice this skill in mathematics class and regularly use quantitative arguments in subjects where writing is taught and critiqued.

Connections

One reason that students think mathematics is useless is that the only people they see who use it are mathematics teachers. Unless teachers of all subjects—both academic and vocational—use mathematics regularly and significantly in their courses, students will treat mathematics teachers' exhortations about its usefulness as self-serving rhetoric.

To make mathematics count in the eyes of students, schools need to make mathematics pervasive, as writing now is. This can best be done by cross-disciplinary planning built on a commitment from teachers and administrators to make the goal of numeracy as important as literacy. Virtually every subject taught in school is amenable to some use of quantitative or logical arguments that tie evidence to conclusions. Measurement and calculation are part of all vocational subjects; tables, data, and graphs abound in the social and natural sciences; business

ANNUAL EDITIONS

> ## My "Aha!" Moment
>
> **Douglas Hofstadter, Distinguished Professor of Cognitive Science, Indiana University, Bloomington.**
>
> I first realized the deep lure of mathematics when, at about age 3, I thought up the "great idea" of generalizing the concept of 2 × 2 to what seemed to me to be the inconceivably fancier concept of 3 × 3 × 3. My inspiration was that since 2 × 2 uses the concept of two-ness *twice,* I wanted to use the concept of three-ness *thrice*! It wasn't finding out the actual value of this expression (27, obviously) that thrilled me—it was the idea of the fluid conceptual structures that I could play with in my imagination that turned me on to math at that early age.
>
> Another "aha" moment came a few years later, when I noticed that $3^2 \times 5^2$ is equal to $(3 \times 5)^2$. Once again I was playing around with structures, not trying to prove anything. (I didn't even know that proofs existed!) It thrilled me to discover this pattern, which of course I verified for other values and found mystically exciting.
>
> I believe that teachers should encourage playfulness with mathematical concepts and should encourage the discoveries of patterns of whatever sort. Any time a child recognizes an unexpected pattern, it may evoke a sense of wonder.

requires financial mathematics; equations are common in economics and chemistry; logical inference is fundamental to history and civics. If each content-area teacher identifies just a few units where quantitative thinking can enhance understanding, students will get the message.

The example of many otherwise well-prepared college students refraining from using even simple quantitative reasoning to buttress their arguments shows that students in high school need much more practice using the mathematical resources introduced in the elementary and middle grades. Much of this practice should take place across the curriculum. Mathematics is too important to leave to mathematics teachers alone.

Contexts

One of the common criticisms of school mathematics is that it focuses too narrowly on procedures (algorithms) at the expense of understanding. This is a special problem in relation to fractions and algebra because both represent a level of abstraction that is significantly higher than simple integer arithmetic. Without reliable contexts to anchor meaning, many students see only a meaningless cloud of abstract symbols.

As the level of abstraction increases, algorithms proliferate and their links to meaning fade. Why do you invert and multiply? Why is $(a + b)^2 \neq a^2 + b^2$? The reasons are obvious if you understand what the symbols mean, but they are mysterious if you do not. Understandably, this apparent disjuncture of procedures from meaning leaves many students thoroughly confused. The recent increase in standardized testing has aggravated this problem because even those teachers who want to avoid this trap find that they cannot. So long as procedures predominate on high-stakes tests, procedures will preoccupy both teachers and students.

There is, however, an alternative to meaningless abstraction. Most applications of mathematical reasoning in daily life and typical jobs involve sophisticated thinking with elementary skills (for example, arithmetic, percentages, ratios), whereas the mainstream of mathematics in high school (algebra, geometry, trigonometry) introduces students to increasingly abstract concepts that are then illustrated with oversimplified template exercises (for example, trains meeting in the night). By enriching this diet of simple abstract problems with sophisticated realistic problems that require only simple skills, teachers can help students see that mathematics is really helpful for understanding things they care about (Steen, 2001). Global warming, college tuition, and gas prices are examples of data-rich topics that interest students but that can also challenge them with surprising complications. Such a focus can also help combat student boredom, a primary cause of dropping out of school (Bridgeland, Dilulio, & Morison, 2006).

Most important, the pedagogical activity of connecting meaning to numbers needs to take place in authentic contexts, such as in history, geography, economics, or biology—wherever things are counted, measured, interred, or analyzed. Contexts in which mathematical reasoning is used are best introduced in natural situations across the curriculum. Otherwise, despite mathematics teachers' best efforts, students will see mathematics as something that is useful only in mathematics class. The best way to make mathematics count in the eyes of students is for them to see their teachers using it widely in many different contexts.

> **The best way to make math count is for students to see their teachers using it widely in many different contexts.**

References

American Diploma Project. (2004). *Ready or not. Creating a high school diploma that counts.* Washington, DC: Achieve. Available: www.achieve.org/files/ADPreport_7.pdf

Barton, R E. (2005). *One third of a nation. Rising dropout rates and declining opportunities.* Princeton, NJ: Educational Testing Service. Available: www.ets.org/Media/Education_Topics/pdf/onethird.pdf

Best, J. (2001). *Damned lies and statistics: Untangling numbers from the media, politicians, and activists.* Berkeley: University of California Press.

Best, J. (2007, June). *Beyond calculation: Quantitative literacy and critical thinking about public issues.* Paper presented at Johnson Foundation Conference on Quantitative Literacy and Its Implications for Teacher Education, Milwaukee, WI.

Bridgeland, J. M., Dilulio, J. J., & Morison, K. B. (2006). *The silent epidemic: Perspectives of high school dropouts.* Washington, DC: Peter D. Hart Research. Available: www.gatesfoundation.org/nr/downloads/ed/TheSilentCpidemic3-06FINAL.pdf

Carnevale, A. P. & Desrochers, D. M. (2003). *Standards for what? The economic roots of K–16 reform.* Princeton, NJ: Educational Testing Service. Available: www.transitionmathproject.org/assets/docs/resources/standards_for_what.pdf

Committee on Science, Engineering, and Public Policy. (2007). *Rising above the gathering storm: Energizing and employing America for a brighter economic future.* Washington, DC: National Academies Press. Available: www.nap.edu/catalog/11463.html

Greene, J. P. & Winters, M. (2005). *Public high school graduation and college readiness rates, 1991–2002.* New York: Manhattan Institute for Policy Research. Available: www.manhattan-institute.org/html/ewp_08.htm

Haycock, K. (2007). Kati Haycock's Testimony before the Subcommittee on Labor, HHR, and Education, House Appropriations Committee [Online press release]. Washington, DC: Education Trust. Available: www2.edtrust.org/EdTrust/Press+Room/Haycock+Appropriations+Testimony.htm

Lutsky, N. (2006). Quirks of rhetoric: A quantitative analysis of quantitative reasoning in student writing. *Proceedings of the section on statistical education, American Statistical Association* (pp. 2319–2322). Available: www.statlit.org/pdf/2006lutskyASA.pdf

Lutzer, D. J., Maxwell, J. W., & Rodi, S. B. (2007). *CBMS (Conference Board of Mathematical Sciences) 2005: Statistical abstract of undergraduate programs in the mathematical sciences in the United States.* Providence, RI: American Mathematical Society.

Ma, L. (1999). *Knowing and teaching elementary mathematics.* Mahwah, NJ: Erlbaum.

McCrory, R. (2006, January). Mathematicians and mathematics textbooks for prospective elementary teachers. *Notices of the American Mathematical Society, 53*(1), 20–29. Available: http://meet.educ.msu.edu/documents/McCroryNotices.pdf

National Center for Education Statistics. (2005a). Table ED4-A. In *America's children: Key national indicators of well-being.* Washington, DC: U.S. Department of Education. Available: www.childstats.gov/pdf/ac2007/ac_07.pdf

National Center for Education Statistics. (2005b). *The nation's report card: Long-term trends.* Washington, DC: Institute of Education Sciences, U.S. Department of Education. Available: http://nces.ed.gov/nationsreportcard/ltt/results2004/nat-math-perf.asp

Noddings, N. (2007, March 20). The new anti-intellectualism in America. *Education Week, 26*(28), 29, 32. Available: www.edweek.org/ew/articles/2007/03/20/28noddings.h26.html?qs=Noddings

Schield, M. (2002). *Statistical literacy inventory: Reading and interpreting tables and graphs involving rates and percentages.* Minneapolis, MN: Augsburg College, W. M. Keck Statistical Literacy Project. Available: http://web.augsburg.edu/~schield/MiloPapers/StatLitKnowledge2r.pdf

Schield, M. (2006, July). *Statistical literary survey analysis: Reading graphs and tables of rates and percentages.* Paper presented at the International Conference on Teaching Statistics, Salvador Bahia, Brazil. Available: www.StatLit.org/pdf/2006SchieldICOTS.pdf

Steen, L. A. (Ed.). (2001). *Mathematics and democracy: The case for quantitative literacy.* Princeton, NJ: National Council on Education and the Disciplines, Woodrow Wilson National Fellowship Foundation. Available: www.maa.org/ql/mathanddemocracy.html

Swanson, C. B. (2004). *Who graduates? Who doesn't? A statistical portrait of public high school graduation, class of 2001.* Washington, DC: Urban Institute. Available: www.urban.org/publications/410934.html

Taylor, C. (2007, June). *Preparing students for the business of the real (and highly quantitative) world.* Paper presented at Johnson Foundation Conference on Quantitative Literacy and Its Implications for Teacher Education, Milwaukee, WI.

Tucker, A. (2006). *Preparing for fractions* [Discussion paper]. Washington, DC: Mathematical Association of America. Available: www.maa.org/pmet/resources/PrepForFractions.pdf

Wu, H. (2005). Chapter 2: Fractions (Draft). Berkeley: University of California—Berkeley. Available: http://math.berkeley.edu/~wu/EMI2a.pdf

Zinth, K. (2006). *Mathematics graduation requirements, classes 2006 through 2011.* Denver, CO: Education Commission of the States. Available: www.ecs.org/clearinghouse/67/07/6707.pdf

Assess Your Progress

1. Make a list of all the ways mathematics appear in your content area. Prepare a brief explanation of what you would do to help students understand the importance of math. If you teach in a special area such as music, physical education, art or dance/theater, you might do this exercise for either reading or math.

2. Search Internet sites for teachers of math, look for lesson plans that would help you emphasize the importance of math in daily life.

LYNN ARTHUR STEEN is Professor of Mathematics at St. Olaf College, 1520 St. Olaf Ave., Northfield, MN: steen@stolaf.edu.

From *Educational Leadership,* November 2007, pp. 9–14. Copyright © 2007 by ASCD. Reprinted by permission. The Association for Supervision and Curriculum Development is a worldwide community of educators advocating sound policies and sharing best practices to achieve the success of each learner. To learn more, visit ASCD at www.ascd.org.

Article 16

Textbook Scripts, Student Lives

A math teacher goes beyond the standardized curriculum.

JANA DEAN

Three years ago my school district invested in a new, highly structured math program. At the same time, the central office vowed to invest in its teachers. Those taking on the program got the opportunity to co-plan with others teaching the same grade level. Because I love teaching math and like collaborating, I agreed to be part of this centralized bid to support student success.

The school board approved the purchase of the *Connected Mathematics 2* series, published by Prentice Hall. The back of the textbooks promised: "Classroom tested, proven effective!" The publishers claimed that the curriculum as packaged would spiral elegantly through three grade levels and leave no gap in anyone's understanding. My heart sank at our first collaboration meeting. The hired consultant took up all the talk time and then handed us teacher's editions and proclaimed that we had nothing to worry about: 70 percent of the content in the books matched state standards, and all we had to do was open the books to page one and follow the pacing guides he'd provided.

During my first year of teaching, I learned what an asset a textbook can be. I taught in a school without books. I wrote every single math, language arts, social studies, and science lesson, and also taught music, physical education, and art. My students moved on to 7th grade, their skills improved, and I required a weeklong solo stay at the beach to recover. (I watched daytime television and did jigsaw puzzles.)

Since then, I've also come to realize that a textbook can provide continuity for students. There's no way, however, that textbook authors can know what happened in my classroom the day before yesterday. Nor can they listen to my students' stories in order to connect academics to the daily and local struggles of their families and community. I want to teach responsively and with hope for a better future for my students. Textbooks, published by corporations that have much to gain by maintaining business as usual, aren't likely to press students to envision a future any different from the past and present. I want students not only to master the concepts and procedures that will be on the next standardized test, but also to be able to use the mathematics they learn to examine how race, environmental issues, and economics affect their lives and their world. If I'm to do that, the textbook can come along for the ride, but I've got to be in the driver's seat.

The students I teach live in Tumwater, Wash. Ours is the smallest of three towns surrounding the state capital, Olympia. Interstate 5 cuts our county in half and connects it to Seattle—just an hour's drive to the north when the traffic is not bad. When I first moved here 20 years ago, log trucks rumbled to the bay and plywood mills lined the waterfront. Now, with the easy reach of the deep-water ports of Tacoma and Seattle and the loss of most of our Western Washington big trees, ship-to-shore container trailers and warehouses outnumber log trucks and mills. Most people work for the state, in the service sector, or in the trades. Some commute up or down the freeway. We have few private schools. Almost everyone goes to public school, and families tend to trust teachers with the task of teaching their children to read, write, and do mathematics.

In contrast, the curriculum choices of school districts around the country seem to show a distrust of teachers' ability to get students where they need to go. Many new textbooks provide detailed instructions about exactly how each lesson is to be delivered, complete with predicted and scripted classroom dialogue. Even open-ended questions often have a "correct" answer. School districts pay good money for this "learning insurance" and understandably, given the investment they've made, expect teachers to follow whatever program they've purchased.

Although not the only culprit, No Child Left Behind has exacerbated the trend toward this kind of top-down control. School districts, in their bid to ensure quick success on standardized tests, seek "guaranteed" programs, creating a national curriculum appetite. A national market makes the investment in developing the materials worthwhile. Textbook publishers have lined up to profit from selling ready-made packages linked to CDs, websites, and automated, standards-linked lesson planning software. On the surface, it would seem that ample, predesigned resources would be in the interest of student learning. When the rubber hits the road, however, teachers, not the textbooks, know their students. And teachers do the teaching. My first year in the classroom, I met a tow truck driver. He told me as he hooked up my Honda Civic (seized cam shaft) that he loved driving a tow truck because it was just like fishing: He never knew what he'd haul in. I wouldn't know until I had taught for a few years how much like driving a tow truck classroom life would be. While the rudiments of the job remain the same, every class is different. Some years the combination of personalities makes for dozens of blissful permutations of the seating chart. Projects get a life of their own and the only students failing are those who never make it to school. Other years, you stagger through the weeks and months, pulling every trick you know out of your bag to massage a collection of challenges into a productive community. The first few years of teaching I hoped that I'd "get it down." I desperately wanted some kind of script to follow just to make the job a little easier. To rely on a fixed curriculum presumes uniformity from day to day, year to year, and student to student, from now into the foreseeable future. Eventually I learned that while I repeat lessons and units from year to year, the way students respond undoes any notion of a foolproof pace and predictable script.

For me, teaching starts with my commitment to showing my students that they have the power to bring beauty and justice to their lives. While it's my job to provide students with an opportunity to learn what's outlined by the state standards, the only way I know to get them there is to listen to my class so that I can teach in a way that helps them use academics to make their world a better place. *Connected Mathematics 2,* the series our district purchased, does do more to engage students in learning than most books, but the problems don't invite students to apply mathematics to analyzing the institutions and social and environmental issues that matter in local communities.

According to the charts provided by the publisher, the pace of the program also looked problematic. It assumed more classes per week and longer class meetings than any of us teachers had ever had. In addition, on a good week in middle school, at least one day out of five, things just don't go as planned. We routinely have bad-weather late starts, a death in the family, fire drills, or a frank refusal to learn on Tuesday. Even under the best circumstances, the events in a lively, engaging classroom simply can't be predicted years in advance and from five states away. Teaching at the proposed pace would have been like going on a road trip with a remote-control driver. I wanted to drop the new books and retreat to my closet full of math resources. I didn't. Instead, I grimly picked up my stack of books and resolved to try.

We teachers taking on the challenge had also taken on supporting each other to succeed. The fear of letting down my colleagues made it hard to trust my experience and instincts. Rather than carefully building classroom community that is closely tied to mathematics in students' lives like I usually do, I jumped in and started with the books open to page one. Like my colleagues, I found that following the program strictly as written and paced wouldn't reach my students. I had to address their misconceptions, and often, the cumbersome or directive language of the book got between me and my students and between my students and the math. In addition, we were right about the pace: it was simply too fast to keep without losing half the crowd to confusion that leads to disengagement.

Also, while textbook authors do their best to create "student-friendly" texts, these books presumed experience my students simply hadn't had. Many of the problems touched on the familiar: car washes, T-shirt sales, and planning for school events. Others, however, built on contexts that required background knowledge most of my students didn't have. I remember an early lesson that derailed into a long explanation of rental fees for bicycles while on vacation. Renting bikes is an expensive proposition, one which most of my students hadn't encountered. The objective of the lesson had to do with rates and linear equations, but the distance of the context from my students' lives made the math harder rather than easier to access. I don't have anything against bike rentals, and I don't object to building background knowledge to help my students access math, but if I am going to do so I want it to be about something that can lead to critical thinking about the conditions of their own lives and the lives of others.

While textbook authors do their best to create 'students-friendly' texts, these books presumed experience my students simply hadn't had.

Another problem especially dogged me. Many of my students simply weren't engaged. And they were the same ones most at risk for failing our state's standardized test and missing out on the chance for higher math or dropping out of high school. Here's my theory: Curricular resources designed for "typical" students work best for those students who have accepted school as an institution. They tend to come from families who've been successful in school. When resources reflect upper-middle-class and middle-class experiences, they normalize those experiences and marginalize others. This can serve to reinforce the gap in my grade book between students who see their lives reflected by the curriculum and those who don't.

I quickly learned to shift contexts as I aimed to reach all my students. My early attempts were simply bids for engagement through the familiar. When we came to a problem in the math textbook about yogurt shops, for example, rather than explaining a phenomenon absent from our community, I turned the yogurt shop into Eagan's Drive-In, one of the last remaining local joints amidst a growing maze of national chains. Another set of problems had to do with Walk-a-Thons. Instead of following a five-day thread that I didn't think would interest most of my crowd, I got a copy of Johnny Cash's "Walk the Line" and we playfully walked and tracked rates and paces to the music. Instead of buying a cookstove on time, as suggested by the book, I researched skateboard prices. Each of these shifts in context took preparation time. I could no longer rely on the book for student-friendly instructions. Instead, I rewrote tasks and projected them on the wall. In spite of the extra upfront work, I found it paid off in less of the mop-up work generated by missed homework, confusion, and lack of student interest.

For each of these early departures, I relied heavily on the purchased program for the structuring and sequencing of questions and problems. This helped keep me "on the same page" as my colleagues during collaboration meetings. While my students hadn't "covered" the pages, I'd studied the lessons and the state standards so closely that I could bring my students through the concepts apace with other classes. That way I could still exchange observations with colleagues. In this way, the common text served as an advantage. We teachers learned from each other about how students struggled with specific concepts. We were also able to commiserate about the pacing mandated by the district office. Together, we eventually made a successful bid to the math curriculum coordinator for pacing charts that better matched our school calendar.

Staying close to—but not following—the text improved my teaching. In order to shift contexts, I had to see the math underlying each set of problems in the textbook through my students' eyes. I had to ask and answer the question, "What would help them care about learning these concepts?" I took on understanding the assumptions and sequencing of the text as a professional development project.

As I gained confidence balancing text, my desire for collaboration, and each year's "haul" of students, I got more ambitious. The second year, rather than studying fictitious peanut butter prices, students compared the ages of their oldest living relatives. In the process, I learned about my students' heritage and families in the first weeks of school. More importantly, students learned about each other. Later, I shifted a series of lessons in nonlinear relationships from interest rates on savings to interest rates on loans. I challenged students to respond to the question, "Is interest fair?" They compared rates for payday loans, auto loans, and student loans. They also grappled with the injustice of realizing that people who have less money often pay more for college due to interest on loans.

More recently, I have begun to design whole units around topics that touch students' lives, as well as supporting them to think critically and see connections to local, national, and international issues. Students studied fossil fuel depletion, local driving habits, and gas prices while learning statistics. (See "The Future of Driving," *Rethinking Schools,* Vol. 21 No. 2.) Living wages became a backdrop for linear relationships. (See "Living Algebra, Living Wage," *Rethinking Schools,* Vol. 21 No. 4.) This year's class compared life expectancy in the United States with life expectancy in other parts of the world and applied statistics to understand the underlying environmental and economic causes for the inequity they observed. Each of these "redesigns" uses the textbook as a point of departure. I study the scaffolding of concepts provided by the purchased program and use it to frame my students' learning while massaging the culture of the class with questions that open their eyes to the world and to each other.

Sometimes I think my life would be easier if I abandoned the book altogether. But I don't throw it down and march off independently because I value the opportunity to talk math with my colleagues. Also, while I question much of the motivation behind standardization, I accept the premise that the sequencing of content makes sense. Students' time oughtn't be wasted by needless repetition. If I operate within the sequence of the purchased program, my students' education will have more continuity. And sometimes the text provides the most direct access to important concepts. The book series also affords valuable experience in reading "academic English" which is also the language of standardized tests, higher math, and the path to a diploma. My most at-risk students need as much practice with that as I can give while keeping them engaged in learning. I also have my selfish reasons for hanging onto the book: Using it usually frees me from writing homework assignments. I still remember that first year in the classroom.

Sometimes I consider backing off from my ambitious redesigns of entire units to rely more heavily on my district's structured program. But then I remind myself of the hush that came over the room when I introduced statistics and life expectancy with the sad and too-early death of my own father. Students proceeded to listen to each other's memories of lost family and friends. They heard about Dustin's cousin and former student of mine who had died in a car wreck a few years before. They heard about stillborn babies. They heard about whole families gone, and blankets on fire with houses that followed, and family members lost in Vietnam, the Gulf, Iraq. They heard about Riva's little brother, hit by a car on his bike when he was 10. By the time students' stories filled the room, the math learning we were about to do was already more about my students and less about the textbook. And better yet, the connection they made between math and their own families later allowed them to connect to the struggle for clean water and health care in Bangladesh and Malawi.

Sometimes I naively think that the hard work is over and maybe I've "got it down." And then I remember: A script, no matter how good, isn't teaching and learning. When I asked Sammie a few weeks ago what she thought about learning math by collecting statistics about families, she tilted her head to the side and said slowly, "Well, I think that making it about our families makes comparing histograms and box-plots more interesting." Her response twice reassured me. Not only did she find the learning engaging because it tapped into her classmates' stories, she'd used the academic language required by our state test. While the books contain lessons to meet the standards and plenty of well-organized problems, they just don't contain my students' lives. And as importantly, they don't contain questions that help my students analyze how wealth and power function in our world, let alone push them to envision a future much different from the present.

Like my tow truck driver, I love my job. Every day is different. And unlike my carefully edited teacher's guide, I never know what I'll haul in.

Assess Your Progress

1. What suggestions or strategies will you take away from the Steen and Dean articles? Provide a reason for your selections.

2. Synthesize the major issues surrounding both print and math literacy expressed in these articles? Cite information from the articles to support your choices.

JANA DEAN (jdean@reachone.com) *teaches algebra to 8th-grade students at Bush Middle School in Tumwater, Wash. She contributes regularly to* Rethinking Schools *and is co-editing a Rethinking Schools book on environmental justice and climate change.*

From *Rethinking Schools Online,* Spring 2008, pp. 37–40. Copyright © 2008 by Rethinking Schools, Ltd. Reprinted by permission.

UNIT 4

Creating Caring Communities of Learners

Unit Selections

17. **Creating Intentional Communities to Support English Language Learners in the Classroom,** Judith Rance-Roney
18. **Cultivating Optimism in the Classroom,** Richard Sagor
19. **Teachers Connecting with Families—In the Best Interest of Children,** Katharine C. Kersey and Marie L. Masterson
20. **How Not to Talk to Your Kids: The Inverse Power of Praise,** Po Bronson
21. **Democracy and Education: Empowering Students to Make Sense of Their World,** William H. Garrison

Learning Outcomes

After reading this unit, you will be able to:

- Restate the good news-bad news issues that No Child Left Behind legislation presents to English Language Learners.
- Relate one teacher's experiences to your teaching and your content to support learning of English Language Learners.
- Develop a plan for an *intentional community* in your classroom.
- Explain the importance of optimism for retention of students and prevention of drop-outs.
- Determine how you will help students have faith in the future and gain personal efficacy.
- Select strategies and actions that are appropriate for your classroom or content area to cultivate optimism.
- State reasons why involving parents in your classroom is important to student learning.
- Describe how you will make and maintain a relationship with families of your students or future students.
- Point out the pitfalls of being a *praise junkie*.
- Discriminate between effective praise statements and inappropriate, meaningless praise statements.
- Examine the link between democracy and education.
- Defend the need for democracy in all classrooms.

Student Website

www.mhhe.com/cls

Internet References

Read Write Think Connection
www.readwritethink.org/lessons/lesson_view.asp?id=987

Education World
www.educationworld.com/a_curr/curr302.shtml

Teacher Vision
www.teachervision.fen.com/education-and-parents/resource/3730.html

Coalition of Essential Schools
www.essentialschools.org

The National Coalition for Parent Involvement in Education (NCPIE)
www.ncpie.org

All of us are situated in social, political, and economic circumstances, which inform and develop our values. Our values are usually derived from principles of conduct that we learn in each of our histories of interaction with ourselves (as they form) and in interaction with others. This is to say that societal values develop in a cultural context. Teachers cannot hide all of their moral preferences. They can, however, learn to conduct just and open discussions of moral topics without succumbing to the temptation to indoctrinate students with their own views. In democratic societies, such as the United States, alternative sets of values and morals co-exist.

What teachers perceive to be worthwhile and defensible behavior informs our reflections on what we as educators should teach. We are immediately conscious of some of the values that affect our behavior, but we may not be as aware of what informs our preferences. Values that we hold without being conscious of them are referred to as tacit values: these are values derived indirectly after reasoned reflection on our thoughts about teaching and learning. Much of our knowledge about teaching is tacit knowledge, which we need to bring into conscious cognition by analyzing the concepts that drive our practice. We need to acknowledge how all our values inform, and influence, our thoughts about teaching. Teachers grapple with the dilemma of their own values versus the values of their students. Is it ethical to try to change character, values and beliefs of our students?

Students need to develop a sense of genuine caring both for themselves and others. Teachers need to help student develop within themselves a sense of critical social consciousness and a genuine concern for social justice. Rance-Roney suggests that we form intentional learning communities. The suggestion in this article will help teachers support English Language Learners (ELL) as well as invest all students in creating an inclusive classroom culture.

Another concept that is essential to building a caring community is a student who believes that her efforts will make a difference and that the future holds promise for her life. These are the important aspects of Sagor's articles on cultivation optimism. He asks us to consider why some students are motivated to do well and others are not. His answer is optimism. Motivated students believe in the future. These students believe that investing in today will bring a positive payoff in the future. His examples from popular movies about teachers to personal examples of his own children illustrate how we might cultivate optimism in our students.

Schools have an obligation to individual students and to their families as well. Sometimes teachers engage in the classist idea that families are uncaring, uninformed, distracted, or too disorganized to offer educational and behavioral support to their children. What may be missing is a teacher who knows and understands that caregivers may have valid reasons for their lack of involvement. We have long standing research that says when parents are involved in schools, their child's achievement improve. How can a teacher connect with all parents? Kersey and Masterson offer practical suggestions for building bridges and strong ties to families; including suggestions to overcome parent reluctance, share information, and maintain parent involvement throughout the year.

As we are cultivating optimism and building bridges, Bronson cautions us to think about the way we talk to children. While this article is written primarily for parents, teachers can use this message as well. We are often admonished to avoid using red pens when grading student papers because red is an angry color. We are told to write two nice comments for every criticism when commenting on those papers. But have we carried this too far? Should we be careful about the praise we use? Bronson state that as a parent he had become a "praise junkie" and notes that offering praise had become a panacea for the anxieties of parenting. Once Bronson realized his praise dilemma, he looked to research to find answers. Are there implications for teachers in this article? You decide.

© Getty Images/Image Source

Teaching students to respect all people, to revere the sanctity of life, to uphold the right of every citizen to dissent, to believe in the equality of all people before the law, to cherish freedom to learn, and to respect the right of all people to their own convictions—these are principles of democracy and ideals worthy of being cherished. An understanding of the processes of ethical decision making is needed by the citizens of a democratic nation; thus, this process of learning to live in a democracy should be taught in a free nation's schools. Some believe that, as teachers, we must allow students to assume the freedom and responsibility to make choices which might include directing their own learning experiences.

So, for whom do the schools exist? Is a teacher's primary responsibility to his or her client, the student, or to the student's parents? Do secondary school students have the right to study and to inquire into subjects not in officially sanctioned curricula? We present this group of articles to help teachers answer the questions in the paragraph above and to support their efforts.

Article 17

Creating Intentional Communities to Support English Language Learners in the Classroom

Judith Rance-Roney calls on teachers to form intentional learning communities within their classrooms. The Culture Share Club, initially conceived to provide scaffolding for ELL students to acquire English and pass the statewide test in English, legitimized student knowledge by benefitting all students as they prepared materials for lessons and invested in shared experiences and responsibilities for classroom learning.

JUDITH RANCE-RONEY

Earlier in my career, I taught in a large suburban district in New Jersey. In my junior English class, side by side in the front row sat Tu and Phan, two Vietnamese brothers whom I estimated knew a few hundred words other than "Hello, how are you?" I thumbed through my minutely planned unit on *Beowulf* and early English and I felt like crying. How would I teach *Beowulf* to these brothers who were struggling to learn the basics of English grammar and vocabulary? How could I teach the new language of early English to my "regular" students while teaching "real" English to these young men? I was an English teacher and I was stumped. I know that more and more teachers are facing these questions.

According to Diane August, there has been a significant increase in the percentage of teachers who will encounter at least one English language learner in the mainstream classroom (August and Shanahan). In 1991–92, only 15 percent of all teachers would instruct an English language learner, but in 2001–02, the percentage had risen dramatically to 42.6 percent (45). In addition, statewide mandates moving the English language learner out of bilingual and ESL classrooms into the mainstream English curriculum have occurred in some of the states with the greatest populations of English language learners (ELLs), such as California and Arizona.

Federal legislation, too, has put the spotlight on these students. For the English language learner (LEP—limited English proficient in government terms), No Child Left Behind (NCLB) legislation means good news and bad news. The good news is that these students can no longer remain in the darker corners of our classrooms, exempted from state achievement testing because of their English as a second language status. Schools have had to implement a more effective and grade-appropriate education for ELLs. However, the bad news contained in such legislation is that for new learners of English entering high schools for the first time in the United States, meeting the grade-level content standards, especially in English language arts, is difficult or nearly impossible for all but the most educationally ready learners who arrive in our schools with strong literacy and content knowledge in their first language. Key researchers Jim Cummins and Virginia Collier contend that it takes five to seven years of English exposure before English language learners can demonstrate academic English proficiency equal to their native English speaking peers. However, in spite of this finding, NCLB demands that ELLs who have been enrolled in US schools for more than one year must demonstrate progress on English proficiency measures *and* meet grade level content mastery determined for high school graduation. For Tu and Phan to graduate with a high school diploma, they must earn enough credits but also pass the rigorous state assessment, a requirement similar to that of about half the states. While the more rigorous standards take a toll on students, the effect on school districts and teachers can be equally challenging. Thus, the welcome mat, by and large, has not been rolled out for students like Tu and Phan at the macrolevel of district and school nor at the microlevel of the classroom community.

Key researchers Jim Cummins and Virginia Collier contend that it takes five to seven years of English exposure before English language learners can demonstrate academic English proficiency equal to their native English speaking peers.

Article 17. Creating Intentional Communities to Support English Language Learners in the Classroom

NCLB makes districts accountable for ensuring that subgroups, such as English language learners, achieve Annual Yearly Progress (AYP) targets or risk penalties. School districts with significant populations of ELLs may be labeled as schools in need of improvement because of the performance of the ELL subgroup alone; this designation will then trigger schoolwide interventions even though only the subgroup has failed to meet the target. According to the 2005 NAEP (National Assessment of Educational Progress) reading reports, while 74 percent of non-ELL twelfth-grade students score at or above the basic level, only 31 percent of ELLs score at or above the basic level and of those students, only 5 percent are deemed proficient or advanced. Finger pointing has escalated at the English language arts teachers who may be facing the daunting task of bringing these learners to proficient level, yet language arts teachers may be untrained or minimally trained in fostering language development for ELLs.

Thus, at the school level, a shuffling game often occurs; teachers who are untenured or who have the most to lose strategize to avoid these students. English teachers who in past years have been sensitive to the needs of ELLs find their classes filled with students who are struggling with the language, but they also find that they are not fully prepared, lack support systems, and are unable, even with their best effort, to adequately help these students with language development needs. In this climate of rigorous accountability, English language learners are often seen as liabilities and not as resources in the daily life of a school.

When Tu and Phan entered the doors of my classroom, I must honestly admit that I, too, saw them for a fleeting moment as yet another chore in my stress-filled day even though I had a strong background in TESOL. The other members of the classroom community, their fellow students, merely stared dispassionately past them. How could I create a learning community where these English language learners were defined, not by "lacks," but by the potential resources they brought to the classroom: diverse experiences with the world, novel perspectives of the world, and linguistic and cultural knowledge to be shared with others including their fellow students?

Marginalization and Interaction

Tu and Phan, like many other new immigrants (newcomers), arrived mid–high school with little English, with little knowledge of how to "do school" in American culture, and with a realization that they may not be welcomed socially into the school community. In her book about newcomers in an American high school, *Made in America: Immigrant Students in Our Public Schools,* Laurie Olsen writes, "The point from which newcomer students observe, learn about, and begin to interact with 'America' is always from the sidelines. . . . Their view of the other students and of the life of the school is truly a view from afar, a view from the margins of the life of the school" (44). In the first few weeks, Tu and Phan remained together but alone, sitting by themselves in the corner of the cafeteria, walking together silently in the halls, and talking sometimes to me in class, but never to the non-ELL classmates sitting around them.

From the perspective of second language acquisition, this spells disaster. Researchers have begun to explore the synergy among the language skills of reading, writing, listening, and speaking. There is an obvious practice effect; when learners engage in academic conversations and listen to others, the syntax and vocabulary of academic English is internalized and becomes automatic. But also, recent research points to the role of oral language development and aural comprehension in the fostering of reading comprehension skills. Talking to others about deep questions and co-constructing knowledge seems to increase comprehension, perhaps because of the exercise of critical-thinking skills and a motivation for deeper inquiry (Meltzer and Hamann 27).

Tu and Phan were immersed in a language they could barely understand throughout the long school day. As most language learners, they paid attention to critical messages that they judged would immediately affect their well-being. However, like most language learners, "listening fatigue" would set in quickly and so they seemed to take the sensible route of staying in the bubble of silence they were able to build around them. Some ESL advocates will allow the bubble of silence to stay intact, citing references to the existence of a "silent period" (the preproduction phase) in which ELLs are building critical language mass before having to produce the language. However, the advisability of allowing this period to continue for more than a few weeks in adolescents has been questioned by practitioners because, for many, the silent period becomes a habit that may extend to the end of the high school years.

As most language learners, they paid attention to critical messages that they judged would immediately affect their well-being. However, like most language learners, "listening fatigue" would set in quickly and so they seemed to take the sensible route of staying in the bubble of silence they were able to build around them.

Adding to the challenges of teaching ELLs in the mainstream, Tu and Phan, like others, had experienced what has been labeled "interrupted formal education" and had not been in a content classroom in almost two years. Back in Vietnam, their schooling may have been strong but their sense of cultural dislocation and the real challenges of setting up life in the United States had also influenced their ability to concentrate on academic work even if their English had been proficient.

The diversity of prior background knowledge and schema development among all learners is a challenge that English teachers face when teaching the language of *Beowulf* and Chaucer; but for Tu and Phan, the cultural connection to monsters, to the Viking images, and to the history of the English language required taking a further step back.

83

Tu and Phan came to school every day and appeared motivated to succeed, but the language, new content forms, and their reticence to talk to their classmates were hampering their acquisition of English and the new culture. How could I help them to acquire English, and how could I leverage the English skills they were able to grasp so that they could pass the statewide test in English required for graduation that would be administered in the spring?

An Intentional Classroom Learning Community

Seeing the marginalization of Tu and Phan in my classroom, I soon realized that it would be important to re-envision the dysfunctional culture of the classroom community that was rapidly solidifying and allowing the brothers to exist in the bubble of silence. I recognized that I needed to take steps not only to support my two English language learners in their English acquisition, but also to invest all the students in creating a classroom culture that encouraged shared experiences and a construction of knowledge that legitimized all class members. In the second language field, there has been an increasing awareness that a web of potent social factors and the motivation that follows from those factors is a strong predictor of second language acquisition. Bonnie Norton Peirce talks in terms of "investment" (17): For a new learner of English to take the risk of using the fledgling language in spite of the fear of being misunderstood or laughed at, the learner must believe that there is a substantive payoff in language use. The user's social identity in the new language and new culture is being formed, and for the time being, the new identity is fragile. By creating the bubble of silence, Tu and Phan were protecting their fragile identities but were also missing valuable chances to practice and experiment with their new language and were not building confidence in social English. They did not see themselves as authentic users of English.

> **I recognized that I needed to take steps not only to support my two English language learners in their English acquisition, but also to invest all the students in creating a classroom culture that encouraged shared experiences and a construction of knowledge that legitimized all class members.**

In the high school English classroom, English language learners need to see themselves as worthy and legitimate contributors to co-constructed knowledge and to possess the deep belief in their ability to interact in the English language. Thankfully, the teacher can take intentional steps in fostering that environment; it not only takes a classroom to support an English language learner but it also takes the English language learner to support a classroom.

Challenging Conventional Classroom Dynamics and Values: The Culture Share Club

I began by observing the subtle classroom interactions that started before the bell rang. Tu and Phan were always the first to leave the chatter of the hall and choose their front-row seats. I observed Renee, a smart and popular young woman, smile and say hi to the brothers as she passed by. Edgar, whom I suspect may have once learned English himself, tapped Phan on the shoulder saying, "What's up, man." With those simple acts, I found hope that I could still alter classroom dynamics. I started the process by handing out a flyer announcing that I was forming an informal Culture Share Club of volunteer student helpers who were willing to work collaboratively on special projects in class and to meet twice during the school year to talk and to journal about what they were learning from each other. I encouraged those thinking about a career in teaching to join a group. I promised to print certificates at the end of the year and promised to write college recommendation letters for all who gave their best effort. I felt I needed an initial vehicle to legitimize the classroom moves I would soon be making. By the end of the week I had five enrollees in addition to Tu and Phan, whom I had "strongly encouraged" to join. From the volunteer group, I formed two smaller groups to act as support systems for each of the brothers. As a firm believer in controlled seating, I physically surrounded each of the brothers with their group members. I put Renee, Edgar, and Phan in a triad. When I gave out project assignments, I provided the option for either individual work or for Culture Share group collaborative projects. As the year progressed and more students wanted to do projects in collaborative groups, I formed more groups.

My first assignment was for all students to interview a class member whom they felt had a background different from their own and to write an essay about that person. For the Culture Share groups, the assignment was to interview one another and to put together a multimedia presentation about the similarities and contrasts among the members of the group. For this first assignment, I became a participating group member of each of the Culture Share groups for several reasons. I wanted not only to model effective group interaction when a member has limited English (drawing, writing words in addition to saying them, using a two-way bilingual dictionary for all group members to translate unknown words, talking about cultural differences in power-neutral language) but also to allow Tu and Phan to get to know me as a person and for me to get to know Tu and Phan. One of the most critical steps in the education of an English language learner is for the teacher to understand the learner's unique needs and motivations and for the learner to develop a personal relationship with the teacher. From the learner's perspective, a mutual interview begins the establishment of a mentor relationship with the teacher and provides a culturally responsive connection between home and school. Many ELLs come from cultures in which the teacher is *in loco parentis* and respect for the teacher is a motivating factor in academic achievement.

The Culture Share group interview project assignment served several purposes. First, because the report was to be in a multimedia format, the new English learners could assist the group in finding images and writing the abbreviated script needed for the slides. This differentiated format used their artistic strengths and the English language resources they had. The collaborative discussion that went into the preparation of the project and their role in the class presentation gave Tu and Phan a chance to practice their spoken English. Further, this presentation allowed them to begin speaking about their Vietnamese culture and to teach others, thereby establishing their legitimacy as contributors to co-constructed knowledge. Their group was building a global view of community and developing critical-thinking competence as the members tried to describe cultural differences and similarities. This competence would serve all the members well when they faced statewide testing in the spring.

> **Their group was building a global view of community and devolping critical-thinking competence as the members tried to describe cultural differences and similarities.**

Learning Support Projects

For each major unit in my eleventh-grade English class, students had to complete a unit project. The project could be either a prequel (pre-unit) or a sequel (post-unit) project. I asked the Culture Share groups to consider prequels that were service-learning projects, thus helping each other as learners by developing learning support materials.

Jump-Start Files

To provide content access for English language learners, Jana Echevarria, MaryEllen Vogt, and Deborah J. Short advocate the use of "jump-start" lessons (32), which entails pre-teaching small groups of struggling students the background material and vocabulary needed to understand the upcoming lesson. In my teaching practice, what I have found equally effective is a jump-start packet, a collection of preview materials that the English learner would take home or cover in a tutoring session prior to the start of the whole-class instruction in that unit. There are typically three components in a jump-start packet: (1) a preview of essential vocabulary; (2) visual scaffolding of the content; and (3) proficiency-appropriate prereading text that parallels the upcoming class readings.

For a prequel unit project, I asked that a group member of each Culture Share prepare a jump-start packet for the group. Two weeks ahead of the unit, he or she compiled important words, collected and labeled pictures relating to the unit, made a list of helpful websites about the topic, and found simple articles or printouts about the key ideas in the topic. This would constitute the unit project requirement. Before our Shakespeare unit, several students prepared elaborate file folders filled with labeled pictures, maps, history timelines, and even videotapes of Shakespearean plays. I used these files as jump-start material for Tu and Phan before beginning the unit.

Adapted-Text Files

Another popular choice for the prequel assignment was adapting or scaffolding the text in some way for greater comprehensibility for English language learners and struggling readers.

Text highlighting and annotating are some of the strategies that are least time intensive. The teacher sets aside one or two textbooks for ELLs or makes photocopies of text pages on which a student helper highlights key terms and elaborates on difficult concepts. This helps English learners who know little English to focus exclusively on the highlighted text and translate as needed. They can begin to make sense of the text that otherwise seems overwhelming. I found that when the student helper explains a concept, the comments are audience-sensitive and scaffold the reading for English language learners. For the final act of *Julius Caesar,* one student not only highlighted important lines in the play but also drew a graphically accurate storyboard of the various actions in the scenes.

Another adapted-text technique that students chose included the audiotaping of text material. I taught the student helpers to read with expression and to highlight verbally important terms or words. I found that the student helpers, being aware of the audience, also made parenthetical comments, defining a word that they felt would be difficult for an ELL to understand or explaining an American or British cultural tradition that may be unknown to the newcomer student. I made copies of the audiotapes of the literature and distributed them to Tu and Phan and kept copies for use with future English learners.

Turning the Tables

While initially it was obvious that the service-learning projects were designed to scaffold the English language learners, the student helpers soon realized the value of the projects for their own learning. They reported that doing these prequel projects led them to read more critically and to think more clearly about the key ideas of the literature. The students seemed more engaged in the classroom as an outcome of sharing responsibility for the learning of the Culture Share members, most notably for Tu and Phan.

Later in the year, as Tu and Phan became more confident about their linguistic and social skills, I introduced a unit on contemporary Vietnamese poetry. This time, I asked the brothers to create a jump-start file for the class to prepare them for the experience of reading this lyrical verse, and I gave them the opportunity to co-teach the file material with me. That morning in my classroom two crocks of soup, a large pile of Vietnamese spring rolls, and a platter of cakes appeared along with an assortment of cultural objects the family had carried from Vietnam. In class, we all learned how to wrap a delicate spring roll and about holidays and the education system in that country. A few days later, I handed out a poem in Vietnamese to the students, and Tu and Phan read the poem to their classmates and worked with the class translating the poem into English and comparing this poem to the British poetry of the same time period.

English Language Learners as Resources

Tu and Phan graduated with their class the next year in spite of the predictions that it would take much longer to master academic English. Their English expanded and so did the social network that was forming around the brothers. Tu and Phan demonstrated Bonny Norton and Kelleen Toohey's contention that "the proficiencies of the good language learners . . . were bound up not only in what they did individually but also in the possibilities their various communities offered them" (318).

What is the bottom line? When teachers reorient their beliefs about the nature of English language learners, seeing them as authentic and legitimate participants in constructing classroom knowledge even when their English is limited, these students are able to grow academically and develop language proficiency. However, beliefs alone will not change the secondary classroom culture that isolates and marginalizes these students. Teachers need to form intentional communities of learners that both support these students and integrate the resources that ELLs bring to the English classroom.

Works Cited

August, Diane, and Timothy Shanahan, eds. *Developing Literacy in Second-Language Learners: Report of the National Literacy Panel on Language-Minority Children and Youth.* Mahwah: Erlbaum, 2006.

Collier, Virginia P. "How Long?: A Synthesis of Research on Academic Achievement in a Second Language." *TESOL Quarterly* 23.3 (1989): 509–31.

Cummins, Jim. *Language, Power and Pedagogy: Bilingual Children in the Crossfire.* Clevedon, UK: Multilingual Matters, 2000.

Echevarria, Jana, MaryEllen Vogt, and Deborah Short. *Making Content Comprehensible for English Learners: The SIOP Model.* 2nd ed. Boston: Pearson, 2004.

Meltzer, Julie, and Edmund T. Hamann. *Meeting the Literacy Development Needs of Adolescent English Language Learners through Content-Area Learning: Part One: Focus on Motivation and Engagement.* Providence: Education Alliance at Brown U, 2005. 11 Jan. 2008 www.alliance.brown.edu/pubs/adlit/adell_litdv1.pdf.

National Assessment of Educational Progress. "Average Reading Scores and Achievement-Level Results for English Language Learners." *The Nation's Report Card.* 2005. 11 Sept. 2007 http://nationsreportcard.gov/reading_math_grade12_2005/s0211.asp?subtab_id=Tab_2&tab_id=tab1#chart>.

Norton, Bonny, and Kelleen Toohey. "Changing Perspectives on Good Language Learners." *TESOL Quarterly* 35.2 (2001): 307–22.

Norton Peirce, Bonny. "Social Identity, Investment, and Language Learning." *TESOL Quarterly* 29.1 (1995): 9–31.

Olsen, Laurie. *Made in America: Immigrant Students in Our Public Schools.* New York: New Press, 1997.

Assess Your Progress

1. What does an intentional community look like in P-12 classrooms?
2. Rance-Roney makes suggestions for creating intentional learning communities. Select up to five of those suggestions that you think would be appropriate for your classroom. Provide a rationale for each selection.
3. Based on Rance-Roney's suggestions, what would your intentional community look like? Describe the actions you would take and explain why you selected each.

JUDITH RANCE-RONEY is assistant professor in the Department of Secondary Education at the State University of New York at New Paltz and is on the English Language Learner Leadership Team of the National Writing Project. She teaches education courses across the disciplines, but her primary work is in TESOL graduate education. *email:* ranceroj@newpaltz.edu.

Creating Intentional Communities to Support English Language Learners in the Classroom from *English Journal*, by Judith Rance-Roney, May 2008, pp. 17–22. Copyright © 2008 by National Council of Teachers of English. Reprinted by permission.

Article 18

Cultivating Optimism in the Classroom

Students are motivated to put forth their best effort when they have faith in the future and themselves.

RICHARD SAGOR

There's a proverb, "The best predictor of the future is the past." This notion isn't lost on Hollywood and helps explain the attractiveness of such movies as *Stand and Deliver* and *Freedom Writers,* which turn it on its head. *Stand and Deliver* tells the story of math teacher Jaime Escalante, whose previously underachieving students went on in great numbers to pass the advanced placement (AP) test in calculus; and *Freedom Writers* tells the story of Erin Gruwell, who inspired her inner-city students to transform their lives through journal writing. Audiences are captivated by seeing poor, alienated teenagers who are well behind their peers in basic skills and have a near total disdain for the education process unexpectedly emerge a few years later with top AP scores, published books, and a desire for a college education.

Unfortunately, what makes this storyline so compelling is that it's so rare. A more familiar scene is this: angry, low-income teenagers with a history of school failure wandering the school hallways with little apparent interest in academics, the curriculum, or their teachers. For too many of them, gangs are more attractive than school activities, drugs are more valuable than learning, and the streets are more appealing than school.

We know the facts. Nearly 50 percent of Latino, black, and American Indian youth leave school before graduating (Orfield, Losen, Wald, & Swanson, 2004). The academic performance of students in low-income communities lags well behind that of students living in more privileged enclaves. The message most often taken from movies like *Stand and Deliver* is that these students' success was the result of the magical powers of a few special, charismatic teachers.

Hollywood wants us to think that Escalante and Gruwell are superheroes, but I'd rather think of them as colleagues who have demonstrated an important lesson regarding what it takes to motivate all our diverse students to strive for the best.

Building Optimism

Whenever we face a choice, we intuitively make a calculation. Typically, we assess the potential costs and benefits—both short- and long-term—of doing one thing instead of another. On the basis of that assessment, we act.

As parents, we are delighted when we see our children defer immediate gratification to achieve a more important long-range goal. At school, we often deliberately teach the merit of investing now for returns in the future. For example, teenage athletes learn the relationship between hard work at practices and success at the game on Friday night. Other students elect to do well in school out of a firm belief that getting good grades will lead to admission to a selective college, which will lead to a happy adult life.

We might wonder why this calculation isn't convincing for all students. Why aren't they buying in? The reason is simple: Investing today for a payoff tomorrow requires believing in your future. Put succinctly, motivation requires optimism.

Investing today for a payoff tomorrow requires believing in your future.

Sometimes it appears that optimism—a positive belief in the future—is a genetic trait. This is one explanation for why children of successful people tend to be successful themselves. And, conversely, it helps explain why children from families that must continually struggle to just get by often find themselves engaged in similar struggles on reaching adulthood.

But the good news, dramatically demonstrated by teachers like Jaime Escalante and Erin Gruwell, is that optimism can be taught and learned. Two key variables are the building blocks of optimism: faith and efficacy.

Building Block 1: Faith in the Future

For me to invest time and energy today for a benefit I won't realize until tomorrow, I need to have a good reason to believe that my investment will pay off. Clearly, it's much easier to acquire that faith when one's immediate environment regularly shows concrete evidence of return on investment. John Ogbu (1991) has written extensively about how children tend to look to the experience of adults in their communities and extended families to predict what lies ahead for them.

If children see despair around them, it's likely that they will fear that this represents their destiny. Many children simply have no good reason to expect tomorrow to be any better than today. There are many legitimate reasons for despair: the impact of poverty, chemical dependency, bigotry, family break-ups, and so on.

If the picture is rosier, however, children have a better chance of being optimistic about their futures. One powerful demonstration of the positive influence of faith in the future was the experience of philanthropist Eugene Lang (White, 1987), the founder of the "I Have a Dream" Foundation. In an impromptu speech, Lang promised a free college education to 61 6th graders at a New York public school if they stayed in school and graduated. Although statistics showed that 75 percent of the students wouldn't go on to graduate from high school, more than 90 percent of Lang's dreamers graduated, with more than two-thirds attending college. What these students had lacked was sufficient reason to believe in their futures. Once they had a justification for faith, they did what it took to realize success.

> **Efficacy is a deep-seated belief in our own capabilities. It explains the phenomenon of success breeding success.**

Building Block 2: Personal Efficacy

In general, it takes more than faith to commit to a difficult pursuit. Optimistic people have the fortitude to persevere with complex tasks because they are confident that if they work long and hard enough and apply enough creativity, they will, in fact, succeed.

Efficacy is a deep-seated belief in our own capabilities. It explains the phenomenon of success breeding success. Every time people attack a problem and succeed, they have authentic evidence of their capability. The more data I have about my capabilities, the more confident I will be of my potential to achieve future success.

Early in my teaching career, I decided to expect every student to produce work deserving of an *A* or *B*; otherwise, his or her grade would be *NYE*—not yet excellent. Occasionally it took extra time, but every student was ultimately able to leave my class with evidence of his or her capability.

There's a reason why so many parents love the story of The Little Engine That Could. We all know that if someone keeps hearing a credible inner voice repeating, "I think I can, I think I can, I think I can," that person will start believing it.

Building Faith and Efficacy in School

Empowered Preschoolers

My daughters went to the Montessori preschool in the local Catholic church. They loved it, as did all their classmates, and they happily got up each morning to go to school. Donna Hargraeves was their teacher, and in her classroom, the children had continual opportunities to explore and learn. She directed the students to activities at a level at which, with effort, they could achieve success.

I can still vividly recall the first open house we attended. I was expecting to hear a teacher presentation, receive handouts, or engage in a conference with the teacher. It was nothing like that. As I entered the room, it looked no different from when I dropped Ellisa off each morning. An aide greeted my daughter and handed her a 3 × 5 index card that listed all the lessons she had mastered. She was then invited to show us what she could do.

For the next 40 minutes, Ellisa led us around the room and treated us to demonstrations of things she had learned. Her pride in her accomplishments was palpable, and as I looked around, I saw the same scene repeated child after child. It was clear to me that the teacher was developing optimism in that room every day with every child.

This was my first experience with student-led parent-teacher conferences, this one brilliantly directed by a 4-year-old. In 40 minutes, I learned more about what my daughter could do, what she had accomplished, and what she was still working on than I ever could have gotten from a traditional conference. But, most important, I witnessed the development of a powerful sense of efficacy on Ellisa's part. She was sharing *her* accomplishments, which were the result of *her* efforts, and she was deservedly beaming with pride and confidence.

Now a junior in college, Ellisa takes on any challenge placed in front of her. There is no doubt in my mind that those crucial early experiences in Donna Hargraeves's classroom empowered her with the conviction that when she sets her mind to something, she can do it.

Sixth Grade Astronauts

Every May at Liberty Middle School in Camas, Washington, approximately 125 6th graders spend a long 10-hour day in space. This extraordinary simulation is a collaborative project that has evolved over several years.

Each space station crew includes five specialists—a mission commander, a life sciences specialist, a health and nutrition specialist, a robotics specialist, and a communications officer. Immediately after spring break, students must prepare written applications for at least two different positions. The teachers then select students for the five crews, and over the next 10 weeks, the students prepare for the mission. At times, all the students who have the same position work with one another in a group—all the mission commanders meet, all the life sciences specialists meet, and so on. At other times, students work with their crewmates, training for the work required during their day in space.

When parents bring their kids to school on the morning of the mission, the gymnasium is a sight to behold. In one corner is mission control, a bank of computers, monitors, and microphones from which the teachers and mission control officers (older students who have been through the program) monitor the astronauts' work. Most of the gym is filled with the space station, which is made up of six connected modules. Soon the students don their spacesuits and gather for the preflight briefing from their teacher. Then, like clockwork, every five minutes another crew enters the space shuttle for the short flight to the International Space Station. For the next 10 hours, the only people each crew will interact with are fellow crew members and mission control.

The five crews rotate through the different modules and carry out their work without ever seeing or interacting with one another. They prepare and eat food in the galley, manipulate objects outside the spacecraft with robotic equipment, conduct experiments on plants and animals, observe rest periods, and even follow exercise routines to keep fit.

The day in space ends with a press conference conducted from the space station. Parents and guests get to see their children on the monitors and listen as the "astronauts" describe what transpired and what they learned on their long and grueling mission. After the press conference, the astronauts board the shuttle and return to earth.

The teachers have structured this 10-week experience in a manner that enhances the academic program rather than detracts from it. Each crew member must do a great deal of reading, writing, math, science, and social studies to prepare for the mission; and this intensive training pays off. Invariably, the mission succeeds, and the crews do their work well. Most important, each crew member possesses concrete evidence of his or her success as a leader, learner, and teacher, engendering a powerful sense of optimism. This optimism lasts quite a while; several former 6th grade astronauts are now in college studying aerospace.

Middle School Reformers

At a large middle school in Southern California that serves a racially, economically, and ethnically diverse community, an English teacher and a doctoral student invited interested students to join them as coresearchers in an investigation of the obstacles to learning at their school (SooHoo, 1993). Twelve students agreed to meet for regular lunchtime discussions. The student researchers were mostly a diverse group of immigrant and minority students, with several English language learners among them. These students weren't particularly comfortable with their place in society or school. Armed with cameras and sketch pads, the students set out to record areas of concern and discuss them at their lunch meetings.

After a few months of deliberation, the student researchers began to see a pattern in their data. Some aspects of the school program weren't working as well as they should. Students had ideas about changing the school's discipline and reward policy as well as the physical education program. They began developing ideas for program improvement.

They soon realized that they lacked power to bring about the desired changes. Together with their adult mentors, the students requested the opportunity to present their research to the faculty. In a faculty meeting at which they served cookies, cupcakes, and soft drinks, the students presented their research. Later that spring on a scheduled professional development day, the 12 students were invited to work side by side with their teachers in making plans for the new school year. On the basis of the students' input, the school revised the discipline and reward process and redesigned the physical education program.

Article 18. Cultivating Optimism in the Classroom

I met these students a few years later when they presented their research to an audience of university professors at the annual American Educational Research Association conference. The students—now high school sophomores—were articulate, confident, and absolutely certain they were headed to college and professional careers. After they learned as middle school students that they had powerful voices and were capable of persuading adult professionals with their arguments, nothing could stop them from achieving their goals.

> **After they learned as middle school students that they had powerful voices, nothing could stop them from achieving their goals.**

An Environmental Advocate

A high school student named Sam recently became interested in the movement to design and build environmentally sound "green" buildings. He was not a good student academically, had few friends and little status, and didn't fit in with or have much respect for the social activities that defined the traditional high school experience.

But he didn't lack confidence. He went to the high school administrators with an elaborate written proposal describing an independent study he wanted to do on the potential conversion of a recently built public building to meet green building standards. He worked hard on his proposal and was excited about pursuing this work. Unfortunately, the school didn't see it the same way. As a result, Sam decided to leave to attend a nearby alternative school in the hope that its community-based learning model might be a better fit.

The teachers' reaction to his proposal at the alternative school was markedly different. The school made arrangements for Sam to intern at one of the largest and most prestigious architectural firms in the region. One day in a meeting with several of the firm's top architects, a lead architect commented that the constraints of school construction limited possible energy efficiencies.

Sam spoke up. His research had revealed that six buildings recently built in Los Angeles now operated completely off the grid. Impressed, the architects asked Sam to do more research. The next day Sam presented this "new information" to some of the leaders in the field.

Sam has now graduated and is making plans to attend college. Although he readily admits that he is the proverbial square peg that people try to push through a round hole, he has no doubt about his ability to accomplish whatever he sets his mind to.

Great Expectations

It is naive to think there could be an easy answer to all our student motivation problems. But one thing is clear: Young people are more likely to invest their energy in pursuit of what they view to be an achievable dream than in what they sense is futility.

That's why students need continuous encouragement and hope from schools—so they can believe in their futures and themselves. Every day as students leave our classrooms we need to ask ourselves two questions: As a result of todays experience, will these students be more or less confident that their futures are bright? Will students walk out of the classroom feeling more capable than when they walked in?

> **Will students walk out of the classroom feeling more capable than when they walked in?**

Every morning an alarm clock goes off, a student awakes, and thoughts begin to form. What should the student expect from the upcoming day? If he or she were lucky enough to have had a teacher like Jaime Escalante or Erin Gruwell, or had been promised a college education by Eugene Lang, that student may well be looking forward to a bright future. But optimism shouldn't depend on having a superhero as a teacher or on receiving help from a philanthropist. We teachers can nurture optimism in all our students by creating routine education experiences in which hard work leads to success and a world of possibilities.

References

Ogbu, J. U. (1991). Immigrant and involuntary minorities in comparative perspective. In M. A. Gibson & J. U. Ogbu (Eds.), *Minority status and schooling: A comparative study of immigrant and involuntary minorities* (pp. 3–33). New York: Garland.

Orfield, G., Losen, D., Wald, J., & Swanson, C. B. (2004). *Losing our future: How minority youth are being left behind by the graduation rate crisis.* Cambridge, MA: The Civil Rights Project at Harvard University. Available: www.urban.org/uploadedPDF/410936_LosingOurFuture.pdf

SooHoo, S. (1993). Students as partners in research and restructuring schools. *The Educational Forum, 57*(4), 386–393.

White, J. (1987). Eugene Lang: Dream-maker to the kids of Harlem. *AGB Reports, 29*(3), 10–17.

Assess Your Progress

1. Consider that cultivating optimism might be a deterrent against bullying. Prepare to debate this issue from either side: agree or disagree.
2. Think of the person who helped you have faith in the future and gain personal efficacy. What did that person do for you?
3. What will you do for students to build faith and efficacy? Select strategies and actions that are appropriate for your classroom or content area to cultivate optimism.

RICHARD SAGOR is Professor and Director of the Educational Leadership Program at Lewis and Clark College, Portland, Oregon; sagor@lclark.edu.

Article 19

Teachers Connecting with Families—In the Best Interest of Children

KATHARINE C. KERSEY AND MARIE L. MASTERSON

When parents are involved in school, their children's achievement improves. Children make friends more easily and are more successful learners (NCPIE, 2006).Children whose families participate in school activities stay in school longer and take more advanced classes (Bamard 2004). But the greatest benefit to children of a successful home-school partnership is that children are more motivated to succeed (Hoover-Dempsey et al. 2005).

To connect parents with school, teachers need to learn the best ways to share information and thereby build bridges and strong ties with families. They need to find ways to establish positive relationships by shifting from a focus on children's problems to affirming children's strengths. Such approaches can improve classroom-home communications and encourage all families to become involved.

Knowing and Understanding Families

Most parents can remember what it felt like to take their child to school for the first time. Those hours seemed endless. Was she OK—smiling, crying, or hurt? Could you hardly wait to see her? What positive things did her teacher have to say when you picked up your child after her first day at kindergarten? If you waited to learn what she did on her first day and the teacher didn't say anything at all, were you crushed? Had you hoped that she would tell you what a nice little girl you had (in other words, that you'd done a good job)?

There are reasons a parent might feel intimidated by a teacher or hesitant to come to a conference. One parent expressed frustration that he left a meeting at work and drove 45 minutes during the worst traffic of the day, only to have 10 or 15 minutes with his child's teacher! Other parents say that they did not feel welcome at their children's school. Sometimes, parents can feel a teacher is questioning their competence, and so when they come for a meeting, they are defensive. Parents could be anticipating bad news. They may be surprised if the teacher has something nice to say. Teachers need to build parents' confidence that their school encounters will result in positive interactions and success for their child.

At times, when parents hesitate to become involved, it may be because they feel inadequate in terms of their education or perhaps are unable to read. Teachers may use language a parent doesn't understand or describe a child's progress in educational jargon, which the parent is reluctant to admit confuses him. Parents may cringe at the thought of being asked questions they can't answer. And most of all, parents don't want to feel judged for their child's problems, behaviors, or poor progress.

Distrust and uncertainty work both ways. Teachers themselves can feel intimated by parents. In some cases, a parent's strong personality comes across as demanding or accusatory, Teachers may worry about being caught off guard or asked a question not easily handled. They too could fear being judged or embarrassed. One teacher said that at the end of a parent teacher conference, she experienced an awkward moment when she tried to shake hands with the parent, a practice she didn't know was considered disrespectful in the family's culture. She now takes the time to learn about the cultures of the children in her class. Setting parents at ease and helping them know that as teachers we want the same things they want for their children is well worth the time and energy it takes.

Sharing Information with Families

The positive interactions teachers use to create connections with parents are in the best interest of the child (Hamre & Pianta 2005). Successful teachers make it their business to connect with families and plan ways to build strong relationships with children and parents. Setting up an open and positive system of teacher availability supports cooperative and productive teacher-parent relationships.

The following suggestions illustrate some specific ways to build bridges and strengthen the bond between teacher and parent. Using strategies such as these can ensure that when challenges come, a strong foundation is already in place.

Before School Starts

- **Send a personalized postcard** to every child saying " See you soon at school You'll make friends and enjoy learning!"
- **Make a phone call** to each child: "I am calling to talk to Maria. I am your new teacher, and I look forward to seeing you."
- **Have an open house** for children and families as an orientation to school. Let the children explore the room so they will feel safe. Join the children at their level when you talk to set them at ease. Introduce children and families with common interests.
- **When the school year begins,** hold a Welcome Parents meeting [AQ3a Indicate when this takes place.] to show families that you care about their ideas and interests. Ask each family to complete a questionnaire to help you learn children's interests, strengths, pets, and hobbies. Ask for information about allergies and special concerns.

Begin the meeting with a Family Introduction Circle: "Whose mom or dad are you?" "Tell us something about _____ [child's name]." "what would you like everyone to know?" "Do you have something you would like to share with the children about your job, hobby, or a special interest?" Hand out copies of daily schedules, menus, and other items. Provide copies in the home languages of the families in the group. Plan time for a group of parents to get to know each other, and help them find ways to connect.

Make and share a "Me Bag." Bring special items that show and tell about you personally. Let families get to know you and about the things you love. You can share the same Me Bag with the children when school begins, and let the children bring in their Me Bags as well.

Throughout the Year

- **Call children at home.** Leave a message on the home answering machine during the school day. "Jamal, I am calling to say I noticed you help Brandon on the playground. He seemed grateful for your help." It takes 15 seconds, and Jamal may never want to erase it. Set aside a time each week to make these calls, and keep a list to make sure to include every child.
- **Send home a Great Moments! Certificate.** Attach a digital photo to the certificate and highlight a special contribution, a kind gesture, or clever words a child has used. Send three to five certificates each day to ensure each child receives one during the week.
- **Use the phone to share news.** Ask parents to let you know when they are available, and then set up a schedule so they can look forward to hearing from you. Be available for parents to call you at a set time if they have questions or want to talk. When a child is sick, it is appropriate to call her home to let her know she is missed.
- **Send e-mail communications.** "Today we had a picnic. We went outside under a tree. Ask Carmen to tell you what she did." Do this frequently so parents come to associate e-mails with memories of their children's experiences.
- **Say at least one positive thing each** time you see a parent. "Danny has such a wonderful sense of humor." "Teresa told me about your camping trip." Run after a parent to say, "I want to tell you . . . !" Parents will enjoy hearing about interesting things their child has done and learned.
- **Record the positive things children do.** Place them on 3 × 5 cards in a notebook you can share each time you see a parent—another opportunity to connect. Focus on conveying the message, "I notice your child!"
- **Encourage parent volunteers**. Any time you invite a parent to class, the child will feel excited and special. Encourage parents to read, share some expertise, or tell about a special interest. Let the parent's child help. Find creative ways for parents to make meaningful contributions to the classroom that can fit in their schedules (organizing child portfolios, photo copying, planning parties, or preparing for an art, music, or dramatics activity).
- **Send home weekend project packs** with activities parents and children can do together. An example could be a class mascot—a stuffed animal that takes turns going home with the children and have the families keep a diary of his activities. Children will take pride in bringing home the pet and then sharing their diary entry with classmates when the mascot returns to school.

During Parent Conferences

- **Focus on a child's natural strengths.** Affirm the child. Share special traits and unique capabilities. "Judy's block buildings are complex and inventive." "Joey shows compassion to his peers." "Jasmine enjoys exploring new aft materials." A teacher can help parents see the potential in their child and encourage them to support and nurture the child's gifts at home.

- **Always get the parent to talk first.** Say, "Tell me about your child?" The parent may ask, "What do you want to know?" You can respond, "Anything you want to tell me." Such an approach lets parents take the lead and feel relaxed and open to a conversation.
- **Ask parents for their perspectives.** Parents are experts about their child and may describe a child's strength or need. When they mention a strength, ask, "How do you support her at home?" When they tell you about a problem, ask, "How do you deal with that?"
- **Ask for help!** If the child is experiencing difficulty at school and you think the parent needs to get involved, you might introduce your concern by saying, "There is something I'd like your help with."
- **Focus on one important issue.** When you have concerns, choose one that you think can be helped or fixed. First, identify it, and then brainstorm some solutions. Together with the family you can agree to a plan. "I will work on this at school, while you work on it at home. Let's set an appointment to get together again in two weeks." This tells parents that by working together you can help the child succeed.
- **Start and end on positive notes.** Tell something good first. It lets the parents relax and know you notice special things about their child. Make sure to end with a commitment. "I appreciate and value the time that I share with your child, and I want to help her develop and learn."
- **Send a reminder.** Call or send an e-mail the day before to confirm the next appointment. "If you can't come that day, when is it convenient for you to come?"

When Parents Are Not Able to Come to School

- **Share successes immediately.** With parental permission, allow a child to call a parent during the day to tell about something great he just did. You can call also: "I want you to know that Joshua counted to six in Spanish today!"
- **Videotape children's activities,** presentations, and special accomplishments. Send the tape home on loan for parents to appreciate what they see their child learning and doing. Or upload the video to the school or classroom website.
- **Send home daily sheets.** Use photos and descriptions to show parents the activities and learning in which the children are engaged.
- **Fill a class newsletter with highlights** of community activities, parenting and positive guidance tips, and information about the class curriculum. Children can help write the news for this newsletter!

Use Affirmations to Connect with Families

With parents, use every opportunity to connect positively: "I can't wait to see you and tell you all of the wonderful things your child is doing!" When a teacher adopts this attitude in her interactions with parents, they will eagerly join in to support school and classroom activities for their child. Tell parents what the child is learning about himself, new friends, the world, and the outdoors. Parents need to hear what children are learning socially and how they are becoming successful. It is our job as teachers to help each child navigate the world successfully. We can give parents hope and confidence that their child is well on his way to achieving that goal.

It is always in the best interest of the child to connect with parents. When teachers and parents build connections and work together, children are more successful—both academically and socially. The relationships teachers form early with parents help children become socially and emotionally competent and do better in school (Walker et al. 2005). As a result, children have fewer behavior problems both at school and at home (NCPIE 2006). Family connections built, when children are young pay off in a lifetime of rich dividends for the child.

Teachers can tell families, "I hear about you all the time. I heard what a great thing you all did together last night." These positive affirmations make a parent feel relaxed and stand up tall. You're the teacher, are building bridges. You have a lasting impact on parents when you share your values and your goals for their children. You empower parents to be more successful in their parenting role when you connect them positively to their child's teacher and to school.

Once families feel comfortable and understand how important they are to their child's success, a strong relationship begins. The partnership strengthens as school and teacher become a source for positive information. Through this approach to building connections, teachers create authentic, caring relationships with families, and parents become active participants in their child's success.

References

Barnard, W.M. 2004. Parent involvement in elementary school and educational attainment. *Children and Youth Services Review* 26 ( ):39–62.

Gladwell, M. 2005. Blink: *The power of thinking without thinking.* New York: Little, Brown.

Hamre, B., & R. Pianta. 2005. Can instructional and emotional support in the first-grade classroom make a difference for children at risk of school failure? *Child Development* 76 (5): 949–67.

Hoover-Dempsey, K., M. Walker, H. Sandler, D. Whetsel, C. Green, A. Wilkins, & K. Closson. 2005. Why do parents become involved? Research findings and implications. *Elementary School Journal* 2 (106): 105–30.

NCPIE (National Coalition for Parent Involvement in Education). 2006. What's Happening. *A new wave of evidence: The impact of school, family and community connections on student achievement.* www.ncpie.ore/WhatsHappening/researchJanuary2006.html

Walker, J.M., A.S. Wilkins, J.R. Dallaire, H.M. Sandler, & K.V. Hoover-Dempsey. 2005. Parental involvement: Model revision through scale development. *The Elementary School Journal* 106 (2): 85–104.

Assess Your Progress

1. Give three reasons why involving parents in your classroom is important to your teaching and student learning. Cite information from articles in this unit.
2. Which of the authors' suggestions for connecting with parents will you adopt? Share your reasons.

KATHARINE C. KERSEY, EdD, is professor of early childhood, an educator, and the director emeritus of the Child Study Center, Old Dominion University (ODU), in Norfolk, Virginia. She is the former chair of ODU's Department of Early Childhood, Speech Pathology, and Special Education and is a child behavior expert, TV consultant, teacher and parent educator, author, and speaker. kkersev@odu.edu

MARIE L. MASTERSON, PhD, is the early childhood specialist for the Virginia Department of Education and adjunct professor of early childhood education at Old Dominion University. She is coordinator of the ODU Director's Institute and an educational researcher, child behavior consultant, and speaker. mmasters@odu.edu

---

From *Young Children*, September 2009. Copyright © 2009 by National Association for the Education of Young Children. Reprinted by permission.

Article 20

How Not to Talk to Your Kids

The inverse power of praise.

PO BRONSON

What do we make of a boy like Thomas? Thomas (his middle name) is a fifth-grader at the highly competitive P.S. 334, the Anderson School on West 84th. Slim as they get, Thomas recently had his long sandy-blond hair cut short to look like the new James Bond (he took a photo of Daniel Craig to the barber). Unlike Bond, he prefers a uniform of cargo pants and a T-shirt emblazoned with a photo of one of his heroes: Frank Zappa. Thomas hangs out with five friends from the Anderson School. They are "the smart kids." Thomas's one of them, and he likes belonging.

Since Thomas could walk, he has heard constantly that he's smart. Not just from his parents but from any adult who has come in contact with this precocious child. When he applied to Anderson for kindergarten, his intelligence was statistically confirmed. The school is reserved for the top one percent of all applicants, and an IQ test is required. Thomas didn't just score in the top one percent. He scored in the top one percent of the top one percent.

But as Thomas has progressed through school, this self-awareness that he's smart hasn't always translated into fearless confidence when attacking his schoolwork. In fact, Thomas's father noticed just the opposite. "Thomas didn't want to try things he wouldn't be successful at," his father says. "Some things came very quickly to him, but when they didn't, he gave up almost immediately, concluding, 'I'm not good at this.'" With no more than a glance, Thomas was dividing the world into two—things he was naturally good at and things he wasn't.

For instance, in the early grades, Thomas wasn't very good at spelling, so he simply demurred from spelling out loud. When Thomas took his first look at fractions, he balked. The biggest hurdle came in the third grade. He was supposed to learn cursive penmanship, but he wouldn't even try for weeks. By then, his teacher was demanding that his homework be completed in cursive. Rather than play catch-up on his penmanship, Thomas refused outright. Thomas's father tried to reason with him. "Look, just because you're smart doesn't mean you don't have to put out some effort." (Eventually, he mastered cursive, but not without a lot of cajoling from his father.)

Why does this child, who is measurably at the very top of the charts, lack confidence about his ability to tackle routine school challenges?

Thomas is not alone. For a few decades, it's been noted that a large percentage of all gifted students (those who score in the top 10 percent on aptitude tests) severely underestimate their own abilities. Those afflicted with this lack of perceived competence adopt lower standards for success and expect less of themselves. They underrate the importance of effort, and they overrate how much help they need from a parent.

When parents praise their children's intelligence, they believe they are providing the solution to this problem. According to a survey conducted by Columbia University, 85 percent of American parents think it's important to tell their kids that they're smart. In and around the New York area, according to my own (admittedly nonscientific) poll, the number is more like 100 percent. Everyone does it, habitually. The constant praise is meant to be an angel on the shoulder, ensuring that children do not sell their talents short.

But a growing body of research—and a new study from the trenches of the New York public-school system—strongly suggests it might be the other way around. Giving kids the label of "smart" does not prevent them from underperforming. It might actually be causing it.

For the past ten years, psychologist Carol Dweck and her team at Columbia (she's now at Stanford) studied the effect of praise on students in a dozen New York schools. Her seminal work—a series of experiments on 400 fifth-graders—paints the picture most clearly.

Dweck sent four female research assistants into New York fifth-grade classrooms. The researchers would take a single child out of the classroom for a nonverbal IQ test consisting of a series of puzzles—puzzles easy enough that all the children would do fairly well. Once the child finished the test, the researchers told each student his score, then gave him a single line of praise. Randomly divided into groups, some were praised for their intelligence. They were told, "You must be smart at this." Other students were praised for their effort: "You must have worked really hard."

Why just a single line of praise? "We wanted to see how sensitive children were," Dweck explained. "We had a hunch that one line might be enough to see an effect."

Then the students were given a choice of test for the second round. One choice was a test that would be more difficult than the first, but the researchers told the kids that they'd learn a lot from attempting the puzzles. The other choice, Dweck's team explained, was an easy test, just like the first. Of those praised for their effort, 90 percent chose the harder set of puzzles. Of those praised for their intelligence, a majority chose the easy test. The "smart" kids took the cop-out.

Why did this happen? "When we praise children for their intelligence," Dweck wrote in her study summary, "we tell them that this is the name of the game: Look smart, don't risk making mistakes." And that's what the fifth-graders had done: They'd chosen to look smart and avoid the risk of being embarrassed.

In a subsequent round, none of the fifth-graders had a choice. The test was difficult, designed for kids two years ahead of their grade level. Predictably, everyone failed. But again, the two groups of children, divided at random at the study's start, responded differently. Those praised for their effort on the first test assumed they simply hadn't focused hard enough on this test. "They got very involved, willing to try every solution to the puzzles," Dweck recalled. "Many of them remarked, unprovoked, 'This is my favorite test.'" Not so for those praised for their smarts. They assumed their failure was evidence that they weren't really smart at all. "Just watching them, you could see the strain. They were sweating and miserable."

Having artificially induced a round of failure, Dweck's researchers then gave all the fifth-graders a final round of tests that were engineered to be as easy as the first round. Those who had been praised for their effort significantly improved on their first score—by about 30 percent. Those who'd been told they were smart did worse than they had at the very beginning—by about 20 percent.

Dweck had suspected that praise could backfire, but even she was surprised by the magnitude of the effect. "Emphasizing effort gives a child a variable that they can control," she explains. "They come to see themselves as in control of their success. Emphasizing natural intelligence takes it out of the child's control, and it provides no good recipe for responding to a failure."

In follow-up interviews, Dweck discovered that those who think that innate intelligence is the key to success begin to discount the importance of effort. *I am smart,* the kids' reasoning goes; *I don't need to put out effort.* Expending effort becomes stigmatized—it's public proof that you can't cut it on your natural gifts.

Repeating her experiments, Dweck found this effect of praise on performance held true for students of every socioeconomic class. It hit both boys and girls—the very brightest girls especially (they collapsed the most following failure). Even preschoolers weren't immune to the inverse power of praise.

Jill Abraham is a mother of three in Scarsdale, and her view is typical of those in my straw poll. I told her about Dweck's research on praise, and she flatly wasn't interested in brief tests without long-term follow-up. Abraham is one of the 85 percent who think praising her children's intelligence is important. Her kids are thriving, so she's proved that praise works in the real world. "I don't care what the experts say," Jill says defiantly. "I'm living it."

Even those who've accepted the new research on praise have trouble putting it into practice. Sue Needleman is both a mother of two and an elementary-school teacher with eleven years' experience. Last year, she was a fourth-grade teacher at Ridge Ranch Elementary in Paramus, New Jersey. She has never heard of Carol Dweck, but the gist of Dweck's research has trickled down to her school, and Needleman has learned to say, "I like how you keep trying." She tries to keep her praise specific, rather than general, so that a child knows exactly what she did to earn the praise (and thus can get more). She will occasionally tell a child, "You're good at math," but she'll never tell a child he's bad at math.

But that's at school, as a teacher. At home, old habits die hard. Her 8-year-old daughter and her 5-year-old son are indeed smart, and sometimes she hears herself saying, "You're great. You did it. You're smart." When I press her on this, Needleman says that what comes out of academia often feels artificial. "When I read the mock dialogues, my first thought is, *Oh, please. How corny.*"

No such qualms exist for teachers at the Life Sciences Secondary School in East Harlem, because they've seen Dweck's theories applied to their junior-high students. Last week, Dweck and her protégée, Lisa Blackwell, published a report in the academic journal *Child Development* about the effect of a semester-long intervention conducted to improve students' math scores.

Life Sciences is a health-science magnet school with high aspirations but 700 students whose main attributes are being predominantly minority and low achieving. Blackwell split her kids into two groups for an eight-session workshop. The control group was taught study skills, and the others got study skills and a special module on how intelligence is not innate. These students took turns reading aloud an essay on how the brain grows new neurons when challenged. They saw slides of the brain and acted out skits. "Even as I was teaching these ideas," Blackwell noted, "I would hear the students joking, calling one another 'dummy' or 'stupid.'" After the module was concluded, Blackwell tracked her students' grades to see if it had any effect.

It didn't take long. The teachers—who hadn't known which students had been assigned to which workshop—could pick out the students who had been taught that intelligence can be developed. They improved their study habits and grades. In a single semester, Blackwell reversed the students' longtime trend of decreasing math grades.

The only difference between the control group and the test group were two lessons, a total of 50 minutes spent teaching not math but a single idea: that the brain is a muscle. Giving it a harder workout makes you smarter. That alone improved their math scores.

"These are very persuasive findings," says Columbia's Dr. Geraldine Downey, a specialist in children's sensitivity to rejection. "They show how you can take a specific theory and develop a curriculum that works." Downey's comment is typical of what other scholars in the field are saying. Dr. Mahzarin Banaji, a Harvard social psychologist who is an expert in stereotyping, told me, "Carol Dweck is a flat-out genius. I hope the work is taken seriously. It scares people when they see these results."

Since the 1969 publication of *The Psychology of Self-Esteem,* in which Nathaniel Branden opined that self-esteem was the single most important facet of a person, the belief that one must do whatever he can to achieve positive self-esteem has become a movement with broad societal effects. Anything potentially damaging to kids' self-esteem was axed. Competitions were frowned upon. Soccer coaches stopped counting goals and handed out trophies to everyone. Teachers threw out their red pencils. Criticism was replaced with ubiquitous, even undeserved, praise.

Dweck and Blackwell's work is part of a larger academic challenge to one of the self-esteem movement's key tenets: that praise, self-esteem, and performance rise and fall together. From 1970 to 2000, there were over 15,000 scholarly articles written on self-esteem and its relationship to everything—from sex to career advancement. But results were often contradictory or inconclusive. So in 2003, the Association for Psychological Science asked Dr. Roy Baumeister, then a leading proponent of self-esteem, to review this literature. His team concluded that self-esteem was polluted with flawed science. Only 200 of those 15,000 studies met their rigorous standards.

I am smart, the kids' reasoning goes; I don't need to put out effort. Expending effort becomes stigmatized—it's public proof that you can't cut it on your natural gifts.

After reviewing those 200 studies, Baumeister concluded that having high self-esteem didn't improve grades or career achievement. It didn't even reduce alcohol usage. And it especially did not lower violence of any sort. (Highly aggressive, violent people happen to think very highly of themselves, debunking the theory that people are aggressive to make up for low self-esteem.) At the time, Baumeister was quoted as saying that his findings were "the biggest disappointment of my career."

Now he's on Dweck's side of the argument, and his work is going in a similar direction: He will soon publish an article showing that for college students on the verge of failing in class, esteem-building praise causes their grades to sink further. Baumeister has come to believe the continued appeal of self-esteem is largely tied to parents' pride in their children's achievements: It's so strong that "when they praise their kids, it's not that far from praising themselves."

By and large, the literature on praise shows that it can be effective—a positive, motivating force. In one study, University of Notre Dame researchers tested praise's efficacy on a losing college hockey team. The experiment worked: The team got into the playoffs. But all praise is not equal—and, as Dweck demonstrated, the effects of praise can vary significantly depending on the praise given. To be effective, researchers have found, praise needs to be specific. (The hockey players were specifically complimented on the number of times they checked an opponent.)

Sincerity of praise is also crucial. Just as we can sniff out the true meaning of a backhanded compliment or a disingenuous apology, children, too, scrutinize praise for hidden agendas. Only young children—under the age of 7—take praise at face value: Older children are just as suspicious of it as adults.

Psychologist Wulf-Uwe Meyer, a pioneer in the field, conducted a series of studies where children watched other students receive praise. According to Meyer's findings, by the age of 12, children believe that earning praise from a teacher is not a sign you did well—it's actually a sign you lack ability and the teacher thinks you need extra encouragement. And teens, Meyer found, discounted praise to such an extent that they believed it's a teacher's criticism—not praise at all—that really conveys a positive belief in a student's aptitude.

In the opinion of cognitive scientist Daniel T. Willingham, a teacher who praises a child may be unwittingly sending the message that the student reached the limit of his innate ability, while a teacher who criticizes a pupil conveys the message that he can improve his performance even further.

New York University professor, of psychiatry, Judith Brook explains that the issue for parents is one of credibility. "Praise is important, but not vacuous praise," she says. "It has to be based on a real thing—some skill or talent they have." Once children hear praise they interpret it as meritless, they discount not just the insincere praise, but sincere praise as well.

Scholars from Reed College and Stanford reviewed over 150 praise studies. Their meta-analysis determined that praised students become risk-averse and lack perceived autonomy. The scholars found consistent correlations between a liberal use of praise and students, "shorter task persistence, more eye-checking with the teacher, and inflected speech such that answers have the intonation of questions."

Dweck's research on overpraised kids strongly suggests that image maintenance becomes their primary concern—they are more competitive and more interested in tearing others down. A raft of very alarming studies illustrate this.

In one, students are given two puzzle tests. Between the first and the second, they are offered a choice between learning a new puzzle strategy for the second test or finding out how they did compared with other students on the first test: They have only enough time to do one or the other. Students praised for intelligence choose to find out their class rank, rather than use the time to prepare.

In another, students get a do-it-yourself report card and are told these forms will be mailed to students at another school—they'll never meet these students and don't know their names. Of the kids praised for their intelligence, 40 percent lie, inflating their scores. Of the kids praised for effort, few lie.

When students transition into junior high, some who'd done well in elementary school inevitably struggle in the larger and more demanding environment. Those who equated their earlier success with their innate ability surmise they've been dumb all along. Their grades never recover because the likely key to their recovery—increasing effort—they view as just further proof of their failure. In interviews, many confess they would "seriously consider cheating."

Students turn to cheating because they haven't developed a strategy for handling failure. The problem is compounded when a parent ignores a child's failures and insists he'll do better next time. Michigan scholar, Jennifer Crocker, studies this exact scenario and explains that the child may come to believe failure is something so terrible, the family can't acknowledge its existence. A child deprived of the opportunity to discuss mistakes can't learn from them.

My son, Luke, is in kindergarten. He seems supersensitive to the potential judgment of his peers. Luke justifies it by saying, "I'm shy," but he's not really shy. He has no fear of strange cities or talking to strangers, and at his school, he has sung in front of large audiences. Rather, I'd say he's proud and self-conscious. His school has simple uniforms (navy T-shirt, navy pants), and he loves that his choice of clothes can't be ridiculed, "because then they'd be teasing themselves too."

After reading Carol Dweck's research, I began to alter how I praised him, but not completely. I suppose my hesitation was that the mind-set Dweck wants students to have—a firm belief that the way to bounce back from failure is to work harder—sounds awfully clichéd: Try, try again.

But it turns out that the ability to repeatedly respond to failure by exerting more effort—instead of simply giving up—is a trait well studied in psychology. People with this trait, persistence, rebound well and can sustain their motivation through long periods of delayed gratification. Delving into this research, I learned that persistence turns out to be more than a conscious act of will; it's also an unconscious response, governed by a circuit in the brain. Dr. Robert Cloninger at Washington University in St. Louis located the circuit in a part of the brain called the orbital and medial prefrontal cortex. It monitors the reward center of the brain, and like a switch, it intervenes when there's a lack of immediate reward. When it switches on, it's telling the rest of the brain, "Don't stop trying. There's dopa [the brain's chemical reward for success] on the horizon." While putting people through MRI scans, Cloninger could see this switch lighting up regularly in some. In others, barely at all.

What makes some people wired to have an active circuit?

Cloninger has trained rats and mice in mazes to have persistence by carefully *not* rewarding them when they get to the finish. "The key is intermittent reinforcement," says Cloninger. The brain has to learn that frustrating spells can be worked through. "A person who grows up getting too frequent rewards will not have persistence, because they'll quit when the rewards disappear."

That sold me. I'd thought "praise junkie" was just an expression—but suddenly, it seemed as if I could be setting up my son's brain for an actual chemical need for constant reward.

What would it mean, to give up praising our children so often? Well, if I am one example, there are stages of withdrawal, each of them subtle. In the first stage, I fell off the wagon around other parents when they were busy praising their kids. I didn't want Luke to feel left out. I felt like a former alcoholic who continues to drink socially. I became a Social Praiser.

Then I tried to use the specific-type praise that Dweck recommends. I praised Luke, but I attempted to praise his "process." This was easier said than done. What are the processes that go on in a 5-year-old's mind? In my impression, 80 percent of his brain processes lengthy scenarios for his action figures.

But every night he has math homework and is supposed to read a phonics book aloud. Each takes about five minutes if he concentrates, but he's easily distracted. So I praised him for concentrating without asking to take a break. If he listened to instructions carefully, I praised him for that. After soccer games, I praised him for looking to pass, rather than just saying, "You played great." And if he worked hard to get to the ball, I praised the effort he applied.

Just as the research promised, this focused praise helped him see strategies he could apply the next day. It was remarkable how noticeably effective this new form of praise was.

Truth be told, while my son was getting along fine under the new praise regime, it was I who was suffering. It turns out that I was the real praise junkie in the family. Praising him for just a particular skill or task felt like I left other parts of him ignored and unappreciated. I recognized that praising him with the universal "You're great—I'm proud of you" was a way I expressed unconditional love.

Offering praise has become a sort of panacea for the anxieties of modern parenting. Out of our children's lives from breakfast to dinner, we turn it up a notch when we get home. In those few hours together, we want them to hear the things we can't say during the day—*We are in your corner, we are here for you, we believe in you.*

In a similar way, we put our children in high-pressure environments, seeking out the best schools we can find, then we use the constant praise to soften the intensity of those environments. We expect so much of them, but we hide our expectations behind constant glowing praise. The duplicity became glaring to me.

Eventually, in my final stage of praise withdrawal, I realized that not telling my son he was smart meant I was leaving it up to him to make his own conclusion about his intelligence. Jumping in with praise is like jumping in too soon with the answer to a homework problem—it robs him of the chance to make the deduction himself.

But what if he makes the wrong conclusion?

Can I really leave this up to him, at his age?

I'm still an anxious parent. This morning, I tested him on the way to school: "What happens to your brain, again, when it gets to think about something hard?"

"It gets bigger, like a muscle," he responded, having aced this one before.

Assess Your Progress

1. How is it possible to praise too much? Think about your own praise practice or that of teachers you have observed.
2. What are the implications of Bronson's research for teachers?

Copyright © 2007 by Po Bronson. Originally published by *New York Magazine*. Reprinted by permission of Curtis Brown, Ltd. www.pobronson.com

Article 21

Democracy and Education

Empowering Students to Make Sense of Their World

WILLIAM H. GARRISON

Ever wonder why democratic societies are unrivaled in expanding knowledge and creativity? There is a simple yet vital link between democracy and education, and it is found in how we learn best. If you have studied educational psychology or learning theory, you probably have insight into the causes of this phenomenon. If your instructional practices include such things as self-directed learning, self-reflection, or action research, you are probably well aware of the practical mechanism underlying this productivity even if you don't know it by name.

It is a fundamental belief under our system of governance that education is necessary for democracy. Less recognized is the equally important principle that democracy is necessary for education. Looking closely at the relationship between democracy and education reveals a common foundation in a learning mechanism that is as important for classroom practice as it is for a democratic society.

In *Democracy and Education*, Dewey defines education as the "reconstruction or reorganization of experience which adds to the meaning of experience and which increases the ability to direct the course of subsequent experience."[1] Education, like democracy, is fundamentally empowerment. Both provide the participants with the means to shape and direct their experiences.

The educational process in a democratic society, even in the most autocratic of classrooms and institutions, is grounded in basic freedoms. These freedoms exist beyond the particular classroom and institution, if not within them. From a learning perspective, the most important of these freedoms is the freedom to choose, to act on that choice, and to experience the results of those actions. Instructional practices that include self-reflection and action research are based on the idea that we learn by following our thoughts and actions and examining their consequences. By choosing a course of action and experiencing the results, our beliefs and understandings about the world, how it works, and how we fit into it are reinforced or modified.

In describing "intelligence," Jean Piaget echoes this fundamental play between thinking, acting, and learning: "The essential functions of intelligence consist in understanding and in inventing, in other words in building up structures by structuring reality."[2] We learn by constructing meaning from our experiences. We reconstruct, reorganize, and direct our experiences as we attempt to make sense of our world. Our understanding of the world is constructed through what we make of our experiences, how we interpret them, and how these interpretations are integrated into our knowledge and beliefs. These learnings provide the mental structures and dispositions that influence and direct subsequent experience.

We continually make choices in all of our thoughts and actions. Ulric Neisser wrote about the "perceptual cycle" of learning: of all the possibilities presented in our environment, our thought processes or mental structures guide our perceptual awareness, which samples the available information. As we choose to focus our attention, what we experience serves to modify or reinforce these structures, which guide further perceptual exploration and experience.[3]

This fundamental learning mechanism underlies the rich and productive relationship between democracy and education. Learning is the process of constructing meaning or structuring reality. It is necessarily a self-directed process contingent on individual choice and action.

The critical connection between democracy and education is that democratic social institutions are produced and sustained by the same progressive mechanism: the freedom to learn from experience, to build on experience, and to use this knowledge to direct the course of subsequent experience. Learning, individually or as a democratic society, is fundamentally contingent on freedom and self-governance: the ability to make choices and to take action, to formulate understandings and to test those understandings in actual experience.[4]

Formal education, as a system by which society transfers its knowledge and customs from generation to generation, generally does a poor job of teaching students how to learn, specifically a poor job of helping students to develop as self-directed learners, which is so critical in a rapidly changing world. The motivation we provide in school for learning is mostly external and driven by the belief that today's curriculum is essentially preparation for what comes next in the curriculum. But the curriculum is actually the total learning environment that we as educators create. For the future of each student's education, this environment is responsible for what he or she learns about learning. Cultivating the desire to learn is the single most important objective for any instructional strategy.

An often-quoted analysis of a major international study of science and mathematics education criticized the United States for a curriculum that is "a mile wide and an inch deep."[5] Nowhere is this more apparent than in our secondary schools, in which college preparation, including grades and test scores, is too often the only rationale for what and how we teach. In a curriculum that is always focused on what's next, there is little time to connect the subject matter and concepts to student experience. But it is precisely these connections that motivate and engage students and promote the joy of learning that feeds the desire to learn more.

The interests that teachers inspire often arise from their efforts to make the subject matter relevant. Schooling should focus on the connectedness of the subject matter to the student's life and world. The curriculum, as Dewey and others have argued, needs to connect in a meaningful way to the world in which our students live rather than rationalize its pace and content as necessary for the course and sequence ahead.

The primary mission of schooling should not be to prepare for the next grade level but to help students understand, to make sense of, and to be successful in their world today and tomorrow. The skills our students need now and in the future are acquired only through learning. It is learning that needs to be cultivated.

It is really that simple: the best curriculum is structured around helping students make sense of their world. This is a natural drive, a survival instinct that we all share. This does not require a radical change in today's curriculum, just a different mindset.

And the best learning happens under a democratic system, as our ever-maturing students increasingly assume the freedom and responsibility to make choices and direct their learning experiences. As teachers in a democratic society, we should cultivate a learning curriculum by empowering students to make sense of their world.

Notes

1. John Dewey, *Democracy and Education* (New York: Macmillan, 1916; reprint, 1944), p. 76.
2. Jean Piaget, *Science and the Psychology of the Child* (New York: Orion Press, 1970), p. 27.
3. Ulric Neisser, *Cognition and Reality* (San Francisco: W. H. Freeman, 1976).
4. William H. Garrison, "Democracy, Experience, and Education: Promoting a Continued Capacity for Growth," *Phi Delta Kappan*, March 2003, pp. 525–29.
5. A phrase employed by William Schmidt, director of the U.S. National Research Center for the Third International Mathematics and Science Study (TIMSS).

Assess Your Progress

1. When are students ready to accept personal responsibility for their learning? How might you assess their readiness?
2. Examine one of your lesson plans. Now, revise the lesson to support personal responsibility and democracy by providing at least two opportunities for student choice.

WILLIAM H. GARRISON is director of assessment and evaluation for the Palo Alto Unified School District, Palo Alto, Calif.

From *Phi Delta Kappan*, January 2008, pp. 347–348. Copyright © 2008 by Phi Delta Kappan. Reprinted by permission of the publisher and William Garrison.

UNIT 5

Addressing Diversity in Your School

Unit Selections

22. **Meeting Students Where They Are: The Latino Education Crisis,** Patricia Gándara
23. **What Does Research Say about Effective Practices for English Learners?,** Rhoda Coleman and Claude Goldenberg
24. **Becoming Adept at Code-Switching,** Rebecca S. Wheeler
25. **The Myth of the "Culture of Poverty,"** Paul Gorski
26. **Books That Portray Characters with Disabilities: A Top 25 List for Children and Young Adults,** Mary Anne Prater and Tina Taylor Dyches

Learning Outcomes

After reading this unit, you will be able to:

- Restate the issues and concerns regarding the academic outcomes of Latino students.
- Select strategies that would be helpful in your local school district's efforts to support Latino students.
- Explain the importance of knowing the academic language skills of the students who are ELL in your classroom.
- Consider which effective teaching practices suggested by Gandara would also be helpful for Latino students. Explain your answer.
- Describe code-switching.
- Explain the importance of code-switching to language acquisition and academic achievement.
- Create a code-switching chart to teach a formal English language pattern.
- Recognize myths about poverty that you have heard or read in public media, from friend, family or teachers, or public figures.
- Develop a strategy that you will use to combat popular myths about poverty.
- Apply research-based guidelines to evaluate books about people with disabilities.
- Select books to use in your classroom to teach acceptance of exceptionalities and diversity.
- Evaluate the ideas presented in this unit to develop classroom activities that stress acceptance and equity.

Student Website
www.mhhe.com/cls

Internet References

The Literacy Web
www.literacy.uconn.edu/index.htm

New Horizons for Learning
www.newhorizons.org

National Association for Multicultural Education (NAME)
www.nameorg.org/index.html

Everything ESL
www.everythingesl.net

The National Research Center on the Gifted and Talented
www.gifted.uconn.edu/nrcgt

Circle of Inclusion
www.circleofinclusion.org

Special Education Law Blog
www.specialedlaw.blogs.com

LD Online
www.ldonline.org

Council for Exceptional Children (CEC)
www.cec.sped.org

The concepts of culture and diversity encompass all the life ways, customs, traditions, and institutions that people develop as they create and experience their history and identity as a community. In the United States, very different cultures coexist within the civic framework of a shared constitutional tradition that guarantees equality before the law. So, many people are united as one nation by our constitutional heritage. Some of us are proud to say that we are a nation of immigrants. We are becoming more multicultural with every passing decade. Each of us is identified by our culture, language, and other socioeconomic factors in our society. However, as educators we have a unique opportunity. We are given the role to encourage and educate our diverse learners. The articles in this unit reflect upon all the concerns mentioned above.

The problem of high levels of poverty in urban and rural areas of our country is of great concern to American educators. One in four American children does not have all of his/her basic needs met, and lives under conditions of poverty. Almost one in three lives in a single-parent home, which in itself is no disadvantage, but under conditions of poverty, it often is. Children living in poverty are in crisis if their basic health and social needs are not adequately met, and their educational development can be affected by crises in their personal lives. We must teach and support these students and their families, even when it appears that they are not fully interested in their education. As a teacher, you may not have much control over the factors that shape the lives of our students. However, you can establish a classroom that is a place of care and nurture for your students, is multicultural-friendly, equitable, and free from bigotry, and where diverse students are not just tolerated but are wanted, welcomed, and accepted. Respect for all children and their capacity is the baseline for good teaching. Students must feel significant and cared for by all members of the classroom. Our diverse children should be exposed to an academically challenging curriculum that expects much from them and equips them for the real world.

On average, Latino students never perform as well as other students, not even in kindergarten. In some states the Latino school-age population has nearly doubled since 1987, and is approaching one-half of all students. Unfortunately these students are more likely to attend a hypersegregated school, where the population is 90–100% minority, and less likely to read or do math on grade level or earn a college degree. In fact they drop out of high school at higher rates than all other student population. After presenting these sad data, Gándara discusses ways in which this trend can be changed. In the end, she remarks that it is in our best interest to take action to help these students. Perhaps one reason Latinos are experiencing difficulty in our school is that we do not have enough teachers to help ELL. Included in this unit, Coleman and Goldenberg discuss the research on academic language proficiency. Learning academic language take several years longer than conversational language, however, sometimes teachers confuse the use of social or conversational language and assume that a student should be able to learn in English. Understanding this and what to do about teaching students who do not have strong academic English will help teachers know how to help ELL in their classes.

Gorski contends that there is no such thing as a *culture of poverty*. He addresses four stereotypes that may create inequality in how teachers respond to, work with, and teach students from impoverished circumstances. Most importantly he concludes that with a list of actions, teachers and others can take to address classism and end inequity. Casas shares her research-in-action with at-risk Mexican and Chicano students; many of whom had been recently released from a juvenile detention center. She notes the rise in student achievement when they were fully engaged in their own learning, used multicultural materials, and lessons were linked to their real-life experiences.

Wheeler summarizes research that suggests that teachers are not trained to understand the linguistic differences that exist in urban African Americans' daily language. This lack of understanding can cause teachers to think these students have reading and writing deficits. She presents a set of strategies to build on the informal language structures students already know and lead them to accurate use of Standard English. Code-switching is also a skill the students who are ELL must achieve as they move from home to school and from academic English to conversational English.

Diversity includes students who learn differently from their typical same-age peers. So we have included an article that could be helpful for general education teachers who want to help their students understand why Joey is using a Braille book, Billy is listening to an audio book, or Jamal is checking his blood sugar after recess. Prospective teachers often ask me, "What do I tell the other children about Joey's disability?" I always tell them to ask the school librarian to buy books that realistically portray students with disabilities in a variety of situations and use these in their teaching. In their article, Prater and Dyches have constructed a list of award winning books that include both text content and pictures about children and youth with disabilities. Teachers and parents will find these books well written, with positive examples of students with disabilities and teachers will find them useful for teaching their student how others live with disabilities.

Article 22

Meeting Students Where They Are: The Latino Education Crisis

PATRICIA GÁNDARA

They're the fastest-growing ethnic group but the most poorly educated. Do we have what it takes to close the gap?

From their first day of kindergarten to their last day of school, Latinos, on average, perform far below most of their peers. They now constitute the largest minority group in the United States and the fastest growing segment of its school-age population. As such, they are inextricably bound up with the nation's future.

The Latino public school population nearly doubled between 1987 and 2007, increasing from 11 to 21 percent of all U.S. students (National Center for Education Statistics [NCES], 2009b). The U.S. Census Bureau predicts that by 2021, one of four U.S. students will be Latino. In key states in the U.S. Southwest, such as Texas and California, the Latino school-age population is already approaching one-half of all students. In these states, the future is already here.

But it's a troubling picture. Latinos are the least educated of all major ethnic groups (see Figure 1). Although a large gap exists between the college completion rates of whites and blacks, both groups show steady growth. However, the growth in college degrees for Latinos is almost flat. The failure over more than three decades to make any progress in moving more Latino students successfully through college suggests that what we have been doing to close achievement gaps is not working. This fact has enormous consequences for the United States, as the job market continues to demand more education and Latinos continue to make up a larger and larger portion of the workforce.

Behind at the Start

Can schools close these gaps? It is instructive to look back to the first days of schooling to see the differences that exist at that point. Data from the 1998 Early Childhood Longitudinal Study show that only one-half as many Latino children as white children fall into the highest quartile of math and reading skills at the *beginning* of kindergarten, and more than twice as many fall into the lowest quartile. The gap is even wider between Latino and Asian students (see Figure. 2).

Figure 1 Bachelor's Degree Completion by Ethnicity

	Year				
Ethnicity	1975	1985	1995	2005	2008
White	24	24	29	34	37
Black	11	12	15	18	21
Latino	9	11	9	11	12

The figures represent the percentage of 25- to 29-year-olds in the United States who completed a bachelor's degree or higher.

Source: *Current Population Survey (CPS), Annual Social and Economic Study Supplement,* 1971–2005, previously unpublished tabulation, November 2005, and *American Community Survey 2008,* by U.S. Census Bureau, Washington, DC: U.S. Department of Commerce.

Figure 2 Percentage of Kindergartners Scoring at Highest and Lowest Quartiles, on the 1998 Early Childhood Longitudinal Study

	Reading		Math	
Ethnic Group	Highest Quartile	Lowest Quartile	Highest Quartile	Lowest Quartile
White	30	18	32	18
Asian	39	13	38	13
Black	15	34	10	39
Latino	15	42	14	40
Native American	9	57	9	50

Source: *America's Kindergartners: Findings from the Early Childhood Longitudinal Study,* by J. West, K. Denton, and E. Germino-Hausken, 2000, Washington, DC: National Center for Education Statistics.

Access to preschool education, of which Latino children have less than any other major group (NCES, 2009a), contributes to some of this early gap, but it cannot account for all of it. The evidence shows that poverty is the culprit. Young Latino children are more than twice as likely to be poor as white children and are even more likely to be among the poorest of the poor. At least one-third of Latino families lack health insurance; many Latino children rarely see a doctor, dentist, or optometrist, and so they often go to school with toothaches, uncorrected vision problems, and untreated chronic health problems (Berliner, 2009). Many also go to school hungry. These all constitute serious impediments to learning that schools are often poorly equipped to address.

Latino students are many more times as likely as students from other ethnic groups to come from homes where parents do not speak English well—or at all— and where parental education is low. More than 40 percent of Latina mothers lack even a high school diploma, compared with only 6 percent of white mothers; and only about 10 percent of Latina mothers have a college degree or higher, compared with almost one-third of white mothers (see Figure 3). Although Latino students may come from loving homes, limited education and resources do affect their education outcomes. There is no better predictor of how well children will fare in school than parents' education attainment (Murnane, Maynard, & Ohls, 1981).

It is difficult for parents to impart to their children experiences and knowledge that they do not have. Many studies have shown that school benefits poor children more than middle-class children (Alexander, Entwisle, & Olsen, 1997; Coleman, 1966); in the case of poor children, schools offer what parents cannot, whereas for middle-class children, school supplements what the home and community routinely offer. Under the right conditions, schools could conceivably close the gaps for Latino children, but the schools that serve most Latino students today have not met those conditions.

Figure 3 Mother's Education Level by Ethnicity

Ethnicity	Less than High School	High School	Bachelor's Degree or Higher
Latino	41.3%	28.6%	9.9%
White	5.9%	29.0%	31.7%
Black	18.2%	34.4%	15.3%
Asian	16%	22.2%	44.7%

Asian percentages were based on a small sample, so they may not be entirely representative.

Source: *Current Population Survey (CPS), Annual Social and Economic Study Supplement, 1971–2005,* previously unpublished tabulation, by U.S. Census Bureau, 2005, Washington, DC: U.S. Department of Commerce. Available: http://nces.ed.gov/pubs2007/minoritytrends/tables/table_5.asp

Segregated from the Mainstream

In the United States as a whole, Latinos are slightly more likely than black students (39.5 percent vs. 38.3 percent) to attend hypersegregated schools—those that are 90 to 100 percent nonwhite. In the large central cities in the west, more than 60 percent of Latinos attend hypersegregated schools (Orfield & Frankenberg, 2008).

This means that many Latino students lack access to peers from the mainstream U.S. culture, which inhibits their understanding of the norms, standards, and expectations of the broader society. For example, these students may rarely come into contact with anyone who has gone to college or who intends to go, so the aspirations and knowledge about getting to college never develop. It also means that Latino students are likely to attend underresourced schools with poorer facilities and less-qualified teachers than mainstream students experience.

The Need for Comprehensive Support

Factors like health care; intense neighborhood segregation (which results in school segregation); and the language and resources of the family may seem beyond the scope of what most schools can reasonably address. But other factors— such as teacher quality, school facilities and resources, and a rich curriculum—are very much within the purview of schools.

One key to successfully meeting Latino students' needs is to conceptualize our efforts as a *continuum* of interventions rather than discrete interventions; according to the literature, the effect of a single intervention tends to fade in the absence of sustained supportive environments. Preschool won't, on its own, permanently narrow or close achievement gaps, just as the effects of an intervention in elementary school will probably not last through high school.

The evidence suggests that a continuing net of support for disadvantaged students is likely to significantly improve their academic outcomes and reduce the wide gaps in achievement that now exist. It follows that under these conditions, students will be more likely to graduate from high school and successfully prepare for college.

A Focus on Early Childhood

If Latino children are going to catch up with their more-advantaged peers, they must have access to high-quality preschool. We have never been successful in closing these achievement gaps after students are in elementary school.

A number of studies have demonstrated the effectiveness of high-quality Head Start–type programs that provide comprehensive services to students and their families.

The research on Head Start has demonstrated "moderate effects on pre-academic skills, greater parental awareness of the needs of their children and increased skills in meeting those needs, and provision of health and nutrition services and information" (Gándara & Contreras, 2009, p. 259). Of course, once children leave Head Start, they also lose the health and family support services that are so important for many low-income Latino students.

In his study of Oklahoma's universal preschool program, Gormley (2008) documented that Latino students benefited more than any other category of student from attending preschool. In both reading and math readiness, the Latinos in the program performed approximately one year above those Latino students who did not attend preschool. Students in full-day kindergarten also outperformed those who attended a half-day program. The researchers attributed the score gains to the policy of hiring fully credentialed teachers and paying them at the same salary level as other teachers. The teachers not only were competent, but also were likely to stay and build strong programs at the center over time. Other researchers have found similar gains for low-income preschool students in high-quality programs (Karoly et al., 1998).

The single biggest argument against providing universal preschool—apart from its cost—is that research has shown that the positive effects are not sustained for many students; students show an initial rise in test scores that seems to disappear after one or two years of school (Currie & Thomas, 1995). However, researchers have argued that this is probably because the schools these students attend are too weak to sustain the positive effects of preschool. Research has also shown that students' environments outside school probably contribute more to schooling outcomes than in-school factors do. Compared with all other developed nations of the world, the United States provides the weakest safety net for its low-income students and their families (Rainwater & Smeeding, 2005). This surely contributes to the erosion of positive effects of schooling interventions.

A Focus on K–12 Supports

To sustain the effects of early interventions, it is crucial to strengthen the capacity of K–12 schools to monitor and support students once they arrive at school. Some programs, such as Project GRAD (www.projectgrad.org), have attempted to bundle research-based interventions that follow students as a cohort through their K–12 years. These include well-established programs, such as the University of Chicago School Mathematics Project (http://ucsmp.uchicago.edu) and Success for All (www.successforall.net). In fact, consistent with other studies, the Success for All researchers found good outcomes for Spanish-speaking students in their regular English curriculum but superior outcomes using their bilingual curriculum (Slavin & Cheung, 2005).

Although Project GRAD takes a whole-school reform approach, it also monitors students and their progress. Recent findings indicate that students who stay in the program longer appear to benefit the most and that careful monitoring of individual students is central to the effectiveness of education interventions (Gándara & Bial, 2001).

Dual-Language and Two-Way Immersion Programs

Programs promoting bilingualism have been found to produce superior academic outcomes for both Latino students whose first language is Spanish and for non-Spanish speakers, while also developing a strong competence in a second language (see Genesee, Lindholm-Leary, Saunders, & Christian, 2006). Such programs, whose goal is to transform monolingual speakers of either English or Spanish into fully bilingual and biliterate students, have mushroomed in recent years. Because the programs give equal status to both languages and typically enroll Latino students alongside non-Latino students, they have the additional advantage of fostering positive intergroup relations and increasing Latino students' social capital, as the Latino students are fully integrated with their middle-class peers (Morales & Aldana, 2010). These programs usually have long waiting lists.

Magnet Schools

Magnet schools often specialize in a specific field, such as medicine, the arts, or science. A number of studies have shown that in addition to benefitting from a more desegregated schooling experience, magnet school students tend to outperform students in regular public and private schools in both reading and math scores on standardized tests (Frankenberg & Seigel-Hawley, 2008).

Dropout Prevention and College-Going Programs

High school programs that focus on immediate issues such as dropout prevention and college-going tend to be more successful for Latino youth than those with less focused goals. Effective programs tend to share five components (Gándara & Bial, 2001). They (1) provide at least one key person whose job it is to know, connect with, and monitor the progress of each student; (2) structure a supportive peer group that reinforces program goals; (3) provide access to strong curriculum that leads to college preparation; (4) attend to students' cultural backgrounds; and (5) show students how they can finance their education, providing scholarships when possible.

One high school program that focuses specifically on preparing Latino students for college is the Puente Project, which is active in 36 California high schools. Through a school support team, the program provides a net of services: two years of intensive college-preparatory English, focusing on writing skills and incorporating Latino literature;

intensive college counseling; and a mentor from the community who acts as a guide and role model. The program has doubled the college-going of participating students and has motivated them to attend more selective schools. This is important because Latino students tend to enroll in less selective colleges than they qualify for (Fry, 2004), and students who attend more selective schools tend to have higher graduation rates (Sigal & Tienda, 2005). Key to the success of the program is its strong adult-student connections and the availability of a counselor to advocate for the students.

School Attachment and Belonging

Latino students' extraordinarily high dropout rate is related, in part, to their lack of attachment to school and a sense of not belonging. A crucial means by which students attach to school and form supportive friendship groups is through extracurricular activities—sports, band, newspaper, and other clubs. Unfortunately, Latino students are less likely to participate in these activities, either because they perceive the club to be exclusive or due to logistical problems, like needing to work or help out after school or not having transportation to and from the activity. Latino students' lack of participation is also related to their lack of inclusion in the same circles as their middle-class peers who have a way of being invited into these activities.

Schools that address this issue find ways to incorporate clubs, sports, and other activities into school routines and bring the benefit of these activities into the classroom. For example, some schools mix students in heterogeneous classes and create conditions for students from different groups to interact in conditions in which they are more equal in status (see Gibson, Gándara, & Koyama, 2004).

How School-Community Partnerships Can Help

Schools alone cannot close the yawning gaps in achievement. But schools can partner with other institutions to help narrow those gaps. Collaboration in the following three areas can make a significant difference for many Latino students.

- *Create magnet schools that appeal to middle-class parents.* Some interventions are not costly in terms of dollars but require spending political capital. For example, in gentrifying areas of the inner cities, we could attack the problem of neighborhood and school segregation through thoughtful and progressive planning. The apartments that have sprung up in formerly downtrodden areas typically market to professional single people and young couples without children—the assumption being that young families do not want to live in the city center. We need to create attractive options by offering desegregated, high-quality schools adjacent to open spaces that could serve both the families of young professionals and inner-city residents. Because dual-language programs often appeal to middle-class parents, it would make sense to include such programs as features of new inner-city magnet schools.

- *Work with health and social service agencies.* Because access to health care and social services is an acute problem for Latino families, schools should be the primary contact for these kinds of services for youth. The Center for Health and Health Care in Schools (n.d.) reports that in 2006, there were more than 1,800 school-based health centers around the United States, providing care for children who might otherwise not have been able to access it. Although this is an encouraging number, it represents a small fraction of U.S. schools that serve low-income students and Latinos.

  An evaluation of California's Healthy Start Program, which provides integrated services primarily to Latino children and families, showed that it reduced needs for food, clothing, transportation, and medical and dental care; improved clients' emotional health and family functioning; reduced teen risk behaviors; modestly improved grade point averages; and reduced student mobility (Wagner & Golan, 1996). Nevertheless, the program has progressively lost funding.
  One study found that such programs are difficult to operate because of the need to integrate many services that compete with one another for dollars (Romualdi, 2000). However, if we can stabilize funding, these programs can make a big difference in the lives of Latino children. Placing medical, dental, and social services in an accessible, safe place makes sense if the goal is to help schools do their job of teaching these students. Critics have argued against the "effectiveness" of these centers, in part because research has failed to show that they significantly raise standardized test scores. But children who arrive at school with basic health, emotional, and nutritional needs unmet are not ready to learn. It only makes sense to evaluate the centers on their primary mission—healthier developmental outcomes for children that ultimately lead to better opportunities to learn. Moreover, if such programs can create family attachments to a school, thereby reducing student mobility, this could result in long-term benefits for Latino students.

- *Reach out to parents in culturally appropriate ways.* Many studies have shown that a primary reason that

Latino students do not complete college degrees is because they don't understand how to prepare for college or even why they should attend. Their parents, who have often not completed high school in the United States, are even less familiar with these issues.

However, given the opportunity, most parents are eager to help their children succeed in school. One example of an effective program designed specifically for Latino immigrant parents is the Parent Institute for Quality Education (PIQE). Founded in San Diego, California, in 1987 but now operating in both Washington, D.C., and Texas, PIQE teaches parents, in nine weekly evening sessions, how to monitor their children's progress, advocate on their behalf, and prepare them for college. Many of the staff members who run the program were once parent participants. One evaluation of the program found that participating parents read more with their children and understood more about how they could support their children's education (Chrispeels, Wang, & Rivero, 2000).

Doing Whatever It Takes

No silver bullet or single program can close the enormous gap between Latino students and their peers with respect to academic achievement and attainment. But it's in all of our interests to find ways to begin the process of narrowing those gaps. This will require the collaborative efforts of both schools and social service agencies. It will also take the political courage to acknowledge that schools cannot do this alone—and that the rest of society will need to step up to the challenge.

References

Alexander, K., Entwisle, D., & Olsen, L. (1997). *Children, schools, and inequality.* Boulder, CO: Westview Press.

Berliner, D. (2009). *Poverty and potential: Out-of-school factors and school success.* Boulder, CO, and Tempe, AZ: Education and the Public Interest Center.

Center for Health and Health Care in Schools. (n.d.). *Health services.* Available: www.healthinschools.org/Health-in-Schools/Health-Services.aspx

Chrispeels, J., Wang, J., & Rivero, E. (2000). *Evaluation summary of the impact of the Parent Institute for Quality Education on parent's engagement with their children's schooling.* Available: www.piqe.org/Assets/Home/ChrispeelEvaluation.htm

Coleman, J. (1966). *Equality of educational opportunity.* Washington, DC: U.S. Government Printing Office.

Currie, J., & Thomas, D. (1995). Does Head Start make a difference? *American Economic Review, 85,* 341–364.

Frankenberg, E., & Seigel-Hawley, G. (2008). *Rethinking magnet schools in a changing landscape.* Los Angeles: Civil Rights Project/Proyecto Derechos Civiles.

Fry, R. (2004). *Latino youth finishing college: The role of selective pathways.* Washington, DC: Pew Hispanic Center. Available: http://pewhispanic.org/reports/report.php?ReportID=30

Gándara, P., & Bial, D. (2001). *Paving the way to postsecondary education.* Washington DC: National Center for Education Statistics.

Gándara P., & Contreras, F. (2009). *The Latino education crisis: The consequences of failed social policies.* Cambridge, MA: Harvard University Press.

Genesee, F., Lindholm-Leary, K., Saunders, W., & Christian, D. (2006). *Educating English language learners: A synthesis of research evidence.* New York: Cambridge University Press.

Gibson, M., Gándara, P., & Koyama, J. (Eds.). (2004). *School connections: U.S. Mexican youth, peers, and school achievement.* New York: Teachers College Press.

Gormley, W. (2008). The effects of Oklahoma's pre-K program on Hispanic children. *Social Science Quarterly, 89,* 916–936.

Karoly, L. A., Greenwood, P. W., Everingham, S. S., Hoube, J., Kilburn, M. R., Rydell, C. P., Sanders, M., et al.(1998). *Investing in our children: What we know and don't know about the costs and benefits of early childhood interventions.* Santa Monica, CA: RAND.

Morales, P. Z., & Aldana, U. (2010). Learning in two languages: Programs with political promise. In P. Gándara & M. Hopkins (Eds.), *Forbidden language: English learners and restrictive language policies.* New York: Teachers College Press.

Murnane, R., Maynard, R., & Ohls, J. (1981). Home resources and children's achievement. *The Review of Economics and Statistics, 63*(3), 369–377.

National Center for Education Statistics. (2009a). *The condition of education.* Washington, DC: U.S. Department of Education.

National Center for Education Statistics. (2009b). Racial/ethnic enrollment in public schools. Indicator 7. In *The condition of education.* Washington, DC: U.S. Department of Education.

Orfield, G., & Frankenberg, E. (2008). *The last have become first: Rural and small town America lead the way of desegregation.* Los Angeles: UCLA Civil Rights Project/Proyecto Derechez Civiles.

Rainwater, L., & Smeeding, T. (2005). *Poor kids in a rich country: America's children in comparative perspective.* New York: Russell Sage.

Romualdi, E. V. (2000). Shared dream: A case study of the implementation of Healthy Start (California). (Doctoral dissertation, University of California, Davis). *Dissertation Abstracts International, 61*(09). (UMI No. 9315947).

Sigal, A., & Tienda, M. (2005). Assessing the mismatch hypothesis: Differentials in college graduation rates by institutional selectivity. *Sociology of Education, 78*(4), 294–315.

Slavin, R., & Cheung, A. (2005). A synthesis of research on language of reading instruction for English language learners. *Review of Educational Research, 75,* 247–284.

Wagner, M., & Golan, S. (1996). *California's Healthy Start school-linked services initiative: Summary of evaluation findings.* Menlo Park, CA: SRI International.

Assess Your Progress

1. What is the crisis? How will this crisis impact the communities with high Latino populations?
2. What are the potential social and educational implications of the high dropout rates for Latino students?
3. Which of the strategies mentioned by Gandara do you think would be most effective in your community? Explain your choice and why you think it is best for your community?

Patricia Gándara is Professor of Education at University of California, Los Angeles, and Codirector of the Civil Rights Project. She is the coauthor, with Frances Contreras, of *The Latino Education Crisis: The Consequences of Failed Social Policies* (Harvard University Press, 2009).

From *Educational Leadership*, February 2010, pp. 24–30. Copyright © 2010 by ASCD. Reprinted by permission. The Association for Supervision and Curriculum Development is a worldwide community of educators advocating sound policies and sharing best practices to achieve the success of each learner. To learn more, visit ASCD at www.ascd.org.

Article 23

What Does Research Say about Effective Practices for English Learners?

PART II: Academic Language Proficiency.

Rhoda Coleman and Claude Goldenberg

Using strategies and techniques that make academic content more accessible, classroom teachers can help ELL students keep pace academically.

This is the second in a four-part series written exclusively for the Kappa Delta Pi Record. Each article summarizes what research says about effective practices for ELL. The authors draw on several recent reviews of the research (August and Shanahan 2006; Genesee et al. 2006; Goldenberg 2008; Saunders and Goldenberg, in press). The fust article in the series (which appeared in the Fall 2009 Record) covered research on English oral language instruction. This, the second article, deals with academic language and literacy in English. Article three Record Spring 2010) takes this research into practice by describing an observation tool (the CQeII) that is useful for planning and coaching teachers who want to implement effective strategies in their classrooms. The final article (Record Summer 2010) is about school and district reform and offers practical recommendations for administrators and teacher leaders so that the research can more readily translate into practice.

Academic language is a vital part of content-area instruction and is one of the most pressing needs faced by English Language Learners (ELLs). The fundamental challenge ELLs in all-English instruction face is learning academic content while simultaneously becoming proficient in English. Because of this challenge, we, as educators, do not know to what extent ELLs can keep pace academically with English speakers; nonetheless, our goal should be to make academic content as accessible as possible for these students and promote English language development as students learn academic content.

Academic language differs from everyday language and knowing the differences is important for effective academic instruction. Academic language refers to the sort of language competence required for students to gain access to content taught in English and, more generally, for success in school and any career where mastering large and complex bodies of information and concepts is needed (Fillmore and Snow 2000). Academic language, the language of texts and formal writing, is different from everyday speech and conversation, what Cummins (1984) has referred to as Basic Interpersonal Communication Skills (BICS). BICS, in general, is language used for communication skills in everyday social interactions. In contrast, Cognitive Academic Language Proficiency (CALP) is the oral and written language related to literacy and academic achievement (Cummins 1984).

The terms BICS and CALP have somewhat fallen out of favor, in part because they imply a hard dichotomy that might be misleading. There is likely to be a great deal of grey area, where language has both conversational and academic elements. Nonetheless, BICS and CALP identify a useful distinction between (a) language that is relatively informal, contextualized, cognitively less demanding, used in most social interactions, and generally learned more easily; and (b) language that is more formal, abstract, used in academic and explicit teaching/learning situations, more demanding cognitively, and more challenging to learn.

Fluency in academic language is especially critical for academic achievement. Knowledge of academic disciplines—science, social studies, history, mathematics-is, of course, the primary objective of content-area instruction. Just as important is the language needed to learn about and discuss academic content. Most ELLs eventually acquire adequate conversational language skills, but they often lack the academic language skills that are essential for high levels of achievement in the content areas.

Educators must focus on the academic language needed for academic achievement. Yet, we are lacking a solid research base that identifies effective techniques and approaches. There are, however, promising directions—e.g., Dutro and Moran (2003), Schleppegrell (2001); Lyster (2007), and Zwiers (2008). Educators are strongly encouraged to learn about them, implement them in their classrooms, and try to determine which best meet the needs of English learners.

For both oral and academic language, students need to be taught expressive as well as receptive language.

Article 23. What Does Research Say about Effective Practices for English Learners?

Using sheltered instruction strategies makes grade-level academic content comprehensible; that is, students develop receptive language in order to comprehend or, at least, get the gist of a lesson. From this type of instruction, students do not necessarily develop expressive language so that they can speak and write in the language. Students need to be taught expressive language—"comprehensible output" (Swain 1985)—so that they can answer questions, participate in discussions, and be successful at showing what they know on assessments.

Because content instruction may be an excellent opportunity to teach language skills in a meaningful context, teachers may integrate both types of instruction throughout the day. There is no reason to believe these types of instruction are mutually exclusive. This support for ELLs in the general classroom may be offered in addition to a separate English Language Development (ELD) block.

Academic and conversational English are different . . . and similar!

It is important to note that there is a connection between conversational and academic language; they are not completely distinct from each other. Using students' everyday experiences can help students learn academic language. That is, if students are familiar with a task in a social context, they may be able to adopt appropriate language from that task and transfer it to school-based tasks.

For example, a student might know how to retell what happened on a favorite television show or present an argument for why he should be able to go out and play basketball at the park. Accordingly, that student may be able to transfer the language he or she uses to express cause and effect regarding behavior and consequences to a science experiment, an if-then hypothesis structure, or a historical sequence of causally linked events. If a student can compare and contrast dogs and cats, this same structure applies to comparing and contrasting two systems of government. To help students make these language connections, teachers should bring this skill to a conscious level. Though students may be able to make comparisons in their everyday life, they may need to learn how these structures are transferable to school-based situations. There is not a clear line separating conversational from academic language. describes the differences between conversational and academic language and also shows the grey area where the two overlap. Categories used in the table are based on Goldenberg and Coleman (in press).

Academic language instruction should include not only the vocabulary of the content subjects, but also the syntax and text structures. Schleppegrell (2001) distinguished between academic language and everyday speech and explained how academic language is about so much more than learning content-specific, or technical, vocabulary. Students may know the meanings of individual content-specific words, yet still not be able to understand the larger meaning when reading them in a sentence or be able to combine them to write a sentence.

Academic language and curriculum content are closely intertwined. It is not sufficient for a student to comprehend only text and teacher-talk well—that is, to have receptive understanding. The student also must be able to express his or her complete thoughts orally and in writing using academic language. For example, students need to understand how to construct a sentence or paragraph (orally and in writing) that expresses compare/contrast or cause and effect (Dutro and Moran 2003).

Language development and sheltering techniques should be incorporated into content instruction.

Sheltered instruction strategies, or SDAIE (Specially Designed Academic Instruction in English), provide comprehensible input for any content area. The term comprehensible input refers to strategies that enable ELLs to understand the essence of a lesson by means of context or visual cues, clarification, and building background knowledge that draws on students' experiences (Krashen and Tenell 1983).

What is often overlooked is that sheltered instruction calls for all lessons to have clearly stated language objectives in addition to providing comprehensible input. Short (1994) discussed the importance of explicit language instruction along with content-area instruction. She advocated developing language objectives in addition to content-area objectives for ELLs to provide them access to the core curriculum. The SIOP model for making content comprehensible to English Learners also emphasizes the need for a language objective along with a content objective (Echevarria, Vogt, and Short 2008) and suggests the language goals be adjusted for the students' proficiency levels (Genesee et al. 2006, 191).

For example, students studying how the saguaro cactus survives in the desert in science (content objective) have a language objective of writing cause-and-effect sentences using signal words "because" and "as a result of." For example, "Because its accordian skin holds water, the saguaro cactus can survive in the desert." and "As a result of its shallow roots, which capture surface water, the saguaro cactus can survive in the desert." A social studies teacher having students interview a grandparent or other elder to learn about the past can instruct students on how to correctly phrase interview questions (language objective). An English teacher having students write about setting (content objective) can use this as an opportunity to teach a lesson on adjectives (language objective). However, the language objectives, like the content objectives, should not be chosen randomly. They should be selected based on the proficiency level and grade level standards appropriate to the students.

Educators must take care that ELD does not displace instruction in academic content. Content-based ELD, which is driven by the ELD standards, does not replace content instruction driven by the content standards. In other words, just because an ELD lesson is about a science topic does not mean it meets the requirements for standards-based science instruction in that grade level. A sheltered lesson makes standards-based content instruction accessible. A content-based ELD lesson has language as a focus, but uses a content area as the medium. This type of lesson is not the same as standards-based content instruction.

Closing Thoughts

Most ELLs take years to develop the level of academic English proficiency required for full participation in all English classrooms (Genesee et al. 2006). It does not take much imagination to conclude that if (a) students are functioning at less than high levels of English proficiency; and (b) instruction is offered only in mainstream academic English, these students will not have access to the core academic curriculum. They will have virtually no chance of performing at a level similar to that of their English speaking peers. Whether students are in primary language (that is, "bilingual") or English-only programs, educators must focus intensively on providing them with the academic language skills in English they will need to succeed in school and beyond.

To move this discussion from research to practice, let's take a look at a scenario that incorporates some of these recommendations. This is an actual lesson taught by a 5th-grade teacher.

Elementary Academic Instruction

Mrs. C is teaching a 5th grade social studies lesson on immigration. ELD levels range from early intermediate to fluent English. The language objective is for students to write cause-and-effect sentences about the immigrant experience—e.g., "Because we wanted a better life, my family immigrated to the United States" or "My family immigrated to the United States because we wanted a better life." This lesson is designed to motivate interest in and build background for a chapter on immigration in the history textbook that students will read later.

Before students read the state-adopted history textbook, Mrs. C looks for key passages. She analyzes them for any words, phrases, or concepts that may need clarification and any concepts for which she may need to build background knowledge. She also looks for supportive visuals in the textbook, such as charts, graphs, maps, and photos.

Mrs. C begins the lesson by sharing pictures of her family members who were immigrants. Next she puts on a babushka (Russian for scarf) and a long skirt and becomes her own immigrant grandmother. Speaking in the first person, she tells the story of when, how, and why she came to America. She points to Russia on a map. As she tells her story, "grandmother" holds up vocabulary cards with the words immigrant, motivation, perspective, ancestor, and descendant, and she uses each word in context. For example, "I am an immigrant from Russia. I used to live in Russia, but I came to live in America. My motivation or reason for coming to America was . . ."

Students are then invited to interview her—that is, ask her questions—in preparation for their assignment to interview an immigrant. The person can be a family member or, if that is not practical, a neighbor or teacher. The students and Mrs. C. discuss possible interview questions, using the target vocabulary words, and decide: "From what country did you immigrate to the United States? When did you arrive? What are some things you remember about that experience? What was your motivation for coming/leaving? What was your perspective, or how did you feel about immigrating?" When the students return with their interview responses, Mrs. C records them on a graphic organizer with these headings: Person, Country, Motivation for Immigrating, and Perspective.

Mrs. C models how to turn the answers into cause-and-effect statements, using sentence frames:

_____ because _____.

Because _____, _____.

Students respond with sentences orally and in writing—such as.

My great-grandmother immigrated to the United States from Russia in 1903 because she wanted religious freedom. My grandmother likes it here because she can attend a synagogue.

Because of the potato famine, my ancestors immigrated to the United States from Ireland. They were sad because they had to leave some family members behind.

References

August, D., and T. Shanahan, eds. 2006. Developing literacy in second-language learners: Report of the National Literacy Panel on Language Minority Children and Youth. Mahwah, NJ: Erlbaum.

Cummins, J. I 984. Wanted: A theoretical framework for relating language proficiency to academic achievement among bilingual students. In Language proficiency and academic achievement, ed. C. Rivera, 2–I9. Clevedon, Avon, England: Multilingual Matters.

Dutro, S. 2005. A focused approach to frontloading English language instruction for Houghton Mifflin reading, K-6, 4th ed., Califomia Reading St Literature Project. Santa Cruz, CA: ToucanEd.

Dutro, S., and C. Moran. 2003. Rethinking English language instruction: An architectural approach. In English learners: Reaching the highest level of English literacy, ed. G. C. Garcia, 227–58. Newark, DE: International Reading Association.

Echevarra, J., M. Vogt, and D. Short. 2008. Making content comprehensible for English Leamers: The SIOP* model, 3rd ed. Needham Heights, MA: Allyn St Bacon.

Fillmore, L. W., and C. E. Snow. 2000. What teachers need to know about language. In What teachers need to know about language, ed. C. T. Adger, C. E. Snow, and D. Christian, 7–53. Washington, DC: Center for Applied Linguistics.

Genesee, F., K.Lindholm-Leary, W. M. Saunders, and D. Christian. 2006. Educating English Language Learners. New York: Cambridge University Press.

Goldenberg, C. 2008. Teaching English Language Leamers: What the research does- and does not- say. American Educator 32(2): 8–23,42–44.

Goldenberg, C, and R. Coleman. In press. Promoting academic achievement among English learners. Thousand Oaks, CA: Corwin.

Krashen, S. D., and T. D. Terrell. 1983. The natural approach: Language acquisition in the classroom. Hayward, CA: Alemany Press.

Lyster, R. 2007. Learning and teaching languages through content: A counterbalanced approach. Philadelphia, PA: John Benjamins Pub.

Saunders, W. M., and C. Goldenberg, C. in press. Research to guide English Language Development instruction. In Improving education for English Learners: Research-based approaches, ed. D. Dolson and L. Burnham-Massey. Sacramento, CA: CDE Press.

Schleppegrell, M. J. 2001. Linguistic features of the language of schooling. Linguistics and Education 12(4): 431–59.

Short, D. J. 1994. Expanding middle school horizons: Integrating language, culture, and social studies. TESOL Quarterly 28(3): 581–608.

Swain M. 1985. Communicative competence: Some roles of comprehensible input and comprehensible output in its development. In Input in second language acquisition, ed. S. M. Gass and C. G. Madden, 235–56. Rowley, MA: Newberry House Publishers.

Zwiers, J. 2008. Building academic language: Essential practices for content classrooms, grades S-l 2. San Francisco, CA: Jossey-Bass.

Rhoda Coleman is Research Fellow at The Center for Language Minority Education and Research at California State University, Long Beach, where she also teaches in the College of Education. She was a California State Teacher of the Year and Milken recipient.

Claude Coldenberg is Professor of Education at Stanford University. His research focuses on academic achievement among English learners. He was on the Committee for the Prevention of Early Reading Difficulties in Young Children and the National Literacy Panel.

Portions of this article are based on the authors' forthcoming book Promoting Academic Achievement among English Learners, to be published by Corwin Press in 2011, and are used with permission.

Assess Your Progress

1. Summarize the research presented in this article.
2. Create a resource file of teaching strategies or methods and materials that you can use to teach linguistically or culturally diverse students.
3. What are the positive effects of diversity in our schools? Provide rationales for your challenges based on the articles in this unit.

COLEMAN, RHODA *"What Does Research Say about Effective Practices for ENGLISH LEARNERS?"*. Kappa Delta Pi Record. Find-Articles.com. 30 Mar, 2010. http://findarticles.com/p/articles/mi_qa4009/is_201001/ai_n45882227/

From *Kappa Delta Pi Record* by Rhoda Coleman and Claude Goldenberg, Winter 2010. Copyright © 2010 by Kappa Delta Pi. Reprinted by permission.

Article 24

Becoming Adept at Code-Switching

By putting away the red pen and providing structured instruction in code-switching, teachers can help urban African American students use language more effectively.

REBECCA S. WHEELER

It was September, and Joni was concerned. Her 2nd grade student Tamisha could neither read nor write; she was already a grade behind. What had happened? Joni sought out Melinda, Tamisha's 1st grade teacher. Melinda's answer stopped her in her tracks. "Tamisha? Why, you can't do *anything* with that child. Haven't you heard how she talks?" Joni pursued, "What *did* you do with her last year?" "Oh, I put her in the corner with a coloring book." Incredulous, Joni asked, "All year?" "Yes," the teacher replied.

Although extreme, Melinda's appraisal of Tamisha's performance and potential as a learner is not isolated. In standardized assessments of language acquisition, teachers routinely underrate the language knowledge and the reading and writing performance of African American students (Cazden, 2001; Ferguson, 1998; Godley, Sweetland, Wheeler, Minnici, & Carpenter, 2006; Scott & Smitherman, 1985). A typical reading readiness task asks the student to read five sentences (*The mouse runs. The cat runs. The dog runs. The man runs. Run, mouse, run!*). As Jamal reads, *Da mouse run. Da cat run. Da dog run. Da man run. Run, mouse, run,* his teacher notes 8/15 errors, placing him far below the frustration level of 3/15. She assesses Jamal as a struggling reader and puts him in a low reading group or refers him to special education.

Through a traditional language arts lens, Tamisha's 1st grade teacher saw "broken English" and a broken child. Through the same lens, Jamal's teacher heard mistakes in Standard English and diagnosed a reading deficit. These teachers' lack of linguistic background in the dialects their students speak helps explain why African American students perform below their white peers on every measure of academic achievement, from persistent over-representation in special education and remedial basic skills classes, to under-representation in honors classes, to lagging SAT scores, to low high school graduation rates (Ogbu, 2003).

Across the United States, teacher education and professional development programs fail to equip teachers to respond adequately to the needs of many African American learners. We know that today's world "demands a new way of looking at teaching that is grounded in an understanding of the role of culture and language in learning" (Villegas & Lucas, 2007, p. 29). Unfortunately, many teachers lack the linguistic training required to build on the language skills that African American students from dialectally diverse backgrounds bring to school. To fill this need, elementary educator Rachel Swords and I have developed a program for teaching Standard English to African American students in urban classrooms (Wheeler & Swords, 2006). One linguistic insight and three strategies provide a framework for responding to these students' grammar needs.

One Linguistic Insight

When African American students write *I have two sister and two brother, My Dad jeep is out of gas,* or *My mom deserve a good job,* teachers traditionally diagnose "poor English" and conclude that the students are making errors with plurality, possession, or verb agreement. In response, teachers correct the students' writing and show them the "right" grammar.

Research has amply demonstrated that such traditional correction methods fail to teach students the Standard English writing skills they need (Adger, Wolfram, & Christian, 2007). Further, research has found strong connections among teachers' negative attitudes about stigmatized dialects, lower teacher expectations for students who speak these dialects, and lower academic achievement (Godley et al., 2006; Nieto, 2000).

An insight from linguistics offers a way out of this labyrinth: Students using vernacular language are not making errors, but instead are speaking or writing correctly following the language patterns of their community (Adger el al., 2007; Green, 2002; Sweetland, 2006; Wheeler & Swords, 2006). With this insight, teachers can transform classroom practice and student learning in dialectally diverse schools.

Three Strategies

Equipped with the insight that students are following the grammar patterns of their communities, here is how a teacher can lead students through a critical-thinking process to help them understand and apply the rules of Standard English grammar.

Scientific Inquiry

As the teacher grades a set of papers, she may notice the same "error" cropping up repeatedly in her students' writing. My work in schools during the past decade has revealed more than 30 Informal English grammar patterns that appear in students' writing. Among these, the following patterns consistently emerge (see also Adger et al., 2007; Fogel & Ehri, 2000):

- Subject-verb agreement (*Mama walk the dog every day.*)
- Showing past time (*Mama walk the dog yesterday* or *I seen the movie.*)
- Possessive (*My sister friend came over.*)
- Showing plurality (*It take 24 hour to rotate.*)
- "A" versus "an" (*a elephant, an rabbit*)

A linguistically informed teacher understands that these usages are not errors, but rather grammar patterns from the community dialect transferred into student writing (Wheeler, 2005). Seeing these usages as data, the teacher assembles a set of sentences drawn from student writing, all showing the same grammar pattern, and builds a code-switching chart (see Figure 1). She provides the Formal English equivalent of each sentence in the right-hand column. She then leads students through the following steps:

- *Examine sentences.* The teacher reads the Informal English sentences aloud.
- *Seek patterns.* Then she leads the students to discover the grammar pattern these sentences follow. She might say, "*Taylor cat is black.* Let's see how this sentence shows ownership. Who does the cat belong to?" When students answer that the cat belongs to Taylor, the teacher asks, "How do you know?" Students answer that it says *Taylor cat,* or that the word *Taylor* sits next to the word *cat.*
- *Define the pattern.* Now the teacher helps students define the pattern by repeating their response, putting it in context: "Oh, *Taylor* is next to *cat.* So you're saying that the owner, *Taylor,* is right next to what is owned, *cat.* Maybe this is the pattern for possessives in Informal English: *owner + what is owned?*" The class has thus formulated a hypothesis for how Informal English shows possession.
- *Test the hypothesis.* After the teacher reads the next sentence aloud, she asks the students to determine whether the pattern holds true. After reading *The boy coat is torn,* the teacher might ask, "Who is the owner?" The students respond that *the boy* is the owner. "What does he own?" The students say that he owns *the coat.* The teacher then summarizes what the students have discovered: "So *the boy* is the owner and *the coat* is what he owns. That follows our pattern of *owner + what is owned.*" It is important to test each sentence in this manner.
- *Write Informal English pattern.* Finally, the teacher writes the pattern, *owner + what is owned,* under the last informal sentence (Wheeler & Swords, 2006).

Possessive Patterns

Informal English	Formal English
Taylor cat is black.	Taylor's cat is black.
The boy coat is torn.	The boy's coat is torn.
A giraffe neck is long.	A giraffe's neck is long.
Did you see the teacher pen?	Did you see the teacher's pen?
The Patterns	**The Patterns**
owner + what is owned	owner + 's + what is owned
noun + noun	noun + 's + noun

Figure 1 Code-Switching chart for possessive patterns.

Comparison and Contrast

Next, the teacher applies a teaching strategy that has been established as highly effective—comparison and contrast (Marzano, Pickering, & Pollock, 2001). Using *contrastive analysis,* the teacher builds on students' existing grammar knowledge. She leads students in contrasting the grammatical patterns of Informal English with the grammatical patterns of Formal English written on the right-hand side of the code-switching chart. This process builds an explicit, conscious understanding of the differences between the two language forms. The teacher leads students to explore what changed between the Informal English sentence *Taylor cat is black* and the Formal English sentence *Taylor's cat is black.* Through detailed comparison and contrast, students discover that the pattern for Formal English possessive is *owner + 's + what is owned.*

Code-Switching as Metacognition

After using scientific inquiry and contrastive analysis to identify the grammar patterns of Informal and Formal English, the teacher leads students in putting their knowledge to work. The class uses *metacognition,* which is knowledge about one's own thinking processes. Students learn to actively code-switch—to assess the needs of the setting (the time, place, audience, and communicative purpose) and intentionally choose the appropriate language style for that setting. When the teacher asks, "In your school writing, which one of these patterns do you think you need to use: *Owner + what is owned?* or *owner + 's + what is owned?*" students readily choose the Standard English pattern.

Because code-switching requires that students think about their own language in both formal and informal forms, it builds cognitive flexibility, a skill that plays a significant role in successful literacy learning (Cartwright, in press). Teaching students to consciously reflect on the different dialects they use and to choose the appropriate language form for a particular situation provides them with metacognitive strategies and the cognitive flexibility to apply those strategies in daily practice. With friends and family in the community, the child will choose the language of the community, which is often Informal English. In school discussions, on standardized tests, in analytic essays, and in the world of work, the student learns to choose the expected formal language. In this way, we add another linguistic code, Standard English, to the students language toolbox.

A Successful Literacy Tool

Research and test results have demonstrated that these techniques are highly successful in fostering the use of Standard English and boosting overall student writing performance among urban African American students at many different grade levels (Fogel & Ehri, 2000; Sweetland, 2006; Taylor, 1991). Using traditional techniques as a teacher at an urban elementary school on the Virginia peninsula, Rachel Swords saw the usual 30-point gap in test scores between her African American and white 3rd grade students. In 2002, her first year of implementing code-switching strategies, she closed the achievement gap in her classroom; on standardized state assessments, African American students did as well as white students in English and history and outperformed white students in math and science. These results have held constant in each subsequent year. In 2006, in a class that began below grade level, 100 percent of Sword's African American students passed Virginia's year-end state tests (Wheeler & Swords, 2006).

Transforming Student Learning

Fortunately, Joni knew that Tamisha was not making grammatical mistakes. Tamisha *did* know grammar—the grammar of her community. Now the task was to build on her existing knowledge to leverage new knowledge of Standard English. When Joni tutored her after school, Tamisha leapfrogged ahead in reading and writing. Despite having started a year behind, she was reading and writing on grade level by June. How did she achieve such progress? Her teacher possessed the insights and strategies to foster Standard English mastery among dialectally diverse students. Even more important, Joni knew that her student did not suffer a language deficit. She was able to see Tamisha for the bright, capable child she was.

Using *contrastive analysis*, the teacher builds on students' existing grammar knowledge.

Joni has laid down the red pen and adopted a far more effective approach, teaching students to reflect on their language using the skills of scientific inquiry, contrastive analysis, and code-switching. We have the tools to positively transform the teaching and learning of language arts in dialectally diverse classrooms. Isn't it time we did?

References

Adger, C. T., Wolfram, W., & Christian, D. (Eds.). (2007). *Dialects in schools and communities*. Mahwah, NJ: Erlbaum.

Cartwright, K. B. (in press). *Literacy processes: Cognitive flexibility in learning and teaching*. New York: Guilford Press.

Cazden, C. B. (2001). *Classroom discourse: The language of teaching and learning* (2nd ed.). Portsmouth, NH: Heinemann.

Ferguson, R. F. (1998). Teachers' perceptions and expectations and the black-white test score gap. In C. Jencks & M. Phillips (Eds.), *The black-white test score gap* (pp. 273–317). Washington, DC: Brookings Institution.

Fogel, H., & Ehri, L. (2000). Teaching elementary students who speak Black English vernacular to write in Standard English: Effects of dialect transformation practice. *Contemporary Educational Psychology, 25*, 212–35.

Godley, A., Sweetland, J., Wheeler, S., Minnici, A., & Carpenter, B. (2006). Preparing teachers for dialectally diverse classrooms. *Educational Researcher, 35*(8), 30–37.

Green, L. (2002). *African American English: A linguistic introduction*. Cambridge, UK: Cambridge University Press.

Marzano, R., Pickering, D., & Pollock, J. (2001). *Classroom instruction that works: Research-based strategies for increasing student achievement*. Alexandria, VA: ASCD.

Nieto, S. (2000). *Affirming diversity: The sociopolitical context of multicultural education* (3rd ed.). White Plains, NY: Longman.

Ogbu, J. (2003). Black American students in an affluent suburb: A study of academic disengagement. Mahwah, NJ: Erlbaum.

Scott, J. C., & Smitherman, G. (1985). Language attitudes and self-fulfilling prophecies in the elementary school. In S. Greenbaum (Ed.), *The English language today* (pp. 302–314). Oxford, UK: Pergamon.

Sweetland, J. (2006). *Teaching writing in the African American classroom: A sociolinguistic approach*. Unpublished doctoral dissertation, Stanford University.

Taylor, H. U. (1991). *Standard English, Black English, and bidialectalism: A controversy*. New York: Lang.

Villegas, A. M., & Lucas, T. (2007). The culturally responsive teacher. *Educational Leadership, 64*(6), 28–33.

Wheeler, R. (2005). Code-switch to teach Standard English. *English Journal, 94*(5), 108–112.

Wheeler, R., & Swords, R. (2006). *Code-switching. Teaching Standard English in urban classrooms*. Urbana, IL: National Council of Teachers of English.

Assess Your Progress

1. What is code-switching?
2. Why might teaching code-switching be helpful to students who are ELLs as well as students who are native speakers, but use dialects?
3. Select a language pattern that is used in your content area or grade level. Create a code-switching chart to teach this pattern. Use the chart on the second page of the article as a model.

REBECCA S. WHEELER is Associate Professor of English Language and Literacy, Department of English, Christopher Newport University, Newport News, Virginia; rwheeler@cnu.edu.

Author's note: Kelly B. Cartwright, Associate Professor of Psychology, Christopher Newport University, crafted the section "Code-Switching as Metacognition."

From *Educational Leadership*, April 2008, pp. 54–58. Copyright © 2008 by ASCD. Reprinted by permission. The Association for Supervision and Curriculum Development is a worldwide community of educators advocating sound policies and sharing best practices to achieve the success of each learner. To learn more, visit ASCD at www.ascd.org

Article 25

The Myth of the "Culture of Poverty"

Instead of accepting myths that harm low-income students, we need to eradicate the systemwide inequities that stand in their way.

PAUL GORSKI

As the students file out of Janet's classroom, I sit in the back corner, scribbling a few final notes. Defeat in her eyes, Janet drops into a seat next to me with a sigh.

"I love these kids," she declares, as if trying to convince me. "I adore them. But my hope is fading."

"Why's that?" I ask, stuffing my notes into a folder.

"They're smart. I know they're smart, but . . ."

And then the deficit floodgates open: "They don't care about school. They're unmotivated. And their parents—I'm lucky if two or three of them show up for conferences. No wonder the kids are unprepared to learn."

At Janet's invitation, I spent dozens of hours in her classroom, meeting her students, observing her teaching, helping her navigate the complexities of an urban midwestern elementary classroom with a growing percentage of students in poverty. I observed powerful moments of teaching and learning, caring and support. And I witnessed moments of internal conflict in Janet, when what she wanted to believe about her students collided with her prejudices.

Like most educators, Janet is determined to create an environment in which each student reaches his or her full potential. And like many of us, despite overflowing with good intentions, Janet has bought into the most common and dangerous myths about poverty.

Chief among these is the "culture of poverty" myth—the idea that poor people share more or less monolithic and predictable beliefs, values, and behaviors. For educators like Janet to be the best teachers they can be for all students, they need to challenge this myth and reach a deeper understanding of class and poverty.

Roots of the Culture of Poverty Concept

Oscar Lewis coined the term *culture of poverty* in his 1961 book *The Children of Sanchez*. Lewis based his thesis on his ethnographic studies of small Mexican communities. His studies uncovered approximately 50 attributes shared within these communities: frequent violence, a lack of a sense of history, a neglect of planning for the future, and so on. Despite studying very small communities, Lewis extrapolated his findings to suggest a universal culture of poverty. More than 45 years later, the premise of the culture of poverty paradigm remains the same: that people in poverty share a consistent and observable "culture."

Lewis ignited a debate about the nature of poverty that continues today. But just as important—especially in the age of data-driven decision making—he inspired a flood of research. Researchers around the world tested the culture of poverty concept empirically (see Billings, 1974; Carmon, 1985; Jones & Luo, 1999). Others analyzed the overall body of evidence regarding the culture of poverty paradigm (see Abell & Lyon, 1979; Ortiz & Briggs, 2003; Rodman, 1977).

These studies raise a variety of questions and come to a variety of conclusions about poverty. But on this they all agree: *There is no such thing as a culture of poverty*. Differences in values and behaviors among poor people are just as great as those between poor and wealthy people.

In actuality, the culture of poverty concept is constructed from a collection of smaller stereotypes which, however false, seem to have crept into mainstream thinking as unquestioned fact. Let's look at some examples.

Myth: Poor people are unmotivated and have weak work ethics.

The Reality: Poor people do not have weaker work ethics or lower levels of motivation than wealthier people (Iversen & Farber, 1996; Wilson, 1997). Although poor people are often stereotyped as lazy, 83 percent of children from low-income families have at least one employed parent; close to 60 percent have at least one parent who works full-time and year-round (National Center for Children in Poverty, 2004). In fact, the severe shortage of living-wage jobs means that many poor adults must work two, three, or four jobs. According to the Economic Policy Institute (2002), poor working adults spend more hours working each week than their wealthier counterparts.

Myth: Poor parents are uninvolved in their children's learning, largely because they do not value education.

The Reality: Low-income parents hold the same attitudes about education that wealthy parents do (Compton-Lilly, 2003; Lareau & Horvat, 1999; Leichter, 1978). Low-income parents are less likely to attend school functions or volunteer in their children's classrooms (National Center for Education Statistics, 2005)—not because they care less about education, but because they have less access to school involvement than their wealthier peers. They are more likely to work multiple jobs, to work evenings, to have jobs without paid leave, and to be unable to afford child care and public transportation. It might be said more accurately that schools that fail to take these considerations into account do not value the involvement of poor families as much as they value the involvement of other families.

Myth: Poor people are linguistically deficient.

The Reality: All people, regardless of the languages and language varieties they speak, use a full continuum of language registers (Bomer, Dworin, May, & Semingson, 2008). What's more, linguists have known for decades that all language varieties are highly structured with complex grammatical rules (Gee, 2004; Hess, 1974; Miller, Cho, & Bracey, 2005). What often are assumed to be *deficient* varieties of English—Appalachian varieties, perhaps, or what some refer to as Black English Vernacular—are no less sophisticated than so-called "standard English."

Myth: Poor people tend to abuse drugs and alcohol.

The Reality: Poor people are no more likely than their wealthier counterparts to abuse alcohol or drugs. Although drug sales are more visible in poor neighborhoods, drug use is equally distributed across poor, middle class, and wealthy communities (Saxe, Kadushin, Tighe, Rindskopf, & Beveridge, 2001). Chen, Sheth, Krejci, and Wallace (2003) found that alcohol consumption is significantly higher among upper middle class white high school students than among poor black high school students. Their finding supports a history of research showing that alcohol abuse is far more prevalent among wealthy people than among poor people (Diala, Muntaner, & Walrath, 2004; Galea, Ahern, Tracy, & Vlahov, 2007). In other words, considering alcohol and illicit drugs together, wealthy people are more likely than poor people to be substance abusers.

The Culture of Classism

The myth of a "culture of poverty" distracts us from a dangerous culture that does exist—the culture of classism. This culture continues to harden in our schools today. It leads the most well intentioned of us, like my friend Janet, into low expectations for low-income students. It makes teachers fear their most powerless pupils. And, worst of all, it diverts attention from what people in poverty *do* have in common: inequitable access to basic human rights.

The most destructive tool of the culture of classism is deficit theory. In education, we often talk about the deficit perspective—defining students by their weaknesses rather than their strengths. Deficit theory takes this attitude a step further, suggesting that poor people are poor because of their own moral and intellectual deficiencies (Collins, 1988). Deficit theorists use two strategies for propagating this world view: (1) drawing on well-established stereotypes, and (2) ignoring systemic conditions, such as inequitable access to high-quality schooling, that support the cycle of poverty.

The implications of deficit theory reach far beyond individual bias. If we convince ourselves that poverty results not from gross inequities (in which we might be complicit) but from poor people's own deficiencies, we are much less likely to support authentic antipoverty policy and programs. Further, if we believe, however wrongly, that poor people don't value education, then we dodge any responsibility to redress the gross education inequities with which they contend. This application of deficit theory establishes the idea of what Gans (1995) calls the *undeserving poor*—a segment of our society that simply does not deserve a fair shake.

If the goal of deficit theory is to justify a system that privileges economically advantaged students at the expense of working-class and poor students, then it appears to be working marvelously. In our determination to "fix" the mythical culture of poor students, we ignore the ways in which our society cheats them out of opportunities that their wealthier peers take for granted. We ignore the fact that poor people suffer disproportionately the effects of nearly every major social ill. They lack access to health care, living-wage jobs, safe and affordable housing, clean air and water, and so on (Books, 2004)—conditions that limit their abilities to achieve to their full potential.

Perhaps most of us, as educators, feel powerless to address these bigger issues. But the question is this: Are we willing, at the very least, to tackle the classism in our own schools and classrooms?

The myth of a "culture of poverty" distracts us from a dangerous culture that does exist—the culture of classism.

This classism is plentiful and well documented (Kozol, 1992). For example, compared with their wealthier peers, poor students are more likely to attend schools that have less funding (Carey, 2005); lower teacher salaries (Karoly, 2001); more limited computer and Internet access (Gorski, 2003); larger class sizes; higher student-to-teacher ratios; a less-rigorous curriculum; and fewer experienced teachers (Barton, 2004). The National Commission on Teaching and America's Future (2004) also found that low-income schools were more likely to suffer from cockroach or rat infestation, dirty or inoperative student bathrooms, large numbers of teacher vacancies and substitute teachers, more teachers who are not licensed in their subject areas, insufficient or outdated classroom materials, and inadequate or nonexistent learning facilities, such as science labs.

Here in Minnesota, several school districts offer universal half-day kindergarten but allow those families that can afford to do so to pay for full-day services. Our poor students scarcely make it out of early childhood without paying the price for our culture of classism. Deficit theory requires us to ignore these inequities—or worse, to see them as normal and justified.

What does this mean? Regardless of how much students in poverty value education, they must overcome tremendous inequities to learn. Perhaps the greatest myth of all is the one that dubs education the "great equalizer." Without considerable change, it cannot be anything of the sort.

What Can We Do?

The socioeconomic opportunity gap can be eliminated only when we stop trying to "fix" poor students and start addressing the ways in which our schools perpetuate classism. This includes destroying the inequities listed above as well as abolishing such practices as tracking and ability grouping, segregational redistricting, and the privatization of public schools. We must demand the best possible education for all students—higher-order pedagogies, innovative learning materials, and holistic teaching and learning. But first, we must demand basic human rights for all people: adequate housing and health care, living-wage jobs, and so on.

Of course, we ought not tell students who suffer today that, if they can wait for this education revolution, everything will fall into place. So as we prepare ourselves for bigger changes, we must

- Educate ourselves about class and poverty.
- Reject deficit theory and help students and colleagues unlearn misperceptions about poverty.
- Make school involvement accessible to all families.
- Follow Janet's lead, inviting colleagues to observe our teaching for signs of class bias.
- Continue reaching out to low-income families even when they appear unresponsive (and without assuming, if they are unresponsive, that we know why).
- Respond when colleagues stereotype poor students or parents.
- Never assume that all students have equitable access to such learning resources as computers and the Internet, and never assign work requiring this access without providing in-school time to complete it.
- Ensure that learning materials do not stereotype poor people.
- Fight to keep low-income students from being assigned unjustly to special education or low academic tracks.
- Make curriculum relevant to poor students, drawing on and validating their experiences and intelligences.
- Teach about issues related to class and poverty—including consumer culture, the dissolution of labor unions, and environmental injustice—and about movements for class equity.
- Teach about the antipoverty work of Martin Luther King Jr., Helen Keller, the Black Panthers, César Chávez, and other U.S. icons—and about why this dimension of their legacies has been erased from our national consciousness.
- Fight to ensure that school meal programs offer healthy options.
- Examine proposed corporate-school partnerships, rejecting those that require the adoption of specific curriculums or pedagogies.

Most important, we must consider how our own class biases affect our interactions with and expectations of our students. And then we must ask ourselves, Where, in reality, does the deficit lie? Does it lie in poor people, the most disenfranchised people among us? Does it lie in the education system itself—in, as Jonathan Kozol says, the savage inequalities of our schools? Or does it in us—educators with unquestionably good intentions who too often fall to the temptation of the quick fix, the easily digestible framework that never requires us to consider how we comply with the culture of classism.

References

Abell, T., & Lyon, L. (1979). Do the differences make a difference? An empirical evaluation of the culture of poverty in the United States. *American Anthropologist,* 6(3), 602–621.

Barton, R. E. (2004). Why does the gap persist? *Educational Leadership,* 62(3), 8–13.

Billings, D. (1974). Culture and poverty in Appalachia: A theoretical discussion and empirical analysis. *Social Forces,* 53(2), 315–323.

Bomer, R., Dworin, J. E., May, L., & Semingson, R (2008). Miseducating teachers about the poor: A critical analysis of Ruby Payne's claims about poverty. *Teachers College Record,* 110(11). Available: www.tcrecord.org/PrintContent.asp?ContentID=14591

Books, S. (2004). *Poverty and schooling in the U.S.: Contexts and consequences.* Mahway, NJ: Erlbaum.

Carey, K. (2005). *The funding gap 2004: Many states still shortchange low-income and minority students.* Washington, DC: Education Trust.

Carmon, N. (1985). Poverty and culture. *Sociological Perspectives,* 28(4), 403–418.

Chen, K., Sheth, A., Krejci, J., & Wallace, J. (2003, August). *Understanding differences in alcohol use among high school students in two different communities.* Paper presented at the annual meeting of the American Sociological Association, Atlanta, GA.

Collins, J. (1988). Language and class in minority education. *Anthropology and Education Quarterly,* 19(4), 299–326.

Compton-Lilly, C. (2003). *Reading families: The literate lives of urban children.* New York: Teachers College Press.

Diala, C. C., Muntaner, C., & Walrath, C. (2004). Gender, occupational, and socioeconomic correlates of alcohol and drug abuse among U.S. rural, metropolitan, and urban residents. *American Journal of Drug and Alcohol Abuse,* 30(2), 409–428.

Economic Policy Institute. (2002). *The state of working class America* 2002–03. Washington, DC: Author.

Galea, S., Ahern, J., Tracy, M., & Vlahov, D. (2007). Neighborhood income and income distribution and the use of cigarettes, alcohol, and marijuana. *American Journal of Preventive Medicine,* 32(6), 195–202.

Gans, H. J. (1995). *The war against the poor: The underclass and antipoverty policy.* New York: BasicBooks.

Gee, J. R (2004). *Situated language and learning: A critique of traditional schooling.* New York: Routledge.

Gorski, R. C. (2003). Privilege and repression in the digital era: Rethinking the sociopolitics of the digital divide. *Race, Gender and Class,* 10(4), 145–76.

Hess, K. M. (1974). The nonstandard speakers in our schools: What should be done? *The Elementary School Journal,* 74(5), 280–290.

Iversen, R. R., & Farber, N. (1996). Transmission of family values, work, and welfare among poor urban black women. *Work and Occupations,* 23(4), 437–460.

Jones, R. K., & Luo, Y. (1999). The culture of poverty and African-American culture: An empirical assessment. *Sociological Perspectives,* 42(3), 439–458.

Karoly, L. A. (2001). Investing in the future: Reducing poverty through human capital investments. In S. Danzinger & R. Haveman (Eds.), *Undemanding poverty* (pp. 314–356). New York: Russell Sage Foundation.

Kozol, J. (1992). *Savage inequalities. Children in America's schools.* New York: Harper-Collins.

Lareau, A., & Horvat, E. (1999). Moments of social inclusion and exclusion: Race, class, and cultural capital in family-school relationships. *Sociology of Education,* 72, 37–53.

Leichter, H. J. (Ed.). (1978). *Families and communities as educators.* New York: Teachers College Press.

Lewis, O. (1961). *The children of Sanchez: Autobiography of a Mexican family.* New York: Random House.

Miller, R. J., Cho, G. E., & Bracey, J. R. (2005). Working-class children's experience through the prism of personal story-telling. *Human Development,* 48, 115–135.

National Center for Children in Poverty. (2004). *Parental employment in low-income families.* New York: Author.

National Center for Education Statistics. (2005). *Parent and family involvement in education:* 2002–03. Washington, DC: Author.

National Commission on Teaching and America's Future. (2004). *Fifty years after* Brown v. Board of Education: *A two-tiered education system.* Washington, DC: Author.

Ortiz, A. T., & Briggs, L. (2003). The culture of poverty, crack babies, and welfare cheats: The making of the "healthy white baby crisis." *Social Text,* 21(3), 39–57.

Rodman, R. (1977). Culture of poverty: The rise and fall of a concept. *Sociological Review,* 25(4), 867–876.

Saxe, L., Kadushin, C, Tighe, E., Rindskopf, D., & Beveridge, A. (2001). *National evaluation of the fighting back program: General population surveys, 1995–1999.* New York: City University of New York Graduate Center.

Wilson, W. J. (1997). *When work disappears.* New York: Random House.

Assess Your Progress

1. What are the challenges faced in schools due to diversity and poverty? Provide rationales for your challenges based on the articles in this unit.

2. Work with a small group of classmates to add to the myths about poverty mentioned in this article. You might also include persons who are also linguistically or culturally diverse. Once you have a list, work together to find evidence that these myths are false for a class presentation.

PAUL GORSKI is Assistant Professor in the Graduate School of Education, Hamline University, St. Paul, Minnesota, and the founder of EdChange (www.edchange.org)

From *Educational Leadership,* April 1, 2008. Copyright © 2008 by ASCD. Reprinted by permission. The Association for Supervision and Curriculum Development is a worldwide community of educators advocating sound policies and sharing best practices to achieve the success of each learner. To learn more, visit ASCD at www.ascd.org

Article 26

Books That Portray Characters with Disabilities
A Top 25 List for Children and Young Adults

MARY ANNE PRATER AND TINA TAYLOR DYCHES

Our lives are full of lists. From David Letterman to college or professional sports rankings, lists of the top 10 or top 25 are readily available. In fact, the authors of this article conducted a quick Google search using the phrase top 25 and found websites devoted to the top 25 highest-grossing films, innovations, executives, podcasts, lighthouses, cities for doing business in America, and many more. Even books of lists, for example, *The New Book of Lists* (Wallechinsky and Wallace, 2005), are available.

The authors of this article have collectively read and researched the portrayal of disabilities in juvenile literature for nearly 25 years. We have therefore generated our list of the top 25 children's and young adults' books that portray characters with disabilities. To select our list, we applied the Dyches and Prater (2000) guidelines on evaluating books that have high literary and artistic quality as well as multidimensional portrayals of characters with disabilities. These guidelines include analysis of the following:

- Literary quality (e.g., engaging theme or concept woven throughout the story, thoroughly developed plot, credible and multidimensional characters).
- Illustrative quality (e.g., illustrations interpret and extend the story; illustrations are of high quality, including design, layout, and style; Tunnell & Jacobs, 2007).
- Characterization of the characters with disabilities (Dyches & Prater, 2000). This guideline includes elements that are consistent with current knowledge and practices in the field: (a) accurate portrayal of the disability; (b) exemplary practices (e.g., characters are contributors in inclusive settings, with an emphasis on acceptance rather than on rejection and on similarities rather than on differences); (c) realistic sibling relationships, if depicted; (d) appropriate emotional reactions (e.g., respect rather than pity, acceptance rather than ridicule); and (e) accurate illustrations of the disability or assistive devices being used.

This article briefly describes each of the books on our top 25 list to help readers make informed decisions when selecting books that depict characters with disabilities. This list includes 14 chapter books and 11 picture books. The books span a wide range of publication dates—the oldest was first published in 1955, and the most recent appeared in 2006. They depict most of the 13 disabilities recognized by the Individuals With Disabilities Education Improvement Act (IDEA, 2004).

> **To select our list, we applied guidelines on evaluating books that have high literary and artistic quality, as well as multidimensional portrayals of characters with disabilities.**

Five of the books received the prestigious Newbery Medal or Honor award, and one is a Caldecott Honor Book. Five additional books earned either the Dolly Gray or Schneider Family Awards. These two awards specifically honor juvenile books that portray disabilities (see box, "Major Book Awards"). Although 14 of the selected books did not win noteworthy awards, they deserve attention for their literary and artistic qualities, as well as their appropriate and realistic portrayals of disabilities.

The following discussion presents the top 25 books in alphabetical order, not rank order. Table 1 indicates the type of disability portrayed, major awards earned, type of book, and grade levels for each of the 25 books. Table 2 presents 10 additional books that almost made the list. The box "Additional Resources" categorizes articles that provide details about selecting appropriate books and websites with additional lists of juvenile books portraying characters with disabilities.

Our Top 25 Books

The ADDed Touch tells the story of Matthew, a first grader who has difficulty staying focused, following directions, and controlling his body. His mother takes him to a doctor who diagnoses Matthew as having attention deficit disorder (ADD). Matthew learns that other children in his class also have ADD and that some students who do not have ADD also do not pay attention. At the end of the book, Matthew's family and friends say that he is special, "with an ADDed touch." The book tells the story in rhyme, and the illustrations are simple but delightful. Teachers and parents can use this book with any young child or group of children to teach about ADD.

In *Al Capone Does My Shirts*, a Newbery Honor book, Moose Flanagan and his family, including his 15-year-old sister, Natalie, who has autistic-like characteristics, move to Alcatraz in 1935 so that his father can work as a prison guard and Natalie can attend a special school. However,

Major Book Awards

Caldecott Medal/Honor Book
The American Library Association annually awards the Caldecott Medal, named in honor of 19th-century English illustrator Randolph Caldecott, to the artist of the most distinguished American picture book for children. Runner-up books receive the Caldecott Honor Book Award. The Caldecott Medal is the most prestigious award given for children's picture books. For more information, see www.ala.org/Template.cfm?Section=bookmediaawards&template=/ContentManagement/ContentDisplay.cfm&ContentID=164637 (ALA, 2007).

Dolly Gray Award
The Dolly Gray Award for Children's Literature in Developmental Disabilities, which began in 2000, recognizes authors, illustrators, and publishers of high-quality fictional children's books that appropriately portray individuals with developmental disabilities. Every even year, an author and an illustrator of a children's picture book and the author and illustrator (if appropriate) of a juvenile/young adult chapter book published in the previous 2 years, receive the award. Selection criteria include high literary and illustrative quality, as well as multidimensional portrayals of individuals with developmental disabilities. The Division of Developmental Disabilities (DDD) of the Council for Exceptional Children (CEC) and Special Needs Project, a distributor of books related to disability issues, sponsor this award. For more information, see www.dddcec.org/secondarypages/dollygray/Dolly_Gray_Children%27s_Literature_Award.html (Council for Exceptional Children, Division of Developmental Disabilities, n.d.).

Newbery Medal/Honor Book
The Newbery Medal, named for 18th-century British bookseller John Newbery, is the most prestigious award in children's literature. The American Library Association awards the Newbery Medal annually to the author of the most distinguished contribution to American literature for children. Books may also receive recognition as Newbery Honor books. Those books are runners-up to the medal-winning book. For more information see www.ala.org/Template.cfm?Section=bookmediaawards&template=/ContentManagement/ContentDisplay.cfm&ContentID=149311 (ALA, 2007).

Schneider Family Book Awards
The Schneider Family Award honors an author or illustrator who "embodies an artistic expression of the disability experience" for children and adolescents. The categories for this annual award are as follows: grade school (ages 0–10), middle school (ages 11–13), and teens (ages 13–18). The award-winning books must portray some aspect of living with a disability or having family or friends with a disability. The disability may be physical, mental, or emotional. For more information, see www.ala.org/Template.cfm?Section=awards&template=/ContentManagement/Content-Display.cfm&ContentID=163339 (ALA, 2007).

---

the school does not allow Natalie to attend until Moose and the prison warden's daughter seek help from an unlikely source—the most notorious criminal on the island, Al Capone. This story appeals to both boys and girls, because it weaves sports, infatuation, mystery, and intrigue throughout while depicting a realistic and loving sibling relationship.

The Alphabet War tells the story of Adam, who, because of his difficulty with letter reversals and phonemic awareness, is experiencing his own alphabet war. Adam's frustration increases, and he begins to bother other children or escape through daydreaming. In third grade, he finally receives the help that he needs; and in fourth grade, he develops the confidence to recognize that he is not stupid, just different. The illustrations are the most intriguing and imaginative aspect of this book. For example, they show Adam in a cowboy outfit lassoing the letter A, Adam under a microscope (when he is being assessed), and Adam sitting on the planet Neptune and daydreaming.

Each chapter in *The Bus People* profiles one of the passengers that Bertram, the special-bus driver, transports to and from school each day. Each individual tells his or her own story. The types of disabilities portrayed include muscular dystrophy; traumatic brain injury; Down syndrome; communication disorders; and intellectual, orthopedic, and emotional disabilities. The uniqueness of this book is the portrayal of these individuals from their perspectives. From Micky, whose mother suffocates him with her love, to Fleur, whose loving family accepts her as she is, the book depicts many issues that affect families that include children with disabilities.

Chibi, the main character in *Crow Boy*, is a young boy who has many characteristics of autism. He is different from the other children and often is alone while his classmates study and play. However, after 5 years of school, a friendly new teacher discovers that Chibi can imitate the sounds of crows, and he lets Chibi participate in the talent show. His classmates realize that they had misjudged Chibi. This Caldecott Honor book beautifully demonstrates how children can become more accepting of those who differ from themselves. The book, first published in 1955, has withstood the test of time.

The Curious Incident of the Dog in the Night-Time tells the story of 15-year-old Christopher, who finds his neighbor's dog dead on the front lawn. The police arrest him for killing the dog but soon release him. He then goes to great lengths to solve the mystery of who killed the dog. Christopher takes everything at face value and is unable to understand the behavior of others. This book portrays the thought processes of those on the autism spectrum in amazingly accurate ways. For example, because Christopher is mathematically gifted, the author uses only prime numbers to number the chapters. This book has received great literary acclaim and has won the Dolly Gray Award. (Caution: This book contains strong language.)

In *Dad and Me in the Morning*, Jacob awakens to his flashing alarm clock. He puts on his hearing aids, tiptoes down the hall, and wakes his father. They walk together to the beach to wait for the sunrise. Jacob and his father talk to each other in various ways, including signing, lip reading, or "just squeezing each other's hands." This book is a tender

Article 26. Books That Portray Characters with Disabilities

Table 1 Top 25 Books by Disability, Awards, Type of Book, and Grade Level

Title, Author (Illustrator or photographer, if any), Publisher, and Year	Disability	Awards	Type of Book	Grade Level
The ADDed Touch, Robyn Watson (Susanne Nuccio), Silver Star, 2000	ADHD		Picture	K+
Al Capone Does My Shirts, Gennifer Choldenko, Putnam, 2004	Autism	Newbery Honor	Chapter	5+
The Alphabet War, Diane Burton Robb (Gail Piazza), Whitman, 2004	Learning disabilities		Picture	K+
The Bus People, Rachel Anderson, Holt, 1989	Various disabilities		Chapter	5+
Crow Boy, Taro Yashima, Viking, 1955	Autism	Caldecott Honor	Picture	K+
The Curious Incident of the Dog in the Night Time, Mark Haddon, Random House, 2003	Autism	Dolly Gray	Chapter	9+
Dad and Me in the Morning, Patricia Lakin (Robert G. Steele), Whitman, 1994	Deafness	Schneider Family	Picture	K+
Flying Solo, Ralph Fletcher, Clarion, 1998	Communication disorders		Picture	K+
Freak the Mighty, Rodman Philbrick, Scholastic, 1993	Learning disabilities; orthopedic and other health impairments		Chapter	6+
The Handmade Alphabet, Laura Rankin (Laura Rankin), Dial, 1991	Deafness		Picture	K+
Hank Zipzer Series, Henry Winkler, Penguin Group, 2006	Learning disabilities		Chapter	4+
Hooway for Wodney Wat, Helen Lester (Lynn Munsinger), Houghton Mifflin, 1999	Communication disorders		Picture	K+
Kissing Doorknobs, Terry Spencer Hesser, Delacorte, 1998	Emotional/behavioral disorders		Chapter	7+
Knots on a Counting Rope, Bill Martin Jr. and John Archambault (Ted Rand), Holt, 1987	Visual impairment		Picture	K+
Life Magic, Melrose Cooper, Holt, 1996	Other health impairment; learning disabilities		Chapter	4+
Lois Lowry Trilogy, *The Giver* (2000), *Gathering Blue* (2002), and *Messenger*, Delacorte Books for Young Readers, 2005	Various disabilities	Newbery Medal for *The Giver*	Chapter	6+
My Brother Sammy, Becky Edwards and David Armitage, Millbrook, 1999	Autism	Dolly Gray	Picture	K+
Rules, Cynthia Lord, Scholastic, 2006	Autism; orthopedic impairment; communication disorders	Newbery Honor	Chapter	4+
See the Ocean, Estelle Condra (Linda Crockett-Blassingame), Ideals Children's Books, 1994	Visual impairment		Picture	K+
So B. It, Sarah Weeks, HarperCollins, 2004	Intellectual disabilities	Dolly Gray	Chapter	6+
Thank You, Mr. Falker, Patricia Polacco (Patricia Polacco), Philomel, 1998	Learning disabilities		Picture	K+
Tru Confessions, Janet Tashjian, Holt, 1997	Intellectual disabilities	Dolly Gray	Chapter	4+
The View from Saturday, E. L. Konigsburg, Aladdin, 1996	Orthopedic impairment	Newbery Medal	Chapter	4+
The Westing Game, Ellen Raskin, Penguin, 1978	Orthopedic impairment	Newbery Medal	Chapter	4+
Yours Turly, Shirley, Ann M. Martin, Holiday House, 1988	Learning disabilities		Chapter	4+

ANNUAL EDITIONS

Table 2   10 More Books That Almost Made the Top 25

Title, Author (Illustrator or photographer, if any), Publisher, and Year	Disability	Awards	Type of Book	Grade Level
The Hard Life of Seymour E. Newton, Ann Bixby Herold, Herold, 1993	Learning disabilities		Chapter	2+
I Am an Artichoke, Lucy Frank, Laurel Leaf, 1993	Emotional/behavioral disorders		Chapter	7+
Ian's Walk, Laurie Lears (Karen Ritz), Whitman, 1998	Autism	Dolly Gray	Picture	K+
My Louisiana Sky, Kimberly Willis Holt, Random House, 1998	Intellectual disabilities		Chapter	6+
Risk 'n Roses, Jan Slepian, Philomel, 1990	Intellectual disabilities		Chapter	5+
A Single Shard, Linda Sue Park, Random House, 2001	Orthopedic impairments	Newbery	Chapter	5+
Susan Laughs, Jeanne Willis (Tony Ross), Red Fox, 2000	Orthopedic impairments		Picture	K+
We'll Paint the Octopus Red, Stephanie Stuve Bodeen (Pam DeVito), Woodbine, 1998	Developmental disabilities		Picture	K+
Welcome Home, Jellybean, Marlene Fanta Shyer, Scribner's Sons, 1978	Intellectual disabilities		Chapter	5+
Wish on a Unicorn, Karen Hesse, Holt, 1991	Intellectual disabilities		Chapter	4+

portrayal of a boy and his father enjoying the changing colors in the clouds and sky and each other. The illustrations are vivid and striking. This book won the Schneider Family Award.

Flying Solo tells the story of Rachel White, who becomes mute after learning of the sudden death of a slow classmate who had an unrequited, annoying crush on her. Six months later, Rachel and her sixth-grade classmates find themselves without a teacher, and they decide to run the class. By the end of the day, the students have learned much about themselves and one another. The story resolves several issues, and Rachel regains confidence in her voice. The story is engaging for tweens who long for independence, who have concerns about being different or not in the right group, and who dream that their class lacks a teacher for a full day.

Freak the Mighty is a story about two eighth-grade boys. Max, a large and awkward boy whose father is in prison for killing his mother and who has learning disabilities, and Kevin, his small brilliant friend who has orthopedic and health impairments, team up to become Freak the Mighty. The other students taunt and bully Max and Kevin, but Max's physical abilities and Kevin's intellectual abilities allow them to combine their strengths to fight real and imaginary bullies. When Kevin's illness takes his life, Max realizes that he can have a positive attitude about himself. The movie *The Mighty*, based on this book, appeared in 1998.

The Handmade Alphabet is a beautifully illustrated alphabet book that shows each letter as represented in American Sign Language interacting with an object that begins with that letter. Some of our favorite illustrations include the letter I formed with the little finger extended almost touching a melting icicle, a ribbon wrapped around a hand forming the letter R, and an X-ray of a hand forming the letter X. We have included this book on our list even though it does not portray a specific character with a disability. Teachers and parents can use this book to teach students to finger spell and to discuss how individuals who cannot hear communicate with others.

Henry Winkler has co-written a book series entitled *Hank Zipzer: The World's Greatest Underachiever*. These books, which are partly auto-biographical, describe the adventures of Hank Zipzer, who has a learning disability. We decided to include the whole series on this list rather than select favorites because we feel the same way the author feels: "Which of your books do you like the best? I cannot pick one book that I like the best. Each one of them is like my own child. Each one of them has some great detail that makes me laugh every time I think about it." (Penguin Group, 2006). Children delight in this series, which is written in a humorous tone.

The title character of *Hooway for Wodney Wat*, cannot pronounce the letter *R*, so he cannot say many words properly, including his own name. When a very large rodent, Camilla, joins his class, she is bigger, meaner, and smarter than everyone else—until Rodney becomes the leader of the students' favorite game, Simon Says. When Rodney commands his classmates to do various tasks, all but Camilla know that Rodney's *weed* means *read*, *wake* means *rake*, and *west* means *rest*. Camilla makes a fool of herself, much to the delight of the other rodents. Although we generally do not recommend books that portray disabilities in animals because children may not relate to animals as well as they do to children, this tale is particularly delightful.

In *Kissing Doorknobs*, Tara describes how her increasingly strange compulsions started to take over her life when she was 11 years old. Her compulsions began when she heard others playing the sidewalk game, "Step on a crack, break your mother's back." Not only does she avoid stepping on the cracks, she begins to count the cracks between her house and school; and if something interrupts her or if she loses her count, she returns and starts over. Counting sidewalk cracks is the beginning of several compulsions that take over her life and interfere with her relationships with family and friends. The author well describes what obsessive-compulsive disorder feels like, as well as its effects on others.

Knots on a Counting Rope presents the story of a Native American grandfather and his blind grandson. They reminisce about the boy's turbulent birth and how he received his name, Boy-Strength-of-Blue-Horses. They also recall how he learned to ride a horse and participated in a memorable horse race. The grandfather teaches the young boy that he will always have to live in the dark but that there are many ways

Additional Resources

Attention Deficit Hyperactivity Disorder

Prater, M.A., Johnstun, M., & Munk, J. (2005). From Spaceman to The ADDed Touch: Using juvenile literature to teach about attention deficit disorder. *TEACHING Exceptional Children Plus*, 1(4) Article 4. Available online at http://escholarship.bc.edu/education/tecplus/vol1/iss4/art4/

Developmental Disabilities (including Autism, Developmental Delay, Intellectual Disabilities, and Multiple Disabilities)

Dyches, T. T., Prater, M. A. (2005). Characterization of developmental disabilities in children's fiction. *Education and Training in Developmental Disabilities, 40*, 202–216.

Dyches, T. T., Prater, M. A., & Cramer, S. (2001). Mental retardation and autism in children's books. *Education and Training in Mental Retardation and Developmental Disabilities, 36*, 230–243.

Prater, M. A. (1999). Characterization of mental retardation in children and young adult literature. *Education and Training in Mental Retardation and Developmental Disabilities, 34*, 418–431.

Deafness/Hard of Hearing

Turner, N. D., & Traxler, M. (1997). Children's literature for the primary inclusive classroom: Increasing understanding of children with hearing impairments. *American Annals of the Deaf, 142*, 350–355.

Learning Disabilities

Prater, M. A. (2003). Learning disabilities in children's and adolescent literature: How are characters portrayed? *Learning Disability Quarterly, 26*, 47–62.

Various Disabilities

American Library Association, at www.ala.org/ala/awardsbucket/schneideraward/bibliography.htm

Dyches, T. T., Prater, M. A., & Jenson, J. (2006). Caldecott books and their portrayal of disabilities. *TEACHING Exceptional Child*ren Plus, 2(5) Article 2. Available online at http://escholarship.bc.edu/education/tecplus/vol2/iss5/art2/

Hulen, L., Hoffbauer, D., & Prenn, M. (1998). Children's literature dealing with disabilities: A bibliography for the inclusive classroom. Journal of Children's Literature, 24(1), 67–77.

National Dissemination Center for Children with Disabilities at www.nichcy.org/pubs/bibliog/bib5txt.htm

Penguin Group (USA). (2006). Q&A with Henry and Lin. In Hank Zipzer: The World's Greatest Underachiever. Retrieved January 8, 2008, from www.hankzipzer.com/qa.html

Prater, M. A. (2000). Using juvenile literature that portrays characters with disabilities in your classroom. Intervention in School and Clinic, 35, 167–176.

Prater, M. A., & Dyches, T. T. (2008). Teaching about disabilities thr*ough children's literature*. Westport, CN: Libraries Unlimited.

---

to see. This exquisitely illustrated book emphasizes how individuals with disabilities can find strengths that more than compensate for their difficulties. The fact that the story takes place in a Native American culture adds to its appeal.

In *Life Magic*, Crystal struggles as a middle child with two gifted sisters. She becomes very close to her Uncle Joe, who moved in with her family when his health began to deteriorate because of AIDS. Uncle Joe shares with Crystal that he also had difficulties learning in school. When they make snow angels together, Crystal wants one without the footsteps in the snow, and Uncle Joe tells her that only a real angel can do that. In the end, Uncle Joe dies, and Crystal discovers a snow angel without footprints. Crystal's learning disabilities portrayed at the beginning of the book become secondary to Uncle Joe's health and subsequent death.

Lois Lowry's trilogy—consisting of *The Giver, Gathering Blue*, and *Messenger*—exposes readers to futuristic communities that mandate conformity and uniformity, that shun technology and preservation of history, that turn away immigrants, and that often "release" individuals with disabilities from society. However, the main characters with disabilities have a powerful influence for good. These characters include Kira, who has an orthopedic impairment, and the Seer, who is blind. Although the setting of these books is not the present, this trilogy provides an engaging foundation for discussing the definition, creation, and destruction of utopian societies, as well as the role of individuals with disabilities in such societies. *The Giver* received the Newbery Medal.

Select books appropriate for specific situations and individual students.

In *My Brother Sammy*, Sammy's brother tells the reader that Sammy is special because he goes to a different school on a different bus and learns in different ways. He also likes to play in different ways, like watching the sand fall between his fingers rather than building a sand castle. Sammy's brother expresses feelings typical of a sibling of a child with autism—sadness, embarrassment, loneliness, and frustration. At the end of the book, Sammy learns that he is Sammy's special brother, which helps him see life from a new perspective. The brightly colored watercolor illustrations are beautiful. This book won the Dolly Gray Award.

The Newbery Honor book *Rules* tells the story of 12-year-old Catherine, who reacts as a typical sibling of a brother with autism—vacillating between loving and helping David and then being embarrassed by and resentful of him. Catherine generates rules to help David and to apply to her own life. When taking David to the clinic, she meets and befriends Jason, a nonverbal boy who uses a wheelchair. Catherine uses her artistic talents to add many pictures to Jason's communication book and begins to develop a strong friendship with him. However, she does not want her peers to know about their friendship. In the end, Jason helps Catherine see that her rules may really be excuses, and she begins to look at life differently.

In *See the Ocean*, Nellie is a young girl who is blind; however, her blindness is not evident until the end of the story. The fog is thick when Nellie and her family approach the ocean on their annual visit to the beach; and for the first time, Nellie can "see" the ocean with her other senses before her brothers see it with their eyes. Nellie's blindness does not prevent her from feeding crumbs to the seagulls, throwing pebbles into ponds, and enjoying the feeling of seashells and driftwood. The beautiful oil paintings that illustrate this book hide Nellie's eyes under her hat.

In *So B. It*, which has received the Dolly Gray Award, the character with a disability is 12-year-old Heidi's mother, who has intellectual disabilities and a very limited vocabulary. Heidi and her mother live alone in an apartment but rely heavily on their next-door neighbor, Bernadette, who has agoraphobia. In an attempt to discover her personal and family history, Heidi ventures from their home in Reno, Nevada, to Liberty, New York, discovering who she is and better understanding her mother as well. This book is noteworthy, particularly because it portrays how those with significant intellectual disabilities have the capacity and desire to love and be loved.

Trisha, in the autobiographical book, *Thank You, Mr. Falker*, cannot wait to start school so that she can learn to read. By first grade, however, she becomes frustrated with how easy reading seems for everyone but herself. Trisha begins to feel different and stupid. After her family relocates across the country, Trisha finds that her new school is the same as the previous one, and the other students tease her incessantly. Finally, Mr. Falker, her fifth-grade teacher, recognizes that Trisha cannot read. He and the reading teacher tutor her after school until she learns to read. After 30 years have passed, Trisha sees Mr. Falker again and thanks him for changing her life.

Tru Confessions, tells the story of 12-year-old Tru, who has two primary ambitions in life: to produce her own television show and to cure her twin brother of his intellectual disability. Tru seems tormented that her brother has a disability although she does not. Eventually, Tru realizes that she does not need to cure her brother and that she can move on with her own life. This book is unique in that it intersperses Tru's electronic diary within the text, which makes the book particularly enjoyable to read. This book has won the Dolly Gray Award and was made into a Disney Channel movie.

Mrs. Olinski, who uses a wheelchair in *The View from Saturday*, returns to teaching 10 years after a car accident has paralyzed her. She selects a group of four brilliant, but shy and unlikely, teammates to be her sixth-grade academic bowl team. She does not know why she has selected these four classmates, nor does she understand their repeated success at beating older, more experienced competitors until she, like the reader, learns the story of each member and what draws them together. This book is a good example of including a character with a disability without emphasizing the character's limitations or disabilities. Mrs. Olinski's disability is not a focal point of the story, although it does affect the story line in minor ways. This book won the Newbery Medal Award.

In another Newbery Medal book, *The Westing Game*, the tenants of a new condominium building learn that they are heirs to the estate of Sam Westing. His will states that his murderer is among the heirs. In teams of two, they must use clues to identify the murderer, with the winning team inheriting the Westing fortune. One of the potential heirs is Chris, an adolescent boy who uses a wheelchair. Although the author does not present detailed information about Chris and his condition, it is refreshing to read a very clever and well-written book that integrates a character in a wheelchair without focusing on his disability.

The title character of *Yours Turly, Shirley* compensates for her learning disabilities by being the class clown. When her parents adopt Jackie, a young Vietnamese girl, Shirley helps her learn English and a new culture, including learning about Barbie and Santa Claus. Helping Jackie makes Shirley feel important. Jackie turns into an excellent student who is a wonderful reader, speller, and memorizer and whose schoolwork is far better than Shirley's schoolwork. Now school is not the only thing that Shirley dislikes. The characters in this book are enchanting and lovable. The book is a fast read with a cute and entertaining story that shows how some people use humor to cover up their weaknesses.

Final Thoughts

Parents, teachers, librarians, psychologists, social workers, and others can use books from this top 25 list to share with children the joy of reading exemplary books that include multidimensional characters with disabilities. Given that literary merit alone will not ensure that you have chosen "the right book for the right reader for the right situation" (Kurkjian & Livingston, 2005, p. 790), the books on this list should help you select books appropriate for specific situations and individual students.

References

American Library Association (ALA). (2007). *Awards and scholarships*. Retrieved January 2, 2008, from www.ala.org/Template.cfm?Section=bookmediaawards&template=/ContentManagement

Council for Exceptional Children, Division of Developmental Disabilities. (n.d.). Dolly Gray Award for children's literature in developmental disabilities. Retrieved January 2, 2008, from www.dddcec. org/secondarypages/dollygray/Dolly_Gray_Children%27s_Literature_Award.html

Dyches, T. T., & Prater, M. A. (2000). *Developmental disability in children's literature: Issues and annotated bibliography*. Reston, VA: The Division on Mental Retardation and Developmental Disabilities of the Council for Exceptional Children.

Individuals With Disabilities Education Improvement Act of 2004 (IDEA), 20 U.S.C. §1400 *et seq.* (2004; reauthorization of the Individuals with Disabilities Education Act of 1990).

Kurkjian, C., & Livingston, N. (2005). The right book for the right child for the right situation. *The Reading Teacher, 58*, 786–795.

Tunnell, M. O., & Jacobs, J. S. (2007). *Children's literature, briefly*. Upper Saddle River, NJ: Prentice Hall.

Wallechinsky, D., & Wallace, A. (2005). *The new book of lists: The original compendium of curious information*. Edinburgh, Scotland: Canongate.

Assess Your Progress

1. How might reading books about students with disabilities help diverse students feel more accepted in your classroom?
2. Using the guidelines mentioned in the article, select three to five books about people who are diverse in other ways, such as those who live in poverty, are linguistically or culturally diverse, or have other factors that make them targets for bullies or shunning.

3. Each of the articles presented in this unit addresses a specific issue of diversity. Which of these issues is a major or primary concern in your local schools? Once you have stated the top two or three issues, use the information provided in the unit to determine at least two strategies or teaching practices for each issue.

MARY ANNE PRATER (CEC UT Federation), Professor and Chair; and **TINA TAYLOR DYCHES** (CEC UT Federation), Associate Professor, Counseling Psychology and Special Education, Brigham Young University, Provo, Utah.

Address correspondence to Mary Anne Prater, Counseling Psychology and Special Education, Brigham Young University, 340 MCKB, Provo, UT, 84602 (e-mail: prater@byu.edu).

From *Teaching Exceptional Children,* March/April 2008, pp. 32–38. Copyright © 2008 by Council for Exceptional Children. Reprinted by permission.

UNIT 6

Rethinking Discipline: Getting the Behavior You Want and Need to Teach Effectively

Unit Selections

27. **The Under-Appreciated Role of Humiliation in the Middle School,** Nancy Frey and Douglas Fisher
28. **Tackling a Problematic Behavior Management Issue: Teachers' Intervention in Childhood Bullying Problems,** Laura M. Crothers and Jered Kolbert
29. **The Power of Our Words,** Paula Denton
30. **Marketing Civility,** Michael Stiles and Ben Tyson
31. **Classwide Interventions: Effective Instruction Makes a Difference,** Maureen A. Conroy et al.
32. **Developing Effective Behavior Intervention Plans: Suggestions for School Personnel,** Kim Killu

Learning Outcomes

After reading this unit, you will be able to:

- Discuss the differences between student and teachers responses to the types of humiliation found in schools.
- Summarize the effects of humiliation.
- Analyze the suggestions that may enable teacher to manage problem behavior of bullying.
- Consider the appropriate timing for implementing techniques for managing bullying.
- Explain how language used by adults actually shapes learners.
- Relate the guiding principles for positive language.
- Apply positive language to teaching practices.
- Discuss the research on how communication affects the school climate.
- Synthesize the research and strategies in the two articles by Denton and Stiles and Tyson.
- Describe the correlation between a positive classroom climate and the frequency of behavior problems.
- Review universal class wide interventions suggested in the article.
- Define Functional Behavior Assessment and Behavior Intervention Plan.
- Determine when and why a teacher might decide to conduct a functional behavior assessment.
- Outline the steps for a functional behavior assessment.

Student Website
www.mhhe.com/cls

Internet References

The OSEP Technical Assistance Center of Positive Behavior Interventions & Supports (PBIS)
www.pbis.org/school/what_is_swpbs.aspx

Bully OnLine
www.bullyonline.org

Teaching Tolerance
www.tolerance.org

National Education Association: Classroom Management
www.nea.org/tools/ClassroomManagement.html

Teacher Vision
http://teachervision.fen.com

Center for Safe and Responsible Internet Use
www.cskcst.com

When teachers (and prospective teachers) discuss what concerns them about their roles (and prospective roles) in the classroom, the issue of discipline (how to manage student behavior) will usually rank near or at the top of their lists. Teachers need a clear understanding of what kinds of learning environments are most appropriate for the subject matter and ages of the students. Any person who wants to teach must also want his or her students to learn well, to acquire basic values of respect for others, and to become more effective citizens.

All teachers have concerns regarding the "quality of life" in classroom settings. Teachers and students want to feel safe and accepted when they are in school. There exists today a reliable, effective knowledge base on classroom management and how to prevent unwanted behaviors in schools. This knowledge base has been developed from hundreds of studies of teacher/student interaction and student/student interaction that have been conducted in schools in North America and Europe. We speak of classroom management because there are many factors that go into building effective teacher/student and student/student relationships. If teachers think about managing their classroom rather than controlling or ruling over the classroom, there is a shift in thinking that makes a difference. Managers are collaborative, cooperative, and sensitive to those they manage. Teachers who control are more commanding than cooperative, more punishing than managing, and tend to use fear as the dominant emotion in their classrooms. Furthermore, the term *discipline* is too narrow, and refers primarily to teachers' negative responses to unwanted behavior. We can better understand methods of managing student behavior when we look at the totality of what goes on in classrooms, with teachers' responses to student behavior as a part of that totality.

Teachers' core ethical principles come into play when deciding what constitutes defensible and desirable standards of student conduct. Teachers need to realize that before they can control behavior, they must identify what student behaviors are desired in their classrooms. They need to reflect, as well, on the emotional tone and ethical principles implied by their own behaviors. To optimize their chances of achieving the classroom atmosphere that they wish, teachers must strive for emotional balance within themselves; they must learn to be accurate observers; and they must develop just, fair strategies of intervention to aid students in learning self-control and good behavior. A teacher should be a good model of courtesy, respect, tact, and discretion. Children learn by observing how other persons behave and not just by being told about how they are to behave. There is no substitute for positive and assertive teacher interaction with students in class.

Teachers bear moral and ethical responsibilities for being witnesses to and examples of responsible social behavior in the classroom. We now have a body of research that attests to widespread prejudicial discipline measures being used with African American and Hispanic students. Teachers must examine their practices for such prejudice; do we see threats in the actions and behaviors of black and Hispanic boys and youth? Those of us who teach or have taught in urban settings may have noted that African American and Hispanic males are more often the ones in the hallways with teachers scowling and shaking their fingers. What message does this send to all students, including the ones sitting compliantly in their seats? We must be careful about the silent messages we send that clearly betray our innermost fears.

Furthermore, teachers are responsible for the emotional climate that is set in a classroom. Whether students feel secure and safe and whether they want to learn depend to an enormous extent on the teacher's psychological frame of mind. Teachers must be able to manage their own selves first in order to effectively manage the development of a humane and caring classroom environment. This is why we address the issues of bullying again in this edition. Crother and Kolbert offer eight strategies to address bullying as a management issue. We also offer two articles about dealing with bullying problems that often begins in middle school, but the humiliation can carry through high school and into adulthood as noted in two articles (Frey and Fisher; Stiles and Tyson). Responsible and responsive adults can make a difference. Denton reminds us that respect and caring are attitudes that a teacher must communicate to receive them in return. Open lines of communication between teachers and students enhance the possibility for congenial, fair dialogical resolution of problems as they occur. Several articles in this unit address the bullying issue.

In the course of a teaching career, any one teacher may have one or more children whose behavior requires more than the usual classroom management strategies. Conroy Sutherland, Snyder, and Marsh suggest six classroom tools that work based on effective instructional practices. However, some students may have deeper needs, including emotional or behavioral disabilities, or a conduct disorder. These students may require a Behavior Intervention Plan (BIP), especially if they have an Individual Education Plan (IEP). These plans help guide teachers, families, and students in their treatment and management of serious unwanted behaviors and should be viewed as a positive. These plans should be designed to help students change their behavior rather than being punitive in nature. For example, teachers may have students who have Attention-Deficit Hyperactivity Disorder (ADHD) and a behavior plan that outlines positive self-monitoring methods for helping the student to be more attentive and less active. Since general education teachers should be part of the team that writes these plans, we have included an article about BIPs by Killu.

Helping young people learn the skills of self-control and motivation to become productive, contributing, and knowledgeable adult participants in society is one of the most important tasks that good teachers undertake. These are teachable and learnable skills; they do not relate to heredity or social conditions. They can be learned by any human being who wants to learn them and who is cognitively able to learn them. All that is required is the willingness of teachers to learn these skills themselves and to teach them to their students. In this unit we have included an article on teaching self-regulation in early childhood settings, but some of these methods can generalize to higher grade levels.

Article 27

The Under-Appreciated Role of Humiliation in the Middle School

NANCY FREY AND DOUGLAS FISHER

In his book *The World Is Flat,* Friedman (2005) argued that we have under-appreciated the role that humiliation plays in terrorism. He notes that the reaction humans have when they are humiliated is significant and often severe. If it is true, that humiliation plays a role in terrorism, what role might this under-appreciated emotion play in middle school? If terrorists act, in part, based on humiliation, how do middle school students act when they experience this emotion?

To answer these questions, we interviewed 10 middle school teachers and 10 students. We asked them about times they (or their students or peers) were humiliated and what happened. In each case, they were surprised to be asked about this emotion. They said things like "It just happens; you gotta deal with it" and "You know how kids are, they can be mean." The responses from the teachers and students about the ways that students are humiliated clustered into three major areas: bullying, teacher behavior, and remedial reading. In addition, we searched the ERIC database for documentation about the impact humiliation has on middle school students. In this article, we will begin by discussing the findings from our interviews and surveys, then we will describe the effects of humiliation on middle school learners.

Types of Humiliation

The 10 teachers and 10 students we interviewed worked or attended one of three large urban middle schools in two southwestern states. These schools fit the profile of many schools across America—large (more than 1,000 students), located in major metropolitan communities, with diverse demographic profiles among students and teachers. None of the schools had a formal anti-bullying or character education program. We sought a representative sample of teachers based on experience, gender, and subject area. We chose students who represented different grade levels, genders, and achievement levels. The names of students and teachers are pseudonyms. We conducted individual interviews with each teacher and each student to ensure privacy and promote candor in their disclosures. Based on an analysis of their responses, we identified three themes.

Bullying

Student voices. The most common topic raised in the conversation for both teachers and students was bullying. Many students believed that bullying was part of life, something that was unavoidable. It need not be. "Being bullied is neither a 'part of growing up' nor a 'rite of passage'" (Barone, 1997, p. 80). Every student participant recounted a time in which he or she had been bullied or had witnessed it occurring with other students. Marcus, a sixth grader, described an incident that occurred earlier that school year.

> There're these older guys [eighth grade] who think they're the kings of the school. They talk loud, swear, shove people in the halls. I see them comin' and I bounce [leave]. My first month at this school, they walked behind me, talkin' loud about how I was a little faggot. I tried to ignore them, but they knocked my stuff out of my hand.

Marcus's experience is perhaps the most common type associated with bullying. There was an age and size differential between perpetrators and victim, accompanied by verbal abuse associated with sexual orientation, and some physical contact (Nishina & Juvonen, 2005; Olweus, 1993). This is also consistent with Bjorklund and Pellegrini's (2000) dominance theory of increased bullying directed at those entering a new social group.

Martha, a seventh grader, described a more subtle kind of bullying.

131

There's this girl, and she used to be our friend [named several girls] ... but she's just so weird. What happened to her? We were all friends since second grade, but when she came back to school [entering middle school] she still dressed and talked like such a baby. It's embarrassing to be around her. So, we stopped talking to her.

Martha described relational bullying, memorably chronicled in a number of studies (Bjoerkqvist, Lagerspetz, & Kaukianen, 1992; Crick, Bigbee, & Howe, 1996; Simmons, 2002). Although Martha did not describe herself as a bully, she exhibited prevalent forms of female aggression: relational bullying and avoidance (Crick, Bigbee, & Howe, 1996). The transition from elementary to middle school appears to play a role as well. Pelligrini and Bartini's (2000) study of bullying across fifth and sixth grade noted that the move to larger, more impersonal school environments often interfered with the maintenance of peer affiliations.

We also sought students' perspectives on the reasons bullying exists. Their comments suggest that they accept bullying as a given, a common part of middle school life. "Everyone gets made fun of," remarked seventh grade student Juan. "If you can't take it ... if you let anyone see it bothers you, you just get it even worse." Martha echoed this sentiment. "It's how girls are. One day you're friends, and the next day you're not. Better not be caught lookin' at someone else's man. That'll get you quicker than anything." Beliefs about the normative presence of bullying, verbal taunts, and teasing are prevalent among adolescents, who view these as *de facto* elements of the secondary school experience (Shakeshaft et al., 1997).

We also asked students about their reactions to being humiliated by their peers. Most described deep levels of shame and responses that could be categorized as either violent or avoidant. Students told us they "snapped," "pounded his face in," "blew," or "got my bitch on" to describe verbal or physical retaliation. In other cases, students described attempts to avoid a situation. Similar to Marcus's attempts to "bounce" when bullies were spotted, Al, an eighth grader, reported that he did not use certain restrooms or hallways, because he anticipated that his tormentor would be there. Adriana, an eighth grade student, poignantly recounted the following incident.

When I was in seventh, I made up a boyfriend to my friends. It was stupid. . . . Everyone had a boyfriend and I wanted one, too. I told them I had a boyfriend at [nearby middle school]. When Cindy found out that it wasn't true, she told everybody. They laughed at me, left notes . . . told some of the boys. I told my mom I was sick, and I didn't go to school for two weeks.

Adriana's avoidance of the situation is a common response to the humiliation resulting from bullying. According to the American Psychological Association and the National Education Association, 7% of eighth graders stay home from school at least once a month to avoid a bullying situation (cited in Vail, 1999). Other middle school students, like Marcus and Al, alter their paths in school to avoid encountering bullies (Wessler, 2003).

Teacher voices. The 10 teachers who participated in this study were conflicted about the role of bullying in middle school. All 10 participants expressed concern over the amount of bullying in their schools (i.e., responding positively to the queries, "Bullying occurs frequently at this school," and "Bullying negatively impacts the learning of students at this school"). All were aware of the deleterious effects of bullying on both the victims and the perpetrators. Mr. Lee, a seventh and eighth grade mathematics instructor, noted, "We have to worry about the kid who's doing the bullying as well as the one who's getting it. Those kids that are bullies now end up in trouble in school and in life." In addition, 8 of the 10 instructors reported that they "always" responded to incidents of bullying. Mr. Harper, a music teacher, said, "I had it happen last week. I was outside my class [during passing period] and saw a group of bigger students descend on this smaller boy. You could just see this kid brace himself for what was going to happen. It was like slow motion. . . . I stepped in and made the kids leave him alone." Five other teachers offered anecdotal reports of their personal responses to bullying incidents, although, in all cases, it was related to the threat of physical harm perpetrated by either boys or girls.

Verbal abuse did not prompt such swift responses. "I won't put up with profanity, name-calling. If I hear it, I stop it. I write a referral if I have to," stated Ms. Indria, a sixth grade social studies teacher. However, when probed, all 10 teachers stated that they did not get involved in "personal relationships, friendship stuff." Ms. Indria offered, "Girls just seem to treat each other badly. It's a part of adolescence. . . . I certainly remember doing it when I was that age." Seventh grade science teacher Ms. Anthony echoed a similar response. "I can't keep up with it. One week they're friends; the next week they aren't. Way too much drama. I find that when I have tried to mediate, it ends by consuming too much instructional time." Four other teachers made statements consistent with the belief that negotiating a verbally, or even physically, abusive landscape was a part of growing up. Physical education teacher Ms. Hartford noted,

> You really have to be careful when you choose to interfere. It [teacher involvement] can really make it worse. The kids will just pick more—"teacher's pet." If it looks like the kid is holding his own, I don't get directly involved. I keep an eye on it.

It is also likely that Ms. Hartford and the other teachers interviewed were not cognizant of their relationships with the aggressors. Elias and Zins (2003) found that bullies often hold high social capital with their teachers and are perceived positively, while victims are often perceived as less likable.

Statements like the one offered by the physical education and science teachers illuminate a commonly held belief among middle school educators—that the ability to "take it" is a necessary rite of adolescent passage. Computer instructor Ms. Andersen evoked her own junior high memories to defend this position.

> Face it, being able to dish it out and take it gets you ready for the real world. What's that old commercial? "Never let 'em see you sweat." Teenagers have to learn that you don't wear your emotions on your sleeve. People'll use it against you. I know, I went through it, but I survived. You have to toughen up.

When asked about the role of humiliation in bullying, she replied,

> Yeah, they're good at humiliating each other. I keep an ear on what's going on. But I have to say . . . a lot of times they use it to keep each other in line. In a funny way, they regulate each other's behavior.

Ms. Anderson's beliefs are not entirely misplaced. Tapper and Bolton (2005) used wireless recording equipment to analyze bullying interactions among 77 students. They found that direct aggression (without physical violence) often inspired peer support for the aggressor. The reaction of the victim is a factor in whether the bullying will continue. Perry, Williard, and Perry (1990) determined that displays of distress by the victim increased the likelihood that bullying would occur again. "Never let 'em see you sweat" appears to be accurate.

Teacher Behavior

Student voices. Students had strong feelings about the use of humiliation by teachers. Nine of the 10 student participants could recount times when a teacher had used sarcasm or humiliation to embarrass a student in front of the class. In some cases it was directed at them, while in others they had witnessed it in their classes.

> We had this one teacher in seventh grade; man, she was rough. She had a nickname for every kid in the class. Like, she called this one girl "Funeral," because she said she always looked like she was coming from one.

This story, told by Al, is admittedly an extreme example and not typical of the incidences that were shared by students. However, three students told of times when teachers had "busted someone" in front of the entire class for failing a quiz or test, using insulting language. "I don't know why they do it," said Gail, a sixth grader. "It's not like it makes a difference. Who wants to work harder for someone who embarrasses you that way?"

Other students admitted that the use of humiliation might have a positive effect, at least in the short term.

> My [seventh grade] math teacher reads everyone's quiz grades to the whole class. I failed one, and he said, "Spending too much time looking at girls?" It made me kinda mad . . . but I made sure I didn't fail another math quiz. (Juan, eighth grade)

Veronica, an eighth grade student, said,

> Ms. _____ likes to catch you doing something wrong. Like, we were reading our social studies book out loud and I missed my turn. She goes, "Wake up, Veronica! We're all waiting," in this really stupid way she has [imitates a sarcastic tone]. Everyone laughed as though it never happened to them. I don't let her catch me.

Veronica then used profanity to describe her teacher, evidence of the anger she felt toward this adult and perhaps school in general.

When asked what they thought these teachers hoped to gain with the use of humiliation, their insights were surprising. "They want to be cool, like it's funny," remarked sixth grade student Marcus. Seventh grader Harlan responded similarly. "They don't treat you like little kids. My dad talks the same way. Making fun of kids in the class is just what they do."

The use of sarcasm and humiliation by teachers has been less well documented in the literature than the prevalence and effects of bullying. It is certainly long understood in the teaching profession, as evidenced by Briggs's (1928) article on the prevalence of the use of sarcasm by young secondary teachers. Martin's (1987) study of secondary students' perspectives on this phenomenon was derived from surveys of more than 20,000 Canadian students. Students reported that the use of sarcasm resulted in dislike for the teacher and even anger toward the teacher. Martin also reported that some students described "anticipatory embarrassment," the dread associated with the belief that the teacher would humiliate them again. In addition, this created learning problems, including decreased motivation to study and complete homework, increased cutting of classes, and thoughts of dropping out. Turner and associates (2002) studied the classroom learning environments of 65 sixth grade mathematics classrooms to study factors that promoted or reduced help-seeking behaviors and found that the teacher's classroom discourse, including use of sarcasm, influenced the likelihood that students would seek academic help when needed. Classrooms featuring more negative teacher talk, including sarcasm, were associated with high levels of avoidance in asking for assistance.

Teacher voices. Six of the 10 teachers in the study named colleagues who regularly used sarcasm and humiliation with students. Ms. Robertson, a seventh grade language arts teacher, described a colleague as "us[ing] words like a knife. He just cuts kids down to size." Mr. Lee, the math teacher, described an experience when he was a student teacher.

> [The master teacher] was just vicious with students. Everything was a big joke, but kind of mean-spirited, you know? He'd single out kids because of a quirk, like they talked funny, or they had a big nose, or they wore clothes that were kind of different. Kids would laugh, but I saw the cringes, too.

Five of the participating teachers discussed the fine line between humor and sarcasm. Ms. Andersen offered,

> You have to take into account that they're really very fragile, in spite of all their bluster. We all remember what it was like. Worried all the time about sticking out. They're already sensitive to the need for conformity. As teachers, we have to make sure that we don't make them feel different.

Ms. Hartford noted, "It's great to keep it light and fun, but not at someone else's expense." Sarcasm is typically used for three purposes: to soften a criticism, especially through feigned politeness; to mitigate verbal aggressiveness; or to create humor (Dews & Winner, 1995). However, the use of sarcasm in social discourse assumes an equal relationship between parties. This is never the case in the classroom, where the teacher holds the power in the relationship. Therefore, the student cannot respond with a sarcastic reply without consequences. The use of sarcasm with middle school students is ineffective as well, as evidenced by a study of 13-year-olds by the Harvard Zero Project. They found that 71% of the students studied misinterpreted sarcasm as deception. In other words, the majority had not yet reached a linguistically sophisticated developmental level that would allow them to accurately discern the speaker's purpose, even when it was accompanied by a gestural cue (Demorest, Meyer, Phelps, Gardner, & Winner, 1984).

Remedial Reading and Mathematics

Bullying and sarcasm are age-old tools of humiliation, but a more recent (and inadvertent) tool is that of the remedial class created for students who fail to achieve in reading and mathematics. Commonly referred to as "double dosing," it is the practice of increasing the number of instructional hours spent in remediation, at the expense of electives or core classes such as science and social studies (Cavanaugh, 2006). Though well-intended, our student participants were vocal about the negative effects on the lives of adolescents.

Student voices. "Everyone knows who the dumb kids are," explained Martha, a seventh grade student. "All you have to do is look around at who's not on the wheel [elective class rotation]. They're all in reading mastery." At Martha's school, students who score below a cut point on the state language arts and mathematics examinations are automatically enrolled in another section of instruction. Jessika, an eighth grader, is one of those students. "I hate it. We're all the stupid kids. Everyone knows it." Carol, another eighth grade student, described her classmates this way:

> Nobody even tries in my [remedial] reading class. It's like, if you do, you're trying to make yourself look better than you really are. No offense, but it's "acting white." People just sleep in class. You know, pull their [sweatshirt] hood up. If you look like you're trying, you'll catch it from [classmates.]

Marcus and Al are also enrolled in similar classes for mathematics. When asked what others said to them and about them in regard to their participation in these courses, we heard, "retard," "SPED" [special education], "loser," "tard," "spaz," and "window licker." These labels are quite troubling for students with disabilities, because they suggest an accepted intolerance for students in need of academic supports.

Slavin's (1993) review of the literature on remedial classes in middle school found a zero effect size for academic gains. While it is too soon to gauge the long-term effectiveness of double-dosing academic achievement, the voices of middle school students provide a bellwether for assessing the social and emotional repercussions of such practices. In a few short years, these students will have reached an age at which they can voluntarily exit school. There is further evidence that low-achieving students are more likely to use so-called "self-handicapping strategies" such as giving up and refusing to study (Midgely & Urdan, 1995; Turner et al., 2002). In particular, they are more likely to associate with other negative-thinking students. The remediation classroom, it would seem, from Carol's and Jessika's comments, is a perfect environment for breeding this sort of attitude toward school and learning.

Teachers' voices. We were particularly interested in the views of Mr. Lee and Ms. Robertson, both of whom teach a section of remedial math or reading. "No one wants those classes," remarked Mr. Lee. "I got it because I'm new here. They stick the new teachers with these classes. Wouldn't you think that they should be taught by people with lots of experience?" he asked. Mrs. Robertson described her classroom learning environment. "I'm ashamed to say that I dread fourth [period] because of the students. I feel like all the energy gets sucked out of the room, and me. I can't seem to inspire them, and it affects the way I teach." When asked to elaborate, she said, "I know I'm stricter, and I feel like I can't even smile or make a joke. I'm grim, and it makes for a grim period."

Two other teachers explained that, while they saw the logic in double dosing, they worried about the detrimental effects on their students. Mr. Espinosa, a seventh grade social studies teacher, said,

> We're organized in houses here [a cohort model]. But every time we excuse students to go to another class, one that's different from everyone else, it chops away at the concept of a family of students and teachers. I can see the light go right out of their eyes when they have to pass up computer class to go for extra reading or math class.

Ms. Andersen, the computer teacher, expressed concern about the content students were missing. "If I'm not teaching literacy and math, then what am I doing? They'll just get further behind."

The Effects of Humiliation

In addition to the ways in which middle school students experience humiliation, we discussed the impact that humiliation has on young adolescents. Both students and teachers identified a number of outcomes from humiliation, including drug and alcohol use, attendance problems, dropping out of school, pregnancy, and suicide. Let us examine the perspectives of teachers and students on each of these issues.

Drug and Alcohol Use

Most educators recognize that experimentation with alcohol and drugs during adolescence is common. The Youth Risk Behavior Survey (www.cdc.gov/HealthyYouth/yrbs/index.htm) indicated that more than two-thirds of middle school students report ever having had a drink of alcohol and that 26% report ever having used marijuana. However, several students commented on the regular use of drugs and alcohol by students who feel humiliated at school. In the words of Marcus, "I know a kid who drinks every night. He hates school and says they make him feel stupid." One of the teachers noted that the rate of drug and alcohol use was highest for students who were enrolled in remedial reading classes. Mooney (Mooney & Cole, 2000), a student with a disability who subsequently graduated from an Ivy League college, discussed his use of drugs and alcohol to "turn off the shockers" at school.

Attendance Problems

Another outcome of humiliation that both students and teachers discussed was poor school attendance. Mr. Harper, the music teacher, put it eloquently—"They vote with their feet"— meaning that students tell us, by their physical presence in school, whether or not it is a comfortable place to be. Again, most educators acknowledge that there are patterns of problematic attendance, such as is typically seen in urban schools. More important, for our purpose here, is the difference of attendance patterns within the school. It is clear from an analysis of attendance patterns—both tardiness and absence—that students are communicating with which teachers they feel comfortable and with which they do not. While there are many reasons for students feeling comfortable with teachers, one reason is the climate that is created in class. Veronica reported, "Lots of us cut class with Mr. _____ because he makes you feel bad when you try to answer."

Dropping Out

While calculating an accurate drop-out rate has been exceedingly difficult to do, it is important to note that in many states there is no mechanism for capturing middle school drop-outs. It seems that when the data systems were created, people assumed that middle school students either would not or could not drop out of school. Unfortunately, that is not the reality; middle school students are dropping out. In-grade retention (an indicator of either poor academic performance or poor attendance) is the single strongest school-related predictor of dropping out in middle school (Rumberger, 1995). As Ms. Indria reported, "There are students who just leave us. They don't find school fulfilling and are ashamed of their performance, and they stop coming. No one really knows where they go." Turner and associates' (2002) study on the relationship between classroom climate and help-seeking offers further evidence of the role of humiliation. There is also evidence that the overall school climate—the degree that students feel safe to learn and are not threatened by peers or teachers—is directly related to the drop-out problem (Wehlage, 1991). As Al indicated, "If I had to deal with the crap that Jeremy does, I'd just quit. I wouldn't come to this place."

School institutions related to humiliation play a factor as well. According to Goldschmidt and Wang (1999), "Two school policy and practice variables affect the middle school dropout rate significantly: the percentage of students held back one grade, and the percentage of students misbehaving". Here we see the snowballing effects of humiliation. Students retained in grade, attending remedial classes, surrounded by misbehavior (including bullying), with lower rates of attendance and less inclination to seek help from sarcastic teachers appear to be at great risk for dropping out, and humiliation plays a role in each.

Pregnancy

Another issue associated with humiliation, identified primarily by the teachers we interviewed, was teenage pregnancy. While less common at the middle school level than at the secondary level, teen pregnancy is still an issue with this age group. According to the Centers for Disease Control and Prevention, national data suggests that between six and seven of every 1,000 middle school girls become pregnant (Klien, 2005). While there are a number of theories about the causes of teenage pregnancy, including too much free time, poverty, access to alcohol, and physical maturity, Ms. Hartford had another take on the situation. She said, "In this community, pregnancy is one of the acceptable reasons to leave school. If school is a toxic environment for you, you can get pregnant and leave school. Nobody will question your decision."

Suicide

A final outcome of humiliation identified by the participants was suicide and suicidal thoughts. Public health officials have noted a significant increase in youth suicide—more than 300% since 1950 (Bloch, 1999). Suicide is now the third leading cause of death for youth ages 10 to 19 (following accidents and homicides) (Centers for Disease Control and Prevention, 2000). While the suicide rate for high school students has remained fairly stable over the past decade, the suicide rate for middle school students (ages 10 through 14), increased more than 100% during the decade of the 1990s (Bloch, 1999). A haunting thought was shared by Adriana, who said, "Everybody I know has thought about suicide, but the one who did it was bothered all the time by other kids and no one did anything." As Fisher (2005) noted, teachers have to understand the signs and symptoms of suicide and ensure that students feel honored and respected at school. One of the teachers suggested, "I think that they're under a great deal of pressure to perform. If you add humiliation to that, they don't see a way out and might consider taking their own life."

Recommendations for Reducing Humiliation in Middle School

Some of the problems members of our profession discuss about the challenges to achievement in middle school might be explained by students' experiences with humiliation. When students experience humiliation, as these data suggest they do, a series of negative outcomes can be triggered. We recommend that educators make a commitment to reduce the needless opportunities for humiliation that creep into the daily experiences of their students.

Recommendation #1: Assess the School Climate

The first step to reducing humiliation is to recognize that it might, in fact, be present. Schools routinely administer annual school climate surveys, and this can provide an excellent starting point for analysis. For example, the California Healthy Kids Survey contains questions that can shed light on the issue of humiliation. The survey asks respondents to assess the extent to which adults "treat all students fairly" and "listen to what students have to say" and contains several queries about bullying and bully prevention programs (California Department of Education, 2005).

Recommendation #2: Observe and Analyze Curricular and Instructional Interactions

The middle school reform report entitled *Breaking Ranks in the Middle* (National Association of Secondary School Principals, 2006) strongly recommends heterogeneous grouping of students in small learning communities to improve achievement and personalize learning. This requires schools to abandon outdated ability grouping and tracking, which result in lowered expectations and missed opportunities for rigorous curriculum. Some schools cling to tracking and remedial classes because they do not possess the capacity to differentiate instruction for all learners. Building this capacity is not a matter of scattershot inservices, but rather targeted peer coaching, professional development, and administrative accountability. A first step toward realizing this goal is to conduct classroom observations for the purposes of data collection and analysis of needs. The Instructional Practices Inventory developed by the Middle Level Leadership Center is a useful tool for developing a school-wide profile of the instructional practices occurring at the school, including the amount of teacher-led instruction, student-led discussions, and levels of disengagement (www.mllc.org).[1] Classrooms with high levels of student disengagement should be targeted for further analysis to determine contributing factors, especially teacher behaviors and interaction styles. Teachers struggling with disengagement can participate in the Teacher Expectations and Student Achievement (TESA) professional development program developed by the Los Angeles County Office of Education (www.lacoe.edu/orgs/165/index.cfm). This is a five-month experience that involves peer observations and coaching focused on 15 specific instructional behaviors that increase positive student perceptions about learning. Other teachers who are having difficulty with curriculum design for heterogeneously grouped students can benefit from focused professional development and planning on differentiating instruction at the unit level. A beginning step may include the formation of book study groups using materials such as *Differentiation in Practice for Grades 5–9* (Tomlinson & Eidson, 2003). By collecting and sharing data to develop targeted professional development, teachers are able to move beyond "I've heard/read this before" to take specific action. This is further reinforced through administrative accountability and ongoing data collection to measure improvement at the curricular and instructional levels.

Recommendation #3: Make an Anti-bullying Curriculum Part of the School Culture

Much has been written in the past decade about anti-bullying curricula, especially in the wake of high-profile school shootings throughout the nation. Many fine programs exist, and the Olweus Bullying Prevention Program is among the most respected (www.clemson.edu/olweus/content.html). The multi-layered design of this program targets school-wide, classroom, and individual interventions for both bullies and victims. However, anti-bullying curricula are only effective if there is long-term commitment. Perhaps the most common mistake is that after a period of enthusiastic introduction and implementation, programs such as these fall to the wayside as other initiatives command attention. A multi-year plan that includes refreshers for existing staff as well as training for teachers new to the school is essential for sustainability. The anti-bullying program should be written into the school's accountability plan, the new teacher induction program, and as part of the curriculum for each grade level.

Conclusion

The recommendations made are all costly in terms of time, money, and resources. However, the unintended costs of humiliation are much higher for our students. It is time to take another look at the anti-bullying curricula being developed by groups across the country and how they can be sustained for more than one school year. It might also be time to notice our own behaviors and to have hard conversations with our colleagues about appropriate interactions with students—interactions that clearly demonstrate care, honesty, and high expectations. And finally, it may be time to reconsider the ways in which we group students and provide supplemental instructional interventions such that groups of students do not experience school as telling them they are stupid, incompetent, and not worthy. In doing so, we might just see increases in student achievement as well as youth who are more engaged in their educational experience.

Note

1. For a comprehensive assessment of middle school programs, procedures, and processes, readers might want to consider using the School Improvement Toolkit, available from National Middle School Association at www.nmsa.org/ProfessionalDevelopment/SchoolImprovementToolkit/tabid/654/Default.aspx

References

Barone, F. J. (1997). Bullying in school. *Phi Delta Kappan, 79,* 80–82.

Bjoerkqvist, K., Lagerspetz, K. M. J., & Kaukianen, A. (1992). Do girls manipulate and boys fight? Developmental trends in regard to direct and indirect aggression. *Aggressive Behavior, 18,* 117–127.

Bjorklund, D. F., & Pellegrini, A. D. (2000). Child development and evolutionary psychology. *Child Development, 71,* 1687–1708.

Bloch, D. (1999). Adolescent suicide as a public health threat. *Journal of Child and Adolescent Psychiatric Nursing, 12,* 26–38.

Briggs, T. H. (1928). Sarcasm. *The School Review, 36*(9), 685–695.

California Department of Education. (2005). *California healthy kids school climate survey.* Retrieved February 18, 2007, from http://www.wested.org/chks/pdf/scs_05_alpha.pdf

Cavanaugh, S. (2006, June 14). Students double-dosing on reading and math: Schools aim to improve state test scores—and satisfy federal education laws. *Education Week.* Retrieved September 3, 2006, from www.all4ed.org/press/ EdWeek_061406_Students DoubleDosingReadingMath.pdf

Centers for Disease Control and Prevention. (2000). *Youth risk behavior surveillance—United States, 1999.* In CDC surveillance summaries, June 9, 2000, MMRW. Atlanta, GA: Author.

Crick, N. R., Bigbee, M. A., & Howe, C. (1996). How do I hurt thee? Let me count the ways. *Child Development, 67,* 1003–1014.

Demorest, A., Meyer, C., Phelps, E., Gardner, H., & Winner, E. (1984). Words speak louder than actions: Understanding deliberately false remarks. *Child Development, 55,* 1527–1534.

Dews, S., & Winner, E. (1995). Muting the meaning: A social function of irony. *Metaphor and Symbolic Activity, 10,* 3–18.

Elias, M. J., & Zins, J. E. (2003). Bullying, other forms of peer harassment, and victimization in the schools: Issues for school psychology research and practice. In M. J. Elias & J. E. Zins (Eds.), *Bullying, peer harassment, and victimization in the schools: The next generation of prevention* (pp. 1–5). Binghamton, NY: Haworth.

Fisher, D. (2005). The literacy educator's role in suicide prevention. *Journal of Adolescent and Adult Literacy, 48,* 364–373.

Friedman, T. L. (2005). *The world is flat: A brief history of the twenty-first century.* New York: Farrar, Straus and Giroux.

Goldschmidt, P., & Wang, J. (1999). When can schools affect dropout behavior? A longitudinal multilevel analysis. *American Education Research Journal, 36,* 715–738.

Klein, J. D. (2005). Adolescent pregnancy: Current trends and issues. *Pediatrics, 116,* 281–286.

Martin, W. B. W. (1987). Students' perceptions of causes and consequences of embarrassment in the school. *Canadian Journal of Education, 12,* 277–293.

Midgely, C., & Urdan, T. (1995). Predictors of middle school students' use of self-handicapping strategies. *The Journal of Early Adolescence, 15,* 389–411.

Mooney, J., & Cole, D. (2000). *Learning outside the lines: Two Ivy League students with learning disabilities and ADHD give you the tools for academic success and educational revolution.* New York: Simon & Schuster.

National Association of Secondary School Principals. (2006). *Breaking ranks in the middle: Strategies for leading middle level reform.* Reston, VA: Author.

Nishina, A., & Juvonen, J. (2005). Daily reports of witnessing and experiencing peer harassment in middle school. *Child Development, 76,* 435–450.

Olweus, D. (1993). *Bullying at school: What we know and what we can do.* Oxford, UK: Blackwell.

Pellgrini, A. D., & Bartini, M. (2000). A longitudinal study of bullying, victimization, and peer affiliation during the transition from primary school to middle school. *American Educational Research Journal, 37,* 699–725.

Perry, D. G., Williard, J. C., & Perry, L. C. (1990). Peers' perceptions of the consequences that victimized children provide aggressors. *Child Development, 61,* 1310–1325.

Rumberger, R. W. (1995). Dropping out of middle school: A multilevel analysis of students and schools. *American Educational Research Journal, 32,* 583–625.

Shakeshaft, C., Mandel, L., Johnson, Y. M., Sawyer, J., Hergenrother, M. A., & Barber, E. (1997). Boys call me cow. *Educational Leadership, 55*(2), 22–25.

Simmons, R. (2002). *Odd girl out: The hidden culture of aggression in girls.* New York: Harcourt.

Slavin, R. E. (1993). Ability grouping in the middle grades: Achievement effects and alternatives. *The Elementary School Journal, 93,* 535–552.

Tapper, K., & Boulton, M. J. (2005). Victim and peer group responses to different forms of aggression among primary school children. *Aggressive Behavior, 31,* 238–253.

Tomlinson, C. A., & Eidson, C. C. (2003). *Differentiation in practice: A resource guide for differentiating curriculum grades 5–9.* Alexandria, VA: Association for Supervision and Curriculum Development.

Turner, J. C., Midgley, C., Meyer, D. K., Gheen, M., Anderman, E. M., Kang, Y., & Patrick, H. (2002). The classroom environment and students' reports of avoidance strategies in Mathematics: A multimethod study. *Journal of Educational Psychology, 94,* 88–106.

Vail, K., (1999). Words that wound. *American School Board Journal, 186*(9), 37–40.

Wehlage, G. (1991). School reform for at-risk students. *Equity and Excellence, 25,* 15–24.

Wessler, S. L. (2003). It's hard to learn when you're scared. *Educational Leadership, 61*(1), 40–43.

Assess Your Progress

1. Using a Venn why diagram, compare and contrast teacher and student responses regarding humiliation.
2. Frey and Fisher make three recommendations for reducing humiliation in the middle school. Outline a plan of actions using at least two of those recommendations in either your field experiences or future teaching.

NANCY FREY is an associate professor of teacher education at San Diego State University, California. **DOUGLAS FISHER** is a professor of teacher education at San Diego State University, California. Email: dfisher@mail.sdsu.edu

Article 28

Tackling a Problematic Behavior Management Issue
Teachers' Intervention in Childhood Bullying Problems

In coping with and addressing a common child behavioral problem, classroom teachers may benefit from viewing bullying as a behavior management issue in the educational setting. The authors offer eight suggestions that specifically address childhood bullying problems in the classroom. Teachers can add these to their toolkit of behavior management strategies.

LAURA M. CROTHERS AND JERED B. KOLBERT

Child disciplinary problems can be stressful for a classroom teacher. Teachers find accommodating behavioral difficulties more challenging and less feasible than making instructional modifications for academic problems (Ritter, 1989). In fact, researchers have suggested the existence of a relationship between disruptive student behavior patterns (e.g., disrespect, poor social skills) and teacher burnout (Hastings & Bham, 2003).

When asked about managing problematic student behavior, teachers often respond in one of two ways: It is not much of a concern, because their classroom management strategies are typically effective in resolving student behavioral concerns, or they feel overwhelmed and impotent to address behavioral difficulties that threaten to disrupt the learning process and subsequent academic achievement of students (Discipline Problems Take a Toll, 2004). Those in the latter group often explain that they were not adequately trained to manage students with behavior problems or they believe that teachers who are effective classroom managers are inherently talented in rectifying disciplinary issues demonstrated by children at school.

The use of such external attributions or excuses can compromise a teacher's ability to successfully take responsibility for student behavior and learning in the classroom. Early intervention is critically important in preventing and reducing children's behavior problems (Dodge, 1993). Interestingly, the primary difference between successful and unsuccessful behavior managers is not the manner in which they handle discipline problems but rather the number of discipline problems they encounter. Effective classroom managers create a structured environment and manage behavioral antecedents to diminish the likelihood of behavior problems ever occurring (Duke, 1982; Elliott, Witt, Kratochwill, & Stoiber, 2002).

It is from the vantage of behavior management that childhood bullying problems can be addressed, because such issues often demand a significant portion of teachers' behavior modification efforts. Research has established a normative (i.e., routinely occurring) nature of bully–victim relationships in schools (Smith & Brain, 2000). Further, childhood bullying has increasingly been recognized as one of the most common and widespread forms of school violence occurring not only in the United States but in other countries as well. *Bullying* has been defined as repetitive instrumental aggression that results in an imbalance of power between perpetrator and victim (Smith & Brain, 2000), and it involves approximately 30% of U.S. students during their school careers (Nansel et al., 2001).

Victims of bullying behavior suffer from anxiety, depression, low self-esteem, physical and psychosomatic complaints, posttraumatic stress disorder, and suicidal ideation (Kaltiala-Heino, Rimpela, Marttunen, Rimpela, & Rantenan, 1999; McKenney, Pepler, Craig, & Connolly, 2002; Williams, Chambers, Logan, & Robinson, 1996). Perpetrators of bullying also experience negative effects, including an increased risk of mental health disorders, such as attention-deficit/hyperactivity disorder, depression, oppositional defiant disorder, and conduct disorder (Kumpulainen, Rasanen, & Puura, 2001). Children who bully also exhibit a greater likelihood of engaging in criminal behavior, domestic violence, and substance abuse as adults (Farrington, 1993) and are more likely to struggle with poor academic achievement and poor career performance in adulthood (Carney & Merrell, 2001). Finally, researchers have found that childhood bullies are often severely punitive with their own children, who are subsequently more likely to be aggressive with peers (Eron, Huesmann, Dubow, Romanoff, & Yarmel, 1987; Smokowski & Kopasz, 2005).

Much research has documented the prevalence and negative effects of bullying, yet some literature has also suggested that teachers sometimes contribute to or tolerate the problem. According to Olweus (1991), students often report that teachers do not intervene when a student is being bullied in school, and many times teachers are unaware of occurrences of bullying. This is particularly surprising because students frequently indicate that bullying occurs in the classroom while the teacher is present (Olweus, 1991). Olweus (1993) also explained that when teachers recognize that bullying is occurring, they often do relatively little to put a stop to the behavior and make only limited contact with students involved in the bullying to discuss the problem. This lack of intervention may be particularly dangerous because children who engage in bullying may interpret the resulting adult nonintervention as tacit approval of their behavior.

However, because of the incidence and negative effects on victims and perpetrators, school personnel are increasingly recognizing that bullying is a problem that must be addressed in the educational setting. For purposes of empowerment and a sense of control, it may be helpful for classroom teachers to view the problem of bullying as a behavior management issue, similar to off-task or other non–rule-governed behavior. Also, it may be easier to prevent childhood bullying problems rather than react to them, because responding to incidents of peer victimization can be difficult for such reasons as not directly observing the behavior or not being aware of the extent of the problem due to students not reporting bullying to adults (Crothers & Kolbert, 2004). Eight suggestions are offered to enable teachers to add to their toolkit of behavior management strategies, as well as to specifically address childhood bullying problems in their classrooms.

Assessment

Although teachers measure students' scholastic achievement on a daily basis in their classrooms, they often feel reluctant to use assessment methods to investigate nonacademic problems, believing that such domains are best handled by the training and skills demonstrated by school psychologists and counselors. However, engaging in assessment of bullying behavior is an important first step in addressing the problem. The best news about gathering data regarding childhood bullying is that it can be quite simple. Teachers can compile a list of their students' names and divide the children into three groups: *bullies, victims,* and *bystanders*. Similarly, educators can choose to identify which children match certain behavioral descriptors (e.g., aggressive, assertive, passive). After students have been identified as bullies or victims, they can be targeted for individual intervention efforts.

Some researchers have questioned the accuracy of teacher nomination of bullies and victims, believing that teachers may lack objectivity in identifying bullies and victims and may underestimate the amount of bullying that takes place in school (Smith & Ananiadou, 2003; Smith & Sharp, 1994). Also, teachers may be unable to discern between bullying and horseplay and may have biases regarding their students (Hazler, Carney, Green, Powell, & Jolly, 1997; Pellegrini & Bartini, 2000). However, teachers can minimize such problems by spending long periods of time observing their students in a variety of settings (e.g., classroom, playground, lunchroom) as well as engaging in periodic retraining in conducting accurate observations and reliability checks (e.g., comparing perceptions with another teacher). When possible, information provided through teacher assessment should be compared with students' perceptions of which students are bullying others or are frequently victimized; teachers' and students' shared experiences illuminate the problem (Pellegrini & Bartini, 2000).

Guidance Approaches

Whole-school anti-bullying programs typically use guidance lessons, such as drama (e.g., acting out scenarios), watching videos, and reading books as a means of addressing bullying in the classroom. The primary purpose of such activities can be viewed as sensitization to the problem of bullying. Drama, videos, books, and discussions about bullying can give children the language to identify and talk about the experience of bullying. Teachers of young children can act out bullying scenarios using puppets to play the roles of victim and bully. As children mature into adolescence, teachers can encourage children to develop scripts that depict bullying and use puppets to act out the scenarios.

Videos and books are also a helpful medium for educators to introduce awareness of bullying to their students. Children's literature that addresses bullying behavior, such as *Nobody Knew What to Do: A Story About Bullying* (McCain & Leonardo, 2001), can help children understand that bullying is a common problem by emphasizing the need to seek help from adults (Ralston, 2005). There are also nonfiction selections for students, such as *Bullies to Buddies: How to Turn Your Enemies Into Friends!* (Czarnecki, 2005; Kalman, 2004), which teaches children to avoid being victims of bullying by turning anger into humor, fear into courage, and enemies into friends through the use of verbal interactions and body language.

Videos and DVDs on bullying are also available, such as *Bullies Are a Pain in the Brain* (Comical Sense Company, 2005), in which the main character tries to develop solutions to make a bully leave him alone. Selections for older children, such as *End the Silence: Stop the Bullying* (Sunburst, 2004) are appropriate for Grades 7 through 12 and can model solution strategies for students, such as banding together and refusing to tolerate the behavior, as well as implementing a whole-school anti-bullying program. Teachers can use these materials and experiences as a catalyst for discussions about bullying in their classrooms.

Classroom Management Techniques

It may be helpful for teachers to consider classroom management as an aspect of instruction, curriculum, and school climate rather than one of control (Duke, 1982; Levin & Nolan, 2004). Effective instruction is probably the most powerful form of classroom management because children who are actively engaged in learning are less likely to have the time and inclination to engage in bullying. Curricula that encourage children to question their own assumptions and engage in critical thinking will reduce boredom and the opportunity to bully for entertainment purposes. Having activities overlap so that students are continuously busy with learning tasks can diminish the opportunity that children have to assert power over one another.

In conjunction with curriculum and effective teaching, consideration should be paid to creating a classroom climate that is inhospitable to bullying. Thus, one of the first strategies in addressing bullying is to establish rules prohibiting it. Teachers can provide students with information that instructs them on how they should handle bullying behavior (Batsche, 1997; Boulton & Underwood, 1992). As a part of a general classroom management strategy, teachers can also implement whole-class incentive systems that encourage children to control their aggressive behavior and concentrate on meeting behavioral goals. Programs such as *The Winning Ticket* (Floyd, 1985) are based on the notion that socially appropriate behaviors are skills that can be learned.

Another means of addressing bullying is teacher vigilance regarding student behavior in the classroom and throughout the school in general. Teachers need to be constantly aware of student conduct and activities, because bullying often occurs in the classroom without the teacher's knowledge. Behavior problems such as bullying are also as likely to occur during unstructured times, such as the transition from one class or activity to the next, in the gym, in the cafeteria, or on the bus. Consequently, adults responsible for supervising children during those times need to be aware of the signs of bullying behavior and be given the authority to intervene when they suspect bullying is occurring.

Cooperative Learning Activities

One way that teachers can increase student familiarity with and acceptance of others is to use cooperative learning activities in the classroom. Researchers have emphasized that such activities have been effective in improving attitudes and relationships among children in ethnically diverse and special education inclusion classrooms (Boulton & Underwood, 1992; Cowie, Smith, Boulton, & Laver, 1994; Johnson & Johnson, 1980). Classroom teachers can develop cooperative learning groups and offer group rewards to facilitate improved social integration that would not ordinarily occur (Hoover & Hazler, 1991; Johnson & Johnson, 1980). Teachers should strive to balance competitive activities, which focus on individual achievement, with cooperative goals that help emphasize group achievement (Hazler, 1996).

Boulton and Underwood (1992) suggested pairing older children with younger children through joint projects in the classroom or through peer tutoring. Cooperative learning activities encourage friendship, identification, and a sense of protectiveness between the older and younger students. These feelings cause compassion in the children (Pink & Brown, 1988) and may help to lessen victimization. This was evidenced in a Japanese study, in which bullies' moral evaluation, perception and emotion toward victimization were positively related to the reduction of bullying (Honma, 2003).

Teachers should, however, consider power differences between children when planning for group cooperative work in the classroom. Because bullying is associated with both implicit (i.e., wealth, attractiveness, and athletic competence) and explicit (i.e., physical and relational aggression) forms of power, educators need to make sure that students not vastly different in their power status (Vaillancourt & McDougall, 2003). Teachers may be naturally inclined to group bullies and victims together yet may be better off forming groups with individuals who have fewer differences in social power. Alternately, because some bullies have high social status and power, educators may enlist high-status non-bullies to intervene when students are bullied by peers. When assured that a high-status peer will be amenable to advocate for another student, teachers can then feel comfortable assembling the cooperative group (Vaillancourt et al., 2003).

Assertiveness, Self-Esteem, and Social Skills Training for Victims of Bullying

Bullying prevention programs often include long-term interventions for victims of bullying to remedy deficits that are commonly found in this population. Social skills development appears to be an essential skill base because researchers have found that social isolation is a major risk factor for victimization (Boulton, Trueman, Chau, Whitehand, & Amataya, 1999), and perpetrators likely recognize the vulnerability of a student whom no peer will assist. Also, the development of friendships provides the unpopular student with a support network to ease the emotional pain of low social status. Teachers can promote victims' self-esteem by helping them identify their personal strengths that might attract peers as potential friends.

Furthermore, teachers can instruct students to replace negative statements about themselves with more positive or realistic ones, which is likely to increase the child's confidence as well as reduce his or her social anxiety. Victimized students are often realistically pessimistic about their chances of success in developing friendships, and research has suggested that the social status of victimized students is negative and longstanding (Boulton & Smith, 1994; Salmivalli, Lappalainen, & Lagerspetz, 1998). Thus, victimized students often need encouragement to engage in such behaviors in an attempt to establish social connections. One such strategy is to encourage the victimized student to focus on his or her effort and performance to make friends, rather than the results of these efforts, which rarely bear immediate fruit.

increase in victims' self-esteem, which was maintained at a 3-month follow-up but noted that the program did not have a significant impact upon victims' number of friends, peer acceptance, depression, or anxiety. Group interventions for victimized students may result in greater success when role-playing is used, with specific behaviors modeled for students and followed by supervised practice with peers.

Constructive Conversations with Victims of Bullying

When asked what teachers do to stop bullying behavior when it occurs, students are likely to report that teachers intervene in bullying scenarios less often than children would prefer (Crothers & Kolbert, 2004). In particular, victims of bullying may feel that bullies are actually receiving more teacher attention than do those who are being harassed by peers. Olweus (1992) has identified characteristics of those who are frequently victimized by bullying:

> Victims of bullying are more anxious and insecure than students in general. They are often cautious, sensitive, and quiet. When attacked by other students, they commonly react by crying (at least in the lower grades) and withdrawal. They have a negative view of themselves and their situation. They often look upon themselves as failures and feel stupid, ashamed, and unattractive.

Furthermore, Olweus (1993) noted that victims are often unpopular among their peers and lack even one identifiable friend. Because victims of bullying tend not to tease or display aggression toward peers, other students may assume that they will not retaliate when harassed.

Assisting the student who is frequently bullied may require both short- and long-term intervention. Short-term interventions address specific incidents of bullying, whereas long-term interventions involve skill building to increase confidence and avoid the probability of future victimization. Victims are unlikely to report bullying incidents because they fear exacerbation of the problem or retribution, so it is essential that teachers attempt to alleviate the anxiety of the victim during an investigation of bullying (Olweus, 1993). Educators should inform the child that whatever he or she decides to reveal will be held in confidence, while simultaneously building rapport and educating the victim in identifying what emotions he or she is likely to be experiencing. In addition, the teacher can instill hope in children by sharing that he or she has had success in dealing with such incidents in the past. Victims often internalize bullying, attributing the unwanted behaviors to characteristics within themselves. Thus, it is important to help the victim realize that he or she has done nothing to provoke the bullying behavior and that his or her anger regarding the experience is normal and justified.

Once information about the bullying behavior has been gathered, it is important to explain to the victim what the teacher will do with the information, which may include talking with witnesses and the alleged perpetrator, assigning a negative consequence to the perpetrator, and informing other teachers of the behavior so that they more closely observe the students who are involved. If the bullying incident is either severe or is indicative of an ongoing pattern, the teacher can gather additional data by interviewing other students who may have witnessed such incidents. Teachers can ask the victim to identify other students (who are not friends of the victim or the perpetrator) who may have observed such events, explaining to the victim that these witnesses will not be informed of how they were recognized as being involved. In many cases, the victimization has been occurring for several months and thus the victim can often readily identify other students who may have observed such events. Furthermore, victims should be encouraged to approach the teacher if bullying incidents reoccur.

Constructive Conversations with Students Who Frequently Bully

Research on students who frequently bully reveals some common characteristics. Perpetrators of bullying behavior tend to lack empathy (Olweus, 1993), misattribute their peers' actions as being the result of hostile intentions, demonstrate impulsivity, perceive aggression as an acceptable way to resolve conflict, and exhibit a high need for dominance (Graham & Juvonen, 1998; Olweus, 1993; Ross, 1996). Whereas students who are frequently victimized are generally unpopular with peers, perpetrators of bullying tend to have above-average popularity in primary grades and declining popularity in junior and senior high school.

When first meeting with a student who has been bullying peers, it is important to use a serious tone to convey an important message. The teacher should immediately indicate that he or she is speaking with the student because of his or her inappropriate behavior. To gain the trust of the bully, it is best to begin the conversation with the identification of the bullying behavior and the consequence for this behavior—a straightforward delivery ensures that the student will not be trapped in a lie by asking for his or her version of events. Thus, it is important that teachers collect evidence from other student witnesses prior to meeting with the perpetrator. The teacher should also inform the bully that other teachers and school staff will be made aware of the incident to prevent such behaviors from occurring in the future.

At this point, the teacher should shift into using more of a concerned and caring tone, as the objective is to enable the perpetrator to nondefensively evaluate whether his or her behavior is meeting his or her goals. A common misperception among adults is that students who bully have low self-esteem and thus are motivated to bully others in an attempt to feel better about themselves (Olweus, 1993). Rather than attempting to increase the self-esteem of the student who frequently bullies, teachers can affirm the student's strengths and popularity. Research has been suggestive of bullies' need for dominance, so a discussion of the student's high social status may be appealing to students who frequently bully (Graham & Juvonen, 1998; Olweus, 1993; Ross, 1996).

Ideally, this tactic will enable the student who frequently bullies to realize that victimizing peers is unnecessary to achieve his or her desire for social status. It also serves to help build the teacher–student relationship, which increases the likelihood that the student will engage in self-evaluative behavior. As the student begins to develop trust in the educator, the teacher can more assertively discuss the value of having concern for others, encouraging the student to consider what the victim was feeling and what restitution may be owed. It may be helpful to engage peer victimizers in middle/junior high school in discussions regarding the potential ramifications of bullying, such as the negative impact upon friendships in later grades, explaining that the popularity of students who use aggression typically decreases when they enter high school.

Parent–Teacher Collaboration

If students continue to bully after several months of intervention, the teacher may want to involve parents, although students who frequently bully are likely to receive parenting with little nurturance, along with discipline that is physical and severe (Olweus, 1993). Moreover, family members of child bullies often demonstrate a high need for power (Bowers, Smith, & Binney, 1994). Parents of children who bully others may not regard the behavior as a concern, possibly because such a strong power differential is demonstrated in their own family system. In other words, such behavior may appear to parents of bullies as normal and effective. Thus, it is important for teachers to recognize that parents of bullies may become emotionally reactive when attention and criticism is paid to their children's victimizing behavior.

A realistic objective in conferencing with the parents of perpetrators is to gain at least enough of their support so that they will not undermine teachers or administrators by directly or indirectly implying to their children that they do not need to adhere to the rules regarding bullying. In conferencing with parents of bullying students, teachers should use a no-nonsense, factual presentation and avoid engaging in questioning, long discussions, or using a tone that invites blame upon the parents of the bully. Similar to student perpetrators of bullying, it is not uncommon for parents to minimize or deny the bullying incident. For such situations, it is best that the school staff be prepared to offer concrete evidence of such behavior. Furthermore, the teacher may explain to the parents of the bully, in a respectful and non-emotional manner, the possible consequences if their child continues such behaviors, which may include further school sanctions and eventually decreased popularity among peers. Another effective technique is for the teacher to share with the parents some of their child's strengths and invite the parents to do so as well. Then ask the parents what they believe their child needs to learn at this point in his or her development.

Victims who require long-term intervention may also benefit from parental involvement. Research has suggested that students who are frequently bullied may be closely connected to their parents (Bowers et al., 1994; Olweus, 1993), which may actually impede the development of appropriate peer relations. Some parents react to knowledge that their child is being bullied through over-protection. For example, they may attempt to become their child's best friend, engaging in many social activities with the youngster that effectively fail to help the child develop positive peer relations. Teachers can help such parents develop a perspective of their child as competent, able to deal with bullying situations, and able to develop friendships with guided assistance.

Teachers may also encourage parents to think about how they might help to promote their child's social development, such as inviting friends to the home, role playing through social situations, and getting involved in social organizations that relate to their child's strengths. Encouraging non-athletic victimized children to become involved in team sports may lead to further social rejection, so parents of victims can also be encouraged to consider enhancing their child's physical development through supporting participation in individual sports such as karate, bicycling, swimming, and running.

Discussion

One reason that bullying has persisted throughout human history is that it has traditionally been treated as a socially acceptable means of establishing and securing social position as well as cementing power differences between people (Greene, 2003). Calling attention to the problem by encouraging teachers to tackle bullying as a common behavior management issue may help them effectively address peer victimization in the school environment. A variety of strategies have been presented that teachers can use to reduce child bullying. Educators are encouraged to use these techniques in conjunction with one another as researchers have suggested that bullying can be reduced most effectively through a comprehensive effort that addresses both individual incidents of bullying as well as modifying classroom and overall school environments that indirectly support bullying (e.g., Olweus, 1993).

Teachers are also encouraged to carefully consider the timing of implementing these techniques:

1. Assessment would logically precede guidance curricular approaches to both educate children about the nature of the problem and offer solutions for dealing with students who frequently bully.

2. Improving instruction and curriculum, modifying classroom management techniques, and initiating cooperative learning activities should occur alongside guidance lessons.
3. Constructive conversations with perpetrators and students who are frequently victimized should be reserved for when children have been educated about the new norms regarding this form of aggression.
4. Finally, parent–teacher collaboration is best used for the more entrenched cases of bullying problems given the time investment required of this technique.

Teachers have the power and the techniques available to them to make the classroom a socially just environment that is more hospitable to child development and learning. The techniques that have been identified are not complex, but they do require a significant effort on the part of the teacher. Still, such simple but clear efforts on the part of teachers to address the problem are likely to remove some of the tacit support that schools have historically provided to popular students' desire for dominance (Greene, 2003). The potential benefits seem well worth the effort and can be readily justified in the current educational environment given the negative impact bullying has on the social and emotional development and academic achievement of victims.

References

Batsche, G. M. (1997). Bullying. In G. G. Bear, K. M. Minke, & A. Thomas (Eds.), *Children's needs II: Development, problems, and alternatives* (pp. 171–179). Bethesda, MD: National Association of School Psychologists.

Boulton, M. J., & Smith, P. K. (1994). Bully/victim problems in middle school children: Stability, self-perceived competence, peer-perceptions and peer acceptance. *British Journal of Developmental Psychology*, 12, 315–329.

Boulton, M. J., Trueman, M., Chau, C., Whitehand, C., & Amataya, K. (1999). Concurrent and longitudinal links between friendship and peer victimization: Implications for befriending interventions. *Journal of Adolescence*, 22, 461–466.

Boulton, M. J., & Underwood, K. (1992). Bully/victim problems among middle school children. *British Journal of Educational Psychology*, 62, 73–87.

Bowers, L., Smith, P. K., & Binney, V. (1994). Perceived family relationships of bullies, victims, and bully/victims in middle childhood. *Journal of Social and Personal Relationships*, 11, 215–232.

Carney, A. G., & Merrell, K. W. (2001). Bullying in schools: Perspectives on understanding and preventing an international problem. *School Psychology International*, 22(3), 364–382.

The Comical Sense Company (Producer). (2005). *Bullies are a pain in the brain* [Motion picture]. (Available from the Comical Sense Company, www.trevorromain.com/Shop/item/?Videos/DVD00)

Cowie, H., Smith, P., Boulton, M., & Laver, R. (1994). *Cooperation in the multi-ethnic classroom*. London: David Fulton.

Crothers, L. M., & Kolbert, J. B. (2004). Comparing middle school teachers' and students' views on bullying and anti-bullying interventions. *Journal of School Violence, 3*(1), 17–32.

Czarnecki, K. (2005). Bullies to buddies: How to turn your enemies into friends! *School Library Journal, 51*(2), 148.

Discipline problems take a toll. (2004). *American Teacher, 89*(1), 7.

Dodge, K. A. (1993). The future of research on the treatment of conduct disorder. *Development and Psychopathology, 5*, 311–319.

Duke, D. L. (1982). *Helping teachers manage classrooms*. Alexandria, VA: Association for Supervision of Curriculum and Instruction.

Elliott, S. N., Witt, J. C., Kratochwill, T. R., & Stoiber, K. C. (2002). Selecting and evaluating classroom interventions. In M. A. Shinn, H. M. Walker, & G. Stoner (Eds.), *Interventions for academic and behavior problems II: Preventive and remedial approaches* (pp. 243–294). Bethesda, MD: National Association of School Psychologists.

Eron, L. D., Huesmann, R. L., Dubow, E., Romanoff, R., & Yarmel, P. W. (1987). Childhood aggression and its correlates over 22 years. In D. Crowell, I. M. Evans, & C. R. O'Donnell (Eds.), *Childhood aggression and violence* (pp. 249–262). New York: Plenum.

Farrington, D. P. (1993). Understanding and preventing bullying. In M. Tonry (Ed.), *Crime and justice: A review of research* (pp. 381–458). Chicago: University of Chicago Press.

Floyd, N. M. (1985). Pick on somebody your own size. *Pointer, 29*, 9–17.

Fox, C. L., & Boulton, M. J. (2003). Evaluating the effectiveness of a social skills training programme for victims of bullying. *Educational Research, 45*(3), 231–247.

Graham, S., & Juvonen, J. (1998). A social cognitive perspective on peer aggression and victimization. *Annals of Child Development, 12*, 21–66.

Greene, M. (2003). Counseling and climate change as treatment modalities for bullying in schools. *International Journal for the Advancement of Counselling, 25*(4), 293–302.

Hastings, R. P., & Bham, M. S. (2003). The relationship between student behaviour patterns and teacher burnout. *School Psychology International, 24*(1), 115–127.

Hazler, R. J. (1996). *Breaking the cycle of violence: Interventions for bullying and victimization*. Bristol, PA: Accelerated Development.

Hazler, R. J., Carney, J. V., Green, S., Powell, R., & Jolly, L. S. (1997). Areas of expert agreement on identification of school bullies and victims. *School Psychology International, 18*(1), 5–14.

Honma, T. (2003). Cessation of bullying and intervention with bullies: Junior high school students. *Japanese Journal of Educational Psychology, 51*, 390–400.

Hoover, J. H., & Hazler, R. J. (1991). Bullies and victims. *Elementary School Guidance and Counseling, 25*, 212–219.

Johnson, D. W., & Johnson, R. T. (1980). Integrating handicapped children into the mainstream. *Exceptional Children, 47*(2), 90–98.

Kalman, I. (2004). *Bullies to buddies: How to turn your enemies into friends*. Staten Island, NY: Wisdom Pages.

Kaltiala-Heino, R., Rimpela, M., Marttunen, M., Rimpela, A., & Rantenan, P. (1999). Bullying, depression, and suicidal ideation in Finnish adolescents: School survey. *British Medical Journal, 319*(7206), 348–351.

Kumpulainen, K., Rasanen, E., & Puura, K. (2001). Psychiatric disorders and the use of mental health services among children involved in bullying. *Aggressive Behavior, 27*, 102–110.

Levin, J., & Nolan, J. F. (2004). *Principles of classroom management: A professional decision-making model*. New York: Pearson.

McCain, B. R., & Leonardo, T. (2001). *Nobody knew what to do: A story about bullying*. Morton Grove, IL: Albert Whitman.

McKenney, K. S., Pepler, D. J., Craig, W. M., & Connolly, J. A. (2002). Psychosocial consequences of peer victimization in elementary and high school—An examination of posttraumatic stress disorder symptomatology. In K. A. Kendall-Tackett & S. M. Giacomoni (Eds.), *Child victimization: Maltreatment, bullying and dating violence, prevention and intervention* (pp. 15-1–15-17). Kingston, NJ: Civic Research Institute.

Nansel, T. R., Overpeck, M., Pilla, R. S., Ruan, W. J., Simons-Morton, B., & Scheidt, P. (2001). Bullying behaviors among US youth: Prevalence and association with psychosocial adjustment. *Journal of the American Medical Association, 285*, 2094–2100.

Olweus, D. (1991). Bully/victim problems among school children: Some basic facts and effects of a school-based intervention program. In D. Pepler & K. Rubin (Eds.), *The development and treatment of childhood aggression* (pp. 411–438). Hillsdale, NJ: Lawrence Erlbaum.

Olweus, D. (1992). Bullying among school children: Intervention and prevention. In R. Peters, J. McMahon, & V. I. Quinsley (Eds.), *Aggression and violence throughout the lifespan* (pp. 100–125). Newbury Park, CA: Sage.

Olweus, D. (1993). *Bullying at school: What we know and what we can do*. Cambridge, MA: Blackwell.

Pellegrini, A. D., & Bartini, M. (2000). An empirical comparison of methods of sampling aggression and victimization in school settings. *Journal of Educational Psychology, 92*, 360–366.

Pink, H., & Brownlee, L. (1988, March 4). Playground politics: Pairing off. *Times Educational Supplement*, p. 22a.

Ralston, J. (2005). Nobody knew what to do: A story about bullying. *School Library Journal, 51*(5), 50.

Ritter, D. R. (1989). Teachers' perceptions of problem behavior in general and special education. *Exceptional Children, 55*(6), 559–564.

Ross, D. (1996). *Childhood bullying and teasing*. Alexandria, VA: American Counseling Association.

Salmivalli, C., Lappalainen, M., & Lagerspetz, M. J. (1998). Stability and change of behavior in connection with bullying in schools: A two-year follow-up. *Aggressive Behavior, 24*, 205–218.

Smith, P. K., & Ananiadou, K. (2003). The nature of school bullying and the effectiveness of school-based interventions. *Journal of Applied Psychoanalytic Studies, 5*(2), 189–209.

Smith, P. K., & Brain, P. (2000). Bullying in school: Lessons from two decades of research. *Aggressive Behavior, 26*, 1–9.

Smith, P. K., & Sharp, S. (Eds.). (1994). *School bullying: Insights and perspectives*. London: Routledge.

Smokowski, P. R., & Kopasz, K. H. (2005). Bullying in school: An overview of types, effects, family characteristics, and intervention strategies. *Children and School, 27*(2), 101–110.

Sunburst (Producer). (2004). *End the silence: Stop the bullying* [Motion picture]. (Available from Sunburst, www.sunburstvm.com)

Vaillancourt, T., Hymel, S., & McDougall, P. (2003). Bullying is power: Implications for school-based intervention strategies. *Journal of Applied School Psychology, 19*(2), 157–176.

Williams, K., Chambers, M., Logan, S., & Robinson, D. (1996). Association of common health symptoms with bullying in primary school children. *British Medical Journal, 313*, 17–19.

Assess Your Progress

1. Name the reasons why some teachers experience more management problems than others. Offer your opinion about why this may happen.
2. Have you even been a victim of bullying? What effect did it have on you and your relationship to school?
3. Were you a bully? What effect did it have on you and your relationship to school?

LAURA M. CROTHERS, DEd, is an assistant professor of school psychology in the Department of Counseling, Psychology, and Special Education at Duquesne University. Her current research interests include bullying of gay, lesbian, bisexual, and transgender children and adolescents and female adolescent relational aggression. **JERED B. KOLBERT,** PhD, is an associate professor in the Department of Counseling and Development at Slippery Rock University and currently conducts research in bullying and the use of family therapy in responding to adolescent developmental adjustment problems.

Address: Laura M. Crothers, Duquesne University, 106 D Canevin Hall, Department of Counseling, Psychology, and Special Education, 600 Forbes Ave., Pittsburgh, PA, 15282; e-mail: crothersl@duq.edu

---

From *Intervention in School and Clinic,* January 2008, pp. 132–139. Copyright © 2008 by Pro-Ed, Inc. Reprinted by permission.

The Power of Our Words

Teacher language influences students' identities as learners. Five principles keep that influence positive.

PAULA DENTON

Think back to your childhood and recall the voices of your teachers. What kinds of words did they use? What tone of voice? Recall how you felt around those teachers. Safe and motivated to learn? Or self-doubting, insecure, even angry?

Teacher language—what we say to students and how we say it—is one of our most powerful teaching tools. It permeates every aspect of teaching. We cannot teach a lesson, welcome a student into the room, or handle a classroom conflict without using words. Our language can lift students to their highest potential or tear them down. It can help them build positive relationships or encourage discord and distrust. It shapes how students think and act and, ultimately, how they learn.

How Language Shapes Learners

From my 25 years of teaching and my research on language use, I've learned that language actually *shapes* thoughts, feelings, and experiences. (Vygotsky, 1978). Our words shape students as learners by

- *Affecting students' sense of identity.* Five-year-old Don loves to sing but isn't good at it—yet. His music teacher says, "Let's have you move to the back row and try just mouthing the words." Such language can lead Don to believe not only that he is a bad singer, but also that he will always be a bad singer. But suppose the teacher says, "Don, you really love to sing, don't you? Would you like to learn more about it? I have some ideas." Such words support Don's budding identity as one who loves to sing and is learning singing skills.
- *Helping students understand how they work and play.* For example, an educator might comment on a student's writing by saying, "These juicy adjectives here give me a wonderful sense of how your character looks and feels." Naming a specific attribute—the use of adjectives—alerts the writer to an important strength in her writing and encourages her to build on that strength.
- *Influencing our relationships with students.* To a student who—once again—argued with classmates at recess, we might say either "Emory, if you don't stop it, no more recess!" or "Emory, I saw you arguing with Douglas and Stephen. Can you help me understand what happened from your point of view?" The former would reinforce a teacher-student relationship based on teacher threats and student defensiveness, whereas the latter would begin to build a teacher-student relationship based on trust.

Five Guiding Principles for Positive Language

How can we ensure that our language supports students' learning and helps create a positive, respectful community? During the 20 years I've been involved with the Responsive Classroom, I have found this approach to be a good base for using language powerfully. The Responsive Classroom approach, developed by Northeast Foundation for Children, offers language strategies that enable elementary teachers to help students succeed academically and socially. Strategies range from asking open-ended questions that stretch students' thinking to redirecting students when behavior goes off-track. These strategies are based on the following five general principles.

1. Be Direct

When we say what we mean and use a kind, straightforward tone, students learn that they can trust us. They feel respected and safe, a necessary condition for developing self-discipline and taking the risks required for learning.

It's easy to slip into using indirect language as a way to win compliance. For example, as a new teacher, I tried to get students to do what I wanted by pointing out what I liked about other students' behavior. "I like the way May and Justine are paying attention," I would cheerfully announce while impatiently eyeing Dave and Marta fooling around in the corner.

When this strategy worked, it was because students mimicked the desired behavior so that they, too, would win praise from me, not because I had helped them develop self-control or internal motivation. And often, when I pointed out how I liked certain learners' behavior, the rest of the class ignored me. If I liked the way May and Justine were paying attention, that was nice for the three of us, but it had nothing to do with the rest of the class, who had more compelling things to do at the moment.

Moreover, comparative language can damage students' relationships. By holding May and Justine up as exemplars, I implied that the other class members were less commendable. This can drive a wedge between students.

Later in my career, I learned to speak directly. To call the students to a meeting, for example, I rang a chime to gain their attention (a signal we practiced regularly), then said firmly, "Come to the meeting rug and take a seat now." To Dave and Marta in the previous example, I'd say, "It's time to listen now." The difference in students' response was remarkable.

Sarcasm, another form of indirect language, is also common—and damaging—in the classroom. Sometimes teachers use sarcasm because we think it will provide comic relief; other times we're just tired, and it slips in without our even knowing it. If a teacher says, "John, what part of 'Put your phone away' don't you understand?" students will likely laugh, and the teacher may think she has shown that she's hip and has a sense of humor. But John will feel embarrassed, and his trust in this teacher will diminish. The position of this teacher may shift in the other students' eyes as well: They no longer see her as an authority who protects their emotional safety but as someone who freely uses the currency of insult. Much better to simply say, "John, put your phone away." If he doesn't, try another strategy, such as a logical consequence.

2. Convey Faith in Students' Abilities and Intentions

When our words and tone convey faith in students' desire and ability to do well, students are more likely to live up to our expectations of them.

"When everyone is ready, I'll show you how to plant the seeds." "You can look at the chart to remind yourself of our ideas for good story writing." "Show me how you will follow the rules in the hall." These teacher words, spoken in a calm voice, communicate a belief that students want to—and know how to—listen, cooperate, and do good work. This increases the chance that students will see themselves as respectful listeners, cooperative people, and competent workers, and behave accordingly.

Take the time to notice and comment on positive behavior, being quite specific: "You're trying lots of different ideas for solving that problem. That takes persistence." Such observations give students hard evidence for why they should believe in themselves.

3. Focus on Actions, Not Abstractions

Because elementary-age children tend to be concrete thinkers, teachers can communicate most successfully with them by detailing specific actions that will lead to a positive environment. For example, rather than saying, "Be respectful," it's more helpful to state, "When someone is speaking during a discussion, the rest of us will listen carefully and wait until the speaker is finished before raising our hands to add a comment."

Sometimes it's effective to prompt students to name concrete positive behaviors themselves. To a student who has trouble focusing during writing time, a teacher might say matter-of-factly, "What will help you think of good ideas for your story and concentrate on writing them down?" The student might then respond, "I can find a quiet place to write, away from my friends."

There is a place, of course, for such abstract terms as *respectful* and responsible, but we must give students plenty of opportunities to associate those words with concrete actions. Classroom expectations such as "treat one another with kindness" will be more meaningful to students if we help them picture and practice what those expectations look like in different situations.

Focusing on action also means pointing to the desired *behavior* rather than labeling the learner's character or attitude. I had a student who chronically did poor work when he could do better. In a moment of frustration, I said to him, "I don't think you even care!" This allowed me to vent, but it did nothing to help the student change. His energy went toward defending himself against my negative judgment, not toward examining and changing his behavior. Worse, such language can lead students to accept our judgment and believe that they indeed don't care.

It's more helpful in such situations to issue a positive challenge that names the behavior we want: "Your job today is to record five observations of our crickets. Think about what you'll need to do before you start." This moves the focus to what the student can do.

4. Keep It Brief

It's hard for many young children to follow long strings of words like this:

> When you go out to recess today, be sure to remember what we said about including everyone in games, because yesterday some kids had an issue with not being included in kickball and four square, and we've talked about this. You were doing really well for a while there, but lately it seems like you're getting kind of careless, and that's got to change or . . .

By the end of this spiel, many students would be thinking about other things. Few could follow the entire explanation. Students understand more when we speak less. Simply asking, "Who can tell us one way to include everyone at recess?" gives them an opportunity to remind themselves of positive behaviors. If you have taught and led students in practicing the class's expectations for recess, students will make good use of such a reminder.

5. Know When to Be Silent

The skillful use of silence can be just as powerful as the skillful use of words. When teachers use silence, we open a space for students to think, rehearse what to say, and sometimes gather the courage to speak at all.

We can see the benefit of silence if, after asking a question, we pause before taking responses from students. Researchers have found that when teachers wait three to five seconds, more students respond, and those responses show higher-level thinking (Swift & Gooding, 1983; Tobin, 1980).

Three to five seconds can feel uncomfortably long at first. But if we stick to it—and model thoughtful pausing by waiting a few seconds ourselves to respond to students' comments—we'll set a pace for the entire classroom that will soon feel natural. Our reward will be classroom conversations of higher quality.

Remaining silent allows us to listen to students and requires us to resist the impulse to jump in and correct students' words or finish their thoughts. A true listener tries to understand a speaker's message before formulating a response. When we allow students to speak uninterrupted and unhurried, we help them learn because speaking is an important means of consolidating knowledge.

In my current role teaching educators Responsive Classroom strategies, I watch teachers incorporate these five principles of language into their daily communications with students, and I see them build classrooms where students feel safe, respected, and engaged. By paying attention to our language, we can use it to open the doors of possibility for students.

References

Swift, J. N., & Gooding, T. (1983). Interaction of wait time feedback and questioning instruction on middle school science teaching. *Journal of Research in Science Teaching, 20*(8), 721–730.

Tobin, K. G. (1980). The effect of an extended teacher wait-time on science achievement. *Journal of Research in Science Teaching, 17,* 469–475.

Vygotsky, L. (1978). *Mind in society.* Cambridge, MA: Harvard University Press.

Assess Your Progress

1. What was your first reaction when you read the Denton article? How will this affect your use of words with students?
2. With a small group of classmates, make a list of words and phrases that teachers should never use when speaking with students or their parents. Be prepared to defend your list.

PAULA DENTON is Director of Program Development and Delivery for Northeast Foundation for Children, developer of the Responsive Classroom approach; www.responsiveclassroom.org; paula@responsiveclassroom.org. She is the author of *The Power of Our Words: Teacher Language that Helps Children Learn* (Northeast Foundation for Children, 2007).

Author's note—A 2006 study by Sara Rimm-Kaufman and colleagues at the University of Virginia showed that Responsive Classroom practices were associated with students having higher reading and math test scores, better social skills, and more positive feelings about school. The U.S. Department of Education's Institute of Education Sciences has awarded Rimm-Kaufman a $2.9 million grant to further investigate how Responsive Classroom practices contribute to gains in students' math achievement.

From *Educational Leadership*, September 2008, pp. 28–31. Copyright © 2008 by ASCD. Reprinted by permission. The Association for Supervision and Curriculum Development is a worldwide community of educators advocating sound policies and sharing best practices to achieve the success of each learner. To learn more, visit ASCD at www.ascd.org

Article 30

Marketing Civility

How can you improve communication so high school students feel safe and secure?

MICHAEL STILES AND BEN TYSON

Some students rise each morning anticipating another fulfilling and challenging day of high school. Others view their educational experiences differently.

Do these students perceive that the communication that takes place between them is filled with putdowns? Do they want a school climate that allows them to feel more comfortable about being themselves without fear of being judged?

The teen years are difficult for many and too difficult for some. Suicide is the third leading cause of death for people ages 15 to 24, according to a 2006 report from the Centers for Disease Control and Prevention. A 2005 survey conducted by Indiana University stated that 45 percent of students do not feel safe at school. And reports by the National School Boards Association link, at least anecdotally, the relationship between school climate and student achievement in the upper grades.

One's lack of feeling safe can even aggravate asthma. In 2003, research analyzing the connections between victimization and absenteeism found that students who felt unsafe were more likely to experience an asthma episode.

If you look more closely at studies and research over the past decade, it appears that a lack of civility in schools is reaching epidemic proportions. As students observe their peers engaging in uncivil behavior, often with little or no consequences, the behavior is then perceived to be socially acceptable, causing the behavior to be exhibited by more students.

So what can be done? Schools have implemented civility promotion programs and initiatives that promote positive behavior support. And, at least initially, these program interventions have had good results.

What We Learned

For our study, we looked at a high school in Connecticut to determine how students perceived the communication climate on campus and to get guidance on how improvements might be instituted. Even though we examined only one school, we believe our findings provide some strong suggestions that school districts should consider.

Seventy-six percent of the school's student population (563 of 738) completed the survey. Of those who responded, 47 percent were female and 53 percent were male.

Here are some of our findings:

- More than 75 percent of the students claim they "have witnessed students intimidating other students."
- Nearly 70 percent recognize "name-calling" as a common form of intimidation.
- One-third of the students reported that they have "been bullied or made to feel afraid while in school."
- Only 6 percent of the students surveyed either disagreed or strongly disagreed with the statement, "I do not like it when students bully other students."
- Two-thirds said they would like to go to a school where students do not intimidate or bully other students. However, strong feelings against bullying do not translate into taking action against bullying. Only 5 percent believed that students report bullying when they witness it, although the majority say they wish they would report bullying incidents.
- Student perceptions of how teachers and administrators handle bullying are somewhat negative. For example, only 31 percent feel that teachers properly deal with students who bully, and only 34 percent believe the administration properly addresses the problem. And 63 percent agree or strongly agree that teachers are unaware of conflicts that occur between students.
- What are the ramifications of teasing, bullying, rumors, conflicts, or otherwise uncivil behavior? Forty-two percent of students feel their academic performance is affected, and 60 percent feel verbal arguments have a negative impact on the school environment. Seventy-three percent believe rumors contribute to a negative school environment. And nearly 80 percent agree or strongly agree that "most students who are teased feel hurt, even though they may not let it show."
- How do students perceive their school's overall social environment? Only 37 percent feel the environment is

supportive. In terms of emotional and physical safety, 51 percent say they feel emotionally safe at school, and 69 percent say they feel physically safe. That means that significant proportions of students are either unsure or feel unsafe while in school.

What We Recommended

Based on our survey findings, we made several recommendations to improve the communication climate at the school. You might find that these recommendations will help at your schools as well.

Inform your staff: Keep your staff informed, from the time you decide to conduct the survey until after you receive the results. Use the results to raise staff awareness and initiate conversations about how bullying should be addressed.

Utilize students: Not surprisingly, our study found that students are influenced much more by their peers rather than adults. So how do you reach your students? Utilize student organizations within the school to a greater extent to promote your civility message. Your school's peer mediation program should continue to function as an intervention resource to take advantage of the students' ability to help their classmates work through conflicts.

Improve supervision: Better supervision by staff, especially in the hallways, will reduce bullying. Common areas where bullying takes place, according to students, are: hallways, cafeterias, locker rooms, bathrooms, and study halls. All staff should make a greater effort to be visible in the halls between classes. Also, as one student told us, "Teachers should intervene when they see bullying behavior and not ignore the problem."

Share actual "norms": Often the perception of peer behavior, rather than the actual behavior, is the accepted norm. By clarifying misperceptions of norms, students may be more apt to behave in ways that are more in line with their personal values. Student organizations such as peer mediators, peer advocates, members of student council, or a combination of these could plan a campaign to share the actual student norms with the school population. The actual norm is a desire for more civility and less acceptance of bullying.

Clarify discipline reports: At the start of this study, the high school discipline data was viewed with regard to the frequency and type of disciplinary infractions that occurred in the past year. It was difficult to put infractions into distinct categories. Improving the clarity and specificity of the categories will make it easier for the administration to track uncivil behavior.

Monitor and evaluate: Periodic evaluation is necessary to monitor progress and determine the effectiveness of any interventions you choose to make. This helps program leaders recognize progress or setbacks and adjust strategies as necessary. Administer your schoolwide survey each year to examine student perceptions of the school's communication climate. Also, records involving discipline issues should be compared from year to year as a means of tracking your progress.

Consider offering an annual survey to all staff members to determine their perceptions of the school's communication climate. Most important, ask how each staff member feels he or she can work to improve the climate. After all, the perception of your staff is just as important as the perception of your students. And for things to improve, the commitment to a positive and respectful climate will take everyone.

Assess Your Progress

1. Stiles and Tyson suggest that improved communication will increase civility in classrooms. What is your response to their suggestions? Provide a rationale for your answer.

2. With a small group of classmates, make a list of words and phrases that teachers should add to their interactions with students and parents. Be prepared to defend your list.

MICHAEL STILES is a physical and health education instructor in Connecticut. BEN TYSON (tysonc@ccsu.edu) is a professor in the Department of Communication at Central Connecticut State University.

From *American School Board Journal*, March 2008, pp. 36–37. Copyright © 2008 by National School Board Association. Reprinted by permission.

Article 31

Classwide Interventions
Effective Instruction Makes a Difference

MAUREEN A. CONROY ET AL.

Whether teaching in a general education classroom or in a specialized program for students with special needs, teachers face a variety of classroom behaviors that can detract from the learning process. At times, they may spend so much time with a few students who exhibit disruptive and off-task behaviors that they are less available for academic instruction with all students.

The research literature provides numerous examples of effective teaching strategies that can help teachers address problem behavior in their classrooms. These strategies include manipulating *antecedents* (i.e., environ-mental factors that are likely to increase a behavior), such as increasing opportunities to respond to academic requests (OTRs), and manipulating *consequences* (i.e., environmental factors that maintain behaviors), such as providing contingent praise. Unfortunately, some teachers are not skilled at employing these effective teaching tools in their classrooms. Consider the case scenarios "A Classroom That Works" and "A Classroom With Challenges."

Creating a Positive Climate Through Classwide Interventions

Classrooms are dynamic environments in which teachers and students engage in ongoing reciprocal interactions throughout the school day. As indicated in both case scenarios, classes that include classwide effective intervention practices are likely to have positive teacher-student interactions and to promote student learning and engagement while minimizing problem behaviors. However, when classwide interventions are missing from a classroom, teacher-student interactions are likely to become reactively negative [and perhaps even coercive]. Such interactions interfere with learning and create a chaotic and aversive classroom atmosphere.

Classwide interventions are a group of research-based effective teaching strategies used positively and preventively to promote and reinforce social and behavioral competence in students while minimizing problem behaviors (Farmer et al., 2006). Classwide interventions do not represent a single type of intervention; instead, they include a combination of effective behavior management practices that have a long history in our field, such as using contingent and frequent *praise*, providing *OTRs*, and applying *classroom rules*.

Classwide Interventions: Universal Classroom Tools for Effective Instruction

Teachers should consider the following classwide interventions when implementing positive behavior supports:

- Using close supervision and monitoring.
- Establishing and teaching classroom rules.
- Increasing OTRs.
- Increasing contingent praise.
- Providing feedback and error correction and monitoring progress.
- Implementing the good behavior game (GBG).

Close Supervision and Monitoring

Close supervision and monitoring generally means that the teacher has active, frequent, and regular engagement with students. These engagements may include placing students close to the teacher, scanning and moving frequently, initiating and reciprocating purposeful interactions, and providing opportunities for direct instruction and feedback (Colvin, Sugai, & Patching, 1993). When teachers are in proximity to students and monitor students' learning and behavior, they can prevent problem behaviors before they occur and can redirect them before they escalate. For example, when a teacher is near a student who is becoming frustrated and is struggling with a task, the teacher can intervene quickly and provide academic and behavior supports before a problem behavior occurs.

Case Scenario: A Classroom That Works

Collaboration between special and general education teachers in the classroom can be beneficial to students with and without special needs, especially when the collaboration works seamlessly. Ms. Harman and Ms. Easley teach in an urban elementary school. At the beginning of the school year, they worked collaboratively with their students to develop classroom rules that both special and general education students could follow and to identify specific procedures, such as turning in homework and lining up to go to lunch, for regular classroom activities. In addition, they spent a significant amount of time praising their students not just for work done correctly but also for good attempts.

Ms. Harman and Ms. Easley, who continuously sought ways to improve their teaching and help their students learn, took part in an applied research project that facilitated positive changes in their instructional language and methods. They incorporated a group behavior management system called *the good behavior game (GBG:* Barrish, Saunders, & Wolfe, 1969) into their instructional time.

Ms. Harman and Ms. Easley audiotaped an instructional lesson and graphed the numbers of opportunities to respond (OTRs) that they provided, as well as the number of times that they praised their students during the lesson. Through this self-evaluation of their instructional language, they developed a greater awareness of the frequency with which they provided their students with OTRs to instructional requests and of the frequency of their praise statements. Using these self-management procedures enabled Ms. Harman and Ms. Easley to increase the number of OTRs from only 10 per 15 minutes to almost 6 per minute, approximating the recommendations of the Council for Exceptional Children (1987). This change in the OTR rate encouraged student engagement and led to decreased undesirable behavior. In addition, the teachers increased their rate of praise from only 2 per 15 minutes to almost 1 per minute, resulting in further improvements in the behavior of the students. Making small changes in the ways that they instructed their students and rewarding their students more often for work attempted resulted in an improved positive classroom atmosphere and an increase in students' effort.

Implementing close supervision and monitoring may require developing a plan in collaboration with other adults or paraprofessionals in the classroom. For example, a classroom teacher may implement a zone-monitoring and supervision plan during an instructional time when many students need assistance and engage in problem behaviors. With a zone-monitoring plan, adults in the classroom are at strategic locations throughout the classroom, and each of them monitors a small number of students. This system enables adults to closely supervise and monitor students and facilitates students' access to teacher assistance.

Considerable evidence supports the use of close supervision and monitoring as a classwide intervention. For example, research has documented that close supervision and monitoring result in decreases in disruptive behavior across various educational settings, including classroom instruction (DePry & Sugai, 2002); recess (Lewis, Powers, Kelk, & Newcomer, 2002); and transition time (Colvin, Sugai, Good, & Lee, 1997).

Classroom Rules

The development and implementation of classroom rules is another universal classwide intervention that influences the learning environment for all students. Classroom rules serve as behavioral expectations that create an organized and productive learning environment for students and teachers by promoting appropriate classroom behaviors. Without classroom rules, such problem behaviors as aggression and disruption are more likely (Walker, Colvin, & Ramsey, 1995). Research has indicated that effective teachers do the following:

- Establish rules for expected behavior at the beginning of the year.
- Systematically teach the rules to the students.
- Monitor and reward students' compliance with the rules.
- Consistently apply consequences to rule violations (Anderson, Evertson, & Emmer, 1980; Evertson & Emmer, 1982).

Classroom rules serve as behavioral expectations that create an organized and productive learning environment for students and teachers by promoting appropriate classroom behaviors.

Opportunities to Respond (OTRs)

Increasing instructional pacing through OTRs is a questioning, prompting, or cueing technique that begins a learning trial (e.g.. "What number comes after 10?"). This technique helps increase the number of active child responses, which in turn can result in increases in correct responses and engagement of all students in the classroom (Greenwood, Delquadri, & Hall, 1984). Although OTRs vary in type and characteristics (e.g., choral responses, individual responses, and visual or auditory cuing), all types of OTRs generally include the following components:

- Increasing rates of teacher instructional talk that includes repeated verbal, visual, or verbal and visual types of prompts for responding.
- Presenting information in a manner that increases student correct responding (e.g., "This is an *A*. What letter Is this?").
- Implementing individualized instructional modifications appropriate for the students' level of functioning, along with frequent checks for understanding and accuracy.
- Using repeated instructional prompting that incorporates wait time to allow students to respond.
- Providing corrective feedback, error correction, and progress monitoring (Stichter & Lewis, 2006).

When researchers increase rates of OTR, they have found increases in on-task student behavior and in correct responses, as well as fewer disruptive behaviors by students (Brophy & Good, 1986; Carnine, 1976; Greenwood et al., 1984; Sutherland, Gunter, & Alder, 2003). Students who are engaged in learning are less likely to demonstrate problem behaviors (Sutherland et al.) and more likely to engage in active and correct responses (Sutherland & Snyder, 2007).

Contingent Praise

"Catch 'em being good" is a familiar strategy to most teachers. Although many teachers are aware of the powerful effects of praise, they often underuse it. Fortunately, training can help teachers learn to use praise as a reinforcer. Praise is a generalized reinforcer and has a rich research base that demonstrates its effectiveness in increasing social and behavioral competence in students (Alber, Heward, & Hippler, 1999; Sutherland, 2000). *Effective* praise is specific and contingent (Sutherland). *Specific* praise occurs when the teacher specifies the target behavior reinforced within the praise statement (e.g., "Good, you stayed in your seat during the entire reading session"). Praise is *contingent* when it is a consequence for a specific expected behavior, such as completing an assigned task, following a teacher's instruction, or engaging in appropriate social behavior.

Researchers have found that when teachers increase their use of specific and contingent praise, improvement occurs in the number of correct responses by students, task engagement, words read correctly per minute, problems completed, and student engagement (Kirby & Shields, 1972; Luiselli & Downing, 1980; Sutherland, Wehby, & Copeland, 2000). In general, teachers should offer praise statements more often than corrective statements. For example. Good and Grouws (1977) recommend that teachers strive to achieve and maintain a ratio of 4 or 5 positive statements to corrective statement.

Case Scenario: A Classroom with Challenges

Ms. Walters taught 12 students, whose grade levels ranged from second grade to fifth grade, in an urban elementary school. The students had a variety of disabilities—for example, emotional disorders (ED), learning disabilities (LD), and attention deficit hyperactivity disorder (ADHD).

As a group, these students presented many classroom challenges. Each day, Ms. Walters greeted her students by saying "Good morning, class," only to be confronted by disruptive student talk, papers flying at her, and students who were not in their assigned seats. Along with her paraprofessional, Ms. Johnson, Ms. Walters spent the first 45 minutes of every day just trying to get her students to sit down, hand in their homework, and attend to language arts, the first lesson of the day. She had very few doable procedures in place for daily tasks, and most of the students regularly ignored classroom rules. Ms. Walters had assigned students to small groups on the basis of their skill levels; however, she spent a tremendous amount of time correcting disruptive students, who would provoke others. Needless to say, she was frustrated and often raised her voice at her students in an effort to persuade them to pay attention to her. She knew that what she was doing was not working, but she and her students were caught in a negative, coercive interaction cycle.

Discouraged and ready to quit before she had even finished her first year, Ms. Walters agreed to have a behavioral consultant come into her classroom to help her with classroom management. The consultant worked with Ms. Walters to arrange her classroom so that all students could see her and the blackboard. The consultant and Ms. Walters developed procedures for entering the classroom in the morning (e.g., routines for putting away backpacks and homework), and Ms. Walters distributed students with disruptive behavior across the small groups in the classroom. As a reward for good behavior, she assigned a "daily leader" to each group for the next day.

The consultant also trained the paraprofessional to step in when Ms. Walters was having difficulty with a particular student and engage other students in small-group or individualized work so that Ms. Walters was not responsible for the whole class. After Ms. Walters received this support, her teaching strategies improved, and she felt and looked more competent and effective in her ability to manage her students' behavior and promote their learning. Students responded to her effective teaching practices; and as a result, they were more engaged. Although more growth was necessary, the classwide atmosphere improved, and everyone had hope for a better school year.

Feedback, Error Correction, and Progress Monitoring

Providing students with feedback relative to their behavior and performance level is another important classwide intervention. When used effectively, feedback should

- Help students learn the correct response in a timely way.
- Be specific to students' skill and knowledge levels.
- Occur following a student error (i.e., error correction).

Error correction procedures begin with the teacher's providing a corrective model (e.g., "Remember that to determine the area of a square or rec-tangle, multiply length times width"). This corrective model precedes the student's correct response, which the student should base on the teacher's model (e.g., "if the length of a rectangle is 5 feet and its width is 4 feet, I multiply length by width to obtain a result of 20 square feet."). Corrective feedback should accompany continuous monitoring of the student's academic and/or social behavior performance (e.g., curriculum-based measurement), as well as accurate and consistently presented instruction and interventions (i.e., fidelity of implementation).

Effective feedback can take many forms (e.g., answering questions, checking seatwork, and responding directly), and researchers have linked it positively to student engagement and achievement (Fisher et al., 1980). Similarly, when teachers use error correction, increases occur in academic performance (Barbetta, Heron, & Heward, 1993; Barbetta & Heward, 1993) and correct responses (Bangert-Downs, Kulik, Kulik, & Morgan, 1991).

Good Behavior Game (GBG)

The GBG is a group contingency designed to

- Improve the teacher's ability to define tasks, set rules, and discipline students.
- Reduce disruptive, aggressive, off-task, and shy behaviors in elementary-age children.
- Promote good behavior by rewarding teams that do not exceed mal-adaptive behavior standards.

The teacher begins the GBG by assigning each student in the class to a team and selecting team leaders. The teacher and students read and review the class-room rules, and the teacher informs students that each rule violation results immediately in a check mark on the blackboard next to the team's name. In addition, the teacher tells the students that he or she will state the rule that a student has violated, identify the student who has violated the rule, and praise the other teams for adhering to the rules. At the end of an instructional session, the teacher and students review the number of check marks per team, repeat the preset criteria for winning the game, and announce the winning team or teams. Team leaders then hand out rewards to winning team members (e.g., stamps, stickers, or "I did it" badges), and the nonwinning teams must stay in their seats and continue to engage in their lesson. Because teams try to beat the preset limit, more than one—or even all—teams can win.

Researchers initially associated the GBG with reduced rates of out-of-seat and talking-out behaviors of fourth-grade students (Barrish et al., 1969). Over the next 35 years, this finding led to a line of research that has documented the effectiveness of the GBG with students of varying ages and disabilities across many different settings. For example, Dolan and colleagues (1993) examined the effect of the GBG on first graders' disruptive classroom behaviors and found that teacher ratings of aggressive and shy behavior were significantly lower in the spring of the first grade than in the fall. In sum, the GBG is a good example of a classwide intervention that can have an effect on the behavior—and ultimately, on the learning—of many students.

Where Do You Begin? Steps for Creating a Positive Classroom Atmosphere

Creating a positive classroom environment through implementing classwide interventions does not solve all classroom problem behaviors overnight. As illustrated in the classroom of Ms. Harman and Ms. Easley in "Case Scenario: A Classroom That Works," implementing these effective teaching practices requires up-front planning and ongoing problem solving. In addition, teachers must implement these practices efficiently and correctly (i.e., with fidelity) and individualize the practices to make them appropriate for unique aspects of their classrooms. For example, classroom rules may vary from classroom to classroom, depending on the expectations and ability levels of the students. Similarly, the teacher may implement close supervision and monitoring differently depending on the classroom size and layout. Like other behavior support strategies, implementing classwide interventions requires ongoing monitoring and evaluation of the use and effectiveness of these strategies. Thus, teachers will want to monitor their implementation of targeted classwide strategies and student outcomes. Ms. Harman and Ms. Easley demonstrated that collecting data on their own teaching behaviors helped them improve their skills. Additionally, by collecting data on their students' behavior, they obtained enough evidence to know that the practices were working.

Finally, as illustrated by the example of Ms. Walters in "Case Scenario: A Classroom With Challenges," teachers sometimes need a person outside their classroom to teach them classwide interventions and help them discover how to implement these strategies in their classrooms. Teachers

Table 1 Universal Classwide Interventions

Classwide Interventions	What Are You Currently Doing?	What Do You Want to Change to Improve Your Instruction?
Close supervision and monitoring	Are students in proximity to you? Can you visually monitor all the students in your classroom? Do you actively engage with your students? Do students in your classroom have quick and efficient access to teacher assistance? Is the adult-student ratio sufficient to provide close supervision and monitoring?	During which instructional time will you implement closer supervision and monitoring? What staff will you involve in close supervision and monitoring? How will you implement close supervision and monitoring? How will you monitor the effectiveness of close supervision and monitoring?
Classroom rules	Do you have classroom rules? Did you develop your classroom rules in collaboration with your students? Do your students know the classroom rules, and are they able to perform them? Do you communicate classroom rules to your students in an effective and efficient manner? Do adults in the classroom contingently and regularly provide reinforcement to students for adhering to the rules? Do you apply consequences consistently when students break classroom rules?	Do you and your students implement the classroom rules effectively? Do you need to rewrite or adapt your classroom rules? How will you communicate your classroom rules to your students? How will you monitor whether the rules are working? How will you provide positive reinforcement to students for complying with the rules? What will you do if students do not comply?
Opportunities to respond (OTRs)	Do you use various types of OTRs in your classroom [e.g., choral, individual]? Do you provide students with an adequate rate of OTRs? What type of instructional delivery model do you use (direct, whole group, small group, etc.)?	Can you increase the number of OTRs for your students? Can you "switch up" the delivery method you use to offer more OTRs? How can you use more direct instruction?
Contingent praise	Do you regularly praise students for answering correctly? Do you praise students for an attempt to answer, even if it is not correct? Are you specific about what you are praising a student for (rather than simply "good girl" or "good boy")? Do you praise students for desirable social behavior?	Can you increase your positive interactions with your students? Can you increase your use of specific praise statements? Can you increase your use of contingent praise? Can you find reasons to praise all students in your class more frequently than you reprimand them?

may want to begin by assessing their current use of classwide interventions (see Table 1) and systematically identifying and targeting specific classwide interventions for classroom application.

Final Thoughts

When teachers systematically implement classwide interventions, teacher–student interactions become more positive, students are more engaged, and teachers are able to focus on teaching appropriate behaviors—all these result in a positive classroom environment that promotes student learning and engagement.

> **When teachers systematically implement classwide interventions, teacher–student interactions become more positive, students are more engaged, and teachers are able to focus on teaching appropriate behaviors.**

References

Alber. S. R., Heward, W. L., & Hippler, B. J. (1999). Teaching middle school students with learning disabilities to recruit positive teacher attention. *Exceptional Children, 65,* 253–270.

Anderson, L., Evertson, C., & Emmer, E. (1980). Dimensions in classroom management derived from recent research. *Journal of Curriculum Studies, 12,* 343–356.

Bangert-Downs, R. L., Kulik, C. C., Kulik, J. A., & Morgan. M. (1991). The instructional effects of feedback in test-like events. *Review of Educational Research, 61,* 213–238.

Barbetta, P. M., Heron, T. E., & Heward, W. L. (1993). Effects of active student response during error correction on the acquisition, maintenance, and generalization of sight words by students with developmental disabilities. *Journal of Applied Behavior Analysis, 26,* 111–119.

Barbetta, P. M., & Heward, W. L. (1993). Effects of active student response during error correction on the acquisition and maintenance of geography facts by elementary students with learning disabilities. *Journal of Behavioral Education, 3,* 217–233.

Barrish, H., Saunders. M., & Wolfe, M. (1969). Good behavior game: Effects of individual contingencies for group consequences on disruptive behavior in a classroom. *Journal of Applied Behavior Analysis, 2,* 119–124.

Brophy, J. H., & Good, T. (1986). Teacher behavior and student achievement. In M. C. Wittrock (Ed.), *Handbook of research in teaching* (3rd ed.; pp. 328–375). New York: Macmillan.

Carnine, D. W. (1976). Effects of two teacher-presentation rates on off-task behavior, answering correctly, and participation. *Journal of Applied Behavior Analysis, 9,* 199–206.

Colvin, G., Sugai, G., Good, R. H., & Lee, Y. (1997). Using active supervision and pre-correction to improve transition behaviors in an elementary school. *School Psychology Quarterly, 12,* 344–363.

Colvin, G. Sugai, G., & Patching, W. (1993). Precorrection: An instructional approach for managing predictable problem behaviors. *Intervention in School and Clinic, 28,* 143–150.

Council for Exceptional Children. (1987). *Academy for effective instruction: Working with mildly handicapped students.* Reston, VA: Author.

DePry, R. L., & Sugai, G. (2002). The effect of active supervision and pre-correction on minor behavioral incidents in a sixth grade general education classroom. *Journal of Behavioral Education, 11,* 255–267.

Dolan. L. J., Kellam, S. G., Brown, C. H., Werthamer-Larson, L., Rebok, G. W., Mayer, L. S., et al. (1993). The short-term impact of two classroom-based preventive interventions on aggressive and shy behaviors and poor achievement, *Journal of Applied Developmental Psychology, 14,* 317–345.

Evertson, C., & Emmer, E. (1982). Effective management at the beginning of the year in junior high classes. *Journal of Educational Psychology, 74,* 485–498.

Farmer, T. W., Goforth, J., Hives. J., Aaron, A., Hunter, F., & Sgmatto, A. (2006). Competence enhancement behavior management. *Preventing School Failure, 50,* 39–44.

Fisher, C. W., Berliner, D. C., Filby, N. N., Marliave, R., Cahen, L. S., & Dishaw, M. M. (1980). Teaching behaviors, academic learning time, and student achievement: An overview. In C. Denham & A. Lieberman (Eds.), *Time to learn* (pp. 7–32). Washington, DC: U.S. Department of Education, National Institute of Education.

Good, T., & Grouws, D. (1977). Teaching effects: A process-product study in fourth grade mathematics classrooms. *Journal of Teacher Education, 28,* 49–54.

Greenwood, C. R., Delquadri, J. C., & Hall, R. V. (1984). Opportunity to respond and student academic performance. In W. L. Heward, T. E. Heron, D. S. Hill, & J. Trap-Porter (Eds.), *Focus on behavior analysis in education* (pp. 58–88). Columbus, OH: Charles E. Merrill.

Kirby, F. D., & Shields, F. (1972). Modification of arithmetic response rate and attending behavior in a seventh-grade student. *Journal of Applied Behavior Analysis, 5,* 79–84.

Lewis, T. J., Powers, L. J., Kelk, M. J., & Newcomer, L. L. (2002). Reducing problem behaviors on the playground: An investigation of the application of school-wide positive behavior and supports. *Psychology in the Schools, 39,* 181–190.

Luiselli, J. K., & Downing, J. N. (1980). Improving a student's arithmetic performance using feedback and reinforcement procedures. *Education and Treatment of Children, 3,* 45–49.

Stichter, J., & Lewis, T. J. (2006). Classroom assessment: Targeting variables to improve instruction through a multi-level eco-behavioral model. In M. Hersen (Ed.), *Clinician's handbook of child behavioral assessment* (pp. 569–586). Burlington, MA: Elsevier.

Sutherland, K. S., (2000). Promoting positive interactions between teachers and students with emotional/behavioral disorders. *Preventing School Failure, 44,* 110–115.

Sutherland, K. S., Gunter. P. L., & Alder, N. (2003). The effect of varying rates of OTR on the classroom behavior of students with EBD. *Journal of Emotional and Behavioral Disorders, 11,* 239–248.

Sutherland, K. S., & Snyder. A. (2007). Effects of reciprocal peer tutoring and self-graphing on reading fluency and classroom behavior of middle school students with emotional or behavioral disorders. *Journal of Emotional and Behavioral Disorders, 15,* 103–118.

Sutherland, K. S., Wehby, J. H., & Copeland, S. R. (2000). Effect of varying rates of behavior-specific praise on the on-task behavior of students with emotional and behavioral disorders. *Journal of Emotional and Behavioral Disorders, 8,* 2–8, 26.

Walker, H., Colvin, G., & Ramsey, E. (1995). *Antisocial behavior in school: Strategies and best practices.* New York: Brooks/Cole.

Assess Your Progress

1. Review the case scenario of a classroom with challenges in the article on classroom interventions. The behavior consultant had suggested that the paraprofessional could help the teacher. But you don't have a paraprofessional in your classroom. What would you do to solve your challenges? Provide information from this and other articles in this unit to support your answer.
2. Based on what you have learned from the articles in this unit, what do you think are the primary reasons why novice teachers may experience behavior management problems in their classrooms?

MAUREEN A. CONROY (CEC VA Federation). Professor; KEVIN S. SUTHERLAND (CEC VA Federation). Associate Professor: ANGELA L. SNYDER (CEC VA Federation), Collateral Assistant Professor; and SAMANTHA MARSH (CEC VA Federation), Doctoral Student, Department of Special Education and Disability Policy, Virginia Commonwealth University, Richmond.

Address correspondence to Maureen A. Conroy, Department of Special Education and Disability Policy, Virginia Commonwealth University, 1015 W. Main Street, P.O. Box 842020, Richmond, VA 23284 (e-mail: maconroy@vcu.edu).

From *Teaching Exceptional Children*, Vol. 40, No. 6, July/August 2008, pp. 24–30. Copyright © 2008 by Council for Exceptional Children. Reprinted by permission.

Article 32

Developing Effective Behavior Intervention Plans
Suggestions for School Personnel

With federal mandates to develop and implement programs for students with disabilities who have behavior problems that impede their educational performance, school personnel are faced with increasing responsibility for developing individualized interventions. Developing interventions that appropriately, effectively, and efficiently address the relationship between learning and behavior problems is a complex task that requires a host of essential elements and procedures. For intervention team members who lead and design the functional behavior assessment and behavior intervention plans, specific issues to consider in developing and monitoring these plans are discussed.

KIM KILLU

Behavioral difficulties that interfere with a student's school performance have long been a challenge for educators. To address this issue, the 1997 reauthorization of the Individuals with Disabilities Education Act (IDEA) required educators to develop and implement behavior intervention plans (BIPs). When IDEA 1997 was reauthorized in 2004 as the Individuals with Disabilities Education Improvement Act (IDEIA), BIPs were included again. These plans consider the relationship between student learning and behavior problems that impede classroom performance. Behavior intervention plans outline strategies and tactics for dealing with the problem behavior along with the role that educators must play in improving student learning and behavior. Although many students respond positively to conventional classroom behavior management strategies (e.g., establishing classroom rules, redirection) many others require specially designed interventions to address the relationship between learning and behavior (Morgan & Jenson, 1988). Educators are increasingly placed in a position to develop specialized interventions, yet developing an intervention plan that appropriately and effectively addresses the relationship between student learning and the problem behavior is a complex task. Despite good faith efforts to develop a plan that best meets a student's behavioral needs, educators may find that their plans do not achieve desired results. This article examines specific issues that must be considered and addressed by school personnel who design and monitor the BIP process to enhance the effectiveness of BIPs.

Functional Behavior Assessment

With IDEIA 2004, a functional behavior assessment (FBA) is required prior to the development of a BIP for students with disabilities who have behavioral challenges that impede functioning in the educational environment. Practitioners have sought to analyze the factors involved in student behavior, and fortunately for educators, a behavioral technology for the assessment of challenging behavior exists. Functional behavior assessment involves using several methods to determine the causal and maintaining factors for a behavior that lead to the development of intervention strategies to meet the individualized and unique needs of the student. The FBA mandate in IDEIA continues to reflect a change in practice from one-dimensional approaches that simply seek to increase desired responses or eliminate problem behavior, to a multifaceted process that focuses on examining the contextual variables that set the occasion for problem behavior, linking assessment results to intervention planning, and seeking to develop positive instructional or behavioral strategies and supports to address more appropriate and functional skills.

Discussions and examples of FBA methodology are abundant in the literature. Several comprehensive resources on the design and execution of FBAs, and the relationship between the outcomes of an FBA and the subsequent development and execution of BIPs, are available for practitioners (Crone & Horner, 2003; Crone, Horner, & Hawken, 2004; Florida Department of Education, 1999; O'Neill et al., 1997). The underlying theme to the FBA is that all behavior has a function and occurs for a reason. Determining this function is achieved through a process that usually involves a wide variety of strategies. The primary outcome of the FBA that summarizes these findings is a hypothesis statement that describes the problem and the variables correlated with its occurrence and nonoccurrence (Sugai, Lewis-Palmer, & Hagan-Burke, 1999–2000). Developing this hypothesis is achieved through the following:

1. consensus on the problem behavior,
2. a precise definition of the target behavior (Alberto & Troutman, 2006),
3. a review of the student's records and past interventions,
4. interviews with the student or all relevant parties (O'Neill et al., 1997),
5. team discussion,
6. assessment scales (e.g., Durand, 1988),
7. direct observation and measurement of the target behavior,
8. scatterplot data (Touchette, MacDonald, & Langer, 1985),
9. assessment of antecedents to and consequences of the target behavior,
10. identification of reinforcers (DeLeon & Iwata, 1996; Fisher et al., 1992; Holmes, Cautela, Simpson, Motes, & Gold, 1998; Pace, Ivancic, Edwards, Iwata, & Page, 1985),
11. examination of the ecological context to the problem behavior (Greenwood, Carta, & Atwater, 1991), and
12. analog experimentation of the proposed hypothesis (O'Neill et al., 1997).

It should be stressed that conducting an FBA is a comprehensive *process* supported by data and not simply a matter of those involved with a student achieving consensus on the problem and speculated causes. This process may involve multiple sources (teachers, parents, peers) and multiple environments and contexts (e.g., group activities vs. independent activities, different classrooms, classroom vs. playground or lunchroom). Due to the necessity of examining all of these variables, a team-based approach is essential (Todd, Horner, Sugai, & Colvin, 1999). Once the function or reason for the behavior is determined, appropriate intervention strategies can be developed and implemented. The relationship between developing interventions based on assessment information has been established, for example, in the Curriculum Based Measures (CBM) literature where student assessment is linked to instruction (Deno, 1985). Research indicates that using CBM results in more effective instructional plans (Deno, Marston, & Tindal, 1986). Similarly, an established body of research indicates that successful interventions depend on identifying the environmental correlates of problem behavior (e.g., Dunlap et al., 1993) and that identifying function serves to improve the effectiveness and efficiency of behavioral intervention (Lalli, Browder, Mace, & Brown, 1993; Umbreit, 1995).

Mandating FBAs within IDEIA improves the overall effectiveness of behavioral interventions. Failure to conduct a comprehensive FBA may result in programming that is insufficient to deal with the target behavior. Functional behavior assessments provide information on factors such as the most appropriate course of intervention, strategies and support systems, whether there are multiple functions to the target behavior, the conditions under which the behavior occurs, and the most effective reinforcer. Lack of attention to these variables affects the integrity of the plan. The intervention developed may work to change the target behavior, but the strategy developed may not be comprehensive enough to be most efficient, effective, and relevant. For example, often an FBA is conducted and a plan is developed to be used in multiple environments. However, the same behavior may serve different functions in different environments (e.g., different classrooms). Interventions developed within a plan should ensure that the setting events and function are addressed, appropriate and effective supports are designed and made available, and the occurrence or nonoccurrence of the behavior results in consequences that alter the future probability of the behavior. Similarly, the same behavior may also serve multiple functions within the *same* environment. It is context that dictates function, not type or form of the behavior. Conducting the FBA process *across* environments is the most effective means to determine this.

Assess Antecedent Variables and Setting Events

Traditionally, assessment of problem behavior involved examination of antecedents that trigger the occurrence of the target behavior and consequences that serve to maintain it. Subsequent intervention focused on manipulating the antecedent and consequent events to increase the occurrence of a desirable behavior or decrease the occurrence of an undesirable behavior. More recently, however, greater emphasis has been placed on examining behavior within its context (Horner, 1994; O'Neill et al., 1997; Sugai, Horner, & Sprague, 1999; Sugai, Lewis-Palmer, & Hagan, 1998). This emphasis has intensified with the emergence of the philosophy and practices of positive behavioral support. Within the framework of the traditional three-term contingency (i.e., Antecedent-Behavior-Consequence [A-B-C]), events and conditions that are more distant to the target behavior's direct and immediate antecedent (Smith & Iwata, 1997) are a focus of investigation. These conditions or events, referred to as *setting events*, serve to temporarily change the effectiveness of reinforcers and punishers, thus altering a student's response to environmental events and situations. For example, a student's argument with a peer earlier in the morning may serve to affect his or her on-task behavior later in the afternoon, despite modifications made to the curriculum and instructional strategies to facilitate greater on-task behavior. A poor night's sleep resulting in fatigue may serve to make a student more argumentative with peers, despite programming in place designed to promote more prosocial behavior. Setting events may occur just prior to a target behavior, or even days before. They may involve environmental factors (e.g., method and delivery of instruction, curriculum, the physical setting, number of people in the environment), physiological factors (e.g., illness, medical conditions, side effects of meds) or social factors (e.g., family circumstances, interactions with peers on the school bus; Jolivette, Wehby, & Hirsch, 1999; Kern, Childs, Dunlap, Clarke, & Falk, 1994). Assessing for, examining, and evaluating the presence (or absence) of setting events, referred to as a *structural analysis* (see Stichter & Conroy, 2005), is similar to the FBA process with the focus shifted to antecedent and contextual factors rather than maintaining variables.

The implications of examining the setting and contextual factors on the development of an efficient, effective, and relevant BIP cannot be underestimated. Interventions may focus on manipulating setting events (e.g., preventing the occurrence of a setting event, removing a setting event, minimizing/maximizing the effects of a setting event) so as to set the occasion for the occurrence of more desired behavior. Programming may also focus on manipulating other antecedents when setting events are in effect (e.g., modifying events so they are less aversive). Although school personnel may not have access to setting events outside of the school environment (or even be aware of them), operating within the contingencies and context that one does have access to and can control can make a significant difference in the effectiveness of an intervention.

Establish the Validity of Reinforcers

Many intervention plans focus on using rewards, contingent upon the occurrence of desired behavior. By using these rewards, teachers apply the principle of positive reinforcement, where a response is followed by the presentation of a stimulus (i.e., the reward), thereby increasing the future probability of that response (Cooper, Heron, & Heward, 2007). Yet a serious flaw may result from the simple delivery of a reward. Unless the future occurrence of the behavior increases after the reward is presented, reinforcement has not occurred. A common programming strategy is using a reinforcement system or token system where a student receives a reward for desired behaviors. Rewards may not necessarily serve as reinforcers (Maag, 2001). As many intervention plans rely on this strategy for developing or increasing the occurrence of target behaviors, plans may be abandoned or may be seen as ineffective or unsuccessful when there is no resulting increase in behavior. Without a corresponding increase in a target behavior, the presentation of a reinforcer is not reinforcement. An often underutilized strategy in programming is using negative reinforcement (see Cooper et al., 2007). Like positive reinforcement, negative reinforcement results in an increase in the future probability of a response. The difference, however, is that the response is followed by the termination or reduction of a stimulus.

For example, a teacher develops a system in which students receive one homework pass for every 10 consecutive days that homework is submitted. Assuming a student's homework submission rate increases, the process of negative reinforcement has been in operation. The function of the behavior under the negative reinforcement paradigm is to escape or avoid an aversive stimulus. Improving behavior is neither a simple nor a quick fix, but educators have strategies at their disposal to determine what reinforcers (positive or negative) may be more effective under the circumstances (DeLeon & Iwata, 1996; Fisher et al., 1992; Holmes et al., 1998; Northup, George, Jones, Broussard, & Vollmer, 1996; Pace et al., 1985).

The same argument holds true for using punishment in an attempt to discipline a student. The overriding, desired effect is to decrease the future occurrence of the inappropriate behavior. If the behavior did not decrease, then punishment has not occurred. A frequent disciplinary strategy is to send a student to the principal's office when misbehavior occurs. It is assumed that the effect of this action will punish the student and result in a decrease in the future occurrence of the misbehavior. However, if the target behavior did not decrease in frequency, punishment has not occurred. In fact, the strategy may have served to negatively reinforce the target behavior instead. The important consideration for reinforcement and punishment is that they are not *things*, but rather *effects* (Maag, 2001) and these effects impact the occurrence/nonoccurrence of desirable *and* undesirable behaviors. Reinforcement and punishment are not events but a process that results in the increase or decrease of a behavior; reinforcers and punishers must function as such rather than *look like* such.

Describe and Specify Target Behaviors and Intervention Strategies

Oftentimes, several individuals will note problem behavior with a student. The different perspectives and vocabulary of these individuals can lead to a variety of terms used to describe the problem behavior. These terms may be general or specific, but the resulting consensus can have an impact on the effectiveness of a BIP. For example, a student may be described as "aggressive." Such broad descriptors can have different meanings for different people. Does the student hit others, destroy property, or verbally threaten others? Achieving consensus on the target behavior among all of those implementing the BIP ensures that the plan is implemented consistently, under appropriate conditions. A description of a target behavior should be so specific that an individual unfamiliar with the student should be able to identify the student and the target behavior when it occurs. The term *operational definition* (Alberto & Troutman, 2006) has been used to describe the precision with which target behaviors should be identified. To minimize the differing interpretations of the same target behavior, a clear description of the observable and measurable characteristics of the target response is essential. Without a clear definition of the BIP's focus, it is very likely that a plan will be inconsistently implemented, thereby minimizing its overall effectiveness and relevance.

When establishing definitions of target behaviors, the notion of response class (i.e., a set of behaviors that have a similar function but vary in their basic elements or topography) must be considered. For example, a student's attempt to avoid difficult classroom work may take many forms. She or he may verbally refuse to comply with instructions, engage in tantrum behaviors, or slam the book shut. The similarity between all of these responses is that they serve to avoid work. One must not assume, however, that the same response classes will serve the same function in a different environment, or even in the same environment with a different context. Function dictates the type of intervention, not the setting, definition or types of behavior.

Occasionally, generic, nonspecific BIPs are developed and designed to improve a student's behavior without operationally defining the behavior or focusing on specific target behaviors. For example, a student will receive reinforcement or a reward for the absence of any problem behavior in a given period of time (e.g., if the student is good for the entire class period, he or she will receive a reward). These generic approaches may not provide the specificity and results that a more direct focus provides (e.g., providing a student with a reinforcer if 80% of math problems are completed correctly within a class session). Furthermore, as the consequence is not provided for a specific response, such interventions may have minimal impact on the acquisition or development of new target responses. Along similar lines, a lack of specificity in the BIP itself is another cause for concern. Just as target behaviors must be specifically described, the intervention itself must be clearly outlined. For example, designing a BIP that states a teacher will modify the way she or he interacts with a student gives very little information as to how those interactions are modified. Should the teacher modify the delivery of instruction and if so, how? Should the teacher provide more verbal praise or corrective feedback? In addition to delineating the strategies to use, a BIP must indicate the necessary resources and support along with the expectations of those carrying out the outlined procedures. Those implementing the BIP must know what to do and what not to do when the target behavior occurs (or does not occur). Specifically outlining procedures ensures that the plan is implemented as intended with little room for interpretation.

Consistently Collect Data

Although the process of measuring student performance is not new to teachers, the practice is generally limited to measuring academic response by recording students' grades on tests or other measures of work performance. Many teachers see little value in measuring and recording the occurrence of other student behavior in the classroom (Alberto & Troutman, 2006), and behavioral interventions are often developed with little consistency and attention to necessary details such as monitoring and evaluation (Buck, Polloway, Kirkpatrick, Patton, & Fad, 2000). If a student's behavior warrants implementing a BIP, it stands to reason that steps must be taken to evaluate the effectiveness of the plan in changing that behavior. Just as teachers use different strategies to measure students' academic performance in the classroom to evaluate the effectiveness of their instruction, a measurement of student behavior allows for evaluation of student performance and the effectiveness of the plan. Data should reflect progress toward the intervention's goal.

As previously discussed, contributing to the success of a BIP involves developing specific definitions of the target behavior. To effectively evaluate these behaviors, planned observation and measurement of their occurrence is essential. Without observation and measurement, there is no standard, objective method for determining the effectiveness of a BIP. A BIP may be prematurely modified or discontinued, or an ineffective plan may continue and prolong the student's exposure to ineffective strategies. To evaluate the effectiveness of a BIP, the student's behavior should be observed, measured, and recorded before, during, and after implementing the BIP, and the occurrence or nonoccurrence of the target behavior should be continuously assessed. Continuous measurement of student behavior reduces the likelihood of error in the intervention process (Cooper et al., 2007). Without data to represent student performance, the teacher is forced to rely on perception and opinion to assess the effectiveness of a BIP. A myriad of factors can cloud the accuracy of one's perception and opinion. The chance of error in evaluation of performance is much less when direct and objective measures are used.

Without data, no objective basis exists for judging improvement or decline in performance. Furthermore, continuous assessment of student performance and data collection improves the quality and efficiency of the decision-making process (Horner, Sugai, & Todd, 2001). That is, if an intervention is found to be unsuccessful, continuous evaluation allows for the teacher to change the intervention. Data must be used to assist with understanding, analysis, intervention, evaluation, and decision making (Sugai & Horner, 2005). Researchers have suggested that teachers who frequently and continuously collect data are better decision makers than teachers who do not (Fuchs & Fuchs, 1986; Fuchs, Fuchs, & Stecker, 1989).

Maag (2003) outlined several reasons for measuring and recording behavior. First, to accurately evaluate the effectiveness of the intervention, a precount, or baseline, is necessary. Without baseline data, no standard of comparison exists between pre- and postintervention occurrences of behavior, and there is no objective means of determining whether the intervention was effective. Second, measurement of the behavior allows the practitioner to determine whether the behavior targeted for measurement is the problem behavior (Levitt & Rutherford, 1978). Oftentimes, behaviors targeted for measurement may not be the problem. Behaviors targeted for measurement should be those that are the true problem or those targeted for intervention. For example, disruptive behavior is often the focus of intervention. Though disruptive behavior may certainly be a concern, it may also consist of several other responses such as roaming the room, talking with peers, or playing with objects. The true problem, however, is that the student does not complete work or attend to task. By collecting data on one response, other information is indirectly obtained on other related responses (Maag, 2003). As these other responses are better suited for intervention, it is more appropriate to measure their occurrence. Third, measurement of behavior assists with determining the severity of the problem. Because perceptions may be biased, data allow for an objective assessment of the degree to which the behavior occurs and its severity, relative to the occurrence of other students in the classroom. Data collection may reveal that the degree to which the behavior occurred was not as severe as perceived to be.

Implement Plan Accurately and Consistently

Central to the effectiveness of a BIP is the fidelity of the plan's implementation and several issues may contribute to the BIP's integrity. *Procedural integrity* (also referred to as treatment fidelity) refers to the accuracy and consistency of implementation (Baer, Wolf, & Risley, 1968; Gable, Quinn, Rutherford, Howell, & Hoffman, 2000; Peterson, Homer, & Wonderlich, 1982) and can result from factors such as a poorly defined target behavior or a poorly developed plan. As previously discussed, a poorly defined target behavior may affect accurate implementation of the plan. A poorly developed plan, at best, results in inconsistent implementation, and at worst, incorrect implementation; yet both are likely to negatively impact the effectiveness of the intervention. As Gresham, MacMillan, Beebe-Frankenberger, and Bocian (2000) indicated, the degree of treatment fidelity is directly related to the effectiveness of the plan; that is, a more accurately and consistently implemented plan increases the likelihood of producing positive behavior changes. Intervention is effective only to the degree to which it is reliably implemented. Furthermore, if a plan is poorly understood, difficult to implement, or inefficient, and thus poorly implemented, it is unlikely that appropriate decisions regarding the plan and a student's progress can be made. Just as data should be taken on student performance, data on program implementation provides team members with a measure of accountability. With increased emphasis on accountable systems, it would behoove educators and researchers to develop more practical and direct methods of ensuring and monitoring treatment integrity.

A second, and often overlooked reason for poor procedural integrity, is the social validity of the plan. Social validity is defined as an intervention's acceptance by its consumers; those who implement the plan or benefit from its implementation. Gunter and Denny (1996) noted that acceptability is based upon the judgment of those implementing the plan. The complexity of the plan, the perceived effectiveness of the plan, the teacher's knowledge of the plan's implementation, the willingness and ability of school personnel to execute the plan, and the social context of the plan all impact acceptance (Gresham et al. 2000; Gunter & Denny, 1996; Quinn, 2000; Scott et al., 2004; & Sugai & Horner, 2002; Wilson, Gutkin, Hagen, & Oates, 1998). Plans viewed as demanding, ineffective, or those that go against the philosophical beliefs of those who implement them are less likely to be implemented correctly or consistently and may even be abandoned. Furthermore, with a greater focus on accountability being placed on the educational system, treatment integrity is strongly related to treatment effectiveness. It benefits educators to develop and maintain collaborative relationships with all involved in the intervention process and discuss concerns about the intervention process that may impact its utility and acceptance in the classroom. Teachers have indicated that they are better able to solve behavioral problems when collaboration among team members occurs (Giangreco, Cloninger, Dennis, & Edelman, 2000).

Address Student Skill Deficits

Maladaptive behaviors that serve as the focus of BIPs undoubtedly interfere with a student's ability to effectively interact with the environment, yet the reduction of these target behaviors does not necessarily result in a functional improvement in the classroom (Ferritor, Buckholdt, Hamblin, & Smith, 1972). Ferritor et al. (1972) found that reducing disruptive classroom behavior does not always result in a corresponding improvement in academic performance. As important as reducing inappropriate behavior is, it is equally important for BIPs to address instruction in constructive and productive social and classroom behaviors. Knowledge of the inappropriate behavior's function is particularly important here, as knowing the function is critical for identifying relevant replacement behaviors that serve the same function as the target response. Many inappropriate behaviors are the result of a *skill* deficit rather than a *performance* deficit. Simply addressing the removal of an inappropriate behavior fails to address a possible skill deficit because the student has not learned an alternative, appropriate response. Particularly relevant to the classroom is the lack of academic skills that may impede classroom performance and the behavioral problems that often accompany these skill deficits (e.g., a student's off-task behavior during silent reading time is not due to his or her refusal to follow directions but rather to poor reading skills). Rather than developing a plan only to eliminate the undesired behavior, intervention must also focus on remediating the academic deficiencies correlated with the target behavior, the nature of which may be more appropriately addressed in an individualized education program (IEP). Generally the function of a given behavior, though the focus of intervention, is not usually a cause for concern, but rather the behavior used to achieve that function is. A plan that focuses on teaching a functional, alternative replacement behavior (e.g., teaching a student to recruit teacher reinforcement rather than calling out in class) allows the student to receive the same outcomes as the targeted undesirable behavior but by emitting a more desirable and adaptive functional response. A concurrent focus of intervention can address the acquisition of an alternative behavior that serves the same function as the target behavior.

Program for Generalization and Maintenance

The ultimate expectation of a BIP is that the intervention will result in lasting behavior change across a variety of environments that the student is expected to encounter. Unfortunately, simply implementing a BIP and successfully modifying behavior does not guarantee sustained and generalized behavior change. The desired change resulting from the implementation of a BIP may be short-lived, or the target behavior may not extend into other environments. Two types of outcomes are most often the concern with behavioral programming: stimulus generalization and response maintenance.

Stimulus generalization refers to the occurrence of a behavior in a different setting or under different conditions than in which it was trained (Alberto & Troutman, 2006; Cooper et al., 2007). For example, if the focus of a BIP is to teach a student to raise his or her hand rather than call out answers in the classroom, stimulus generalization has occurred when the student raises a hand, rather than calling out answers, in classrooms other than the classroom in which the BIP was in effect. The student also participates in a variety of questions and situations.

The second type of outcome is *response maintenance*, when a learned behavior continues long after the programmed contingencies in a BIP have been removed (Cooper et al., 2007). For example, as in the same situation just discussed, response maintenance would occur if the student continued to raise a hand, rather than call out answers, throughout her or his educational career. Generalization and maintenance rarely occur without specific programming for their occurrence. Unfortunately, a "train and hope" (Stokes & Baer, 1977) approach is often used with BIPs, where the student is taught a skill and those implementing it hope that it remains in the student's repertoire across settings and time. Although a technology for generalization and maintenance is established in the literature (Alberto & Troutman, 2006; Cooper et al., 2007; Stokes & Baer, 1977; Stokes & Osnes, 1988), these strategies are not often addressed in behavioral programming. Addressing generalization and maintenance issues in a BIP has an impact on programming design. When generalization and maintenance are addressed in programming, programming objectives change as generalization and maintenance objectives differ from typical programming objectives that focus on acquisition of behavior (Haring & Liberty, 1990). For example, the conditions under which the behavior occurs, materials used, schedule of reinforcement, or other performance criteria, differ when considering generalization and maintenance. Consequently, the BIP should be designed to reflect the conditions that the student will encounter in the real world environment.

Students may also need to be taught self-monitoring and self-management strategies to maximize generalization and maintenance (see Todd, Horner, Vanater, & Schneider, [1997] for an example of integrating self-management into the BIP process). Within generalization objectives, conditions reflecting the natural environment are addressed rather than objectives that address the successful acquisition of the skill. Thus, the criteria for successful performance differ. Because the criteria are not the same, it stands to reason that the design and execution of a BIP must also differ if these criteria are to be addressed.

Focus on Demonstrated Behavior Change, Not "Just Talk"

The intent of behavioral planning is to change specific student behavior. As such, programming must focus on the student actually emitting a desired response. Rather than focusing on a specified response, a plan may simply focus on the student verbally reporting what the appropriate response should have been. For example, when a student responds to the teacher's request to begin working by throwing the book across the room and tipping over the desk, a BIP may indicate that she or he talks with the school social worker about more appropriate ways to handle anger. Unfortunately, simply focusing on verbalizations as a behavior change strategy is not likely sufficient enough to establish a desired behavior change.

Correspondence training involves individuals making verbal statements about future behavior. Correspondence is established through programming that reinforces the individual's stated intention (Baer, Williams, Osnes, & Stokes, 1984; Guevremont, Osnes, & Stokes, 1986a, 1986b; Stokes, Osnes, & Guevremont, 1987). However, follow-through to the actual emission of the desired response is essential, especially for the acquisition of new behaviors. Without the follow-through established with correspondence training, it is likely the programming will only serve to establish verbal reports of a desired response rather than the actual desired response.

Provide Sufficient Time, Staffing, Resources, and Supports

Despite good faith efforts to ameliorate a student's problem behavior, barriers may exist that prohibit effective implementation. First, time is an important factor to consider. Time refers not only to the time to implement the plan but also time to allow progress to be made. Second, sufficient personnel must be on board to implement the plan, especially if the plan is implemented across multiple environments (e.g., different classrooms, home and community). Some individuals may think that time and resources are insufficient to implement the program while still addressing the needs of other students, but resources are a key factor in the development and execution of BIPs. These may include materials to implement programming, ongoing consultation, or training. Support is not limited to school personnel but to the supports students require to facilitate their social and learning outcomes, to prevent problem behaviors, and to promote positive, appropriate, and functional behavior change (Carr et al., 2002; Horner, Albin, Sprague, & Todd, 1999). Rather than focusing on means to eliminate undesirable behavior, positive behavioral support strategies seek to promote student achievement through understanding of the unique factors involved in a student's behavior, individualizing interventions, and providing the necessary supports to achieve desired and sustained outcomes (see Crone & Horner, 2003; Florida Department of Education, 1999; Sugai & Horner, 2002). Effective practices require sustained support (Sugai & Horner, 2005). Resources may even include feedback on a teacher's performance of the plan's implementation. Codding, Feinberg, Dunn, and Pace (2005) found that providing performance feedback to teachers improved treatment integrity of the plan in the classroom. Moreover, teachers

✓	**Essential BIP Elements**
	Functional Behavior Assessment
	• Consensus on problem
	• Review of records & past interventions
	• Interviews with all relevant parties
	• Team discussion
	• Assessment scales
	• Direct observation & measurement of the target behavior across settings & context
	• Scatterplot
	• A-B-C analysis
	• Reinforcer preference assessment
	• Ecological analysis
	• Hypothesized statement of the behavior's function
	• Analog experimentation of proposed hypothesis
	Antecedent Variables & Setting Events
	• A-B-C analysis
	• Determine the presence or absence of setting events
	• Contextual factors
	• Environmental factors
	• Physiological factors
	• Social factors
	Validity of Reinforcers
	• Reinforcer preference assessment
	• Corresponding increase in the target behavior when reinforcement is used
	• Corresponding decrease in the target behavior when punishment is used
	• Data to verify change in target behavior
	Clear Description of Target Behavior & Intervention Strategies
	• Observable, measurable, definable, & precise definition of the target behavior
	• Examination of similarities & differences between multiple target responses
	• Intervention focuses on a specific response or class of responses
	• Clear outline of BIP's procedures, specifying what one should/should not do when the behavior does/does not occur
	• Specific resources & support necessary to execute the plan
	Consistent Data Collection
	• Data collection system for continuous measurement of the target behavior is established
	• Data & student performance is continuously evaluated
	• BIP is modified, if necessary, based upon evaluation of the data
	Accurate & Consistent Implementation
	• BIP is accurately implemented
	• BIP is consistently implemented
	• Data is collected on BIP implementation
	• Social validity of the plan is established
	• Collaborative process is maintained
	Student Skill Deficits Addressed
	• Skill vs. performance deficits are determined
	• Skill deficits are remediated within a BIP or IEP
	• Establish a functional & adaptive replacement behavior
	Generalization & Maintenance Programming
	• Long-term outcomes for the target behavior are established (environmentally, contextually)

Figure 1 Checklist for designing, implementing, and evaluating effective behavior intervention plans.
Note. BIP = behavior intervention plan; IEP = individualized education program.

rated performance feedback as valuable to the intervention process (Codding et al., 2005; Noell, Duhon, Gatti, & Connell, 2002). It would be inappropriate and naïve to assume that programming can be adopted and accurately implemented without adequate resources, training, or support.

Conclusion

As the practice of intervention planning grows within the educational arena and educators become more comfortable with its development and practice, the necessary and essential requirements inherent in an appropriately developed and effective plan will become more mainstream. Figure 1 provides a summary checklist for designing more effective BIPs. Although this discussion has focused on the development of individual plans, practitioners should be aware that to provide effective interventions, not only must BIPs address issues specific to an individual student, but specific systems inherent to the school that also serve as contextual factors and that may contribute to the occurrence of undesirable behaviors (Todd, Horner, Sugai, & Sprague, 1999). Effective interventions are not developed in isolation, but rather are the product of individual and cumulative efforts and global and specific assessment strategies. Future resources should be directed toward training educators on more effective practices to improve the quality of intervention programming to most effectively meet the educational needs of students with behavior problems in the classroom and other school settings.

References

Alberto, P. A., & Troutman, A. C. (2006). *Applied behavior analysis for teachers* (7th ed.). Upper Saddle River, NJ: Merrill/Prentice Hall.

Baer, D. M., Wolf, M. M., & Risley, T. R. (1968). Some current dimensions of applied behavior analysis. *Journal of Applied Behavior Analysis, 1,* 91–97.

Baer, R. A., Williams, J. A., Osnes, P. G., & Stokes, T. F. (1984). Delayed reinforcement as an indiscriminable contingency in verbal/nonverbal correspondence training. *Journal of Applied Behavior Analysis, 17,* 429–440.

Buck, G. H., Polloway, E. A., Kirkpatrick, M. A., Patton, J. R., & Fad, K. M. (2000). Developing behavioral intervention plans: A sequential approach. *Intervention in School and Clinic, 36,* 3–9.

Carr, E. G., Dunlap, G., Horner, R. H., Koegel, R. L., Turnbull, A. P., Sailor, W., et al. (2002). Positive behavior support: Evolution of an applied science. *Journal of Positive Behavior Interventions, 4,* 4–16.

Codding, R. S., Feinberg, A. B., Dunn, E. K., & Pace, S. M. (2005). Effects of immediate performance feedback on implementation of behavior support plans. *Journal of Applied Behavior Analysis, 38,* 205–219.

Cooper, J. O., Heron, T. E., & Heward, W. L. (2007). *Applied behavior analysis* (2nd ed). Upper Saddle River, NJ: Pearson/Prentice Hall.

Crone, D. A., & Horner, R. H. (2003). *Building positive behavior support systems in schools: Functional behavioral assessment.* New York: Guilford.

Crone, D. A., Horner, R. H., & Hawken, L. S. (2004). *Responding to problem behavior in schools: The behavior education program.* New York: Guilford.

DeLeon, I., & Iwata, B. (1996). Evaluation of a multiple-stimulus presentation format for assessing reinforcer preferences. *Journal of Applied Behavior Analysis, 29,* 519–533.

Deno, S. L. (1985). Curriculum-based measurement: The emerging alternative. *Exceptional Children, 52,* 219–232.

Deno, S. L., Marston, D., & Tindal, G. (1986). Direct and frequent curriculum-based measurement: An alternative for educational decision making. *Special Services in the Schools, 2,* 5–27.

Dunlap, G., Kern, L., dePerezel, M., Clarke, S., Williams, D., Childs, K., et al. (1993). Functional assessment of classroom variables for students with emotional/behavioral disorders. *Behavioral Disorders, 18,* 275–291.

Durand, V. M. (1988). The motivation assessment scale. In M. Hersen & A. S. Bellack (Eds.), *Dictionary of behavioral assessment techniques* (pp. 309–310). Elmsford, NY: Pergamon.

Ferritor, D. E., Buckholdt, D., Hamblin, R. L., & Smith, L. (1972). The noneffects of contingent reinforcement for attending behavior on work accomplished. *Journal of Applied Behavior Analysis, 5,* 7–17.

Fisher, W., Piazza, C., Bowman, L., Hagopian, L., Owens, J., & Slevin, I. (1992). A comparison of two approaches for identifying reinforcers for persons with severe and profound disabilities. *Journal of Applied Behavior Analysis, 25,* 491–498.

Florida Department of Education (1999, November). *Facilitator's guide: Positive behavioral support.* Tampa, FL: Bureau of Instructional Support and Community Services.

Fuchs, L. S., & Fuchs, D. (1986). Effects of systematic formative evaluation: A meta-analysis. *Exceptional Children, 53,* 199–208.

Fuchs, L. S., Fuchs, D., & Stecker, P. M. (1989). The effects of curriculum-based measurement on teachers instructional planning. *Journal of Learning Disabilities, 22,* 51–59.

Gable, R. A., Quinn, M. M., Rutherford, R. G., Howell, K. W., & Hoffman, C. C. (2000). *Addressing student problem behavior: Part III: Creating positive behavioral intervention plans and supports.* Washington, DC: Center for Effective Collaboration and Practice.

Giangreco, M. F., Cloninger, C. J., Dennis, R. E., & Edelman, S. W. (2000). Problem solving methods to facilitate inclusive education. In R. A. Villa & J. S. Thousand (Eds.), *Restructuring for caring and effective education: Piecing the puzzle together* (2nd ed., pp. 293–327). Baltimore: Brookes.

Greenwood, C. R., Carta, J. J., & Atwater, J. (1991). Ecobehavioral analysis in the classroom: Review and implications. *Journal of Behavioral Education, 1,* 59–77.

Gresham, F., MacMillan, D. L., Beebe-Frankenberger, M. B., & Bocian, K. M. (2000). Treatment integrity in learning disabilities intervention research: Do we really know how treatments are implemented? *Learning Disabilities Research and Practice, 15,* 198–205.

Guevremont, D. C., Osnes, P. G., & Stokes, T. F. (1986a). Programming maintenance after correspondence training interventions with children. *Journal of Applied Behavior Analysis, 19,* 215–219.

Guevremont, D. C., Osnes, P. G., & Stokes, T. F. (1986b). Preparation for effective self-regulation: The development of generalized verbal control. *Journal of Applied Behavior Analysis, 19,* 99–104.

Gunter, P., & Denny, K. (1996). Research issues and needs regarding teacher use of classroom management strategies. *Behavioral Disorders, 22,* 15–20.

Haring, N. G., & Liberty, K. A. (1990). Matching strategies with performance in facilitating generalization. *Focus on Exceptional Children, 22,* 1–16.

Holmes, G., Cautela, J., Simpson, M., Motes, P., & Gold, J. (1998). Factor structure of the school reinforcement survey schedule: School is more than grades. *Journal of Behavioral Education, 8,* 131–140.

Horner, R. H. (1994). Functional assessment: Contributions and future directions. *Journal of Applied Behavior Analysis, 27,* 401–404.

Horner, R. H., Albin, R. W., Sprague, J. R., & Todd, A. W. (1999). Positive behavior support for students with severe disabilities. In M. E. Snell & F. Brown (Eds.), *Instruction of students with severe disabilities* (5th ed., pp. 207–243). Upper Saddle River, NJ: Merrill/ Prentice Hall.

Horner, R. H., Sugai, G., & Todd, A. W. (2001). Data need not be a four-letter word: Using data to improve school-wide discipline. *Beyond Behavior, 11,* 20–22.

Jolivette, K., Wehby, J. H., & Hirsch, L. (1999). Academic strategy identification for students exhibiting inappropriate classroom behaviors. *Behavioral Disorders, 24,* 210–221.

Kern, L., Childs, K., Dunlap, G., Clarke, S., & Falk, G. D. (1994). Using assessment-based curricular intervention to improve the classroom behavior of a student with emotional and behavioral challenges. *Journal of Applied Behavior Analysis, 27,* 7–19.

Lalli, J. S., Browder, D. M., Mace, F. C., & Brown, D. K. (1993). Teacher use of descriptive analysis data to implement interventions to decrease students' problem behaviors. *Journal of Applied Behavior Analysis, 26,* 227–238.

Levitt, L. K., & Rutherford, R. B. (1978). *Strategies for handling the disruptive student.* Tempe: Arizona State University, College of Education.

Maag, J. W. (2001). Rewarded by punishment: Reflections on the disuse of positive reinforcement in schools. *Exceptional Children, 67,* 173–186.

Maag, J. W. (2003). Targeting behaviors and methods for recording their occurrences. In M. J. Breen & C. R. Fiedler (Eds.), *Behavioral approach to assessment of youth with emotional/ behavioral disorders: A handbook for school-based practitioners* (2nd ed., pp. 297–333). Austin, TX: PRO-ED.

Morgan, D., & Jenson, W. R. (1988). *Teaching behaviorally disordered students: Preferred practices.* Columbus, OH: Merrill.

Noell, G. H., Duhon, G. J., Gatti, S. L., & Connell, J. R. (2002). Consultation, follow-up, and implementation of behavior management interventions in general education. *School Psychology Review, 31,* 217–234.

Northup, J., George, T., Jones, K., Broussard, C., & Vollmer, T. (1996). A comparison of reinforcer assessment methods: The utility of verbal and pictorial choice procedures. *Journal of Applied Behavior Analysis, 29,* 201–212.

O'Neill, R. E., Horner, R. H., Albin, R. W., Sprague, J. R., Storey, K., & Newton, J. S. (1997). *Functional assessment for problem behavior: A practical handbook* (2nd ed.). Pacific Grove, CA: Brookes/Cole.

Pace, G., Ivancic, M., Edwards, G., Iwata, B., & Page, T. (1985). Assessment of stimulus preference and reinforcer value with profoundly retarded individuals. *Journal of Applied Behavior Analysis, 18,* 249–255.

Peterson, L., Homer, A. L., & Wonderlich, S. A. (1982). The integrity of independent variables in behavior analysis. *Journal of Applied Behavior Analysis, 15,* 477–492.

Quinn, M. M. (2000). Creating safe, effective, and nurturing schools: New opportunities and new challenges for serving all students. In L. M. Bullock & R. A. Gable (Eds.), *Positive academic and behavioral supports: Creating safe, effective, and nurturing schools for all students* (pp. 1–5). Reston, VA: Council for Children with Behavioral Disorders.

Scott, T. M., Bucalos, A., Liaupsin, C., Nelson, C. M., Jolivette, K., & DeShea, L. (2004). Using functional behavior assessment in general education settings: Making a case for effectiveness and efficiency. *Behavioral Disorders, 29*(2), 189–201.

Smith, R. G., & Iwata, B. A. (1997). Antecedent influences on behavior disorders. *Journal of Applied Behavior Analysis, 30,* 343–375.

Stichter, J., & Conroy, M. (2005). Using structural analysis in natural settings: A responsive functional assessment strategy. *Journal of Behavioral Education, 14,* 19–34.

Stokes, T. F., & Baer, D. M. (1977). An implicit technology of generalization. *Journal of Applied Behavior Analysis, 10,* 349–367.

Stokes, T. F., & Osnes, P. G. (1988). The developing applied technology of generalization and maintenance. In R. H. Horner, G. Dunlap, & R. L. Koegel (Eds.), *Generalization and maintenance* (pp. 5–19). Baltimore: Brookes.

Stokes, T. F., Osnes, P. G., & Guevremont, D. C. (1987). Saying and doing: A commentary on a contingency-space analysis. *Journal of Applied Behavior Analysis, 20,* 161–164.

Sugai, G., & Horner, R. H. (Eds.). (2002). Introduction to the special series on positive behavior support in schools. *Journal of Emotional and Behavioral Disorders, 10*(3), 130–136.

Sugai, G., & Horner, R. H. (2005). Schoolwide positive behavior supports: Achieving and sustaining effective learning environments for all students. In W. L. Heward, T. E. Heron, N. A. Neef, S. M. Peterson, D. M. Sainato, G. Cartledge, et al. (Eds.), *Focus on behavior analysis in education: Achievements, challenges, and opportunities* (pp. 90–102). Upper Saddle River, NJ: Pearson.

Sugai, G., Horner, R. H., & Sprague, J. (1999). Functional assessment-based behavior support planning: Research-to-practice-to-research. *Behavioral Disorders, 24,* 223–227.

Sugai, G., Lewis-Palmer, T., & Hagan, S. (1998). Using functional assessments to develop behavior support plans. *Preventing School Failure, 43*(1), 6–13.

Sugai, G., Lewis-Palmer, T., & Hagan-Burke, S. (1999–2000). Overview of the functional behavior assessment process. *Exceptionality, 8*(3), 149–160.

Todd, A. W., Horner, R. H., Sugai, G., & Colvin, G. (1999). Individualizing school-wide discipline for students with chronic problem behaviors: A team approach. *Effective School Practices, 17*(4), 72–82.

Todd, A. W., Horner, R. H., Sugai, G., & Sprague, J. R. (1999). Effective behavior support: Strengthening school-wide systems through a team-based approach. *Effective School Practices, 17*(4), 23–27.

Todd, A. W., Horner, R. H. Vanater, S. M., & Schneider, C. F. (1997). Working together to make change: An example of positive behavioral support for a student with traumatic brain injury. *Education and Treatment of Children, 20,* 425–440.

Touchette, P. E., MacDonald, R. F., & Langer, S. N. (1985). A scatterplot for identifying stimulus control of problem behavior. *Journal of Applied Behavior Analysis, 18,* 343–351.

Umbreit, J. (1995). Functional assessment and intervention in a regular classroom setting for the disruptive behavior of a student with attention-deficit hyperactivity disorder. *Behavioral Disorders, 20,* 267–278.

Wilson, P. C., Gutkin, T. B., Hagen, K. M., & Oates, R. G. (1998). General education teacher's knowledge and self-reported use of classroom interventions for working with difficult-to-teach students: Implications for consultation, prereferral intervention and inclusive services. *School Psychology Quarterly, 13,* 45–62.

Assess Your Progress

1. Define Functional Behavior Assessment and Behavior Intervention Plan.
2. Under what circumstances might a teacher decide to conduct a functional behavior assessment?
3. For future reference, create an outline of the steps for a functional behavior assessment.
4. Why would a teacher develop a Behavior Intervention Plan?
5. Based on what you have learned from the articles in this unit, develop a mission statement that expresses your management philosophy.

KIM KILLU, PhD, is an associate professor of special education at the University of Michigan–Dearborn. Her current interests include applied behavior analysis, the assessment and treatment of severe behavior disorders, and functional behavior assessment/behavior intervention planning policy and practice.

Address: Kim Killu, University of Michigan–Dearborn, School of Education, 19000 Hubbard Dr., Dearborn, MI, 48126; e-mail: kimkillu@umd.umich.edu

From *Intervention in School and Clinic*, January 2008, pp. 140–149. Copyright © 2008 by Pro-Ed, Inc. Reprinted by permission.

UNIT 7

Technology: Are We Effectively Using Its Potential in Our Schools?

Unit Selections

33. **"For Openers: How Technology Is Changing School,"** Curtis J. Bonk
34. **Tech Tool Targets Elementary Readers,** Katie Ash
35. **Digital Tools Expand Options for Personalized Learning,** Kathleen Kennedy Manzo
36. **Effects of Video-Game Ownership on Young Boys' Academic and Behavioral Functioning: A Randomized, Controlled Study,** Robert Weis and Brittany C. Cerankosky

Learning Outcomes

After reading this unit, you will be able to:

- Consider the ways that technology can and will change schooling.
- Examine trends in technology that will allow blended learning as well as fully online learning.
- Discuss the six technologies that experts have determined will have a major impact on education.
- Identify the challenges that schools will face in the near future.
- Explain how a gaming device can be used to help struggling elementary readers.
- Determine how gaming technology might be used for other educational purposes.
- Describe how technology can be used to differentiate instruction.
- Evaluate the methods used by schools to use technology to meet individual learning needs.
- Restate outcomes of research study on effects of playing video games on academic skills.
- Prepare suggestions for parents and caregivers regarding video gaming.
- Explain why schools block social media websites.
- Demonstrate the validity of using social media for teaching and learning activities.
- Describe the results of research that looks at how children use social media and interest driven information searches.
- Determine how teacher can use student-centered activities with social media to harvest student knowledge.

Student Website
www.mhhe.com/cls

Internet References

Educational Technology
www.edtech.sandi.net

Curriculum Connections
www.edtech.sandi.net/old305/handouts/digitalclassroom/curriculumconnections.html

Open Thinking Wiki
www.couros.wikispaces.com/TechAndMediaLiteracyVids

No limits 2 learning: Celebrating human potential through assistive technology
www.nolimitstolearning.blogspot.com

Quest Garden
www.questgarden.com

Go2web20
www.go2web20.net

We have added a technology unit to *Education 11/12* because technology can and has been a change agent in education. After experiencing early motion pictures in 1913, Thomas Edison declared that books would soon be obsolete in schools because soon we would be able to learn everything from movies. Most recently we have heard similar claims about digital books from advocates of Kindle, Nook, and iPad and other e-reader and sellers of audio books. What is really happening in our schools? Are textbooks disappearing? Is everyone connected? Are our students sitting all day laboring over a keyboard and staring at a screen? In this unit we will explore both the potential of the digital technology and the challenges of using this technology for teaching and learning.

There are significant trends noted by Bitter and Pierson (2002) that are important to this discussion. The first is the shift in demographics within our student population of increased numbers of students who do not live in traditional family structures, who have special needs at both the high and low ends of achievement, who are English Language Learners, and who live in poverty. For many of these students the ability to access sophisticated technology may not exist in their homes or neighborhoods. Hence, schools are the only place where they can be exposed to and made to learn about the usage of technology. These students, many of whom will need technology to access the curriculum, will pose a considerable challenge to public schools. An additional challenge according to Better and Pierson will be the acceleration of technological change that correspondingly increases the pace of change in our knowledge base. Keeping up in one's field of expertise or areas of interest has become a full time job of its own.

In most schools regardless of where the school is regionally or economically, most teachers who use computers do so because computers make their jobs easier and complete tasks more efficiently. The computer can do things the teacher cannot or is unwilling to do. We use them to keep digital grade books that will correctly calculate final grades in a flash, search for information to use in lectures, photos and clip art to illustrate our PowerPoints, and lesson plans to meet state standards and to communicate with peers down the hall, the principal, and even with parents. But too often our computer may be the only computer in a classroom, or even a classroom with a LCD projector and white board. There may be a computer lab down the hall or a few computers in the media center, but very few schools have laptops or handheld devices for all students. So almost 100 years ago, Thomas Edison may have been a bit hasty to declare books a thing of the past. In fact, just 11 years ago, we published an article, *The Silicon Classroom* by Kaplan and Rogers (1996), in the *Education 98/99,* in which they declared that schools were rushing to spend billions on computers without a clue on what to do with them. In this issue, we are publishing an article that outlines the challenges that schools face today in implementing computer use in classroom. Why is this happening? We hope the articles presented in this unit will challenge you to consider how you should and will use technology to provide access to information and your content area curriculum.

The first article is meant to provide a glimpse of what is possible and what challenges still remain. Bonk notes that schooling and learning did not stop in the aftermath of Katrina and Rita, but instead took on a new configuration. He suggests this is a model we should strive to attain in all schools.

But on the other hand, we can find examples of interesting technology use described by Ash in *Tech Tool Targets Elementary Readers.* Companies are working to develop lost cost devices that will put digital technologies into the hands of every student in a school district. Manzo found teachers using digital tools to individualize education plans for every student, regardless of ability. One example is a middle school that provides customized math lessons to every student every day using face-to-face instruction, software-based activities, and online lesson.

We have heard in the main stream media that playing video games is not good for children for any number of reasons. But where was the data? It is here in the article by Weis and Cerankosky describing their naturalistic research study of 64 boy, ages 6–9. They studied the effects of playing games on development of reading and writing skills. The results are what you might expect, but are the reasons what you thought?

It seems that we are faced with two possibilities, being wrong in our predictions or being irrelevant luddites. It might be best if schools were to somewhere along that continuum, but not at either extreme.

Reference

Bitter, G. & Pierson, M. (2002). *Using technology in the classroom.* Boston, MA: Allyn and Bacon.

Article 33

"For Openers: How Technology Is Changing School"

Whether you're sailing around the world, homebound with the flu, or just in the market for more flexible learning, thanks to the Internet, schooling never stops.

CURTIS J. BONK

Sometimes it takes a major catastrophe to transform how we deliver schooling. In 2005, in the aftermath of Hurricanes Katrina and Rita, websites went up in Louisiana, Texas, and Mississippi to help educators, students, families, and school districts deal with the crisis. The Mississippi Department of Education (2005) announced free online courses at the high school level, and institutions from 38 states provided more than 1,300 free online courses to college students whose campuses had been affected by the hurricanes (Sloan-C, 2006).

Health emergencies in recent years have also caused educators to ponder the benefits of the Web. In 2003, during the SARS epidemic in China, government officials decided to loosen restrictions on online and blended learning (Huang & Zhou, 2006). More recently, as concerns about the H1N1 virus mounted, many U.S. schools piloted new educational delivery options, such as free online lessons from Curriki (www.curriki.org) and Smithsonian Education (www.smithsonianeducation.org). Microsoft has even offered its Microsoft Office Live free of charge to educators dealing with H1N1. The software enables teachers to share content, lesson plans, and other curriculum components, while students access the virtual classroom workspace, chat with one another on discussion topics, and attend virtual presentations.

Blended Learning Is Here

The focus today is on continuity of learning, whether learning is disrupted because of a hurricane or the flu—or because of other factors entirely. Schools may have difficulty serving students who live in rural areas; reduced budgets may limit the range of learning that a school can offer; people young and old involved in serious scholarly, artistic, or athletic pursuits may find it difficult to adhere to the traditional school structure.

In light of these developments, some school districts are resorting to blended learning options. They are using tools like Tegrity (www.tegrity.com); Elluminate (www.elluminate.com); and Adobe Connect Pro (www.Adobe.com/products/acrobatconnectpro) to provide online lectures. Many are developing procedures for posting course content and homework online. Some are trying phone conferencing with Skype (www.skype.com) or Google Talk (www.google.com/talk). Others are evaluating digital textbooks and study guides. Still others are sharing online videos from places like Link TV (www.linktv.org); FORA, tv (http://fora.tv); or TeacherTube (www.teachertube.com), with teachers often asking students to post their reflections in blogs or online discussion forums. Many schools have begun to foster teamwork by using Google Docs (http://docs.google.com) and wikis. Although some schools use e-mail to communicate messages district-wide, others are experimenting with text messaging or Twitter (http://twitter.com).

The wealth of information available online is also changing teaching practices. Teachers can access free online reference material, podcasts, wikis, and blogs, as well as thousands of free learning portals, such as the Periodic Table of Videos (www.periodicvideos.com) for chemistry courses and the Encyclopedia of Life (www.eol.org) for biology. Science teachers can use portals devoted to Einstein (www.alberteinstein.info); Darwin (www.darwin-online.org.uk); or Goodall (www.janegoodall.org). English teachers can find similar content repositories on Poe (www.eapoe.org); Shakespeare (http://shakespeare.mit.edu); and Austen (www.janeausten.org), to name just a few.

High School—Online

Tools like these enable great flexibility in learning. When I take a break from work and jog across my campus, smack in the middle of it I come to Owen Hall, home of the Indiana University High School (http://iuhighschool.iu.edu). Indiana University High School (IUHS) students can take their courses online or through correspondence or some combination of the two. Students range from those who live in rural settings to those who are homebound, homeschooled, pregnant, or gifted. Some are Americans living in other countries; some are natives of other countries whose parents want them to have a U.S. education. Some are dropouts or students academically at risk. Still others are teenagers about to enter college who need advanced placement courses or adults who want to finish their high school degrees (Robbins, 2009). Across the board, many of the 4,000 students enrolled in IUHS simply did not fit in the traditional U.S. high school setting.

Take 16-year-old Evren Ozan (www.ozanmusic.com), the Native American flute prodigy whose music I've enjoyed for several years. I'm listening to him as I write this sentence. Many of Evren's vast accomplishments—he's been recording music since he was 7 years old—would not have been possible without the online and distance education experiences he benefited from during his teen years when most of his peers were attending traditional high schools. Also attending IUHS is 15-year-old Ania Filochowska, a Polish-born violinist who has studied with several great masters of the violin in New York City since 2005. Similarly, Kathryn Morgan enrolled in IUHS so she could continue her quest to become a professional ballerina. With the flexibility of online courses and degrees, Kathryn danced full-time and pursued an apprenticeship with the New York City Ballet.

Then there is the amazing story of Bridey Fennell. Bridey completed four IUHS courses while enjoying a five-month sailboat journey with her parents and two sisters from Arcaju, Brazil, to Charleston, South Carolina. Ship dock captains and retired teachers proctored her exams in port, and she practiced her French lessons on different islands of the Caribbean. Her sister Caitlin posted updates about their daily activities to her blog, and elementary students in the Chicago area monitored the family's journey and corresponded with Caitlin.

We All Learn

All this raises the question of why so many people only see the benefits of online learning for musicians, dancers, athletes, and other performers or for those affected by some calamity. I personally benefited from nontraditional education a quarter of a century ago when I was taking correspondence and televised courses from the University of Wisconsin. Back then, I was a bored accountant, and distance learning was my only way out. It got me into graduate school and changed my life. I now speak, write books, and teach about the benefits of distance learning.

The 21st century offers us far more options to learn and grow intellectually. Today more than a million people in the United States alone are learning online.

To make sense of the vast array of Web-based learning opportunities possible today, I have developed a framework based on 10 *openers*—10 technological opportunities that have the potential to transform education by altering where, when, and how learning takes place. The openers form the acronym WE-ALL-LEARN.[1] They include

- **W**eb searching in the world of e-books.
- **E**-learning and blended learning.
- **A**vailability of open-source and free software.
- **L**everaged resources and open courseware.
- **L**earning object repositories and portals.
- **L**earner participation in open information communities.
- **E**lectronic collaboration.
- **A**lternate reality learning.
- **R**eal-time mobility and portability.
- **N**etworks of personalized learning.

Online and blended learning opportunities are just one opener (opener #2). Lets look at two more.

Web Searching in the World of e-Books

A decade ago, books were limited to being physical objects. Today, all that has changed. Government, nonprofit, and corporate initiatives are placing greater emphasis on digital book content.

The digital textbook project in Korea (www.dtbook.kr/eng), for instance, is being piloted in 112 schools with hopes of making textbooks free for all Korean schools by 2013. Digital textbooks include such features as dictionaries, e-mail applications, forum discussions, simulations, hyperlinks, multimedia, data searching, study aids, and learning evaluation tools.

Right behind Korea is California, which is steeped in a huge deficit. Governor Arnold Schwarzenegger is seeking ways out. One direction is a greater emphasis on digital education (Office of the Governor, 2009). By using digital books, California not only addresses its budgetary problems, but also assumes a leadership role in online learning. Officials in the state plan to download digital textbooks and other educational content into mobile devices that they will place in the hands of all students.

Some digital book initiatives are taking place at the district level. Vail School District in Arizona has adopted an approach called Beyond Textbooks (http://beyondtextbooks.org), which encourages the use of Web resources and shared teacher lesson plans geared to meet state standards (Lewin, 2009). Rich online videos, games, and portals of Web materials as well as podcasts of teacher lectures extend learning at Vail in directions not previously possible.

Innovative companies and foundations are also finding ways to offer free textbooks. Flat World Knowledge (www.flatworldknowledge.com) offers free online textbooks and also sells print-on-demand softcover textbooks, audio textbooks, and low-cost ancillary or supplemental materials, such as MP3 study guides, online interactive quizzes, and digital flashcards connected to each book. Using an open-content, Web-based collaborative model, the CK-12 Foundation (http://ckl2.org) is pioneering the idea of free FlexBooks that are customizable to state standards.

Digital books on mobile devices will move a significant chunk of learning out of traditional classroom settings. Hundreds of thousands of free e-books are now available online. You can search for them at places like Google; Many-Books.net (http://manybooks.net); LibriVox (www.librivox.org); the World Public Library (http://worldlibrary.net); the Internet Archive (www.archive.org); Bookyards.com (www.bookyards.com); and other e-book sites. Ironically, the majority of the top 25 best sellers on the Kindle are actually free (Kafka, 2009). We have entered the era of free books.

Real-Time Mobility and Portability

Mobile learning is the current mantra of educators. More than 60,000 people around the planet get mobile access to the Internet each hour (Iannucci, 2009), with 15 million people subscribing each month in India alone (Telecom Regulatory Authority of India, 2009). Also, if just one percent of the 85,000 applications for the iPhone (Marcus, 2009) are educational, thousands of possible learning adventures are at one's fingertips. It's possible to access grammar lessons, language applications, Shakespearean plays or quotes, physics experiments, musical performances, and math review problems with a mobile phone.

Online classes and course modules as well as teacher professional development are now delivered on mobile devices. As mobile learning advocate John Traxler (2007) points out, mobile professional development options are especially important in developing countries in Africa.

Mobile learning is not restricted to phones, of course. Laptops, iPods, MP3 players, flash memory sticks, digital cameras, and lecture recording pens all foster mobile learning pursuits as well as greater learning engagement. Educators need to thoughtfully consider where, when, and how to use such devices.

For instance, rather than ban mobile technologies, school officials might encourage students to record lectures with their pens or digital devices and listen to them while studying for quizzes and final exams. Or teachers might make available snippets of content that students can download to their mobile devices—such as French grammar lessons or quick guides to concepts in the study of chemistry, the human nervous system, or cell biology (Bonk, 2009).

When we think about mobile learning, we often just think of a mobile learner. But the deliverer of the learning might also be mobile. With the Web, our learning content might come from a climb up Mount Everest, expeditions to the Arctic or Antarctic, research at the bottom of an ocean, NASA flights far above us, or sailing adventures across the planet.

Michael Perham (www.sailmike.com) and Zac Sunderland (www.zacsunderland.com), for instance, each blogged and shared online videos of their record-setting solo sailing journeys around the globe. Amazingly, they each completed their adventures last summer at the tender age of 17. I could track their daily experiences and post comments in their blogs. They were my highly mobile teachers. I also learn from Jean Pennycook, a former high school science teacher who now brings scientific research on penguins in the Antarctic to classrooms around the world (see www.windows.ucar.edu/tour/link=/people/postcards/penguin_post.html).

Trends in the Open World

Given these myriad learning opportunities on the Web, you might wonder what is coming next. Here are some predictions.

- *Free as a book.* Digital books will not only be free, but readers will also be able to mix and match several of their components. E-books and classrooms will increasingly embed shared online video, animations, and simulations to enhance learning.
- *The emergence of super e-mentors and e-coaches.* Super e-mentors and e-coaches, working from computer workstations or from mobile devices, will provide free learning guidance. As with the gift culture that we have seen in the open source movement over the past two decades, some individuals will simply want to share their expertise and skills, whereas others may want practice teaching. Many will be highly educated individuals who have always wanted opportunities to teach, coach, or mentor but who work in jobs that do not enable them to do so. Those with the highest credibility and in the most demand will have human development or counseling skills (perhaps a master's degree in counseling); understand how to use the Web for learning; and have expertise in a particular domain, such as social work, nursing, accounting, and so forth.
- *Selecting global learning partners.* Peers don't need to live down the street; they could be anywhere on the planet. Tools like Ning (www.ning.com) and Google Docs and resources like ePals (www.epals.com) and iEARN (International Education and Research Network; www.iearn.org) make global interactions ubiquitous. Global peer partners will form mini-school communities and unique school-based social networking groups. Projects might include learning how to cope with natural disasters, engaging in cultural exchanges, designing artwork related to human rights, exploring the effects of global warming, and learning about threats to animal habitats.
- *Teachers everywhere.* Soon students will be able to pick their teachers at a moment's notice. Want a teacher from Singapore, the Philippines, the United Kingdom, or Israel? They will be available in online teacher or mentor portals as well as preselected and approved by local school districts or state departments. Some will be displayed on a screen as students walk into school; students might consult this individual during a study hall period or review session.
- *Teacher as concierge.* The notion of a teacher will shift from a deliverer of content to that of a concierge who finds and suggests education resources as learners need them.
- *Informal = formal.* Informal learning will dramatically change the idea of "going to school," with a greater percentage of instructors being informal ones who offer content, experiences, and ideas to learners of all ages. Such individuals will include explorers on expeditions, researchers in a science lab, and practitioners in the workplace.
- *International academic degrees.* Consortia of countries will band together to provide international education using online courses and activities with the goal of offering a high school or community college degree.
- *Dropouts virtually drop back in.* The U.S. government will offer free online courses for high school dropouts and those needing alternative learning models (Jaschik, 2009). Such courses, as well as multiple options for learning, may lure students back to pick up a secondary or postsecondary degree. Interactive technology enhancements will appeal to teenagers and young adults savvy with emerging tools for learning.
- *The rise of the super blends.* As schools are faced with continued budgetary constraints and with the plethora of free courses, learning portals, and delivery technologies available, blended learning will become increasingly prevalent in K-12 education. Determining the most effective blend will be a key part of effective school leadership.
- *The shared learning era.* In the coming decade, the job of a K-12 teacher will include the willingness to share content with teachers in one's school district as well as with those

far beyond. Teachers will also be called on to evaluate shared content.

- *Personalized learning environments.* Open educational resources (OER) and technologies like shared online videos podcasts, simulations, and virtual worlds will be available to enhance or clarify any lesson at any time (Bonk & Zhang, 2008). For example, Wendy Ermold, a researcher and field technician for the University of Washington Polar Science Center, conducts research in Greenland and in other northern locations on this planet. While out on the icebreakers or remote islands, she listens to lectures and reviews other OER content from MIT, Stanford, Seattle Pacific University, and Missouri State University to update her knowledge of physics and other content areas. The expansion of such free and open course content options will personalize learning according to particular learner needs or preferences.
- *Alexandrian Aristotles.* Learners will emerge who have the modern-day equivalent of the entire ancient library of Alexandria on a flash memory stick in their pocket or laptop. They will spend a significant amount of time learning from online tools and resources, will be ideal problem finders and solvers, and will set high personal achievement standards.

Open for Business

The world is open for learning. In addition to blended learning, e-books, and mobile learning, we are witnessing an increase in learner generation of academic content, collaboration in that content generation, and customization of the learning environment at significantly reduced costs and sometimes for free.

The 10 openers I suggest, push educators to rethink models of schooling and instruction. They are converging to offer the potential for a revolution in education—which is already underway.

Endnote

1. For a full discussion of the We-All-Learn framework, see my book, *The World Is Open; How Web Technology Is Revolutionizing Education* (Jossey-Bass, 2009).

References

Bonk. C.J. (2009). *The world is open: How Web technology is revolutionizing education.* San Francisco: Jossey-Bass.

Bonk, C. J., & Zhang, K. (2008). *Empowering online learning: 100+ activities for reading, reflecting, displaying, and doing.* San Francisco: Jossey-Bass.

Huang, R., & Zhou, Y. (2006). Designing blended learning focused on knowledge category and learning activities: Case sudies from Beijing. In C. J. Bonk & C R. Graham (Eds.), *Handbook of blended learning: Global perspectives, local designs* (pp. 296–310), San Francisco: Pfeiffer.

Iannucci, B. (2009, January 7). *Connecting everybody to everything.* Nokia Research Center, Stanford University POMI (Programmable Open Mobile Internet), NSF research advisory meeting.

Jaschik, S. (2009, June 29). U.S. push for free online courses. *Inside Higher Ed.* Available: www.insidehighered.com/news/2009/06/29/ccplan

Kafka, P. (2009, December). The secret behind the Kindle's best-selling e-books: They're not for sale. *CNET News.* Available: http://news.cnet.com/8301-1023_310422538-93.html

Lewin, T. (2009, August 9). In a digital future, textbooks are history, *The New York Times.* Available: www.nytimes.com/2009/08/09/education/09textbook.html

Marcus, M. B. (2009, October 5). Pull yourself from that iPhone and read this story. *USA Today.* Available: www.usatoday.com/printedition/life/20091005/appaddiction05_st.art.htm

Mississippi Department of Education. (2005, September). *Katrina recovery information.* Available: www.mde.k12.ms.us/Katrina

Office of the Governor. (2009, May 6). Gov Schwarzenegger launches first-in-nation initiative to develop free digital textbooks for high school students (Press Release). Sacramento, CA: Author. Available: http://gov.ca.gov/press-release/12225/

Robbins, R. (2009, June 9). Distance students are "a varied and interesting lot." *Herald Times Online.* Available: www.heraldtimesonline.com/stories/2009/06/08/schoolnews.qp2930970.sto

Sloan-C (2006, August 8). The Sloan Consortium honored for post-hurricane delivery of online courses. The Sloan semester. Available: www.sloan-c.org/sloansemester

Telecom Regulatory Authority of India. (2009, June). Information note to the press (Press Release No 54/2009). Available: www.trai.gov.in/WriteReadData/trai/upload/PressReleases/687/pr1june09no54.pdf

Traxler, J. (2007, June). Defining, discussing, and evaluating mobile learning: The moving finger writes and having writ... *International Review of Research in Open and Distance Learning,* 8(1). Available: www.irrodl.org/index.php/irrodl/article/view/346/875

Assess Your Progress

1. Make a list of the ways that you use technology to learn or teach.
2. Work with a small group of peers to share your technology use lists. Make a team list of the ways all of you use to teach or learn with technology.

CURTIS J. BONK is Professor of Instructional Systems Technology at Indiana University. He is the author of *The World Is Open: How Web Technology Is Revolutionizing Education* (Jossey-Bass, 2009) and coauthor, with Ke Zhang, of *Empowering Online Learning: 100+ Ideas, for Reading, Reflecting, Displaying, and Doing* (Jossey-Bass, 2008). He blogs at TravelinEdMan (http://travelinedmanblogspot.com); curt@worldisopen.com.

From *Educational Leadership*, April 2010. Copyright © 2010 by ASCD. Reprinted by permission. The Association for Supervision and Curriculum Development is a worldwide community of educators advocating sound policies and sharing best practices to achieve the success of each learner. To learn more, visit ASCD at www.ascd.org.

Tech Tool Targets Elementary Readers

A Game Boy-like device now being used by 40,000 students in 15 states aims to improve the reading skills of K-2 students.

KATIE ASH

Much attention has been paid to how mobile-learning devices can be incorporated into middle and high schools, but Seth Weinberger is targeting a different set of students: kindergartners through 2nd graders.

"The sweet spot of literacy is kindergarten to 2nd grade," says Weinberger, the executive director of Innovations for Learning, the Evanston, Ill.-based nonprofit organization that developed a mobile-learning device called the TeacherMate. "If you get them [reading on grade level] early, there's a real chance that you can keep them at grade level."

TeacherMates are now being used by more than 40,000 students in 15 states, says Weinberger, and there are plans to adapt the TeacherMate software into applications for the iPod touch or iPad. And the decision to target the devices at elementary youngsters has attracted the attention of ed-tech researchers, some of whom say the elementary grades are where such devices could have their greatest impact on improving reading skills.

Cathleen A. Norris, a professor of learning technologies at the University of North Texas and the chief education architect for the Ann Arbor, Mich.-based company GoKnow, which provides educational technology, software, and curriculum to K-12 schools, says that "what you must do is catch (the students] at the early grades and make them successful. When children are experiencing success in early grades, they spend more time with [the subject]."

On the heels of the One Laptop Per Child initiative, which aims to provide low-cost laptop computers to students in developing countries, Weinberger wanted to create a relatively affordable, easy-to-use mobile-learning device for students in the United States. "Schools are unbelievably strapped for cash," says Weinberger.

The TeacherMate device itself costs about $40, although with the reading and math software that has been developed for it, the total cost is about $100 per device. That's not cheap, but it's well below the cost of putting a laptop or netbook computer in the hands of all those youngsters.

Evaluating Effectiveness

Preliminary data on the effectiveness of the device are promising, although more research is needed, says William H. Teale, a professor of education in the department of curriculum and instruction at the University of Illinois at Chicago. His review of a pilot program, which put TeacherMates in 176 1st grade classrooms in the 409,000-student Chicago school district, found that students who used the devices performed higher on their end-of-year reading tests in three categories than those who did not have the devices.

Still, Teale cautions in his review: "Because of its design, this study does not speak to the issue of a causal connection between the use of the hand-held learning systems . . . and enhanced early reading achievement."

And no research is currently available on the effectiveness of the math software for TeacherMates.

The Game Boy-like device fits into the palm of a student's hand and is controlled by eight buttons. It includes a speaker that both plays back sounds and allows students to record their own audio, a screen, and a USB slot to synchronize the devices with the teacher's computer.

To use TeacherMates, teachers need a USB cable and a computer with an Internet connection where they can sync the devices, change the levels of the software that the students are working on, check on how well students are using the software, and listen to what the students have recorded during their lessons.

Instead of teachers' needing to incorporate the Teacher-Mate into the curriculum, the TeacherMate is equipped to align directly with whatever math or reading curriculum the teacher is using, says Weinberger. That aspect of the device appeals to Patti Beyer, a 1st grade teacher at the 750-student New Field Elementary School in Chicago.

"The stories that they're working on are the stories we're reading. The letters [on the device] are the letters that we're working on." she says. "Every concept we hit is addressed by the TeacherMate."

And not only is the device easy for teachers to use. it's easy for students to pick up and learn, too, says Jenna Kelsey, a 1st grade teacher at the 750-student James Russell Lowell Elementary School, also in Chicago. She uses the devices for 15 to 20 minutes a day, usually as part of rotating centers where students spend some time reading on their own, with a teacher, and with the TeacherMate.

"They're so used to hand-held games as it is that they are able to just play the game without much assistance," she says. As a result, Kelsey is freed up to work with pupils one-on-one or in small groups.

Reinforce and Practice

Although students can usually navigate the TeacherMate software by themselves, the devices are not designed to be used on their own but to accompany teachers' lessons, says Weinberger of Innovations for Learning, which developed the devices. Rather than being used to introduce new material and concepts to students, TeacherMates are intended to reinforce and practice skills that students are actively learning in their teacher-led classes, he says.

X. Christine Wang, an associate professor of learning and instruction at the State University of New York at Buffalo, is not familiar with the TeacherMate specifically, but she speculates that hand-held devices used for reinforcement and practice may not be making use of their full educational potential.

"The majority of researchers and teachers are now against the drill-practice type of learning" with technology, she says. "When we take children's active thinking out of learning, we take children's curiosity out of learning."

Hand-held tools that allow access to the Internet, which do not include the TeacherMate, not only can be appropriate for elementary youngsters, but also can help foster collaboration and expand the walls of the classroom, says Wang.

But Kelsey, the teacher at Lowell Elementary in Chicago, sees the lack of Internet capability as an advantage of the TeacherMate. Because students can only access the software that she has downloaded and put on the devices, she can be sure that all her students are on task, unlike in the computer lab, where she has to monitor what each child is doing.

"I already know what's going on [the devices] because I put it there," she says.

Because each student has his or her own device, it's easy to differentiate instruction, says Beyer, from New Field Elementary.

"It's all individualized," Beyer says, and it takes away the stigma of some students' needing more reinforcement of a concept than others do.

Throughout the year that Kelsey has used the devices, they have malfunctioned occasionally, but usually just require a restart, she says. Innovations for Learning provides technical support if teachers run into more serious issues, she says.

Going Global

TeacherMates are also making their way into the hands of children around the world, thanks to the efforts of Paul Kim, the chief technology officer for Stanford University. Over the past year, Kim has traveled to Costa Rica, Mexico, Nicaragua, Rwanda, and other countries to provide educational materials, including TeacherMates, to children who are not receiving any formal education.

"I found it very useful because kids love them, and I don't have to teach them anything," he says. Even children who had never seen similar technologies can pick one of the devices up and start learning, he says. The software's game-based approach, says Kim, helps youngsters learn on their own and engages those who may not be used to traditional instructional methods.

The platform that runs the software, which uses Flash, a multimedia platform popular for creating animations and interactivity, also makes it easy to develop new software for the TeacherMate, he says.

The durability of the devices has also made the TeacherMate a good candidate for Kim's project.

"There is a growing digital divide, and we are leaving a big chunk of our society behind," he says. "I like to give these children who have no access whatsoever to have an opportunity to reach their potential by giving them [this technology]."

Assess Your Progress

1. What is a TeacherMate? How is it being used in K-2 classrooms?

2. Do you think that technology is appropriate for children in K-2 classes to use to complete reading activities? Provide a rationale for your answer.

From *Education Week*, March 18, 2010, pp. 18–19. Copyright © 2010 by Editorial Projects in Education. Reprinted by permission.

Article 35

Digital Tools Expand Options for Personalized Learning

Digital tools for defining and targeting students' strengths and weaknesses could help build a kind of individualized education plan for every student.

KATHLEEN KENNEDY MANZO

Teachers have always known that a typical class of two dozen or more students can include vastly different skill levels and learning styles. But meeting those varied academic needs with a defined curriculum, time limitations, and traditional instructional tools can be daunting for even the most skilled instructor.

Some of the latest technology tools for the classroom, however, promise to ease the challenges of differentiating instruction more creatively and effectively, ed-tech experts say, even in an era of high-stakes federal and state testing mandates. New applications for defining and targeting students' academic strengths and weaknesses can help teachers create a personal playlist of lessons, tools, and activities that deliver content in ways that align with individual needs and optimal learning methods.

For educators who struggle to integrate technology into their daily routines and strategies, the notion of a kind of individualized education plan for every student is more pipe dream than prospect. Yet the most optimistic promoters of digital learning say the vision of a tech-immersed classroom for today's students—one that offers a flexible and dynamic working environment with a range of computer-based and face-to-face learning options customized for each student—is not far off.

Several examples of such customization have recently emerged across the country, and are garnering widespread interest and some encouraging results.

"Those examples are a crude picture of a future scenario, where there's a student playlist of learning experiences, some of which happen in something that looks like a classroom, some with a computer, and some at a community resource, like a library, museum, college, or workplace," says Tom Vander Ark, a former executive director of education for the Seattle-based **Bill & Melinda Gates Foundation** who has advocated for years that schools should take a more individualized approach to learning. He is now a partner in **Vander Ark/Ratcliff,** an education venture-capital firm. "Their day could look like an interesting variety of activities, driven by their learning needs, not by the school's limitations."

'Feedback to Children'

Vander Ark says that supplemental-service providers, like private tutoring companies or after-school programs, have taken the lead in offering tailored instruction. The ways those providers use assessment tools to gather and process data and then suggest a roster of activities for each student could pave the way for similar approaches within the school day, he says.

Creating a Custom Playlist for Learning

Technology experts recommend that teachers utilize a variety of tools and activities to address individual student learning needs:

Class Lessons
Traditional lessons for the whole class help introduce a lesson or reteach material as needed.

Assessments
Teachers conduct regular formative assessments, using some quick digital applications and analytic tools, to determine students' skills and academic needs.

Skill-Building Games
Computer-based games that focus on developing specific skills like vocabulary or multiplication facts.

Group Projects
Students collaborate on assignments using technology and traditional research and presentation tools.

Online Courses
Virtual learning could give students access to credit-recovery or accelerated courses, as well as enrichment and intervention activities.

Tutoring
One-on-one or small-group tutoring sessions, on-site or virtually, aid students who are struggling academically.

Museum Site Visit
Students can tap into outside educational resources, such as museums, libraries, and local historical sites.

Blogs
Students can write blog entries to demonstrate what they've learned, outline their research, and communicate with their teachers.

Independent Research
Assignments outside of class using online and traditional resources give students the chance to guide their own learning.

He points to one widely publicized model: New York City's **School of One.**

The pilot program at Dr. Sun Yat Sen Middle School in Chinatown provided math lessons that were customized every day to meet the individual needs, and progress, of the 80 incoming 7th graders who volunteered to attend the five-week session this past summer. The School of One combined face-to-face instruction, software-based activities, and online lessons designed to move each new 7th grader through a defined set of math benchmarks at his or her own pace.

As students entered school each morning, they could view their schedules for the day on a computer monitor—similar to the arrival-and-departure monitors at airports—and proceed to the assigned locations. A student's schedule could include traditional lessons from a certified teacher, small-group work, virtual learning, or specific computer-based activities, most of them offered in converted space in the school library.

After each half-day of instruction, teachers entered data on students' progress and instructional needs into a computer program that recommended the next day's tasks.

Preliminary data showed significant student progress toward mastering the skills targeted in the program, officials say. The district is continuing to track participants' progress.

The school—named one of the 50 best inventions of 2009 by *Time* magazine—expanded in the fall to three middle schools in the city as an after-school program, and is set to guide the school-day math course at one of them this spring.

"When we ask ourselves how much instruction during the course of a typical school day does each student get exactly on the skill they're working on, and in the amount that is right for them, the answer is very little," says Joel Rose, a former teacher who has been instrumental in the development and expansion of the School of One.

"By leveraging technology to play a role in the delivery of instruction," he says, "we can help to complement what live teachers do."

The San Diego Unified School District is betting that the bulk of a recent $2 billion bond measure for technologies designed to transform teaching and learning through a more personalized approach will yield academic improvements.

The five-year plan for the 135,000-student district started this school year in 1,300 math classrooms. The students, in grades 3 and 6 and in high school, were issued netbook computers, and teachers were required to complete 39 hours of training on instructional strategies using technology. Classrooms throughout the district were also equipped with a variety of interactive technology tools.

After introducing content, teachers can immediately test students using remote devices attached to their netbooks. Students are then assigned to appropriate practice activities or more in-depth lessons.

"The wait time for getting feedback to children is sliced significantly. This is about the speed of learning and the depth of learning," says Sarah Sullivan, the principal of San Diego's Pershing Middle School. "This is the first time I've seen the promise of technology appearing to be paying the dividends we want."

San Diego plans to expand the program next year to other grades and into other subject areas.

Making the Transition

Experts caution, however, that instituting such large-scale change is not simply a matter of putting new tools in place. As in San Diego, most teachers will need extensive professional development to use digital tools and learn the best ways of teaching with technology.

"In many ways, the challenge we face with technology is similar to the challenge we face with data," says Stephanie Hirsh, the executive director of the Dallas-based **National Staff Development Council.** "We have more and more of both with little support to help educators know how to use it . . . to advance their effectiveness and student success."

A number of teachers have found their own ways to harness some of technology's potential to get a closer gauge of their students' work, and to provide a range of options for them to consume required content and demonstrate knowledge.

For several years, Shelly Blake-Plock has asked students in his Latin, English, and art history classes to summarize what they've learned from class and document their progress on assignments in daily blog entries. The students at The John Carroll School, a Roman Catholic secondary school in Bel Air, Md., can post Web links they used in their research, photos and drawings, or short videos that show their work.

Blake-Plock, who writes the popular **Teach Paperless** blog and has a large following among educators on social-networking sites, says the entries are a continuous source of formative data that he can use to evaluate how students are doing.

If he observes a lack of basic understanding or language skill in some students' work, he says, he can suggest online resources and activities to get them on track. When students reveal their personal interests—such as one student's passion for painting and another's talent for music—he can craft assignments that allow them to explore the content through those areas.

"Before I went paperless and used the blogs to get information from them, I would only see students' work if they wrote an essay or turned in a quiz or test," Blake-Plock says. "Now I'm seeing what they're working on all the time, . . . and I'm finding it's a lot easier for me to tell if a student is having problems early on."

'Lack of Innovation'

The advantages for students are potentially more compelling, given the widespread enthusiasm among young people for using technology to create and consume media, ed-tech experts say.

"We have this generation of students that yearns to customize everything they come into contact with," says Steve Johnson, a technology facilitator at J.N. Fries Middle School in Concord, N.C. His book *Engaging All Learners With 21st Century Tools* is due out from Maupin House Publishing this coming summer.

The educational technology market is slowly responding with the kinds of products that can help teachers track and target their students' learning needs.

Wireless Generation Inc., a New York City-based technology company, created its **Burst Reading** program in response to teachers' comments about the need to vary basic literacy lessons for the many students who did not fit the developmental patterns assumed by lockstep reading lessons.

The company, which helped build the technology applications for the School of One, designed an assessment schedule for K-3 reading schedules that gives feedback and recommends lessons for small groups of similarly skilled students every 10 days. Although the Burst program suggests only face-to-face lessons for students, its underlying assessment relies on sophisticated digital tools for gathering and analyzing data from individual students.

"It's this model of deeply analyzing the data in a way that no human teacher would have time to do, and mapping lessons to kids' abilities, that's fundamental to what education is going to look like in the future," predicts Wireless Generation's chief executive officer, Larry Berger. (Berger serves on the board of Editorial Projects in Education, the nonprofit corporation that publishes *Education Week Digital Directions.*)

The company is working on similar products for middle school reading and elementary math.

At the same time, traditional textbook publishers are starting to adapt their products for greater personalization as well. **McGraw-Hill Education,** for example, has developed the K-6 CINCH math program for use on interactive whiteboards that includes differentiation options.

The slow pace of development of customizable content and tools is frustrating, though, to some in the field, particularly in light of the widespread adoption of such strategies for training in the U.S. military, or their entrance into the mainstream in public schooling in other developed countries, Vander Ark says.

"This is not science fiction," he says. "None of the technology we're talking about is really advanced, . . . but the fact that it doesn't exist yet on a large scale in education is just a reflection of a lack of innovation in that sector."

Assess Your Progress

1. Write a 50–75 word abstract for the article regarding tools for individualizing instruction.
2. Review the list of digital tools that are suggested as options for individualizing instruction. Select three of these tools to research. Go to the Internet and find two or three examples of each tool. Create an annotated bibliography of these tools to share with peers in your class.

From *Digital Directions*, February 3, 2010, pp. 16–17, 19–20. Copyright © 2010 by Editorial Projects in Education. Reprinted by permission.

Effects of Video-Game Ownership on Young Boys' Academic and Behavioral Functioning: A Randomized, Controlled Study

ROBERT WEIS AND BRITTANY C. CERANKOSKY

Exposure to violent video games is associated with aggressive behavior among children (Anderson & Bushman, 2001; Carnagey, Anderson, & Bushman, 2007). Meta-analyses show significant associations between violent video-game play and aggressive thoughts ($r = .27$), feelings ($r = .18$), and actions ($r = .20$). These associations can be seen in experimental, correlational, and longitudinal studies involving children, adolescents, and adults (Anderson et al., 2008; Anderson, Gentile, & Buckley, 2007; Carnagey & Anderson, 2005). Furthermore, theoretical models based on learning, social cognitive, and neoassociative network theories have been developed to explain how violent video games might prime immediate aggressive behaviors and make them more accessible and appealing to children over time.

Although parents and children are beginning to recognize the risks of overtly violent video-game exposure, the risks associated with less violent video games, particularly those marketed to young children, are not as evident (Kutner, Olson, Warner, & Hertzog, 2008). Emerging data indicate that video games marketed to young children may also have adverse effects on child development by interfering with academic functioning. Assuming that time spent in after-school activities is zero-sum, recreational video-game play may displace activities that might have greater educational value (Vandewater, Bickham, & Lee, 2006). Indeed, recent studies have found significant relationships between the duration of video-game play and the academic performance of students in elementary school (Anderson et al., 2007), middle and high school (Gentile, 2009; Gentile, Lynch, Linder, & Walsh, 2004; Willoughby, 2008), and college (Anderson & Dill, 2000).

Further support for the displacement hypothesis comes from several recent population-based studies that have monitored children's time use. These studies indicate that children who own video games spend more time playing these games, spend less time engaged in after-school educational activities, and earn lower grades than comparison children (Schmidt & Vandewater, 2008).

For example, Sharif and Sargent (2006) found that middle-school students' exposure to video games on weekdays, but not weekends, was associated with their academic performance. Similarly, Valentine, Marsh, and Pattie (2005) determined that adolescents' after-school video-game play competed with the time they devoted to studying. In their analysis, video-game exposure was associated with decreased academic achievement scores on standardized tests. Most recently, Cummings and Vandewater (2007) found that video-game players spent 30% less time reading and 34% less time completing homework than did children who did not play video games.

Data supporting the displacement hypothesis are limited by the fact that they have been obtained chiefly through cross-sectional research (Cummings & Vandewater, 2007). It is possible that struggling students may simply decide to spend less time reading and completing homework and more time playing video games. Without data from randomized, controlled studies that monitor children's functioning over time, we cannot infer a causal relationship between video-game ownership, increased play, and changes in academic performance.

To remedy this limitation, we conducted a randomized, controlled study of the short-term effects of video-game ownership on the academic and behavioral functioning of young boys. At baseline, none of the boys owned a video-game system, but all of their parents expressed an interest in purchasing a system for them. To control for participant bias, we told parents that the purpose of the study was to examine boys' development, not to study the effects of video-game ownership. Parents were promised a video-game system as incentive for participation. After baseline assessment of boys' functioning, families were randomly assigned to an experimental group, in which members received the video-game system immediately, or to a control group, in which members received the system 4 months later, after follow-up assessment.

Evidence supporting displacement would come from significant differences in boys' duration of video-game usage, duration of after-school academic activities, and academic achievement as a function of experimental condition. Additional support would come from data showing video-game play mediating the relationship between experimental condition and achievement outcomes. We also examined whether boys in the experimental group showed more behavior problems at follow-up than boys in the control group. Such evidence would indicate that video-game ownership places young children at risk for behavior problems, even when they play games marketed to children their age.

Method

Participants

Sixty-four boys, 6 to 9 years of age ($M = 7.89$, $SD = 0.82$) participated. Boys were included in the study if they (a) were enrolled in a first-grade (33%), second-grade (44%), or third-grade (23%) class; (b) did not have a video-game system in their home; (c) had a parent interested in purchasing a system for their use; and (d) had no history of developmental, behavioral, medical, or learning problems. Ethnicities included White (89%), African American (6%), Asian American (3%), and Latino (2%). Approximately 79% of boys came from two-parent families. Paternal education included elementary school (5%), high school (70%), college (15%), and graduate or professional education (10%).

Measures

The Kaufman Brief Intelligence Test—2nd edition (KBIT–2; Kaufman & Kaufman, 2004) was used to estimate boys' intellectual ability ($M = 100$, $SD = 15$). The Woodcock–Johnson—III: Tests of Achievement (WJ–III; McGrew & Woodcock, 2001) were used to assess boys' academic functioning. The WJ–III yields three composite scores ($M = 100$, $SD = 15$): Broad Reading, Broad Mathematics, and Broad Written Language.

The Parent Rating Scale (PRS) and Teacher Rating Scale (TRS) were used to assess boys' behavior at home and school, respectively (Reynolds & Kamphaus, 2004). Both scales yield three composite scores ($M = 50$, $SD = 10$): Externalizing Problems, Internalizing Problems, and Adaptive Skills. The TRS yields one additional composite, School Problems, indicative of Attention Problems (i.e., distractibility, difficulty concentrating) and Learning Problems (i.e., difficulty reading, writing, spelling).

The Afterschool Time Diary (Hofferth, Davis-Kean, Davis, & Finkelstein, 1997) was used to estimate the duration of boys' video-game play and academic activities after school. Parents were asked to report boys' activities from the end of the school day until bedtime for the 2 previous weekdays. Average duration of video-game play was calculated by summing the duration of video-game play across the 2 days and dividing by 2. Average duration of academic activities was calculated by summing the total time spent engaged in after-school education, homework, reading, listening to stories, and writing, divided by 2.

Procedure

In early autumn, boys were recruited through newspaper advertisements to participate in an "ongoing study of boys' academic and behavioral development." In exchange for their participation, parents were promised a PlayStation II (PSII), controllers, and three games rated E (Everyone) by the Entertainment Software Rating Board. The games, *Nicktoons: Battle for Volcano Island*, *Shrek Smash N' Crash Racing*, and *Sonic Riders*, reportedly contain mild cartoon violence and comic mischief.

Only boys were included in the study, to increase the effectiveness of the experimental manipulation. Because our study was naturalistic, we could not directly manipulate the frequency and duration of children's video-game play. We worried that girls assigned to the experimental condition might not play significantly more than girls assigned to the control condition or play enough to potentially influence their academic or behavioral functioning. Indeed, naturalistic studies often show restricted range in girls' frequency and duration of video-game play (Gentile, Saleem, & Anderson, 2007). In contrast, boys play video games more often and for longer duration than do girls (Roberts, Foehr, & Rideout, 2005). Boys are also more likely to select games with violent content and display physical aggression (Ostrov, Gentile, & Crick, 2006). Furthermore, survey data indicate that boys are more likely to displace after-school academic activities with video games (Cummings & Vandewater, 2007), and approximately twice as many boys as girls report skipping homework or performing poorly on tests because of their video-game play (Gentile, 2009).

All parents who expressed an interest in the study were interviewed by telephone to determine whether their children met demographic criteria. Researchers also informed parents of the incentive for participation and asked, "Does your child want a PSII or do you already have a video-game system in your home?" Only parents who reported that the family did not own a system and who said that they intended to give the PSII to their child were scheduled for baseline assessment.

Children completed the KBIT–2 and WJ–III, and parents completed the PRS. The TRS was mailed to teachers. After baseline assessment, boys were randomly assigned to experimental or control conditions. Only boys whose baseline scores indicated academic achievement within normal limits and no significant behavior problems were randomized. Parents of boys assigned to the experimental condition were telephoned the day after randomization and told that the PSII was available immediately and that it would be delivered to their home.

Families participated in follow-up assessment 4 months after baseline. Boys completed the WJ–III, parents completed the PRS and Afterschool Time Diary, and teachers were mailed the TRS. Boys in the control condition were awarded the PSII, and parents were debriefed. Figure 1 provides a flowchart of the steps in the experimental procedure and the number of participants after each step.

Results

Baseline Characteristics and Manipulation Check

There were no significant differences between the experimental and control groups at baseline (see Table 1). Time from baseline to follow-up was similar for boys in the experimental ($M = 135$ days, $SD = 18.34$ days) and control ($M = 133$ days, $SD = 19.11$ days) conditions, $t(62) = 0.240$, $p = .811$. At follow-up, all of the boys in the experimental condition continued to play the video-game system. Ninety percent of boys in the experimental condition acquired additional games ($M = 2.28$, $SD = 1.49$). The most popular games were

Article 36. Effects of Video-Game Ownership on Young Boys' Academic and Behavioral Functioning

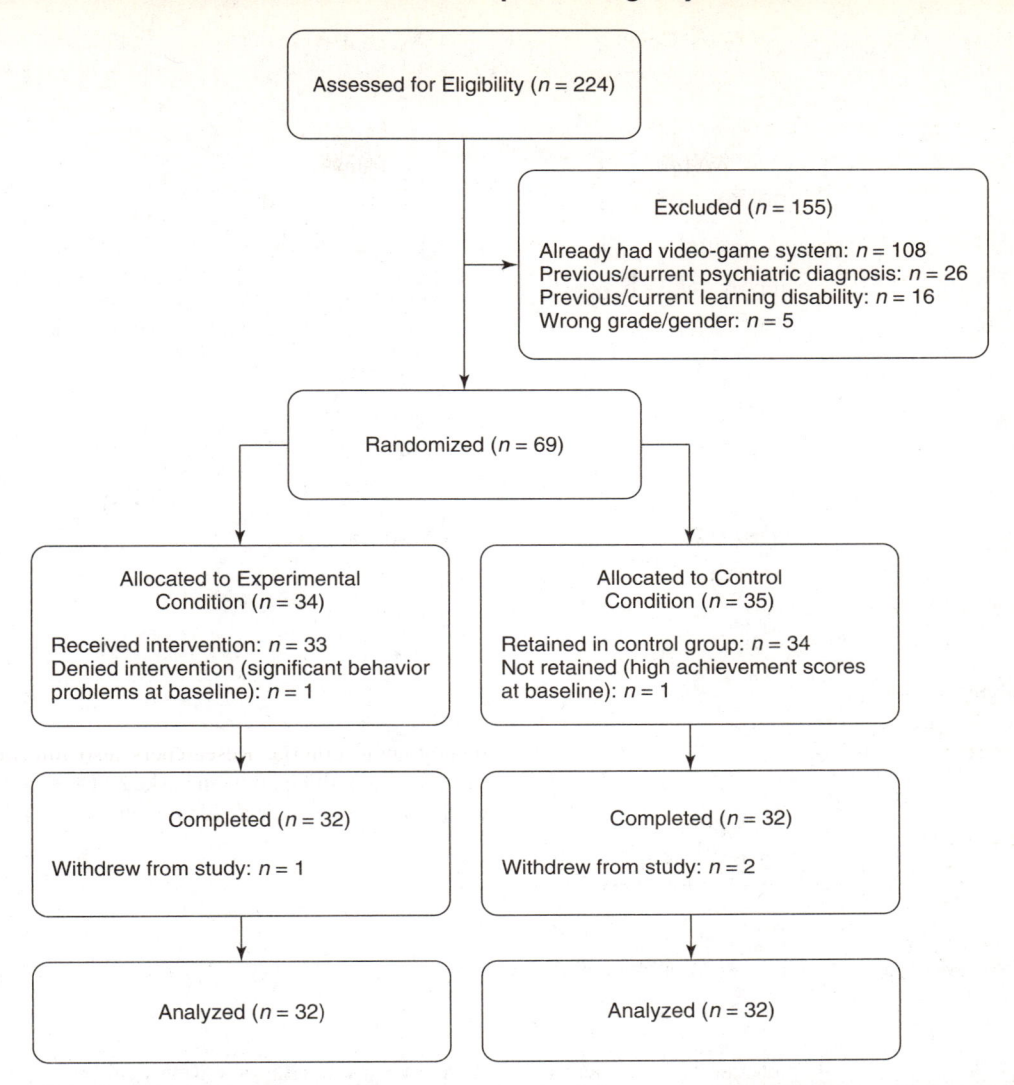

Figure 1 Consolidated Standards of Reporting Trials flowchart of the procedure. Eligible participants were assigned to either the experimental condition, in which they immediately received the video-game system, or the control condition, in which they received the system 4 months later, after assessment. All participants were assessed at follow-up.

rated E (Everyone): *Madden NFL, Lego Star Wars,* and *Pac-Man World 3*. The latter two games reportedly contain mild cartoon violence. Fifty-three percent of boys acquired at least one game rated E10+ (Everyone 10 and older); the most popular game was *Lego Star Wars II*, which reportedly contains cartoon violence and crude humor. Two boys acquired *Pirates of the Caribbean,* rated T (Teen), which reportedly contains alcohol references and violence. No boy in the experimental group owned games rated M (Mature), and no boy in the control group acquired a video-game system during the study.

Average duration of video-game play was longer for boys in the experimental condition ($M = 39.38$ min/day, $SD = 22.13$ min/day) than the control condition ($M = 9.37$ min/day, $SD = 12.65$ min/day), $t(62) = 6.65$, $p < .001$, $d = 1.66$. Also at follow-up, average duration of after-school academic activities was lower for boys in the experimental condition ($M = 18.28$ min/day, $SD = 15.11$ min/day) than for boys in the control condition ($M = 31.64$ min/day, $SD = 20.05$ min/day), $t(62) = 3.01$, $p = .004$, $d = 0.75$.

Effects of Video-Game Ownership

Three multivariate analyses of covariance (MANCOVAs) were conducted to determine the effects of video-game ownership on boys' functioning. In these MANCOVAs, the dependent variables were boys' (a) academic achievement, (b) parent-reported behavior, and (c) teacher-reported behavior at follow-up, respectively. The independent variable was experimental condition. Boys' baseline scores and IQ scores served as covariates. In each analysis, we followed up significant multivariate effects with univariate tests using Bonferroni adjustment to control for family-wise error.

In the first analysis, boys' three achievement scores at follow-up served as dependent variables. Results yielded a significant multivariate effect, Wilks's $\Lambda = .749$, $F(3, 56) = 6.26$, $p = .001$, $\eta_p^2 = .25$. Analyses of covariance (ANCOVAs; see Table 2), evaluated at $p < .017$ to control for error, indicated that boys in the experimental condition earned significantly lower Reading and Written Language scores at follow-up than did boys in the control condition.

Table 1 Characteristics of the Participants at Baseline

Variable	Experimental (n = 32)	Control (n = 32)	χ^2
Child's age (in months)	M = 95.36 (SD = 9.52)	M = 93.92 (SD = 10.16)	
Child's intelligence[a]	M = 100.97 (SD = 9.24)	M = 102.22 (SD = 9.02)	
Child's grade in school			0.790 (df = 2)
First	n = 10 (31.3%)	n = 11 (34.4%)	
Second	n = 13 (40.6%)	n = 15 (46.8%)	
Third	n = 9 (28.1%)	n = 6 (18.8%)	
Child's ethnicity			0.160 (df = 1)
White	n = 28 (87.4%)	n = 29 (90.6%)	
African American	n = 2 (6.3%)	n = 2 (6.3%)	
Asian American	n = 2 (6.3%)	n = 0	
Latino	n = 0	n = 1 (3.1%)	
Parents' marital status			0.097 (df = 1)
Married	n = 26 (81.3%)	n = 25 (78.1%)	
Father's education			0.721 (df = 1)
Finished college	n = 7 (21.9%)	n = 10 (31.3%)	
Child taking medication[b]	n = 3 (9.4%)	n = 4 (12.5%)	0.160 (df = 1)

Note: The experimental and control groups did not differ in age, $t(62) = 0.584$, or intelligence, $t(62) = 0.547$.
[a]Intelligence was estimated using the Kaufman Brief Intelligence Test—2nd edition (Kaufman & Kaufman, 2004).
[b]All children were taking nonpsychotropic medication for medical problems (e.g., asthma).

In the second MANCOVA, parent-reported behavioral outcomes were the dependent variables. Results did not show a significant multivariate effect, Wilks's $\Lambda = .947$, $F(3, 56) = 1.04$, $p = .384$. ANCOVAs (see Table 2) revealed no differences in parent-reported outcomes as a function of condition.

In the final MANCOVA, the four teacher-reported behavior scores served as dependent variables. Results did not show a significant multivariate effect, Wilks's $\Lambda = .882$, $F(4, 54) = 1.81$, $p = .141$. However, ANCOVAs (see Table 2), evaluated at $p \leq .0125$ to control for error, indicated a tendency for boys in the experimental condition to display greater School Problems than boys in the control condition. To explore this finding, we conducted two ANCOVAs (controlling for IQ and baseline scores) examining differences on the Attention Problems and Learning Problems subscales as a function of experimental condition. Results showed no difference in Attention Problems at follow-up, $F(1, 60) = 0.030$, $p = .857$. However, boys in the experimental condition showed greater Learning Problems at follow-up ($M = 52.99$, $SD = 11.33$) than did boys in the control condition ($M = 45.88$, $SD = 7.00$), $F(1, 60) = 9.37$, $p = .003$, $\eta^2 = .12$.

Mediation

We examined whether average duration of video-game play would mediate the relationship between video-game ownership and boys' Reading and Written Language scores at follow-up, adjusting for scores at baseline (Baron & Kenny, 1986; MacKinnon & Fairchild, 2009).

A test of the unmediated model showed that experimental condition predicted boys' Reading scores at follow-up, $b = -5.17$, $\beta = -0.208$, $F(1, 58) = 9.55$, $p = .003$. Experimental condition predicted duration of video-game play, $b = 29.23$, $\beta = 0.629$, $F(1, 58) = 42.29$, $p < .001$, and play predicted Reading outcomes, $b = -0.158$, $\beta = -0.296$, $F(1, 57) = 12.59$, $p = .001$. After controlling for video-game play, the relationship between condition and Reading outcomes was no longer significant, $b = -0.542$, $\beta = -0.022$, $F(1, 57) = 0.073$, $p > .05$. Confidence intervals at 95% (95% CIs) for the indirect effect fell outside zero, indicating significant mediation (95% CI = −7.78, −1.93).

A test of the unmediated model showed that experimental condition predicted Written Language scores at follow-up, $b = -6.21$, $\beta = -0.287$, $F(1, 58) = 12.17$, $p = .001$. A test of the mediated model showed that condition predicted video-game play, $b = 29.23$, $\beta = 0.629$, $F(1, 58) = 42.29$, $p < .001$, and play predicted Written Language outcomes, $b = -0.134$, $\beta = -0.288$, $F(1, 57) = 7.36$, $p = .009$. After controlling for video-game play, the relationship between experimental condition and Written Language was not significant, $b = -2.29$, $\beta = -0.106$, $F(1, 57) = 1.07$, $p > .05$. Confidence limits for the indirect effect also fell outside zero (95% CI = −5.67, −0.81).

Table 2 Academic Achievement and Behavior as a Function of Condition and Time (N = 64)

	Experimental		Control				
Variable and testing time	M	SD	M	SD	F[a]	p	η²
Academic achievement							
Reading							
Pretest	97.81	9.57	98.37	11.20	0.05	n.s.	
Posttest	96.43	12.66	101.60	11.83	9.55	.003	.042
Mathematics							
Pretest	102.69	9.68	102.19	10.26	0.04	n.s.	
Posttest	104.29	11.04	106.24	9.75	1.67	n.s.	
Written Language							
Pretest	94.09	8.80	95.53	9.71	0.39	n.s.	
Posttest	95.19	9.28	101.40	11.29	12.17	.001	.081
Parent-reported behavior							
Externalizing Problems							
Pretest	52.47	8.01	50.75	7.29	0.81	n.s.	
Posttest	51.76	9.20	52.12	8.69	0.07	n.s.	
Internalizing Problems							
Pretest	48.16	8.97	48.59	6.39	0.05	n.s.	
Posttest	49.13	9.71	47.15	8.54	2.49	n.s.	
Adaptive Skills							
Pretest	50.34	8.20	48.13	8.62	1.11	n.s.	
Posttest	49.89	8.07	50.55	7.83	0.32	n.s.	
Teacher-reported behavior							
Externalizing Problems							
Pretest	47.88	6.45	50.84	7.30	2.97	n.s.	
Posttest	50.33	6.89	50.89	9.14	0.19	n.s.	
Internalizing Problems							
Pretest	47.38	7.69	47.22	6.05	0.01	n.s.	
Posttest	50.13	8.39	50.02	7.52	0.06	n.s.	
School Problems							
Pretest	46.53	5.71	48.69	6.64	1.94	n.s.	
Posttest	51.87	9.37	47.47	7.31	5.89	.018	.064
Adaptive Skills							
Pretest	51.13	8.22	48.88	7.62	1.29	n.s.	
Posttest	50.13	6.56	51.90	7.91	2.56	n.s.	

Note: Pretest means are unadjusted; posttest means are adjusted for pretest and Kaufman Brief Intelligence Test—2nd edition (KBIT–2) scores (Kaufman & Kaufman, 2004). The same number of participants was analyzed at pretest and posttest; change in degrees of freedom from pretest to posttest reflects adjusting for pretest and KBIT–2 scores in posttest analyses. All scores are standardized. The mean score was 100 for achievement (SD = 15) and 50 for behavior (SD = 10). Eta-squared was calculated by hand so that total variance explained equals 1.00.

[a] The degrees of freedom for the analyses of variance were as follow—academic achievement and parent-reported behavior: df = 1, 62 for the pretest and df = 1, 58 for the posttest; teacher-reported behavior: df = 1, 62 for the pretest and df = 1, 57 for the posttest.

Discussion

Our study represents the first randomized, controlled test of the effects of video-game ownership on the academic and behavioral functioning of young boys. Our findings provide initial support for the notion that video-game ownership among boys is associated with decreased academic achievement in the areas of reading and writing. Overall, boys who received the video-game system at the beginning of the study showed relatively stable and somewhat below average reading and writing achievement from baseline to follow-up. In contrast, boys in the control group showed increased reading and writing achievement across the duration of the study.

The effect size for reading was moderate, reflecting approximately two fifths of a standard deviation difference in achievement scores at follow-up, whereas the effect size for written language was large, reflecting more than one half of a standard deviation difference at follow-up (Cohen, 1988). Furthermore, the lower academic achievement scores displayed by boys in the experimental condition were observable by teachers; boys who received the video-game system earned significantly higher Learning Problems scores, which reflect delays in reading, writing, spelling, and other academic tasks. These early reading and writing problems are particularly salient to young, elementary-school age children, because they can interfere with the acquisition of more advanced reading comprehension and writing composition skills later in development (Rayner, Foorman, Perfetti, Pesetsky, & Seidenberg, 2001). Altogether, our findings suggest that video-game ownership may impair academic achievement for some boys in a manner that has real-world significance.

Our findings also support displacement as a mechanism by which video-game ownership might influence boys' academic achievement. Boys in the experimental condition spent more time playing video games and less time engaged in after-school academic activities than did boys in the control condition. Furthermore, video-game play mediated the relationship between video-game ownership and boys' reading and writing outcomes. Our findings are consistent with survey research that shows video-game play to be extensive among young boys who own video-game systems (Roberts et al., 2005) and with cross-sectional studies indicating that video games displace children's after-school academic activities (Cummings & Vandewater, 2007; Schmidt & Vandewater, 2008; Vandewater et al., 2006).

Boys' Mathematics scores did not differ as a function of experimental condition. One explanation is that the displacement of homework by video games may not affect the development of math skills as much as reading and writing skills. For example, in one population-based study, the amount of time young children spent completing homework was strongly associated with their basic reading skills but not their math calculation or problem-solving skills (Hofferth & Sandberg, 2001). Another possibility is that young children may not engage in many math-based after-school activities in the first place. Whereas it is easy to imagine a young child reading or listening to stories at bedtime, it is more difficult to imagine a child completing math worksheets for pleasure. Young children may simply have fewer math-based recreational activities for video games to displace.

In our study, video-game ownership was not associated with increased behavior problems among boys. It is likely that boys in the experimental condition were exposed to at least moderate levels of video-game violence, given the tendency of the Entertainment Software Rating Board to underestimate the degree of illegal, harmful, and violent behavior in games rated E and E10+ (Walsh & Gentile, 2001). It is possible that these games did not have enough violent content to prime, model, or reinforce behavior problems. It is also possible that boys' behavior did change, but the omnibus rating scales used in this study were not sensitive to these changes. A third possibility for the null findings is that the study lacked sufficient power to detect differences in boys' behavior as a function of game ownership. Given the extensive evidence supporting the association between violent video-game play and aggression, future experimental studies conducted in naturalistic settings are necessary to explore these possibilities.

Future research is also necessary to replicate and extend the current study to examine the long-term effects of video-game ownership on children. For example, we do not know whether video-game ownership would continue to displace academic activities and impair achievement beyond 4 months. Furthermore, we do not know whether video-game ownership might influence the academic and behavioral functioning of girls. Girls appear to play video games for different reasons, to select games with different content, and to manifest aggressive behavior following play in different ways than boys (Ostrov et al., 2006). Although recent research has shown few gender differences for the effects of violent video-game play on children's behavior, the base rate of girls' video-game play and physical aggression may be too low to observe a relationship between video-game ownership and girls' functioning in naturalistic settings (Gentile et al., 2007).

Finally, future research might also explore other mechanisms, besides displacement, that might explain the relationship between video-game ownership and boys' academic outcomes. For example, video-game play may affect the development of executive functioning or information-processing skills. Children may become accustomed to the fast pace of video games and have difficulty engaging in slower, academic tasks that require sustained concentration (Bailey, West, & Anderson, 2009). Alternatively, children may become conditioned to the frequent and immediate schedule of reinforcement inherent in many video games and show low motivation to learn academic skills that are reinforced in a less consistent and more delayed fashion (Ennemoser & Schneider, 2007).

We believe that our study extends the existing research literature through its focus on games marketed to young children, its examination of academic outcomes, and its reliance on experimental methodology in naturalistic settings. Our findings provide the first experimental evidence that video-game ownership may displace academic activities and hinder the academic achievement of young boys. We hope that our findings can be added to this growing body of research so that parents can make informed choices regarding their family's media consumption.

Acknowledgments

Portions of the data were presented at the 2009 meeting of the Midwestern Psychological Association, Chicago, Illinois.

Declaration of Conflicting Interests

The authors declared that they had no conflicts of interest with respect to their authorship or the publication of this article.

Funding

This research was supported by the J. Reid and Polly Anderson Fund for Science Research and the Fairchild Foundation of Denison University.

References

Anderson, C.A., & Bushman, B.J. (2001). Effects of violent video games on aggressive behavior, aggressive cognition, aggressive affect, physiological arousal, and prosocial behavior: A meta-analytic review of the scientific literature. *Psychological Science, 12,* 353–359.

Anderson, C.A., & Dill, K.E. (2000). Video games and aggressive thoughts, feelings, and behavior in the laboratory and in life. *Journal of Personality and Social Psychology, 78,* 772–790.

Anderson, C.A., Gentile, D.A., & Buckley, K.E. (2007). *Violent video game effects on children and adolescents: Theory, research, and public policy.* New York: Oxford University Press.

Anderson, C.A., Sakamoto, A., Gentile, D.A., Ihori, N., Shibuya, A., Yukawa, S., et al. (2008). Longitudinal effects of violent video games on aggression in Japan and the United States. *Pediatrics, 122,* e1067–e1072.

Bailey, K., West, R., & Anderson, C.A. (2009). A negative association between video game experience and proactive cognitive control. *Psychophysiology, 47,* 34–42.

Baron, R.M., & Kenny, D.A. (1986). The moderator-mediator distinction in social psychological research: Conceptual, strategic, and statistical considerations. *Journal of Personality and Social Psychology, 51,* 1173–1182.

Carnagey, N.L., & Anderson, C.A. (2005). The effects of reward and punishment in violent video games on aggressive affect, cognition, and behavior. *Psychological Science, 16,* 882–889.

Carnagey, N.L., Anderson, C.A., & Bushman, B.J. (2007). The effect of video game violence on physiological desensitization to real-life violence. *Journal of Experimental Social Psychology, 43,* 489–496.

Cohen, J. (1988). *Statistical power analysis for the behavioral sciences.* Mahwah, NJ: Erlbaum.

Cummings, H.M., & Vandewater, E.A. (2007). Relation of adolescent video game play to time spent in other activities. *Archives of Pediatric and Adolescent Medicine, 161,* 684–689.

Ennemoser, M., & Schneider, W. (2007). Relations of television viewing and reading: Findings from a 4-year longitudinal study. *Journal of Educational Psychology, 99,* 349–368.

Gentile, D.A. (2009). Pathological video-game use among youths ages 8 to 18: A national study. *Psychological Science, 20,* 594–602.

Gentile, D.A., Lynch, P.J., Linder, J.R., & Walsh, D.A. (2004). The effects of violent video game habits on adolescent hostility, aggressive behaviors, and school performance. *Journal of Adolescence, 27,* 5–22.

Gentile, D.A., Saleem, M., & Anderson, C.A. (2007). Public policy and the effects of media violence on children. *Social Issues and Policy Review, 1,* 15–61.

Hofferth, S., Davis-Kean, P.E., Davis, J., & Finkelstein, J. (1997). *The Child Development Supplement to the Panel Study of Income Dynamics.* Ann Arbor, MI: Institute for Social Research.

Hofferth, S.L., & Sandberg, J.F. (2001). How American children spend their time. *Journal of Marriage and the Family, 62,* 295–308.

Kaufman, A., & Kaufman, N. (2004). *Kaufman Brief Intelligence Test, Second Edition manual.* Circle Pines, MN: American Guidance Service.

Kutner, L.A., Olson, C.K., Warner, D.E., & Hertzog, S.M. (2008). Parents' and sons' perspectives on video game play. *Journal of Adolescent Research, 23,* 76–96.

MacKinnon, D.P., & Fairchild, A.J. (2009). Current directions in mediation analysis. *Current Directions in Psychological Science, 18,* 16–20.

McGrew, K.S., & Woodcock, R.W. (2001). *Woodcock-Johnson III technical manual.* Itasca, IL: Riverside.

Ostrov, J.M., Gentile, D.A., & Crick, N.R. (2006). Media exposure, aggression and prosocial behavior during early childhood: A longitudinal study. *Social Development, 15,* 612–627.

Rayner, K., Foorman, B.R., Perfetti, C.A., Pesetsky, D., & Seidenberg, M.S. (2001). How psychological science informs the teaching of reading. *Psychological Science in the Public Interest, 2,* 31–74.

Reynolds, C.R., & Kamphaus, R.W. (2004). *Behavior Assessment System for Children, Second Edition manual.* Circle Pines, MN: American Guidance Service.

Roberts, D.F., Foehr, U.G., & Rideout, V. (2005). *Generation M: Media in the lives of 8–18 year-olds.* Washington, DC: Kaiser Family Foundation.

Schmidt, M.E., & Vandewater, E.A. (2008). Media and attention, cognition, and school achievement. *The Future of Children, 18,* 63–85.

Sharif, I., & Sargent, J.D. (2006). Association between television, movie, and video game exposure and school performance. *Pediatrics, 118,* 1061–1070.

Valentine, G., Marsh, J., & Pattie, C. (2005). *Children and young people's home use of ICT for educational purposes.* London: Department for Education and Skills.

Vandewater, E.A., Bickham, D.S., & Lee, J.H. (2006). Time well spent? Relating television use to children's free-time activities. *Pediatrics, 117,* 181–191.

Walsh, D.A., & Gentile, D.A. (2001). A validity test of movie, television, and video-game ratings. *Pediatrics, 107,* 1302–1308.

Willoughby, T. (2008). A short-term longitudinal study of Internet and computer game use by adolescent boys and girls: Prevalence, frequency of use, and psychosocial predictors. *Developmental Psychology, 44,* 195–204.

Assess Your Progress

1. Summarize the data from the research study on the effects of video game ownership. What do you conclude from this data?
2. A father, who enjoys playing video and Facebook games, is seeking your advice about allowing his son to play games and use social media. What will you tell him?

From *Psychological Science,* February 18, 2010, pp. 1–8. Copyright © 2010 by the Association for Psychological Science. Reprinted by permission of Wiley-Blackwell.

Test-Your-Knowledge Form

We encourage you to photocopy and use this page as a tool to assess how the articles in *Annual Editions* expand on the information in your textbook. By reflecting on the articles you will gain enhanced text information. You can also access this useful form on a product's book support website at www.mhhe.com/cls

NAME: DATE:

TITLE AND NUMBER OF ARTICLE:

BRIEFLY STATE THE MAIN IDEA OF THIS ARTICLE:

LIST THREE IMPORTANT FACTS THAT THE AUTHOR USES TO SUPPORT THE MAIN IDEA:

WHAT INFORMATION OR IDEAS DISCUSSED IN THIS ARTICLE ARE ALSO DISCUSSED IN YOUR TEXTBOOK OR OTHER READINGS THAT YOU HAVE DONE? LIST THE TEXTBOOK CHAPTERS AND PAGE NUMBERS:

LIST ANY EXAMPLES OF BIAS OR FAULTY REASONING THAT YOU FOUND IN THE ARTICLE:

LIST ANY NEW TERMS/CONCEPTS THAT WERE DISCUSSED IN THE ARTICLE, AND WRITE A SHORT DEFINITION:

We Want Your Advice

ANNUAL EDITIONS revisions depend on two major opinion sources: one is our Advisory Board, listed in the front of this volume, which works with us in scanning the thousands of articles published in the public press each year; the other is you—the person actually using the book. Please help us and the users of the next edition by completing the prepaid article rating form on this page and returning it to us. Thank you for your help!

ANNUAL EDITIONS: Education 11/12

ARTICLE RATING FORM

Here is an opportunity for you to have direct input into the next revision of this volume.
We would like you to rate each of the articles listed below, using the following scale:

1. **Excellent: should definitely be retained**
2. **Above average: should probably be retained**
3. **Below average: should probably be deleted**
4. **Poor: should definitely be deleted**

Your ratings will play a vital part in the next revision.
Please mail this prepaid form to us as soon as possible.
Thanks for your help!

RATING	ARTICLE
	1. 'Quality Education Is Our Moon Shot'
	2. Duncan's Strategy Is Flawed
	3. Response to Intervention (RTI): What Teachers of Reading Need to Know
	4. Responding to RTI
	5. Reluctant Teachers, Reluctant Learners
	6. Musing: A Way to Inform and Inspire Pedagogy through Self-Reflection
	7. All Our Students Thinking
	8. Start Where Your Students Are
	9. Should Learning Be Its Own Reward?
	10. Learning to Love Assessment
	11. Print Referencing during Read-Alouds: A Technique for Increasing Emergent Readers' Print Knowledge
	12. You Gotta See It to Believe It: Teaching Visual Literacy in the English Classroom
	13. You Should Read This Book!
	14. Do Girls Learn Math Fear from Teachers?
	15. How Mathematics Counts
	16. Textbook Scripts, Student Lives
	17. Creating Intentional Communities to Support English Language Learners in the Classroom
	18. Cultivating Optimism in the Classroom
	19. Teachers Connecting with Families—In the Best Interest of Children
	20. How Not to Talk to Your Kids: The Inverse Power of Praise
	21. Democracy and Education: Empowering Students to Make Sense of Their World

RATING	ARTICLE
	22. Meeting Students Where They Are: The Latino Education Crisis
	23. What Does Research Say about Effective Practices for English Learners?
	24. Becoming Adept at Code-Switching
	25. The Myth of the "Culture of Poverty"
	26. Books That Portray Characters with Disabilities: A Top 25 List for Children and Young Adults
	27. The Under-Appreciated Role of Humiliation in the Middle School
	28. Tackling a Problematic Behavior Management Issue: Teachers' Intervention in Childhood Bullying Problems
	29. The Power of Our Words
	30. Marketing Civility
	31. Classwide Interventions: Effective Instruction Makes a Difference
	32. Developing Effective Behavior Intervention Plans: Suggestions for School Personnel
	33. "For Openers: How Technology Is Changing School"
	34. Tech Tool Targets Elementary Readers
	35. Digital Tools Expand Options for Personalized Learning
	36. Effects of Video-Game Ownership on Young Boys' Academic and Behavioral Functioning: A Randomized, Controlled Study

ANNUAL EDITIONS: EDUCATION 11/12

BUSINESS REPLY MAIL
FIRST CLASS MAIL PERMIT NO. 551 DUBUQUE IA

POSTAGE WILL BE PAID BY ADDRESSEE

McGraw-Hill Contemporary Learning Series
501 BELL STREET
DUBUQUE, IA 52001

NO POSTAGE
NECESSARY
IF MAILED
IN THE
UNITED STATES

ABOUT YOU

Name _____ Date _____

Are you a teacher? ☐ A student? ☐
Your school's name _____

Department _____

Address _____ City _____ State _____ Zip _____

School telephone # _____

YOUR COMMENTS ARE IMPORTANT TO US!

Please fill in the following information:
For which course did you use this book?
_____

Did you use a text with this ANNUAL EDITION? ☐ yes ☐ no
What was the title of the text?
_____

What are your general reactions to the Annual Editions concept?
_____

Have you read any pertinent articles recently that you think should be included in the next edition? Explain.
_____

Are there any articles that you feel should be replaced in the next edition? Why?
_____

Are there any World Wide Websites that you feel should be included in the next edition? Please annotate.
_____

May we contact you for editorial input? ☐ yes ☐ no
May we quote your comments? ☐ yes ☐ no